The Moral Frameworks of Public Life

THE MORAL FRAMEWORKS OF PUBLIC LIFE

Gender, Politics, and the State
in Rural New York, 1870–1930

PAULA BAKER

New York   Oxford
OXFORD UNIVERSITY PRESS
1991

Oxford University Press

Oxford   New York   Toronto
Delhi   Bombay   Calcutta   Madras   Karachi
Petaling Jaya   Singapore   Hong Kong   Tokyo
Nairobi   Dar es Salaam   Cape Town
Melbourne   Auckland

and associated companies in
Berlin   Ibadan

Published by Oxford University Press, Inc.,
200 Madison Avenue, New York, New York 10016

Oxford is a registered trademark of Oxford University Press.

Library of Congress Cataloging-in-Publication Data
Baker, Paula
The moral frameworks of public life :
gender, politics, and the state
in rural New York, 1870–1930 / Paula Baker.
p. cm. Includes bibliographical references and index.
ISBN 0-19-506452-6
1. New York (state)—Politics and government—1865–1950.
2. Women in politics—New York (State)—History.
3. New York (State)—Rural conditions.
4. Sex role—New York (State)—History.
I. Title. JK3495.B35 1991
974.7'04—dc20   90-39867

9 8 7 6 5 4 3 2 1

Printed in the United States of America
on acid-free paper

To Helen and Daniel Baker and Sophie Kozak

Preface

This is a study of the lives and political ideas of men and women in rural New York State. The initial impulse behind the research was to understand how introducing gender to the study of politics might change the way we see public life. I had been struck by the extent of nineteenth-century women's public activism and by the masculine imagery of nineteenth-century partisan politics. These observations raised a series of questions: What were the differences between how men and women thought about politics and government and acted politically? How did ideas about gender shape the public lives of men and women? Did women and gender figure in the transformation of politics and government in the early twentieth century? The answers matter to women's history, where new work is just beginning to assess the impact of women and gender on politics, the welfare state, and public life as a whole; and to political history, where work is barely underway.

This work takes on these questions—and more. As the research unfolded, it became clear to me New York State could not stand simply as a case study of the relationships between gender and politics. Listening to nineteenth-century men's and women's concerns about taxes, roads, liquor, and schools suggested complications: the actions of government itself helped to shape New Yorkers' ideas about politics and gender. Any disciplined conviction that I might have held about focusing solely on gender and politics unravelled further as I learned more about life in rural New York. So this book is a history of people in a particular place and time, as well as an analysis of gender, politics, and government. Seeing it this way has made the work messier than it would have been otherwise; I hope it is richer as well.

To the extent that I have been able to capture the lives and thoughts of New Yorkers, I have current residents of New York to thank. I can trace some of my understanding of New York State to people who sat in diners, bars, laundromats, inns, and on front porches and told men about their towns, life in rural New York, and connections between the past and present. I was able to study New Yorkers' ideas and deeds because some of them recorded the events of their lives and organizations, and local historians preserved their words. My thanks to the staffs of the Adams Center

Free Library, Darwin R. Barker Library Historical Museum, Belfast Town Hall, Castile Historical Society, Cazenovia Public Library, Chautauqua County Historical Society, Cortland County Historical Society, Cortland Free Library, Delaware County Historical Society, Esperance Historical Museum, Friendship Free Library, Historical Society of South Jefferson, David A. Howe Public Library, Madison County Historical Society, Middleburgh Public Library, Patterson Library, Thelma Rogers Historical and Genealogical Society, Volney Town Hall, Wide Awake Club Library, Warsaw Public Library, and Wyoming County Historical Center. Helene Farrell, former Director of Schoharie County's Old Stone Fort Museum, took the time to help me locate photographs and other materials in the county.

Other archivists also responded graciously to my sometimes vague requests. I appreciate the efforts of the staff at New York State Historical Association Library at Cooperstown, especially Amy Barnum and Sara Clark. Gould P. Colman guided me through the vast collection of material on rural New York at the Department of Manuscripts and University Archives, Olin Library, Cornell University, and shared his considerable knowledge of New York agriculture. Thanks, too, to the archivists and librarians at Alfred University, Michigan State University, New York Public Library, New York State Library, State University of New York at Oswego, Wayne State University, and Yale University. Special acknowledgments are due to those in charge of interlibrary loans at the Royal Oak (Michigan) Public Library, and Robert R. Dykstra of SUNY Albany, who invited me to speak at a seminar he conducted on New York villages in 1984 and made the papers available to me. James Perkins prepared the maps under a tight deadline. Financial assistance from a New York State Historic Sites Research Stipend and the American Association of University Women helped give me the time to travel and write.

It has been a pleasure to work with Oxford University Press. I am grateful for Sheldon Meyers's interest in my work, continued well after the point at which he might have forgotten about it, and Gail Cooper's skillful copyediting. Perhaps more than most historians who have worked with Oxford, I appreciate their standards and professionalism.

The criticisms of colleagues and friends improved my work. The chastening skepticism of John F. Reynolds and Michael McGerr encouraged me to retract some of my balder generalizations and to rethink numerous points; Jack and Liz Lennon also supplied conversation and a place to stay when they lived in Albany. Gould Colman saved me from embarrassing errors. Suzanne Lebsock provided very helpful comments on Chapters 2 and 3 and an example of how local histories can illuminate larger concerns. Paul G. E. Clemens, Sallie Pisani, Gerald Pomper, Susan Mernitz, and Traian Stoianovich also furnished thoughtful suggestions. David McDonald told me about a fascinating collection of photographs in Fillmore, New York. Toward the end, Elizabeth Faue's humor and questions restored my perspective.

Conversations with colleagues and students at the University of Massachusetts at Amherst have made this a better book and taught me a great deal. I would like to thank in particular those who commented on all or part of my manuscript: Joyce Berkman, Gerald McFarland, Ronald Story, and Jack Tager. Bruce Laurie not only had excellent ideas for strengthening the book, but also gave solid advice and encouragement on practical matters. I am grateful to everyone at the University of Massachusetts who listened to my stories and tales of woe and helped me think about my research in new ways.

Two other debts stand out. Throughout, Kathleen W. Jones has been a source of good ideas about style, structure, and content. Equally important, her understanding of the value and meaning of complaint and her sense of humor about academic work have kept me sane. Richard L. McCormick directed the dissertation that was the basis for this book. I have benefited from his careful reading of it and my other writings and his confidence in my work. I have also gained from his example of what being a professional historian might mean and, most of all, from his friendship.

Finally, my parents, Helen and Daniel Baker, have extended moral and material support. With my grandmother, Sophie Kozak, they also have given me ways of understanding the past. James DeHullu read some chapters, helped prepare some of the maps, and listened to both my good and indifferent stories more than once. Although he inexplicably has been unable to see that a trip to Hume, Lowville, or even Cooperstown is properly understood as a vacation, I am grateful for his consistent support and affection.

Contents

Introduction: Private Values and Public Life

Much time has passed since anyone suggested we might gain virtue by emulating the lives of politicians. But ordinary men and authors of advice books until the late nineteenth century did just that. Aging members of the Grand Army of the Republic post in Walton, New York, memorialized fellow veteran and former president Rutherford B. Hayes in 1893. "We point to him as the type of lofty character of a true American citizen," they announced. "He was a patriotic, cultured, Christian soldier, and as such we will cherish his memory and imitate his virtue." Writers of tracts for boys also turned to the lives of politicians for examples of manly character that might inspire youthful readers. "These lives show what may be done among us, in short, what we ourselves may do," affirmed one. Through the late nineteenth century, politics remained a field upon which true manhood might be demonstrated and rewarded.[1]

Women, meanwhile, had examples of their own. Should a girl have opened one of her brother's biographies of public figures, she would have found equally flattering portraits of a man's wife and mother. Benjamin Harrison's mother "was a most devout Christian woman of remarkable sweetness of temper, and her spirit pervaded the house," assured a campaign biography. Another biographer noted that Mrs. James G. Blaine "was a model wife and mother," and cryptically, that "more is due to her strong judgment, quick perception, and heroic courage than the world will ever know." Sweet or strong, those women exercised their virtues in the private sphere: in sacrificing for their soon-to-be-famous sons, in extending to their husbands encouragement, affection, and moral guidance. Female virtues may have had public implications, but they were exercised in the context of the home.[2]

The accounts of the lives of public figures and their families offer a glimpse into a nineteenth-century political world where gender roles found expression in politics. Politicians embodied ideal masculine traits: loyalty, strength, fortitude, boldness, industry, and honesty. Men followed politicians' careers with a zeal for politics and respect for public figures that would be lost in the twentieth century as men turned away from avid partisanship and journalists scrambled to unearth the sordid sides of political leaders. While formal politics—voting and office-holding—belonged to men, biographers heeded the dictum that women belonged in the home. From within those walls, women might direct moral influence outward, but their sphere excluded them from formal politics and masculine virtues. Like the notion that politicians personified the best of "manhood," women's special nature, too, was a questionable doctrine by the 1920s. Nineteenth-century assumptions about the proper division of labor between the sexes and about the purposes of politics dissolved in doubt and debate in the twentieth century.

The campaign biographers were not misguided in seeing fundamental separations between nineteenth-century men's and women's public lives. When state governments extended the franchise to all white men and political parties grew more powerful in the early nineteenth century, voting and office-holding indeed became a man's world. Because partisan clubs resembled urban gangs as much as party organizations, and violence was an almost routine feature of elections, antebellum electoral politics seemed perhaps even more hostile to women than the less raucous contests of the Gilded Age. A tradition of women's activism grew up alongside the aggressive masculinity of electoral politics. White middle-class women in the early nineteenth century founded relief societies, hospitals, and schools; they joined together to elevate men's morals, protest slavery, and demand political rights. Much, although not all, of this activity sprang from a conviction that women's superior moral sense demanded expression both inside and outside the house. Such morally inspired voluntary activity persisted—even grew—through the course of the nineteenth century.[3]

To concentrate on the separateness of men's and women's public lives, however, would be to risk missing how ideas about politics and gender interacted. Ideas about gender roles shaped both men's and women's public involvement. By paying attention to explicitly masculine themes in electoral politics and to the ways ideas about womanhood both constrained and justified female politics, we can recover a more complete picture of nineteenth-century political traditions and their gradual transformation. The proper behavior of the sexes in the public world furnished definitions of manhood and womanhood in the late nineteenth century, even as politics provided a forum for acting out those roles. Gender roles figured less prominently in the public life of the twentieth century, when men and women shared political methods and language. The pages that follow, then, analyze how gender shaped male and female political traditions in the nineteenth century and the emergence of a more rationalized and, in some ways, homogeneous public life in the twentieth.

Examining the links between gender and politics leads to a more abstract problem: the relationship between public and private life. I do not see this issue as one of either how retreat into the private sphere gutted public life or how the extension of government's role drained private life. Rather, I want to understand how the boundaries between what Americans considered "public" and "private" have shifted over time. This is a story of internal contradictions and discontinuities in theory and practice. Nineteenth-century men regarded political participation as an occasion for enunciating an imaginative vision of a properly ordered social world and exercising personal male attributes. White activist women, meanwhile, used the idea of domesticity as a wedge to gain political influence usually accessible only to men. Nineteenth-century combinations of the personal and the political changed in the twentieth. As government's purview widened, both men and women came to see politics, not as a public space that validated personal virtues, but as a means to guarantee representation of their moral and material interests. Public policy in the twentieth century also helped sharpen the distinctions between men's and women's private roles. Government thus assisted in the transformation of private lives and political expectations. By revealing some of the ways the state and society changed each other, we can examine the origins of a perception in public and private life that held until the 1960s and 1970s.

This account of gender and politics and public and private life begins in the late nineteenth century, when male partisanship and female activism were at their height. It concerns a specific group of people—men and women who lived in rural New York.[4] They were not "typical" Americans, rural people, or Northerners. Rural New York attracted few newcomers; thus its people remained mostly white, native-born, and Protestant. The cacophony of languages and cultures common in urban areas grew fainter in rural New York, and the state's farmers also differed from many in the South and West. Most New Yorkers did not rely on single "cash" crops: they practiced diversified agriculture, but increasingly relied on dairying for steady income. The region's politics, meanwhile, was as uniform as its population. Republicans could count on large majorities year after year in the late nineteenth century, although even the staunchest Republican counties contained "Democratic" towns. While the rural population showed greater religious and ethnic diversity in the twentieth century, upstate New York became more consistently Republican.[5]

Yet rural New Yorkers obviously shared some experiences and perceptions with other Americans. The hallmarks of Gilded Age electoral politics—party loyalty, campaigns in which men demonstrated their fidelity through parades and pole raisings, and high voter turnout on election days—were as much in evidence in rural New York as anywhere in the North.[6] Some village women organized to battle intemperance and to win the right to vote. The diversity of rural New York townships—prosperous specialized farms and near-subsistence agriculture, salt mining, forestry, and light industry grounded the economies of different areas—makes it possible to discuss how people facing varied economic circumstances understood the transformations of politics and gender.[7]

Whatever their differences from or similarities to other Americans, a single group's experiences can tell us much about broader political and social transformations—as social historians have demonstrated over the past two decades. We know, for example, that the Gilded Age was the high tide of partisan politics: at no time before or since did a larger percentage of eligible voters go to the polls and seem so devoted to the parties. While New York men also voted and wore their party affiliation prominently, they remained skeptical about politicians and government. As loudly as they praised the virtues of party leaders like Rutherford B. Hayes, they criticized and ridiculed politicians whose sole mission seemed to be winning office and government that benefited only the rich and powrful. Even partisan newspaper editors occasionally chimed in. One greeted the 1884 campaign: "Whiskey will be drunk, crime will be committed, boys ruined, industrious men made politicians, bad blood engendered, bad passions excited, and when it is all over, there will come a wild scramble for the loaves and fishes."[8] Perhaps the inconsistency of honoring parties while denigrating politicians did not trouble rural men—they would be neither the first nor the last group to harbor incompatible opinions—but they found a painless settlement that allowed both partisanship and cynicism. By retaining as many governmental functions as possible at the local level and out of the reach of the parties, men maintained an imaginative politics where manhood received its reward, while they nursed contempt for politicians and government.[9]

Rural men's cynicism about Gilded Age partisan politics (if not its consequences) was perhaps shared by other men: only further research can tell.[10] Rural women in New York, meanwhile, departed from patterns of political involvement set by urban female activists. Expanding on the tradition of female institution-building of the early nineteenth century, some urban women organized temperance, charity, and suffrage societies in the Gilded Age; by the first decades of the twentieth century, even formerly staid women's clubs dropped the study of literature in favor of addressing community problems.[11] A relative handful of women in rural New York joined organizations that tackled public issues. Most women had neither the time nor the means to participate in any group. While urban middle-class women focused on their cities, village activists avoided problems that were near at hand other than intemperance. Without enough money and community support, village activists looked beyond their communities to urban, state, and national women's groups. This habit of sidestepping their villages led activist rural women to see merit in expanded government power: the state could accomplish tasks that localities dodged.

Differences between characteristically male and female political ideas and behavior had diminished by the 1920s. Rural men organized to press the state to provide particular benefits to rural places, just as activist women, when denied the franchise, had done. Woman suffrage, a cause many upstate men had opposed, meant that after 1917 electoral politics was no longer an exclusively male preserve. Some twentieth-century rural women devoted more of their time than men did to moral issues—making sure that children saw the "right" movies and Prohibition was enforced. But convictions about gender made a less substantial contribution to differences in how men and women understood the political process, asked for political favors, and spoke about politics in the twentieth century than they had in the Gilded Age. Politics was no longer a public space where the ideals of manhood and womanhood could be acted out.

To chart the passage from nineteenth- to twentieth-century politics, we must abandon the notion of separate spheres that historians, as much as nineteenth century Americans, have clung to.[12] It is only by examining men's and women's politics together that we can understand how both were changed. The work of men and women—especially in cities—encouraged the state government to regulate myriad activities formerly left to individuals or to men's frugal and nonpartisan local governments. New rules regarding how children would be educated, milk would be processed, liquor would be sold, and taxes would be levied in the early twentieth century left rural politicians in a quandary. "Good" local government had been the phlegmatic dispatch of the most essential business, but the new laws required both unpopular spending and difficult choices. By the early twentieth century, rural politicians turned to the state for funding and further administrative rules to resolve their dilemma. As politicians abandoned nineteenth-century creeds, their male constituents slowly adopted a view of politics recommended by nineteenth-century women: nonpartisanship in politics and a more powerful state government staffed by politicians who attended to their constituents' concerns. While the state government thus helped change rural men's minds about the functions of government and politics in the twentieth century, it also organized rural men and women into groups that worked for local reforms and state policies that addressed rural problems. Nonpartisanship, special-interest groups, heightened expectations for government—hallmarks of Progressive-era politics—came to rural New York via government action. Rural men's and women's politics changed in response to each other and to new state initiatives.

The new politics included revised conceptions of the relationships between gender roles and politics and public and private life. By the 1920s, politics, ideally, engaged the efforts of educated citizens interested in the good of the whole; or, in less rarified moments, involved with advancing personal welfare. The personal still intersected with the political—one's material interests or moral vision were obviously personal affairs—but older ideas of manhood and womanhood seemed out of place, even signs of backwardness. The new politics, so devoted to presumed neutral "expertise," allotted women little additional political power; an ironic turn, since women suffragists had argued for precisely this vision of politics throughout the nineteenth century. Gender roles no longer found their ideal representation in public life. Instead, they were contested in private. To the extent that politics retained an imaginative aspect, it was at the highest reaches, such as the Presidency, where twentieth-century concerns about personality and nineteenth-century expectations of personal rectitude and virtue joined.

Yet it would be impossible to understand the interactions of gender, politics, and government in rural New Yorkers' lives without looking outside of those categories to men's and women's everyday lives. This is true because their ideas about other parts of their world—religious beliefs, economic circumstances, and ideas about the future and change—informed their political attitudes. Moreover, the inevitable messiness of men's and women's particular experiences could not be tidied into a study of three areas alone, and they deserve attention in their own right. Many New Yorkers experienced the late nineteenth century, not as a time of exciting economic possibilities, but as a period of decline. Long before 1920, when the rural population in the United States officially became a minority, rural New York saw its population drain away. Farming the state's abundant acres of inferior land was not particularly lucrative for those who remained behind.[13] Both men and women believed that politics ought to reflect moral convictions, and they also shaped it to fit their declining material circumstances. To understand connections between gender and politics, we must first turn to those convictions and circumstances.

The Moral Frameworks of Public Life

CHAPTER 1

The Limited Horizons of Rural Life, 1870–1900

Gilded Age boosters saw "progress" when they surveyed America's burgeoning population and industrial and agricultural production. Yet critics of various persuasions had no trouble spotting persistent problems beneath exuberant paeans to the nation's growing economic might: deepening class divisions, unassimilable immigrants, urban squalor, political corruption, intemperance, disease, and sapped moral will. The countryside, once virtue's bastion against urban vice, did not escape the critical attention of middle-class reformers. They noted with alarm what they called the "exodus" from the country to the city. This movement seemed especially serious in the Northeast, where it left behind abandoned farms, rotting villages, and demoralized—if not depraved—men and women. With only the slow, the old, and the dull left to maintain formerly tidy and prosperous farms and villages, "The Doom of the Small Town" seemed assured.[1]

Such overstated pronouncements had a basis in fact. It was not the harbinger of decadence in the countryside, but fewer people chose to try to make a living in the rural Northeast. The region's farmers, many of them working marginal land, faced stagnant prices and competition from efficient Western and Midwestern producers. While not convinced that the countryside had been beaten in a Darwinian struggle, upstate New Yorkers shared social commentators' worries about the impact of population decline and searched for ways to stanch the flow of people to the cities. Members of the Grange discussed how to keep children on the farm. Newspaper editors pleaded with readers to patronize local stores in order to ensure a future for their villages. Businessmen and politicians tried to attract or build small factories. Nonetheless, rural population in New York began to fall in 1880 and continued to fall throughout the twentieth century.[2]

Rural New Yorkers stitched together an ideology that suited agricultural people facing population decline and economic difficulties. They clung to Protestant teachings, although not all with the same tenacity. They learned to judge grand plans to be hubris and change to be a suspect event, although not all did so with the same thumping certainty.

Their ideas were shared perhaps by the many Americans who failed to go West, join protest movements, amass great wealth, or otherwise participate directly in the great events of the late nineteenth century. A sense of limits—both in the material growth rural New York experienced and in many upstaters' views of their world—informed their social thought, and in turn, their views of politics and government.

Conditions varied from county to county and from town to town, but most areas of rural New York did not enjoy a buoyant economy in the late nineteenth century. The greatest percentage of land in farms was recorded in 1880, when the farm population nearly reached the peak levels recorded in 1855. Reasons for the shrinking number of farms and farmers in New York mirrored those for the Northeast in general. The growth of cities contributed, both directly, by drawing rural people away, and indirectly, by incorporating. When the state government granted city charters, areas formerly considered villages or towns now had their residents counted in the "urban" total. In the same way, villages that grew beyond 2,500 people also reduced the rural total. The decline in New York's rural population is somewhat deceptive, since some portion of that loss is explained, not by the movement away of rural people, but by their absorption into growing towns and villages.[3]

Even if part of the rural to urban shift was more statistical than actual, some rural New Yorkers left their farms—and for good reasons. Many New York farms held their ground against the competition from newer Western and Midwestern farms. But Northeastern farmers who worked plots of the region's abundant marginal land found slight incentive to stay and work the depleted soil for small profits. Improvements in agricultural machinery often failed to make Northeastern farmers more productive, since these implements helped little in hilly and rocky soil. Agricultural techniques that gradually improved New York farmers' productivity—new fertilizers and upgraded dairy herds—only briefly bettered their lot. Even as higher productivity in dairying improved income for a time, it encouraged competition from producers of butter and cheese in the upper Midwest who enjoyed lower production costs. New York's total agricultural production slipped behind that of Midwestern and Western states, while the economic returns New Yorkers received declined relative to those of urban workers.[4]

Some advantages balanced New York farmers' difficulties. They lived relatively close to major markets and practiced diversified farming. The agricultural depressions of the 1870s and 1890s, which brought plummeting prices for staples like cotton, corn, and wheat, passed without the severe problems faced by farmers in the South and West. Most New York farmers had given up extensive market production of corn and wheat in the early nineteenth century. But they did not escape unscathed. Some New Yorkers left the countryside, while those who remained turned to perishable products, such as fluid milk and fruit, less subject to Western competition, and planted corn, hay, and oats for animal feed. Dairy prices remained relatively stable (although low) in the late nineteenth century. Other farmers turned to specialty crops—hops, small fruits, and vegetables—with uneven success. On the whole, New York farmers missed the roller-coaster markets for corn, wheat, and cotton—both the peaks and valleys.[5]

State and regional patterns, however, disguise variations in population trends and economic conditions in different parts of the state. Many villages that secured railroad service grew in the late nineteenth century and developed small industries—the manufacturing of such items as carriages and cheese boxes, for example. Natural resources also shaped the economic futures of villages. Forests drew lumber mills and firms that made doors, sashes, and shingles, especially in the 1870s. Discoveries of oil and gas in the western part of the southern tier forestalled decline in that region until the early twentieth century. Salt deposits in Wyoming County (in western New York) granted stable employment until the 1890s. In other villages, state institutions—schools, hospitals, and prisons—underwrote a steady prosperity. As centers of political, social, and economic activity for surrounding farms, villages continued to gain population, even as farms and farmers disappeared.[6]

Agricultural townships (called "towns" in New York and New England) fared worse that townships with substantial villages in the late nineteenth century, but conditions in those places, too, varied considerably. Soil quality, topography, access to transportation, and proximity to cities and large villages differed even within townships. Areas with the least desirable farming conditions—steep hillsides, acid topsoil, relatively high elevations, and an abundance of stones—lost the largest number of people. Population decline in many such places began as early as the 1850s. The flatter lands and fertile expanses alongside rivers and creeks continued to be farmed and supported roughly the same number of people from 1870 to 1900. Agricultural conditions suited to commercial dairy and vegetable farming and access to transportation and markets tended to be found together, and the combination of the two separated stable from declining rural townships.

While the writers who anticipated doom in the countryside exaggerated the deleterious effects of population decline, they did make a valid point: the movement of people had important consequences for township and village life. Using population change as a guide to economic circumstances, New York rural townships can be divided into five groups. A small number of townships grew rapidly in the late nineteenth century (by twenty-five percent or more) while still not including villages with more than 5,000 people. Only 94 townships fell into this category, most of them in the Adirondack region, a mountainous area where only a handful of people lived before 1870. The rest of the townships that attracted newcomers did so because of villages within their borders. Other areas of the state experienced moderate growth—an increase of ten to twenty-four percent. Moderately growing townships also were usually sites of prosperous villages that served as trading centers, contained small industries, or within which townspeople persuaded the state to build a school or hospital. The majority of growing townships were found in western New York and the southern tier.

Most rural townships lost population or remained relatively stable. Nearly one third of New York townships experienced no notable population change: they showed a ten percent loss or gain. Stable townships were chiefly in western and central New York, south of the shores of Lake Ontario and Lake Erie. Such townships provided first-class agricultural conditions—a good fortune present only in scattered patches elsewhere in the state. In the southern tier, however, stability proved fleeting. After 1890, those townships would join the ranks of the majority of rural townships that lost population; today those townships are among the poorest in the state. In the late nineteenth century, numerous rural townships lost twenty-five percent or more of their population. The substantially declining townships had the worst farming prospects. These towns were clustered in east–central New York, a block extending as far north as Lewis County and west to the edge of the Finger Lakes. Cortland, Chenango, Tompkins, Madison, Oswego, Oneida, Lewis, Columbia, and Washington counties all contained a good proportion of substantially declining townships. Poor soil and hilly terrain encouraged few families to take the places of migrants. These conditions, in slightly less pronounced form, also held in townships that lost between ten and twenty-five percent of their population. Moderately declining townships were concentrated in the Finger Lakes region, but were also scattered throughout the state.

Population growth or decline influenced local policies and social prospects. In declining townships, tax assessments were lower than in more prosperous areas, and residents fought to keep taxes down and services limited. Farmers hestiated to purchase the latest machinery or to practice the latest methods; they even seemed less likely to join such farmer's organizations as the Grange. With few people choosing to move to declining townships, challenges to established political and social patterns were infrequent. Growing New York townships displayed the characteristics associated with nineteenth-century small towns—characteristics largely absent in declining areas. Local newspapers engaged in boosterism, for example, explaining the town's advantages and tracing the signs that suggested it would soon become a small city. In 1880, the editor of the *Cuba Patriot* looked forward to Cuba's future as "a city of 10,000 in the next ten years . . . the metropolis of Allegany." In the late nineteenth century, some villages indeed rose to the status of small city, although most, like Cuba, failed in this ambition.[7]

More important for local politics, growing townships supported a much wider variety of voluntary societies than declining townships, and conflicting opinions on local issues more easily gained a hearing. With a sufficient number of people, citizens organized the men's lodges, temper-

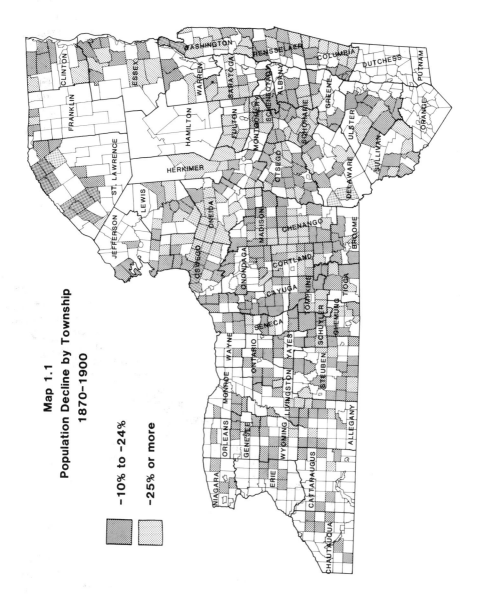

Map 1.1
Population Decline by Township
1870–1900

-10% to -24%

-25% or more

ance organizations, suffrage clubs, and women's clubs that were vital parts of nineteenth-century social and political life. New York's larger Granges and more active church societies emerged in such villages. The presence of the full array of voluntary organizations, along with the steady influx of new residents, encouraged villagers to consider conflict a normal part of public life. Acceptance of conflict appeared both in how voluntary societies conducted their business and in township and village politics. Greater confidence in their township's future apparently allowed residents of growing townships to admit that differences existed on various issues.[8]

This kind of pluralism was not customary among the residents of stable or declining townships. Prosperous agricultural townships resembled growing townships in that they sustained strong farmers' organizations, active church societies, fire companies, and perhaps temperance societies. But residents of stable townships, like those of declining ones, sought consensus and came to decisions extremely slowly in their associations and local governments. Advocates of controversial new programs (and most new programs were controversial) could expect a less than enthusiastic response. Without pressure from an expanding population or new residents with different ideas, departures from established practice and admissions of clashing points of view came infrequently in declining townships.[9]

Many individuals and communities in rural New York adjusted to a stable or shrinking economy in the late nineteenth century. Except in villages, rapid—or sometimes even modest—expansion was a memory, and people in many rural townships came to terms with a smaller population and diminished economic opportunities. Decline or qualified growth ran against the grain of received national wisdom, which stressed the possibilities and problems of unprecedented expansion. Optimism about further social and economic progress—while hardly universal—seemed to be a widely shared feeling about America's immediate future. It is fair to ask how men and women who remained in rural townships understood what was happening to their communities and how they saw their place in them. While the unsystematic quality of the sources prevents a comparison among types of townships, a few themes that grounded rural political ideas turn up time and again. Most prominent among these was Christianity—more specifically, Protestantism—which served as the foundation for the social thought of many New Yorkers. Among the major derivations from Protestantism was a theory of limits—the notion that one's expectations for the present and future ought to be stated in the most minimal terms, to avoid disappointment or the appearance of foolishness. This view of limits, in different ways, shaped the political ideas of rural men and women.

That rural New Yorkers grounded their beliefs and expectations in Protestant doctrine hardly set them apart in the late nineteenth century.

Ministers may have debated the fine points and, with others, wrestled with the problems posed by science, but most Americans could assume that the vast majority of their countrymen followed Christian tenets. Protestantism, that is, Christianity outside of Catholicism that posited the divinity of Jesus Christ, occupied a central place in the everyday lives of rural New Yorkers.[10] Few people actually belonged to congregations, according to limited evidence for a number of townships. But membership did not determine churchgoing, and nonmembers went to services on a regular basis. For those who missed services, newspapers featured a weekly sermon, news of local congregations, and items from national Protestant magazines. At least one man in fact preferred the published sermons to those of local pastors, and satisfied his religious obligations by reading sermons.[11] Even seemingly secular columns taken from other newpapers on topics like "success" also had a Christian content. Whatever they taught, Protestant viewpoints were virtually inescapable.

Rural New Yorkers took seriously what they heard in church and read in newspapers. Following a practice common in the eighteenth and early nineteenth centuries, people often used diaries as spiritual ledgers. Men and women charted their spiritual progress or decline and chided themselves for their shortcomings. After a prayer meeting, a central New York woman took stock: "That I were a better Christian, always shielded from sin by Gods Holy Word, but oh first after I got home I said something rash." Some also regarded God as a close participant in everyday life. "Praise God for a little rain last night," one woman offered. She wondered what she had done for Jesus each day, and thanked "the Good Father" who "gave me strength [to do her work] this morning I was sick." Other diarists reported conversations and arguments with friends and family about God's character or the timing of the Second Coming. Diarists who monitored the state of their souls were more likely to be women than men, but for both sexes, spiritual matters figured in ordinary concerns.[12]

Protestantism pervaded everyday language. The Bible stood as the one book of universal experience. References to Scripture surfaced in letters to politicians, newspaper articles on secular subjects, and discussions of agricultural practices. According to members of the Central New York Farmers' Club, "a higher power than that of man regulates the product of the soil."[13] Biblical metaphors appeared seemingly wherever some illustration was necessary to make a point. Women usually used religious appeals in making political demands. Even for those who avoided church and Bible study, Protestant language was a normal part of speech.

In community life, as well as in personal experience, Protestantism guided. Social life in rural townships and villages revolved around churches. Numerous diaries describe Sundays that began with church services in the morning followed by Sunday School, which drew adults as well as children. Dinner with friends or family came next, with an additional evening sermon to end the day.[14] For the more active, church agendas could keep a believer busy every night of the week. For women, home and foreign missionary societies met monthly or bimonthly, and some supplemented these meetings with prayer, Bible study, or young people's groups that assembled more frequently. This array of organizations existed in nearly every town of suitable size for the pious who could afford the time; one woman, a teacher who moved almost yearly, replicated the round of Methodist activities everywhere she lived. In addition, church groups ran socials and picnics that drew people from both inside and outside their congregations.[15]

Protestantism itself, of course, housed many variants. Yet those devoted to a particular persuasion were not hostile to members of other Protestant churches: New York townships seemed remarkably free of sectarian discord. Within congregations, members quarrelled at times over which language should be used and which minister should be hired, for example. And different denominations were associated with specific ethnic groups or classes. Such distinctions applied only to membership, however, and people attended services and social functions of churches regardless of their affiliation. Attending different churches was especially common in small or declining communites. In such places, it was unlikely that the townspeople could support a number of resident pastors; so men and women gathered at the church that happened to hold services in a given week. Even in larger places, congregants went to a variety of churches. New ministers drew crowds, as did visiting ministers or speakers with particularly good reputations. The absence of doctrinal disputes helped churches to act as the centers of community social life. Such acceptance, however, did not extend to Catholics or to Seventh-Day Adventists. Mainstream Protestants who visited those churches left with their negative assumptions confirmed. "I thank God I was not born under that religion," affirmed one woman after attending a Catholic Mass. In the other denominations, the old battles had been won or lost; members held on to their separate churches, but earlier bitterness had dissipated.[16]

If doctrine seemed to have such a slight impact in the religious life of rural communities, what, then, was the content of Protestantism? For the Grange, with its ritual that dramatized the passing of the seasons, God's and Nature's laws combined in a seamless, mystical unity. At the 1876 state meeting, the Committee Upon the Good of the Order hoped that the Grange would be "the abode of love and charity, let virtue and uprightness be there enshrined, and our children will bless God for the Order." Meanwhile, the sermons diarists said they enjoyed and the books of the Bible they most commonly read suggests that rural New Yorkers leaned decidedly toward prophecy. Along with the New Testament in general, they indicated a special fondness for the books of Daniel and Revelation. Men and women copied entire books in their diaries next to the weather and chores. They noted their pleasure after hearing an especially good sermon—one, usually, that taught lessons about sin and redemption rather than advised on community or national affairs. To this concern with the future they added an element of literalism—a belief in the physical existence of heaven and hell and in a God who closely watched His faithful for evidence of sin.[17]

Rural Protestantism aspired to discover and follow God's laws: humans possessed only limited power to control their fate. After a debate, members of one Grange concluded in 1888 that man was not "his own architect." Good works seemed only a minor part of Christian practice. Rural churches in the late nineteenth century evidenced slight involvement in community problems, with the major exception of congregations that sponsored temperance work. They sponsored socials and encouraged members' organizations, but otherwise spent little time in community service; the social gospel would not arrive until the late 1910s and 1920s. The diarists who monitored their own spiritual health worried about sinful thought and behavior, not charitable acts. Personal—and sometimes community—avoidance of sin loomed larger in securing salvation. Protestantism, for rural New Yorkers, commanded unswerving faith and curbing one's bad behavior—and only incidentally encouraged right action.[18]

Theirs was a religion expected to furnish guidance and comfort. Prophecy assisted in this end. Whether or not one believed in the imminent second coming of Jesus, prophecy provided a vision of a just future and indicated how justice would be meted out. It made sense of life and of history. An interest in prophecy perhaps explains why many New Yorkers were intrigued by spiritualism but rejected other deviations from Protestantism. When the legislature debated strict licensing of medical practicioners in 1901, one woman insisted: "If God has endowed any one with such a gift, of course, it is right that they should use the power to heal. . . . You cannot fight against God, for such a law shall not stand, with God against it."[19] Protestantism also explained death and misfortune. Diarists accounted for illness and economic setbacks either as results of their sins or as part of a test of their faith. They did not attempt to apply such thinking beyond themselves or their immediate community. Outsiders—wealthy people in Manhattan and public officials, for example, who may have been both sinful and successful—seemed exempt from the rule that ambition and selfishness brought failure.[20]

While religion furnished answers to important problems, it occupied a definite and limited sphere. Many New Yorkers restricted the areas in which religious values applied. Where the line marking the boundaries of religious influence ought to be drawn, however, occasioned disagreement. For some, religious beliefs offered a set of general guidelines but not specific directions about how to run one's home or work. Religion, rightly understood, showed how to achieve salvation after death and should remain free of economic or political entanglements. Such connections would only do churches harm, as a newspaper editor argued in explaining the waning influence of Protestant churches in the 1910s.

Men go to church to be told of God and spiritual matters. They want to pray, to put their house in order. . . . [When] a minister delivers a political talk . . . the religious man rightfully resents the assumed leadership of the preacher and, as a result, stays at home to commune with his God.

Spiritual concerns mattered in this view, but they occupied a separate space.[21]

Other members of rural communities—often women—envisioned more direct applications of religion to worldly matters, and their opinion had an impact on local politics. More than mere talk, religious values, they felt, ought to have a place in public as well as private decisions. For a male newspaper editor with Prohibitionist leanings, "[t]he united moral force of the religious element of this country is the only power that can check the tide of corruption and save the country. . . . [W]ill they strike deep and lay the foundation for a moral breakwater which shall say to these waves of devastation, 'thus far shalt thou come and no further.' " Religious concerns appeared in public discussions of temperance, charity, punishment of criminals, and even economic policy. What the connections were between religious teachings and practical problems—most often a nonpartisan question—remained a source of conflict in late nineteenth-century New York.[22]

Even for those who allowed Protestantism only a circumscribed area of influence, religious beliefs shaped what they expected of themselves and their communities. A plastic creed, Protestantism could have taught endless lessons, and the use of religious imagery by Populists and Socialists suggests some remembered the radical implications of Christianity. Rural New Yorkers, however, took away the idea that their expectations should be modest. "Everyone has a range sufficiently wide in which to accomplish something," a newspaper article counseled, "provided he has sense enough to acquiesce in those conditions which he can not alter, and enter upon the labor which nature and circumstances indicate to be his." The writer went on to explain a consequence of inflated expectations: "Many are not satisfied to do that particular work which is thus prescribed for them, but desire to do something else, and complain and make themselves miserable because they can not." New Yorkers expressed a sense of resignation about the inevitability of ill fortune. "Life," wrote one woman, "is just one long succession of horrors." At the Manchester Grange, a member read a paper, "To Be, To Do, To Suffer," which concluded that "in whatsoever condition we find ourselves the proper attitude of our minds is one of gratitude to the Giver of every good and perfect gift." By keeping expectations low, men and women could at least count on avoiding disappointment.[23]

An understanding of personal limitations involved a realistic assessment of one's place. An 1879 editorial in the *Cortland Democrat* drew out the lessons of a scandal involving Senator Roscoe Conkling and a Washington socialite: people should "be content with their simple surroundings and peaceful homes instead of courting grandeur and display indulged in by the so-called aristocracy at the expense of conscience and good regulation. Truly a contented mind is a continual feast." Reasonable expectations brought security and contentment, both of which were highly regarded. A Grange secretary summarized a discussion of happiness by remarking that "*Godliness* with *contentment* is great gain." The highest praise the editor of the *Cuba Patriot* could offer to the people of the town was that "[t]hey did their work well and were content."[24]

Wise people lived within their means and avoided anticipating good fortune. An editor in Penn Yan claimed in 1895 that some of the nation's problems could be traced to a desire for luxuries.

> During the times of our great prosperity, we have shown less disposition to practice economy and accumulate a comfortable surplus than to indulge in luxuries and expensive pleasures. . . . Cheap living does not seem an attractive course for some of our ills but it would prove an effective one. . . . When the spirit of wastefulness which is part of our national spirit is overcome, a long stride will have been taken toward overcoming some of our besetting troubles.[25]

Farmers sometimes argued that inflated desires created their economic problems. A speaker at the 1886 meeting of the state Grange denounced the "folly of reaching for attainments unwise." Men who so tempted fate inevitably found themselves back where they began, "singed, scorched and blackened, from the merciless fire." The speaker advised "a well-guarded perseverance" as the "only way to gain the gracious and successful end of this uncertain and fleeting . . . life."[26]

Ruin more extreme than economic failure visited men and women who clung to exalted ideas about themselves or refused to check their desires. Newspaper editors cited such flawed thinking as the cause of suicides in rural towns in the late nineteenth century. Accounts of suicides appeared almost weekly in rural newspapers; editors usually traced them to disappointment in love, or illness or pain. When none of these reasons applied, misguided expectations explained "the rash act." One editor deplored a series of suicides in 1888 because "six to eight in the last week were for mere trifles." These frivolous suicides pointed to serious social and ethical problems: people wanted too much and were too devoted to material comfort.

> The moral fiber and stamina of a community is getting pretty rotten when a disappointment over a church drives a clergyman to death. . . . The modern world, men and women together, have gone crazy in the desire for a soft life and the lesser luxuries of living. . . . [E]ach want creates a lower desire, until human natures rot in the furnace-heated air of mere material comforts.[27]

If suicide waited for those who failed to regulate their aspirations, death loomed as the single expectation one could entertain without fear of retribution. "It is the last and most important event that awaits us all," wrote Berne lawyer Edward J. Filkins in 1872. A man who could not be accused of excessive optimism, he later wrote that '[i]t does really seem to me that very many things getting worse,' during a year when he mused unremittingly about death and sickness. For others, death, even under unusual circumstances, warranted a matter-of-fact mention, as if in death, too, one had to guard against extravagance. "Wm Frost dropped dead on the street," ran a Delhi farmer's droll entry in 1876.[28] *"Father died at 1 o'clock to day.* Very hot sultry Thunder Showers Lightening struck near H H Whitney's place and near stone schoolhouse," Wellington Richards recorded in 1894. Death, like the weather, inexplicably and inevitably happened. Unlike suicide, it afforded no moral lessons, aside from a reminder of human powerlessness.[29]

The belief that one's expectations ought to be limited—and its corollaries—was the core of many New Yorkers' ideas about society and politics. To be sure, not all concurred. Each town had its boosters, its believers in science and progress, and its renegades who in fact entertained big ideas and served as foils for the traditionalists. But perhaps because it fit the circumstances of gradual economic decline, the idea that limited expectations were appropriate appeared with great regularity. This belief shaped rural New Yorkers' ideas about fundamental concepts: work and change.

The notion that virtue inhered in hard work brought together an unlikely group of people in the late nineteenth century. Populists, union leaders, writers of advice manuals for boys and girls, and industrial and business magnates all agreed on the moral rewards of work, although they drew different conclusions from that idea. New Yorkers, too, celebrated the regenerative quality of work. Readers of country weeklies wrote letters praising Carlyle's essays on work; Grangers revered its moral and economic benefits. Hard work, however, was more than an abstract, unquestioned good thing. It was a brute fact, as tangible and imposing as a mountain. Rural men and women wrote of "their work"— something that was completed some days and not others, but existed nonetheless. Source of both pain and contentment, work never abated and it existed independently of the worker.[30]

To this specific and immediate understanding of work, rural New Yorkers added the more abstract and commonplace late nineteenth-century truisms. Work supplied moral instruction, brought success, and provided the basis for virtue in the producer's republic. Accepting all of these interpretations, New Yorkers also added that one's expectations ought to be limited. "The ability to labor is no small blessing, and it should be so regarded by every sensible and grateful person," a correspondent for the Cooperstown *Freeman's Journal* declared.[31] In a place where bad news lurked everywhere, work might be counted as a small favor.

Of all the values that work taught, New Yorkers put greatest emphasis on the lesson that life was hard. "Men do not learn from their enjoyments," a newspaper quoted a "rural philosopher." In the end, life did not consist of good times, and the sooner a person appreciated this, the better off he was. A newspaper correspondent described the ideal woman as one who understood that "every day and all day cannot be devoted to holiday making, but that life holds duties without number."[32] Difficulty imparted important truths about the world. At a meeting of the Cortland County Farmers' Club, a member offered his opinion that "adversity [was] good for farmers. They had things their own way during the war; grew restless and lived beyond their income, and should put up with the hard times and do the best that circumstances would allow." An appreciation of the necessity of work and the difficulty of life was a sign of maturity; accordingly, men and women debated the optimum amount of work children should do so that its lessons might be learned. "[T]he sooner young people come to know that life is made up of reality and not romance, the better it is for their future welfare and usefulness," a speaker at a state Grange meeting warned. Lazy people—the loafers and idlers, tramps and politicians—were, in turn, contemptible, since such people expected others to care for them.[33]

Views of the value of work and the dangers of laziness varied in New York in the late nineteenth century, especially between farmers and villagers. While the writings of both groups attacked idlers, for example, the reasons for their displeasure differed. Farmers' condemnations of laziness carried criticisms of those who profited from the labor of others—produce dealers, speculators, lawyers, politicians, and so forth. Villagers connected laziness with the serious national problem of weakening character in the wake of more widely available luxuries. A Cortland minister's Thanksgiving sermon in 1880 asserted that most problems would be solved if parents taught their "boys to work . . . and girls that to make a good loaf of bread is more important, and as much a sign of a lady, as to play the piano. . . . We want MEN and not FOPS. WOMEN, and not DOLLS."[34]

Aside from arming men and women to cope with life's trials, work and sacrifice contributed to success, according to some villagers. "When I was a young man," a Cooperstown merchant recalled in 1896, "I worked one year on that farm, for my board and $10 a month; at the end of the year I had saved $75 of my wages." The moral was that the older generation "indulged in few useless luxuries, wasted no money, and practiced strict economy; they did not wait for something to 'come up' that would suddenly make them rich—and so always remain poor." Items from popular magazines and local lectures asserted the link between hard work and success. In keeping with popular wisdom, the writers saw personal character as the basis of success. Asked to describe the necessary elements of prosperous agriculture, a farmer dourly listed "economy, silence, discretion."[35] To a certain extent, New Yorkers believed in the common late nineteenth-century argument about success being available to all men willing to make the necessary effort.

Even newspapermen, however, recognized that despite the hopeful moralizing of advice books, work alone did not always bring success. Hard times further strained the connection between work and reward.[36] But if not a sufficient condition for success, a reputation as a hard worker was essential in gaining respect. Eulogies reprinted in newpapers or delivered at meetings of voluntary organizations stressed hard work as one of the subject's important attributes. A lawyer in Nineveh who attended a staggering number of funerals noted the respectable turnout for one in 1885 and added that the "poor woman had gone through with her troubles in this world and I think she is at rest she has worn herself out here working for her family." Through her perseverance and work, she earned recognition for good character.[37]

Whatever its sterling qualities, work brought nearly incessant complaints, particularly among farmers. The grinding routine of farm and home chores wore away happy moralizing about work's rewards. A Grange in 1893 concluded that work led to illness and even death.

> Overwork is the great lowering element among our rural population. Now many of our Government officials only work five or six hours out of 24 while at the same time the busy farmer and their wives will work 12 to 16 hours. . . . And then again how many homes are presided over by invalid wives and mothers. The sole cause is overwork.

Those who kept diaries always recorded chores (along with weather)—and often nothing else. Complaints about work in part illustrated the writer's virtue: he or she had earned the right to grumble. Long lists of chores also proved that something had changed, progress of a sort had been made, and the day had not been wasted. Nonetheless, diarists called for relief. As one woman protested, "Am tired and sick of everything. . . . Am tired of living always at home at work."[38]

Even when difficult to bear, arduous work was a source of pride to rural New Yorkers. Farmers liked to argue that they worked harder than most people and for less reward. Like Populists, the Knights of Labor, and Socialists, rural New Yorkers proposed a labor theory of value: labor produced all wealth; agriculture was the backbone of the economy; and workers embodied all that was good in the nation. In 1889, a number of local Granges resolved that

> we view with increasing alarm the efforts of both corporate and official greed to absorb the last vestage of the profits of agriculture, the industry which is [the] basis of not only all other industries including trade and Commerce but makes Christianity possible and even life itself, is the only real home of freedom and of virtue but now so depressed and paralized by the greed of capital under official or legal sanction as to cause Republican institutions to tremble.

Farmers' work was harsher than everyone else's, and they were even closer to God, but organized greed conspired to take away the earnings of their labor.[39]

Petitions like this lend support to the arguments offered by some historians about the resilience of republicanism. Grangers saw themselves defending the republic, the virtue it depended on, freedom, and even Christianity from the illegitimate power exercised by the combined forces of capital and corrupt politicians. Yet republican language could support an astounding number of causes. Grangers drew pinched conclusions from the republican tradition: they protested what they considered the outrageous salaries of public officials. They also narrowly applied their ideas about work. Farmers believed they worked harder than villagers and factory workers who put in limited hours. Their labor was more demanding than that of Western farmers, who received special advantages from both the railroads and Nature. New York farmers, in short, selectively applied the idea that productive labor deserved reward; indeed, they denigrated the labor of others. Few rural men in New York would see a way to make common cause with farmer and labor political parties in the late nineteenth century.[40]

New Yorkers' truncated vision and use of republicanism reflected their insistence that one must limit one's expectations. They shrank from finding a positive solution for farm families who worked too much and received less than their fair share in return. In a similar way, rural New Yorkers cast a skeptical glance at the truism that hard work brought success. In their modifications of both the success and the producer ideologies, they revealed a more basic ambivalence about change itself, a chancy thing that could just as easily bring bad as good consequences.

Some rural New Yorkers offered qualifications to the enthusiasm for progress and change characteristic of the late nineteenth century. "Progress" was a stock topic for lyceum lecturers and speakers at community Chautauquas, but in the tradition of the jeremiad, some locally produced talks took dark turns. The main speaker at the Centennial Celebration of the Settlement of the Schenevus Valley, prominent Democrat Walter H. Bunn, chose as his topic "One Hundred Years of Progress." The bulk of the talk, however, decried the decay in virtue and character from the settlement to 1891. Prior to 1800, he claimed, "there were no drones or idlers," and men were not "ambitious for political place, holding, doubtless, that the post of honor was the private station." While material conditions had improved somewhat, those gains came at the expense of the ultimately more important elements of moral character. In the same way, speakers at Granges or at public meetings sometimes spoke of how conditions in the late nineteenth century had improved over those fifty or one hundred years earlier. But it would be pushing common opinion too hard to ignore that in important ways, the quality of life had deteriorated. Women, too, wondered if their lot had improved, but for a different reason. In response to a male Granger's view that new agricultural machinery brought "increased cares," the women countered that they had seen few advances in their work. Their lives might have been somewhat easier than their grandmothers', but too few changes had occurred to talk about progress.[41]

Misgivings about change in a general sense appeared as a common theme in the writings of rural New Yorkers. Individuals seemed wary of changes in their own lives: it appeared most often as an unfortunate disruption, and they expressed few hopes for improvement. Diary entries that noted a new year or a birthday voiced minimal expectations for the future and cited the writers' mistakes of the previous year. A man from Knoxboro indicated his gratitude that "our lives are spaired & all is well" on New Year's Eve, 1880. In 1884, a woman who experienced almost constant depression wrote on New Year's Day that she felt "old and tired," while her family "watched the old year out and the new year in." A twenty-two-year-old woman of a more romantic bent reflected on her birthday: "O how can I comprehend my life! . . . One more year of life and health, one more year to enjoy the society and intercourse of friends and these friends have all been spared, to me another year, thank God." Still others considered their spiritual decline. For those given to reflection, thankfulness for life and health and hope that they would continue passed for positive statements. The absence of change was a wish fulfilled.[42]

While men and women viewed change in their own and their families' lives as probable turns for the worse, farmers often regarded changes in their work with somewhat less suspicion. The merits of scientific agriculture were seriously debated in the late nineteenth century. On one side, men cited the productivity, profits, and increased leisure that would follow from scientific farming, continuing an effort begun more than a century before to modernize farmers' habits. Agricultural societies and farmers' clubs did their best to promote new practices in the nineteenth century, through prizes given at fairs and efforts to disseminate information. Granges also encouraged members to "give their experience" with various methods and crops. By the end of the nineteenth century, the state Agricultural Experiment Station and College of Agriculture worked to spread the idea that modern methods pointed the main route to profitable farming.[43]

For every booster of new methods, another felt that change should not be introduced too hastily and that the old methods were good enough. Grangers debated the practicality of scientific advice, and one woman wondered why farmers had been singled out for so much attention. "Are [farmers] a class of fools, that they do not know how to manage their own affairs?" she asked, and went on to defend farmers' skills, friendliness, good health, and equitable treatment of their wives. Despite the efforts of the modernizers, changes in agricultural practices in the late nineteenth century came slowly. Especially in declining townships, productivity remained low. Even in more prosperous areas, some farmers questioned new farming methods for practical reasons. Increased productivity that might result from more expensive new farming practices—fertilizers and improved dairy herds—would probably only depress prices and leave farmers in debt. The new methods, moveover, had not yet been sanctioned by long experience. As late as 1895, a Granger in Clymer, New York, argued that "if the farmer would buy a 30¢ hoe and use it all up but the handle, it would give him a greater profit than $30 worth of phosphate." Hard work, claimed traditionalists, rather than science, brought success in farming.[44]

Farmers did not question new methods because of their unbending affection for tradition. Rather, some considered the older methods as surer ways to steady returns and self-improvement; the techniques in use were safe although not wildly profitable. New York farmers even speculated in a conservative manner. Like farmers elsewhere, they became enchanted with numerous agricultural fads that promised quick profits. Hops, mint, sugar beets, and other crops were each believed to be, for a time, *the* crop that would allow New York farmers to make an easy living. Some farmers indeed profited by following fads in farming, although most did not. Those who participated in a fad usually did so in a conservative fashion: putting aside a few acres while depending on dairy products or eggs for a stable income. Hardly an American peasantry, New York farmers sought improvement for themselves and their families. Improvement might only mean the achievement of stability, and they pursued it more often than not through retaining older methods. Improvement was, nonetheless, the goal that traditional methods and slow change were supposed to reach.[45]

Both attitudes about scientific agriculture as well as comments in diaries expressed a suspicion of change and a desire for self-improvement. While progress was unlikely, the struggle to move ahead morally and materially was crucial. Effort separated the lazy men and women from the hard workers, the shiftless from the dependable. Both limited personal aspirations and skepticism about scientific agriculture can be seen as sensible attitudes. By moving slowly in adopting new agricultural practices, many New York farmers maintained low levels of debt and thus suffered less severely from the periodic agricultural depressions in the late nineteenth century other farmers elsewhere endured. Limited personal aspirations were a realistic (albeit defensive) assessment of conditions in the rural areas of the state. Meager expectations were as much a description of life in parts of rural New York as a prescription of how to live. Even the sparest diary mentioned the things that changed from day to day: weather, which varied most days; chores, which changed somewhat; and visits made and received. By reminding themselves of the importance of seemingly small matters, rural New Yorkers defended their choice to stay put in a period that valued progress and mobility.[46]

In the end, the conservative course seemed safe and desirable in rural New York. Conservatism as a personal quality could command respect. In an oration given at a funeral around 1900, the speaker noted that the subject, a businessman active on the fringes of local politics, made decisions that were "always conservative in which there is always an element of safety." By this he set a fine example, the speaker continued. The subject was

> a good man in the community—he may not be loud or outspoken, he may not proclaim his virtue from the housetops, he may not even seek to enforce his precept by word of mouth but his life is a restraining power for good in the community in which he lives.

A good man—or woman—practiced modesty, was not assertive, and did not attempt to draw personal attention. Doubtless a practitioner of personal restraint, a good person also curbed, through example, radical aspirations or ideas in the community. Such conservatism hardly described the views of all New Yorkers in this period. Indeed, a dialogue between conservatives, "progressives," and radicals of various sorts had to be maintained—each group needed the other to justify its existence. But perhaps because it asked and expected so little, conservatism tended to carry the day.[47]

Community life, too, testified to the extent to which rural people valued conservatism. New York's smaller rural communities presented themselves as places of harmony, agreement, and measured growth. Citizens of declining or stable rural townships placed particular importance on the appearance of harmony. Community leaders described evil and disagreement as baleful infusions from outside: from strangers who spread bad ideas, committed crimes, loafed, set bad examples, and so forth. Actual rural townships offered closeness—in the sense of support for neighbors, care for the ill, and the like—along with a kind of claustrophobia that some found stifling. Townships (and groups within them) that insisted on consensus before coming to decisions often tried to muffle disagreements and found it difficult to make any decisions at all.

To claim that consensus was an important goal is not to say that townships across New York were either blessed with harmony or weighed down by conformity. As used here, "consensus" merely describes a way of making decisions. Rural townships that sought consensus did not lack conflict, but they used particular methods to deal with the disputes that inevitably arose. Methods of conflict resolution that aimed at the acquiescence of as many townspeople as possible allowed towns to put off certain changes until something approaching unanimity had been reached—usually a long process. Such methods turned up in voluntary organizations and in local governments in the late nineteenth century.

One could expect to see consensual methods of decision-making in voluntary societies. After all, such groups often took fellowship and harmony as ends; even those that adopted other goals sought to create good feeling among members. In rural New York, the Grange was the largest single farmers' organization in the late nineteenth century. In contrast to those in the Midwest and West, Northeastern Granges put education and social contact before politics and economic benefits. This orientation came about because the Order admitted nonfarmers by the 1880s after most attempts to build purchasing cooperatives had failed. In the Grange, as in Freemasonry, after which it was modeled, a lack of harmony could be understood as an indication of failure.[48] Nonetheless, even Granges went about dealing with differences between members and achieving harmony in different ways.

Levels of prosperity and attitudes toward change shaped the ways that Granges made decisions. The consensual model involved a slow process of gaining near-unity on a given proposal. A second method, more common in relatively prosperous places, required the agreement of a simple majority to take action. No organization practiced either style of decision-making exclusively, but one form or the other tended to predominate. Practitioners of consensus gradually wore down opposition. Typically, after a member proposed an initiative of some sort, a lack of full agreement would stall action. A majority might pass the proposal, but without nearly unanimous consent, it would be brought up again for further discussion. The process could last months or even years. Finally, if a group reached agreement, the measure would pass. If not, the matter would simply be dropped. The person or group who proposed the change carried the burden of securing as close to unanimous opinion as possible. Because it made any departure from established practices difficult—and perhaps, too, because would-be innovators tired of the process—the consensual pattern of decision-making worked against the introduction of new initiatives.

The Bowens Corners Grange in Oswego County, for example, had difficulty coming to any conclusion that required changes in the normal activities of their group, as was typical of Granges in declining townships. They acted with reasonable dispatch on matters that already enjoyed wide agreement: to send petitions to Albany opposing taxes for roads, raises for lawmakers, and weaker liquor laws, for example. But in dealing with immediate problems that revealed differences between their members, the group stalled. With Bowens Corners, as well as other Granges, the most controversial matters involved how their hall was to be used and whether to purchase a hall outright. The members of Bowens Corners pondered whether to buy a hall for nearly a decade; deciding if their officers would wear badges with jewels or ribbons took two years. The Three Mile Bay Grange debated for years if a club that wanted to hold a dance could use the Grange hall; if the Grange should hold dances for their members; and, if so, whether outsiders could also attend. The Charlotte Center Grange could reach no conclusion through the 1890s on whether members not connected with certain programs, such as fire relief, should be allowed to vote on those questions.[49]

On each occasion, a similar pattern developed. An apparent majority of members voted for the change, which then caused "spirited" discussions and motions to rescind; the matter dragged on for a number of meetings. In all of these cases, members who proposed departures from present operations needed to build support for change. Since doing nothing was easiest and safest, they faced real challenges. Indeed, in such Granges, activity soon devolved into running "social hours" for members and practicing the Order's ritual. The decision to take no action itself did not normally mean the end of a proposal; rather, action would more likely be put off than killed outright. Hence, issues would live for years without ever finding firm resolutions one way or the other.

Growing or stable townships usually supported the more active and prosperous Granges. This might be expected, since the men and women in such places were more likely than those in declining townships to take an active interest in the scientific and political aspects of agriculture and to have the resources to support an organization. Such Granges— Manchester in Ontario County, Clymer in Chautauqua, Domestic in Scriba, Oswego County—came to decisions on both political issues and organizational procedures through simple majorities. Because success was a reasonable expectation, new initiatives came forward more frequently. Some Granges published their own newspapers; others engaged in local reform by supporting charity and education. Still others organized agricultural fairs as well as additional social and educational events. All this could be accomplished without absolute consent. In the end, it made for a self-fulfilling prophecy: active Granges achieved that status in part because of their favored geographic position, but also because their work brought a level of excitement that in turn drew new members. And the Granges' ability to take on new projects rested on a willingness to accept something less than complete agreement.[50]

The prosperity and activity of a Grange even in the best agricultural parts of the state often receded as an older generation took less interest in the Order and overall activity declined. Aside from generational change, bitter disputes over cooperative purchasing programs or general direction hastened Granges' retreats. County reports given at meetings of the New York State Grange in the 1870s and 1880s recount incidents of local Granges' dividing, breaking apart, or merely stagnating because of severe disagreements about purchasing policy. At the point of decline, Granges moved toward consensual decisions and little change. When Granges—like townships—declined, the need for consensus grew.[51]

If a Grange existed for any appreciable length of time, it probably passed through consensual and majoritarian phases. Throughout, the link between decline and consensus remained. A move toward consensual decision-making was a defensive act, a reflex when the group lacked the resources to take on new activities and when divisions on public policy might further reduce membership. Consensual decision-making—and the related aversion to new projects—did not usually mean that a local Grange had reached its end. Some of the least-active Granges survived the longest and simply served more limited purposes. A consistent feature of Granges in less-prosperous towns, consensual decision-making worked against change, as a result both of the members' preference and of concrete difficulties in marshalling resources.[52]

Other voluntary associations and local governments also employed the patient methods of consensus when grappling with divisive issues. For poorer groups and townships this course made eminent sense: organizations could not ask citizens to part with additional cash unless most already agreed to do so. Searching for agreement and maintaining the appearance of harmony, however, had significant consequences. For women's groups, the consequences included bypassing community projects—initiatives that might have seemed disruptive and that women lacked the resources to sustain. For the most financially strapped town governments, the outcome would be fending off requests for modernized schools and other public services until forced to change by the state. Thus decision-making by consensus encouraged those who wanted changes to look beyond their communities and led those wary of new initiatives to insist on local control.

Rural New Yorkers' ideas about religion, work, and change at once reinforced and challenged nineteenth-century truisms about politics. Such ideas discouraged most men from seriously considering third-party alternatives to the Democrats or Republicans, while also giving them a language with which to criticize lazy and self-seeking politicians. Protestant convictions extended to rural women a reason to participate in public debate, but that activity also reminded men and women of the distinct missions in life that their gender roles laid out. Moreover, men and women largely agreed about the virtues of stern Protestantism and of reining in one's aspirations, but they differed when it came to determining how those convictions applied to public life. That difference provided the space for men's and women's distinct understandings of nineteenth-century government and politics.

CHAPTER 2

The Moral Vision of Men's
Politics, 1870–1900

Gradually shedding eighteenth-century suspicion of political parties, men turned partisan loyalty into a virtue in the early nineteenth century. During the last third of that century, a politics built upon men's allegiance to their parties reached its zenith. Newspapers did not aim for an "objective" telling of a day's events; instead, editors thundered partisan appeals and accused their enemies of all manner of perfidy and ignorance. Voters, meanwhile, gave every indication that they took to heart Gilded Age newspapermen's directives. On election days, the vast majority of both rural and urban men went to the polls and usually cast ballots for one or the other of the major parties, even in the midst of hard times when third parties may have spoken to their needs more directly. Some men sought out more visible ways than voting to proclaim their partisanship. They marched in parades, attended picnics and pole raisings, and shouted at party rallies. Throughout, they listened to the familiar litany of Gilded Age political issues: that (depending on the source) a high or low tariff pointed the way to lasting prosperity; that the other party's extravagance or greed made for expensive government; and that the various virtues, past and present, of their party and its candidates merited continued support. Nothing in rural men's political behavior departed significantly from prevailing patterns in towns and cities across the North.[1]

We do not want for studies of these patterns. Historians have offered numerous insightful interpretations of why different groups of voters supported the Democrats or Republicans, of what would seem by later standards phenomenal turnouts for late nineteenth-century elections, and of the formation of third parties, national issues like the tariff, and the careers of politicians. Rather than replicate such accounts for rural New York, it seems more valuable to pursue a different line of inquiry, one that illuminates the moral framework that men who were devoted to the parties had in common. Gender was one piece of this framework. It shaped men's politics as much as it did that of women: devotion to party was a male virtue and part of a male culture. To analyze the moral vision of men's politics can illuminate the political ideas of New

York men and challenge prevalent assumptions about Gilded Age partisanship and government.[2]

Rural producers of partisan rhetoric—the countless party workers,
editors, county and state office-holders, and local lawyers—filled newspaper pages and the late October evening air with praise for their parties
and economical government, the two verities of Gilded Age politics.
While voting and perhaps parading for Democratic or Republican candidates, other rural men, the intended consumers of these words, often
expressed contempt for politicians, suspicion of government, and cynicism about the political process. Far from the noble descendants of Jackson or Lincoln, ordinary politicians were lazy men who lied. Government
enriched the wealthy. While a pleasant diversion, elections, at best,
changed little; at worst, they ushered in policies destined to hasten rural
New York's economic decline. Both partisan and cynical male political
talk made use of a common language that pushed issues that would be
considered private by the twentieth century—personal loyalty, friendship, and character—into the center of political speeches, newspaper
editorials, and personal correspondence. Alongside of these personal
considerations appeared assurances of devotion to principle above men
and to the public good. Rural male politics merged partisanship with
cynicism, avid participation with suspicion of government, and personal
concerns with public life.

However complex the interweaving of these attitudes about politics
were, one assumption appeared to be simple: politics meant *electoral*
politics—voting and office-holding, no more and no less. Grange members, for example, talked incessantly about legislation and public issues
and sent countless petitions to Albany and Washington lawmakers. But all
along, Grangers declared they swore off politics—its introduction would
be too divisive for an organization dedicated to fraternity.[3] Yet even this
reduction of politics to the work of parties admitted complexities. Politics
had an imaginative aspect. Party politics created and expressed images
and concepts of good government and leadership, proper relationships
between men, and what American society might ideally be. Party appeals
and participation in the process provided solace and guidance insofar as
they contributed to an idealized view of social and political relations.
Electoral politics also expressed self-interest—voters supported the men
who they believed would most help them.[4] Party politics was more than
symbolism; it addressed practical problems and succeeded or failed in
proffering solutions. Imagination and self-interest did not occupy opposite ends of some scale of political thought. They overlapped and reinforced each other in myriad ways; and appreciating rural men's expectations for both inspiration and performance allows us to understand the
otherwise paradoxical world of rural male politics.

When newspaper editors touted the superiority of their parties' candidates, they produced a catalogue of traits desirable in male politics. In

attempting to persuade the voters of Otsego County to vote for Robert Townsend, the Democratic candidate for district attorney in 1883, the *Freeman's Journal* enlisted all the standard claims. The editor's recommendations of Townsend in 1880, when he first ran for the office, remained the same in his bid for re-election: the candidate was "personally a very popular man; and a Democrat from principle and whose services have been freely given the candidates and his friends at every election." Townsend, in short, had worked for the party in the past and thus had earned the support of Democrats in his own race. His re-election, however, could not be taken for granted. Disgruntled Democrats planned to "knife" his candidacy—to replace his name with that of the Republican candidate, on the Democratic ticket. So the editor of the Cooperstown newspaper stepped up his appeals. Townsend, he wrote, "has always been true to the candidates of his party and the party should be true to him in this conflict." Furthermore, Townsend's "time and service have been at the command of his friends." The editor concluded with a plea for the loyalty that Townsend had earned: "Will any of them for some petty cause of personal feelings, turn against so true a Democrat in this contest, and inflict upon him the stigma of defeat, when it is in the power of the party to elect the entire ticket? We trust not. It would be too ungrateful." Friendship, mutual obligation, gratitude, and loyalty mattered in politics. The man's character and long history of fidelity to the Democratic cause alone recommended him to voters.[5]

Notably absent in this editor's arguments were references to Townsend's qualifications or record, much less any hint of positions Townsend might take if he won. A remark that Townsend's election would give Otsegoians "wholesome law" stood as the lonely exception to the silence on policies. Neither the lack of attention to policies nor the stress on the candidate's personal character made this campaign different from others. In late nineteenth-century politics, as newspapermen portrayed it, the worthy won nomination to office, and only partisan treachery cheated them of victory.[6]

This campaign failed. Townsend came up short by nineteen votes out of the 1,423 cast, although the rest of the Democratic ticket carried Otsego County. He lost, the editor maintained, because of Democrats "in fish suits" who conspired against him. These pseudo-Democrats, significantly, lived not in Cooperstown but in the nearby small city of Oneonta. The editor expediently failed to mention Townsend's prosecution of illegal fishing in Otsego Lake, which had helped make him an unpopular man. For the *Freeman's Journal,* Townsend may have lost, but the election had a happy ending nonetheless: no dishonor came to Democrats, the candidate, or the village. With the entire campaign handled in terms of character and obligation, only the tricks of scheming men could account for failure. That such men lived outside the community made the explanation all the better.[7]

For the party workers who constructed appeals for support, politics was likewise about party loyalty and the personal character of the candidates. A Democratic newspaper advised its readers to vote for Roswell P. Flower for governor in 1891 because he was "a family man, a fatherly man, a homespun man, a consistent man, a God-fearing man and a gentleman." His conservative virtues made him a safe person to administer the state government. Another editor in 1888 described Thomas Collier Platt as a man whose "distinguishing traits are integrity, equilibrium and fidelity—the best qualification, the mental equipoise and the faithful support of principles and friends which make the safe and trusty counsellor." Platt understood the role of friendship in politics and avoided rash action: these traits made him the obvious choice for secretary of the treasury. An assembly candidate was "of good old Revolutionary stock," served in the Union Army, and had "the mental aptitude and right moral quality for public life." A nominee for sheriff was "a typical Schoharie county farmer, honest, intelligent, progressive and laborious." Rural newspapers across the state boosted men in their campaigns because they possessed earnestness, popularity, affability, industry, successful careers, loyalty, and steady habits.[8]

Issues were not forgotten as editors assembled the rosters of estimable traits that their candidates happily owned. Partisan newspapers covered certain issues, especially the tariff question, in great (if repetitive) detail. For the Schoharie County Republican Committee, the choice was stark in 1892. "The choice in this election is clear. Protection and prosperity on one hand or free trade and ruin on the other," the committee reminded loyal Republicans. In the preceding presidential election, an article in a campaign supplement luridly specified what "ruin" might mean. "Chains and Slavery," the headline ran: "A Terrible Picture of Tyranny and Degradation In Saintly England: Women At The Forge!" Yet coverage of the tariff, the political scandal of the moment, or the currency question served chiefly to remind men of the sinister intentions of the enemy and the purity of the office-holders of their own party. Articles that praised candidates' adherence to the verities of their parties also described that commitment as indicative of sterling character. Even positions on issues came back to the question of character.[9]

Were appeals grounded on character calculated attempts to sidestep divisive issues and to cynically lull voters into believing a fantastic set of assertions about public life? To some extent, yes. Surely both politicians and voters understood that men in office made decisions that affected voters' well-being and that character often had little to do with what those men decided. Perhaps it is more to the point to see late nineteenth-century political rhetoric as a recognized formal language—like that of the ministry or the law—that created and perpetuated a vision of men in public office expected by both party activists and voters.

This was the language with which politicians conducted their business at county nominating conventions. The Chautauqua County Republican Party, for example, sustained the junction of character, recognition of

the deserving, and the honor of nomination to public office. One delegate nominated a man for county clerk by describing his "earnest manhood and sterling Republicanism." Ratification of national and state Republican candidates provided the occasion for more elaborate rhetorical
flights. The chairman of the 1900 convention opened a "thrilling address" thus: "The Republican party has placed at the head of the national ticket a man whose name is synonymous with prosperity, a man
who believes that the interest of America is paramount to the interests we
have in any other people on the face of the earth." Even cynical accounts
of nominating speeches let stand the connection between office and
proper reward. In 1884, L. S. Terry, "wound up for an all day speech,"
nominated his friend Sidney M. Hoiser for county treasurer. Terry told
of Hoiser's "numerous excellences," but then "began to expatiate on the
wrongs of political rings and evil course of Sperry, late treasurer," until
the chairman cut him short. It was the length of Terry's speech and his
tendency to veer off on tangents that caused problems; not the form of
his recommendation of his friend. The tie between reward and character
was strong, but not strong enough to withstand windy speeches that
departed from the accepted style. Hoiser lost.[10]

The ability to see elevation to public office as the just reward for good
character and hard work turned up in other contexts as well. A newspaper article—perhaps better described as a parable—illustrated the link
between work and public reward. The columnist for the community of
Little York in the *Cortland Democrat* told the story of a patient boy in Cold
Brook. The boy saw a woodchuck retreat into its hole, so he grabbed a
bayonet and stood watch for the next three hours. When the woodchuck
finally reappeared, the boy stabbed it. "This," the writer intoned, "is the
kind of boy from which Presidents are selected." In the late twentieth
century, such behavior would be taken as a sign of serious emotional
problems. But for the readers of the Cortland newspaper in 1879, the
story's message was clear. Patience and perseverance fitted a man for life,
and especially for politics; such traits were necessary for political success
and were virtues the people's representatives should embody. In politics,
if not in business and farming, the virtuous and hardworking still received their due.[11]

Along with shoring up the notion that hard work and virtue beat a path
to success and respect, partisan politics had close links to nineteenth-
century understandings of gender. It reinforced the doctrine of separate
spheres: men belonged out in the "world"—business and politics—while
women's talents suited them for the care of the home and family. Their
distinct natures fitted men for public life and women for the private
sphere.[12]

More than simply reminding men and women of the proper division
of sexual labor, participation in politics helped to define "manhood."
The ability to exercise the franchise was an important right that all men
shared, despite the class and ethnic differences that separated them.

The attributes of character associated with manhood—courage, loyalty, industry, and independence—were those described as most worthy of public reward, thereby strengthening the connection between manhood and politics. Both voters and politicians ideally possessed such traits. Since voting and office-holding were all that rural men saw fit to include in a definition of politics, tactics like direct application of pressure on officals to change public policies seemed either unmanly or non-political. Each part of the imaginative structure—manhood, character, and partisanship—depended on the other two.[13]

Discussions of party politics inevitably involved language that reminded citizens that politics was men's business. As late as 1905, a Republican Civil War veteran hoped "we will always fill our offices with true men." Successful candidates were routinely praised for their "manliness"; losers received consolation for waging "manly" campaigns. In the faction-marred Democratic campaign of 1891, one man noted that in his county, the Democrats eschewed the temptations of bolting the party: "most of the respectable Democrats . . . stood up manfully." Political language had masculine connotations with particular emphasis on war. Elections were "battles" or "fights," party workers were "lieutenants" who fought hard for a worthy cause. Men who marched in party parades wore military uniforms. Loyalty, discipline, and steadfastness under fire were as desirable in politicians and voters as they were in soldiers.[14]

Conversely, partisans derided their foes for their lack of manly virtues; or, as in "Grover's Lament," imagined them seduced by bad ideas. In this Republican song, Free Trade, as a "voluptuous tempting maid," enticed Grover Cleveland. By the end of the song, she appeared as a tormenting hag who brought him defeat. Bad ideas, like bad women, destroyed manhood; Republicans, presumably, benefited from both good women and sound principles. A letter from a local Republican politician to a state assemblyman dramatized the assemblyman's political problems in a similar way. "When one sees a friend married to some worthless vixen, if we know the fellow has some merit in him, our sense of abhorrence rises and falls in proportion to his suffering." The assemblyman's friends felt "disgrace" in watching an enemy's attempts to "humiliate you and embarrass his constituents." Underhanded politicians lacked the integrity to be called men; they were best compared with "worthless" women.[15]

"Manhood" was also shorthand for a set of traits that men should aspire to and that fitted them for public life. Integrity, self-assertion, loyalty, devotion to principle, and friendship loomed largest in this selection of personal attributes. Despite its basis on character rather than physiology, masculine politics excluded women from participation in electoral politics just as surely as an exclusion justified by biology would have done.

An incident concerning temperance agitation in Hartford Mills illustrates some of the attributes of manhood. A male hotel owner was accused of selling liquor without a license. Before the case got to court, however, some of the community's "best citizens" got up a petition attesting to the hotel owner's innocence. The district attorney dismissed the case with apologies to the jury, calling the false charges an exercise of "malice and spite." A newspaper correspondent summed up the event by claiming that "[a] person who would make such a complaint without cause would poison their neighbor's dogs *for sport,* [and] poke fun during family prayers. . . . It could not have been a man; it must have been some miserable, mischief-making, vinegar tempered old shrew." A man, apparently, would poison dogs only when necessary and maintain proper deference toward religion. Men worthy of the name did not bring false charges; they fought fairly and out in the open. Manhood, in this case, meant integrity and forthrightness—characteristics scarce among women.[16]

A letter from a Granger, R. M. Smith, to then-senator David Bennett Hill highlights other desirable male traits by pointing to their absence. Smith offered his assessment of Lieutenant Governor Edward F. Jones, who was also an officer of the New York State Grange and a speaker at successive Grange meetings. As Smith described it, Jones "gets a hearing because he crowds himself in and a few of his Democratic friends aid him in so doing." Then there was Jones' conceit: "He also comes loaded with his photos, and delights, seemingly, in peddling out his pictures, and as one member aptly expressed himself—'Jones is popular as ever with the women but with the men he is not.' " Jones seemed unmanly because he put himself forward in situations where his presence was not demanded. His assertiveness was out of place because he simply aimed to advance his own cause. Worse, he suffered from vanity. Indeed, for the writer, proof of Jones' weakness was the "Semi-Governor's" popularity with women, who, it seems, were more easily convinced by apperances than men were. While men stuck to the facts of character, women were swayed by charm and presentation.[17]

While Edward F. Jones was too pushy for Smith's tastes, self-assertion nonetheless had a place in both manhood and politics. In 1891, C. F. Peck, a Hornellsville politician, had grown disgusted with what he saw as the partisan wrangling and "the double dealing and outright treachery" of Grover Cleveland's wing, as well as with Senator (and Governor) Hill's unhelpfulness. "Governor, if you expect me to lie down quietly under such a condition of facts, I can assure you, that you are greatly mistaken," he warned. "[M]y sense of justice can always be appealed to and my loyalty to you will continue to be in the future. . . . [B]ut I cannot be bulldozed or tricked. I am of age and must be allowed to assert my manhood, occasionally at least." Manhood meant making one's own decisions, having one's concerns heeded, and being treated with respect regardless of one's position. This point was put more plainly in Democratic editorials on the evil of the "unit rule" in conventions, which required counting the votes of districts, counties, or states instead of the votes of individuals in making nominations. The rule "not only deprives [the delegate] of his manhood but makes him a mere cog in the wheel of a 'machine'. . . . Manhood,

independence and patriotism all plead against the evils of centralization."
Independent action was a privilege of manhood that partisanship threatened to destroy, even while political participation helped to define manhood itself.[18]

The danger that subservience to a party posed to true manhood could
be mitigated by reminding men of the place of loyalty and principle. As
much as manhood required independence, it also required the willingness
to remain loyal to a worthy cause despite disadvantages. Men, ideally,
freely gave this loyalty because of their deep sense of honor and belief in
the righteousness of their party's tenets. A letter written by a Democratic
politician in Owego, John Macklin, is an example of the importance of
loyalty to the ideals of manhood and loyalty's ability to quiet fears of
dependency. Macklin complained of the intraparty discord produced by a
contest between himself and a Mr. Bulger for the county chairmanship in
1891. Bulger spread lies about Macklin; and worse, Macklin claimed, he
threatened to abandon the Democratic ticket unless he gained the chairmanship. Macklin defended the honor of county Democrats by describing
them as men who "do not believe in rewarding with office, men who must
be kept in office to guarantee their loyalty to party nominees." Such
loyalty should be given in recognition of service, not dispensed in return
for favors. Macklin thus asserted that to ask Democrats to make Bulger
county chairman was to "perform an act which would be a shultification of
their Manhood, their Democracy and their love for Democratic Suprem-
acy in the State and Nation." Men would not naturally choose to honor one
so unworthy; to force them to do so would be to attack the basis of partisanship. Men were partisans by choice, not by dictation. Party loyalty, more
than voting for a slate of candidates, was a considered judgment that
bestowed honor on those most deserving. Violating that premise destroyed manhood by removing the prerogative of independent action.[19]

Pleas for men to put principle and loyalty above other concerns appeared most commonly when a portion of one of the parties threatened
to bolt the regular ticket. Party leaders listened attentively for rumblings
of discontent, because neither the Democrats nor the Republicans could
establish dominance in late nineteenth-century New York: statewide
races were usually extremely competitive, so defections often spelled
defeat on election day. Hence party regulars called upon all supporters
to act with honor and to recall the worthiness of their party's cause—to
assert their manhood—however unhappy or attracted to the regional or
class background of an opposition candidate they might be. Yet divisions
within parties occurred on a grand scale in the Democratic Party in the
1880s and 1890s and at the local level in both parties throughout the late
nineteenth century. To save face and promote unity, partisans explained
defections in ways that neither impugned all party voters nor insinuated
that the bolters were unmanly. A newspaper editorial blamed the divisiveness in the Democratic Party in 1891, not on the mass of Democrats, nor
even on the principal actors, but on a venal yet undefined "office-seeking

and man worshiping class." The character required of manhood in politics was an ideal; like true womanhood, it was more often than not
observed in the breach.[20]

When an office-holder stood accused of breaking the bonds of loyalty
and friendship, he felt his career and reputation endangered. In 1898,
Willis H. Tennant, a Chautauqua County supervisor, was rumored to
have insulted his district's assemblyman and fellow supervisor, S. Fred
Nixon. Tennant offered a highly emotional defense. "What you revealed
to me to-day," he wrote Nixon, "hurt my feelings more than you are
aware." He asked Nixon to tell him who spread the stories, so that he
might confront the slanderer face to face. He went on to explain the
importance of character in politics and to defend his honor. "Place and
position to me are nothing in comparison to the opinion of those with
whom I have dealing . . . I am not a liar & villain & unworthy of belief &
confidence." Honor may well not have been as important to a political
career as Tennant claimed. He nonetheless thought it necessary to make
his case for his political worth in terms of his character alone. To renew
his reputation, Tennant claimed that he met some of the requirements of
manhood: fidelity and integrity. As proof he offered his continued concern about the good opinion of others, and his desire to confront the
man who lied about him. For Tennant, political success rested on his
peers' conviction that he possessed the highest degree of manhood.[21]

There was more to political manhood than work and unbending fidelity. At party conventions men could express emotions otherwise confined
to women. They expressed gratitude for the recognition their peers
bestowed on them, and, ideally, celebrated the honorable behavior of
men who kept duty, principle, and the good of the whole as their first
priorities. In Chautauqua County in 1885, two candidates sought the
nomination for county clerk. After two ballots, one candidate, A. H.
Stafford, led with ninety-eight votes, while his closest opponent, Ingersoll, trailed with eighty. After additional informal balloting, the chairman
called for a formal vote when Ingersoll moved that Stafford's nomination be made unanimous. This "carried amid great applause and a
speech [was] demanded of the successful candidate." Here was true nobility in politics, and Stafford responded accordingly. "Mr. Stafford was too
overcome to respond at any length," the secretary reported, "and with
tears in his eyes, simply thanked the Convention for the honor done to
him." From the secretary's record, it appears that politicians did not
consider such reactions unusual. On the contrary, a display of emotion
was permissible—even desirable. A man so honored by his fellows might
well respond with deep gratitude. In this case, the recognition was all the
better since Stafford's rival had sacrificed his ambition for party harmony. Such nobility—the highest expression of manhood—could be
touching enough to inspire tears. At the very least, the man who recorded the event found it perfectly reasonable to talk about a nomination in those terms.[22]

Conventions as well as elections, then, offered opportunities to dramatize the imaginative aspect of politics. If all went well, party politics could bring out the best in men—integrity, assertiveness, loyalty, and attention to principle. At least in partisan rhetoric, manhood made political participation a heroic act. Men made important sacrifices, staked their reputations, stood up for abstract principles, and connected themselves with the grand traditions and personalities of the past. Seeing the traits essential to manhood as crucial to politics reinforced male identity and defined its sphere. Character also had a more mundane use. Putting it at the center of political life rewarded consistent support for regular party candidates. Party leaders urged voters to remain true to regular nominees despite competing loyalties like those of class, occupation, or place. A candidate's specific position on issues, moreover, was beside the point in a politics based on character. Any man could lie about the way he would vote if elected to the assembly. But a man of good character could be counted on to do the best he could.[23]

The mythology of partisan politics thus mirrored that of nineteenth-century business. Character led to success and pointed the surest route to finding good associates. In picking an appointee, character mattered: a good man might not always take the positions one wanted, but he kept his promises and could be dealt with. He was predictable. As one man put it in recommending a friend for an assembly committee, "although he is of opposite politics to yourself, I assure you he is a right, loyal good fellow, and can be relied upon in any particular." Politicians claimed that character—as attested to by trusted friends—was the best filter with which to sift through mountains of letters asking for jobs and requesting favors. Numerous recommendations certified a man's personal qualities. A potential appointee was "honest and straight," a typical letter ran; he "has a family and is a man of good habits." To be sure, the reasoning about political worthiness and character had a circular quality: the signs of a man of good character often included long-lived partisanship. The argument that character merited reward also served as a smoke screen that masked self-interested motives. But that politicians and office-seekers chose such dodges underscores the significance of manhood and character in politics.[24]

Political friendships, like manhood and character, linked mythical and practical politics. In politics, a man could be a friend if he did as little as vote for another man. Thus one man promised to "do all in my power to show my Friendship to you on the day of Election in November" in 1898. The word "friendship" described a relationship characterized by support and obligation that was the basis of partisan politics. Political friendships allowed a sense, however illusory, of reciprocity between office-holders and voters, between leaders and led. Despite the differences in position and power, the office-holder not only potentially owed the voter something, but was implicated in a kind of partnership with him. In a more

practical vein, friendship could make self-interested behavior seem like a
principled act. Politicians were friends of voters who could be called
upon to address all manner of requests; the voter simply cashed an
implicit debt. The voter most often earned the favor through support
and work. "Friendship" thus described an ideal relationship between
representatives and citizens from which both sides drew symbolic and
material benefits.[25]

The term "friendship" appeared repeatedly in men's letters to politicians. But what did it mean? Friendship was a matter of favors given and
returned, a relationship that removed the taint of patronage by implying
that favors sprang from a sense of mutual obligation. In return for
support in the past and the promise of its continuation, a man could
reasonably expect some recognition. Examples of such thinking abound
in requests for jobs. A young man offered his "unswerving fealty to your
political fortunes and personality" as his excuse for asking David Bennett
Hill for work. This interpretation of friendship was not confined to rural
places. William H. Niegel of Baltimore, Maryland, asked Roswell P.
Flower for a thirty-dollar loan until his pension check arrived. He was a
Republican, but "4 years ago, I took advanced ground and labored for
your nomination for the Presidency, and this incurred the displeasure of
some Democrats and the bitter anger of Republicans." Such a friend, he
felt, had earned a small favor.[26]

By far the most common source of friendship and entitlement was a
long record of partisanship. When thwarted in his bid for nomination as
school commissioner in Chautauqua County, Charles W. Hurlburt suggested the proper reward for his acquiescence in defeat. "I am a Republican and I believe I am loyal to my Party," he declared. "And all that I
desire of my friends is to appreciate the position I have taken in this
matter." By refusing to fight further for the nomination, he believed that
he was laying in a stock of favors to be granted in the future. Letters of
support for candidates for postmasterships drew on partisanship and the
entire range of entitlement. Making the case that the present postmaster
in Cassadaga should retain his position, one man touted his friend's work
to "build up Cassadaga," his record "as near as I can learn" as a good
postmaster, and career as "a very ardent Republican." Such qualifications helped, but he also deserved reappointment because his competitor
was "a very ungrateful fellow." Only misguided people who "are continu-
ally wanting change" sought to replace the present postmaster. Respect
for work, community betterment, partisanship, and aversion to change
recommended the incumbent.[27]

Partisan friendship opened politicians to a wide variety of personal
requests. William Bastian needed money to visit his ailing son who lived
in Chicago, so he wrote to Democrat Roswell P. Flower for help. If
Flower sent the money, "It will confer the greatest favor as A true
Friend," Bastian closed. Another man who asked Flower for $150
claimed he "always said if you ever come up for office that I could vote

for you although of diferent Politicks." Flower's reputation had evidently spread South: a Salem, Georgia, man wanted Flower's advice on whether to become a Mason, rather than his money. "I have always admired your personal character. I have eagerly read every thing I could find concerning you and have tried to form my own character upon yours and to conform as nearly as possible to your example as my model." The detailed portraits of even fairly obscure politicians in the partisan press encouraged their political friends to ask favors that went beyond grants of government jobs.[28]

Friendship had its limits, however, as attempts to collect on political debts sometimes illustrated. Such letters even hinted at possible reprisals. H. E. Everhart of Smith's Mills wrote to S. Fred Nixon to alert him to the work Everhart and his friends had done in Nixon's last campaign. "We have worked the best way we knew how, in your favor, and in spite of the Democratic faction which have been by no means down-out, we are proud to inform you that you got a majority of about seventy." Everhart's letter showed confidence in his knowledge of how the game was played. He even felt brash enough to slap at Nixon's character. "During our work on your behalf we have been informed that you were a man who would make great promises and do little toward carrying them out." Everhart dared Nixon to prove those rumors wrong. "This election has cost us a large sum and we trust you will reciprocate by doing all in your power to bring about favorable results, and the mail route we deserve." Because his request was not a personal one, but a favor that would benefit the entire community, Everhart perhaps felt a warning was warranted. Few men committed even veiled threats to paper.[29]

Friendship, rather than hints at reprisals, made a better appeal if men wanted to settle differences. H. W. Thompson, editor of a Republican newspaper, wrote to Nixon to explain why he opposed a man nominated for a county office. He pointed to his own fidelity. "I can assure you that I have never been anything but friendly to you and your interests," he claimed. In fact, the man he opposed had been disloyal to both Nixon and Thompson. The nominee, Thompson asserted, "has never been a friend of yours . . . . He has hurt the ticket by bringing personal matters into it," and he never sent his printing to Thompson's office. As John C. Davies, the state attorney general had it, appointments between friends bound men more closely. He asked Nixon to recommend a lawyer for his office and outlined the qualifications. "I place particular stress upon the man being a close friend of yours. . . as I would want him to feel and feel myself that he came here as your friend, which, of course, would be an additional recommendation to me." The man would be "simply an additional link between us."[30]

The language of friendship appeared in full force in letters between politicians, especially between men who lacked personal ties. Such letters followed a standard format. First the writer explained his problem, then proposed his desired solution and listed the reasons why he should be granted the favor. Those reasons included long-standing partisanship, sterling behavior in the past, inadequate recognition of the writer's county or district, or favors done for the recipient in the past. When a St. Lawrence County assemblyman wrote to Nixon for help in procuring a seat on the Ways and Means Committee, he noted that his county had not been represented on that committee for the past three years. To make matters worse, he had been promised the seat the year before. Assembly leaders had not only broken their pledge; they had taken away his better assignments. "But you know that no murmur or 'kick' came from me," he reminded Nixon. "You also know that I have been loyal to the Organization and party." He closed by reaffirming his loyalty and future gratitude. "If I obtain what I ask for, I will give the credit all to you, and I trust that you have learned, that it is at all times my politics, to stand by my friends, and they are obliged to build, no fences around me, to hold me."[31]

From the assemblyman's perspective, however exaggerated, he had behaved like a good Republican but had been slighted nonetheless. The rules he dutifully followed included believing that politics consisted of personal loyalty—a sentiment he believed Nixon would find admirable, would even expect. For him, friendship made politics possible because it confirmed mutual obligations between men, self-sacrifice, and loyalty to party and to individuals. Other letters expressed this view in even more extreme ways. A man who was next in line for the speakership wanted to know about Nixon's political plans. He disclaimed any self-interest. "In all candor, the loyal and lasting friendship of men like yourself . . . count more with me than all things else in this life. . . . When their best interests have been fully served, then, and then only, will it be time for me to seek self-advancement."[32]

These letters, especially those of job-seekers, highlight the importance of friendship in partisan politics. Friendship reconciled self-serving behavior and loftier matters of principle. In the realm of political imagination, friendships existed between men who recognized mutual obligations—between men of honor. Men asked for political favors because their work and support—their friendship—entitled them to benefits. Office-holders honored only legitimate obligations in dispensing favors to fellow partisans. Political patronage, therefore, was an exchange between equals of a sort: between men who contributed to each other's success and who needed each other's work. With friendship as the center, party politics could be imagined to reach the ideal condition of mutuality and obligation between voters and office-holders, one in which both received rewards for work and character.

For men to maintain political friendships, they had to possess the attributes of manhood. Indeed, out of the connection between party politics and friendship came both a definition of manhood and a reaffirmation of it. Only men could vote and hold office, but the importance of manhood went well beyond just the exclusion of women and children. The characteristics partisan rhetoric deemed necessary for political friendships—loyalty, independence, and self-sacrificing devotion to principle—were also those expected of "true men." Men who possessed them deserved to be honored by the nomination and election of their fellows. Because men possessed the proper traits, they were capable of political friendships. Male capacity for friendship, moreover, eliminated possible contradictions like those between independence and loyalty to party. The friendship that men could honor made devotion to party voluntary and loyalty a point of honor, so no contradiction remained. Through the act of imagination that created the ideal of manhood, electoral politics became more emphatically a male sphere.

As party politics spun an imaginative vision of manly virtues and roles, it created a space for a stylized male expression of emotion curiously similar to nineteenth-century sentimental exchanges between women. Elections, nominations, and requests for favors furnished occasions for male expressions of sentimentality and affection similar to the "female world of love and ritual" described by Carroll Smith-Rosenberg. If nineteenth-century middle-class women directed sentimentality toward home, female friends, and family, men did so at party conventions, polling places, and in letters on political subjects.[33]

If at a county convention men saw nothing unusual about a nominee's being moved to tears by the proceedings, letters, especially those written by men who sought favors, also illustrate the emotional language and personal attachments that partisan politics evoked. Men's political letters lacked the hint of physical intimacy that women's letters included. Instead, they described the writer's friendship, loyalty, and devotion to the addressee and to the party. At the same time, they claimed to regard the recipient with real affection, as well as respect. One man wrote to Roswell P. Flower about the direction of the political wind before the 1891 Democratic convention that would nominate Flower for governor. Confident that Flower's opponents would lose, the writer assured him that "you know very well my friendship for you, and that anything you ask of me I will do if in my power." A Pennsylvania man who wanted Flower's financial advice introduced himself. "I have long been a great admirer of yours, as I have learned to know you from the public prints, and I was ardently in hopes to see you the candidate of your grand old Democratic Party in the last presidential campaign. I have read of your life with so much interest and feel so kindly toward you."[34]

When men wrote to political superiors, a good amount of fulsome praise found its way into the letters, such as comparisons of Senator David Bennett Hill to Parnell and Gladstone. The egalitarianism of partisan politics clearly had limits; such overheated praise put a good deal of distance between writer and reader. John Bacon of Medina wrote to Hill in 1889 in order to encourage him to appoint a man from his county (Orleans) as canal commissioner. He began the letter with praise, describing Hill's "most Efficient Ability" as "the champion of the Intrsts of the Democracy." But Bascom balanced the praise with assurances of his own and his town's loyalty and of his good character. "I have served our Party faithfully these many years and havenot asked for anything. and should I not Recive anything at this time I should work just as faithfully in our Intirsts as heretofore." In the rest ot the letter, he anticipated his and Orleans County's gratitude if the commissioner were a county man, and took pains to show the equity of Orleans' getting the appointment since other counties already had "the Lions share." Fairness, personal loyalty, and the proper reward for work and character all argued for appointing someone from Orleans.[35]

Friendship involved personal feeling, but it also had a purpose. J. Edward Young felt distraught in 1894 when he considered his declining political fortunes in Middleburgh, Schoharie County. While the county normally voted Democratic, the party leadership there had turned away from David Bennett Hill, Young's ally. So while Young had never asked for favors before, he felt he needed one now—in part because Hill had caused his predicament. "[W]henever your interests have been at stake, you have always known where to find me & I *always* was *loyal & true* and did what I could." Now it was Hill's turn.

> There isn't a man here who *dares* to speak your name except in disparagement of you save myself & I am fighting the whole gang who have been persecuting me on every Corner, even removing me as Village Clerk, a position I have filled for 14 years & it is because of my loyalty to you.

He wanted a job—"simply as recognition so I can beat this Cleveland crowd of heelers." Young's request for his due combined appeals to partisanship, personal loyalty, and revenge, all connected by political friendship. He had suffered because of his loyalty to Hill and it was time for Hill to make amends. For Young, the specter of public humiliation, rather than personal need, provided the basis for an emotional appeal.[36]

Such extreme language of persecution and suffering only suited special requests. Public affection, if not public shame, however, routinely filled partisan speeches and writing. New York politician Isaac P. Maynard described his fondness for his fellow partisans and his community when he spoke in an upstate village. "If one man can know another," he said, "you and I must know each other in the bonds of a most sacred, enduring friendship." Even taking into account the overblown style of late nineteenth-century rhetoric, the statement suggests how men expressed a range of emotions connected to public life. Men also troubled themselves about what other men believed about their characters. In a letter soliciting an appointment, one man rambled: "I oft times have thought, 'does Senator Hill take my mirthfullness, and oft times— foolishness, to be the component element of my make up?' " Letters from men to Assemblyman S. Fred Nixon commonly began, "Friend Nixon." Other writers pledged undying loyalty. "There is an understanding here among the fellows that what you want is what we are for," one wrote. "*I am now, as always, ready to follow your standard, no matter where you might lead,*" vowed another.[37]

While letters between men expressed friendship and loyalty (if not love), political campaigns supplied a male ritual. From start to finish, elections immersed men in public displays of partisanship and male virtue. Nominating conventions provided the first opportunities. Party leaders at both the state and local level endeavored to settle nominations before the convention met. In such cases, the affair concentrated solely on ratifying the leaders' choices, praising the nominees' characters, and celebrating the party's decisions. When real contests took place, conventions gave further occasion for speeches that depicted the fine qualities of the contestants, for displays of political heroism, and for expression of the proper gratitude men felt when honored by their peers. Parliamentary procedure was no bar to these celebrations of party and manhood.[38]

Conventions directly engaged relatively few men, however. Campaigns more fully absorbed average men in public rituals. Beginning in early October, the parties staged picnics, pole raisings, and rallies in large and small towns in New York State. Supporters of both parties attended these events, some of which featured free food and drink as well as the chance to meet friends and listen to partisan speeches. In presidential election years, men organized clubs named after the candidates, which sponsored parades and rallies and also canvassed the electorate. Club members donned military uniforms, hired bands, and gathered up other townsmen to march in torchlight parades during the final days of the race.[39]

Election days were social events for rural communities. Both farmers and villagers took at least half the day off, often cast their ballots in male enclaves—saloons or barbershops—and stood about while others came in to vote. Men who did not stay in town late enough to learn the election results often returned in the evening. When the returns came in, rural men, like those elsewhere, collected on bets they had made on the outcome. Men typically bet money or offered a trade of some sort, but wagers also involved public humiliation. One loser found himself pushing a man around town in a wheelbarrow; a newspaper reported that a man married because he was on the wrong end of an election bet. All of the campaign and election activities required male participation; women played a only supportive role, if any. Some women illuminated their homes as parades passed by; church groups prepared dinners. From the descriptions of male character in campaign speeches, to the military overtones of parades and rallies, to the places where towns held elections, electoral politics was a public and male endeavor.[40]

Elections, to be sure, were more than pageantry. They put men in power—office-holders who determined policies that affected men's and women's well-being. But as students of Gilded Age politics have suggested, the ability of late nineteenth-century politics to engage men's interest and energies goes a long way toward explaining why the great majority of men took the trouble to vote year after year. In addition to its social attractions, electoral politics served a larger cultural function: it ratified men's attachments to the party, the nation, and democracy, each of which reinforced an individual's sense of his manhood. While scores of ordinary urban and rural men participated in the rituals of partisan politics, party leaders orchestrated the campaigns. The parties also nominated candidates, printed and distributed ballots, and arranged for voters' transportation to the polls. If only because of the parties' involvement in every step of an election, they became objects of veneration in the newspapers they published and elections they organized. Loyalty to party, partisan editors insisted, was an achievement a man could be proud of.[41]

Because they organized men to participate in public decisions, parties seemed essential to democracy. Observers interpreted the spectacle of all classes of men voting for their governors as evidence that democracy was well in America. Partisan parades drove home the point, since they often consciously included men from most sectors of a community. While partisans asserted in the heat of campaigns that elections determined whether the nation would prosper or evil men would bring it to its knees, late nineteenth-century partisan politics reinforced men's identification with the nation. Issues of national proportions supposedly hung in the balance even in the election of a sheriff. Partisan campaigns reminded men of the great deeds and men in the nation's past and of the possibility of future greatness, especially of the large role parties filled in that grand legacy.[42]

Neither democracy, the nation, nor political parties could long survive, partisan rhetoricians claimed, without manhood. The attributes of manhood made it possible for men to govern themselves and for the nation and the parties to prosper. The ability to make one's own decisions—a kind of independence—indicated a man of good character as well as a proper democratic citizen. But such independence would certainly dissipate into greed and anarchy without the attribute of loyalty. Men could forge political friendships and transfer those loyalties to one of the parties. Integrity made it possible for partisanship to be more than a selfish attachment: by standing for principle or for the good of the party, one could even be heroic. The nation itself ultimately depended on men's character to guarantee its future progress. In that it rested on character, late nineteenth-century politics still carried faint echoes of republicanism. Only through the existence of individual (male) virtue could a democracy survive.[43]

Electoral politics and the ritual it involved had few places for women or for men who strayed from the two major parties, except insofar as they provided a foil that helped sharply define correct male behavior. Indeed, as far as party workers were concerned, men who abandoned the major parties fell below the level of the most deceitful of women.

Highlighting the independents' lack of "manliness," an urban Democrat referred to them as "political hermaphrodites"; while a rural party loyalist scorned a "dandelion" faction. Partisans ridiculed men without secure attachments to one of the major parties as insincere, arrogant, ambitious, and unmindful of the public good. Independents, bolters, and defectors to a third party were men who had no friends. One editor described independents as "tenderfoots" who wandered from camp to camp and pompously believed that they had risen above the grubbiness of politics. Such a haughty man expected that "where he goes good must follow. . . . He puts his personal honesty before any other man's honesty and impunges [*sic*] every motive that his little mind cannot fully comprehend." Women in electoral politics were unthinkable; nonpartisan men were reprehensible.[44]

Complaints about independents came from spokesmen of the major parties. Their venom was doubtless a reaction against the good number of men who bolted, split their tickets, and voted for third parties. Despite such occasional waywardness, rural men shared a commitment to the imaginative construction of partisanship with producers of partisan appeals, though it was not as intense as the devotion of newspapermen who doubled as local party leaders. For all men, party politics remained an inspiring thing. The pageantry of a political campaign had grandeur. The parades, fireworks, speeches, and drama of partisan campaigns could absorb men in politics, and they could see party loyalty as a desirable part of public life. Campaigns provided a unique spectacle in rural townships that only yearly fire company parades came close to matching in excitement and community involvement. Campaigns also projected a cooperative vision of the relationship between voters and office-holders, of government run by men of sound principles and character, and of heroism in the battle for right. In the late nineteenth century, these manly virtues had a gentle, even warm, cast, in contrast to the more raucous and violent partisanship earlier in the century. More than this, political rhetoric described participation in politics as an important universal male role, one that also reinforced treasured beliefs about work, character, gender, and reward for the just.[45]

It was a vision that persuaded rural men, but only to a point. Just as they voted and wrote letters to their representatives that used the language of friendship, manhood, and reciprocity, they admitted serious reservations about the entire package of symbols that surrounded electoral politics. Contempt for, or at least amusement with, politics and politicians surfaced in men's conversations at Grange meetings, in their diaries, and even in partisan newspapers. Rural partisanship also incorporated skepticism.

The notion that politicians were not the virtuous men that they made themselves out to be appeared even in partisan newspapers. As the 1879 campaign began, one newspaper correspondent praised his community by denigrating politicians. "Little York is a sober, virtous, industrious, mind-your-own business locality," the writer declared. "In proof, there is not a candidate for county office in the vicinity. What other post office can say as much?" As the campaign progressed, another groaned that "we are getting lame all over as the effect of so many heart-felt greetings, from these large-minded, far-sighted, kind-hearted men." Contrary to grand descriptions of politicians, actual office-seekers engaged in fakery and intruded on people who merely wanted to attend to their work.[46]

The process of political campaigns also came in for criticism. Grangers expressed relief when one campaign concluded: their meetings now proceeded undisturbed by noisy political gatherings in the downstairs rooms of their hall. A Republican editor braced himself for bombastic talk and unwelcome disruptions sure to come in the 1884 campaign. "In this excitement the pulpit will forget its spiritual profession, the stump speaker will invade the land and clamor as frogs clamor in the spring marsh," the editor warned. Campaigns, he claimed, produced nothing but din, since elections now hung on material interests, not principles. Given what was at stake, he argued that voters should re-elect Republicans. Neither party could guarantee prosperity, but if Republicans remained in office, "less disturbance to the working machinery of government" would result. Elections and campaigns, far from inspiring, disturbed the comfortable rhythms of ordinary life.[47]

Such mild criticisms of elections and politicians registered disappointment in the gulf that opened between actual and imaginative politics. Some men went further. "Our rulers," wrote one man, were "legislating for themselves, and those other greedy ones [millionaires], depleting the people—the common people—to their ruin." Dismissing the argument that better office-holders would produce fairer policies, a Granger claimed that "a majority of the men who are sent to the legislature are in the interests of monopolies. If they are not so when they go they are bought over." Self-seeking, incompetent politicians occupied local as well as state and national offices. Members of a Grange complained about their board of supervisors, which, they said, dismissed their petition regarding the exorbitant costs of housing prisoners. Next election, they vowed, they would "lay aside all party Politics & unaniminously vote for such Supervisors as voted against that Petition to stay at home in the future."[48]

Skepticism about politics and politicians, then, shaded off into outright contempt. Greedy men won public office, and once installed, disregarded the wishes of common people in favor of the needs of the wealthy. To a certain point, men hostile to politics and politicians had different backgrounds from those who celebrated partisanship. The Grange and other farmers' organizations were the richest sources of male antipartisan sentiments. Farmers, however, were not alone in voicing displeasure with partisan politics. Nor did members of agricultural organizations often act on their understanding: like other men, they continued their support of the major parties. But farmers, along with some villagers, identified politicians as the men who created problems for rural New Yorkers.[49]

The more pointed rural complaints about politics focused on office-holders who collected high salaries for taxing those who could least afford to pay. Office-holders' paychecks, one Grange decided, were "altogether too high taking into consideration the burden to tax payers and the salery of other business or profession of others requiring the same or greater qualifications." Another Grange proposed holding candidates account-able: the Patrons pledged to support men who promised to cut their salaries. Attempting to turn these feelings into votes, partisan newspapers accused the other party of raising salaries and otherwise practicing ex-travagance. But criticisms of overpaid politicians transcended party lines. Men circulated petitions and wrote letters by the score denouncing corpu-lent office-holders. The problem was a simple one for one farmer: "we have too many laws & Lawyers, too many offices and office-seekers." Politicians of both parties were barely tolerated nuisances.[50]

In addition to paying themselves more than they were worth, politi-cians enacted measures that worsened economic conditions in rural New York. Most injurious of all, they levied unjust taxes. Rural residents complained with justification that the state government extracted dispro-portionately high levels of its total revenue from them. State and local governments derived most of their income from property taxes, and real estate bore the brunt of this taxation. Farmers felt this was unfair and held that all property, real as well as personal, should be taxed equally. Corporations and railroads should pay more. Some rural men supported a state income tax to replace the property tax entirely. For marginal farmers, such changes in the tax codes might have made a real differ-ence. All farmers hoped that lower (or, as they would put it, fairer) taxes would improve their competitive position.[51]

While the fight for new tax equalization schedules wore on, rural New Yorkers sought to lower the costs of government by cutting spending and services. Indeed, rural men seemingly opposed all new state initiatives in the late nineteenth century. Favorite targets included the Erie Canal and state roads and prisons. Men who lived in townships distant from the Canal tried to block any further funding of its operation. They felt that the Canal merely helped politicians who used it as a patronage source, Western farmers who could ship their produce cheaply, and merchants in New York and Buffalo. The Canal benefited particular groups, not the state as a whole—in fact, by conferring advantages on Western farm-ers, it hurt New York agriculture. As a compromise, farmers' organiza-tions argued that the federal, rather than the state, government should pick up the costs. Similarly, rural groups held that new roads financed by state taxes would not help farmers and villagers, but instead would only amuse "[w]heelmen and fast drivers." Worse, they thought that state funding might mean that decisions about what kinds of roads would be built and how much they would cost would move from the local to the state level. Inevitably, state control meant that politicians would have charge, which would make the roads needlessly expensive.[52]

The issues of spending on prisons and convict labor joined moral with monetary concerns. New state institutions that would be built upstate generally found a warm reception. Prisons, hospitals, and schools regenerated otherwise declining townships. Nonetheless, some New York men regarded these institutions, even ones in their own villages, as a waste of money, and wanted economy to guide the building and staffing of the institutions. As a way of both bringing down the costs of running prisons and of teaching moral truths, convict labor won wide support among rural men. It would be unfair to hardworking taxpayers if prisoners did not work. The end of convict labor would create a "Convict Aristocracy," a rural editor warned. "The taxpayers of the state would be somewhat startled by the naked proposition that hereafter every producer . . . will have to contribute enough to enable the state to support in idleness all its thieves, tramps, and loafers." Such legislation increased crime, wasted workers' efforts, and reinforced criminals' wicked habits. If convicts were made to work, moreover, prisons might eventually become self-supporting.[53]

Local government, too, was the target of endless efforts to economize. Farmers' organizations sought ways to cut back the amount of money spent on "poor farms" that housed the destitute and sometimes investigated the matter themselves. They paid special attention to reducing the number of people employed at county homes to the barest minimum. Bond issues of all sorts faced problems, even in prosperous towns. Proposals to build waterworks and schools, for example, passed only after townspeople spent years debating the costs. Shouldering additional long-term debt was gambling on future income, a wager that demanded a confidence that many rural men lacked.[54]

Rural suspicion of politicians was matched by an equal distrust of government. If a career in politics deserved only slightly more respect than outright thievery, government made public theft and injustice possible. Rural men seemed undecided as to whether bad men in politics made government disreputable or government inevitably brought out the lower motives of men. But in the end, rural distrust of government constrained the proposals men might offer as solutions for their economic and social problems.

Rural men thus faced a difficult choice. What could be done about a system of electoral politics that reinforced cherished values and beliefs but seemed unresponsive to rural interests? The most radical, and ultimately least compelling, solution was to quit the major parties in favor of third parties that promised concrete solutions: the Greenback, Prohibition, and Populist parties. A less drastic step was nonpartisanship—voting for the candidates who promised to support certain measures, whatever their partisan affiliation. Rural men turned fitfully to this solution; but on the whole, nonpartisanship remained an unrealized threat.

Another answer was to shrink government to its smallest possible proportions by taking issues "out of politics"—out of the parties' reach. Politicians and government then could do the least possible harm. By allowing men to keep the rituals of electoral politics, to punish politicians, and to make government equally unresponsive to all groups, this solution achieved the widest following in rural New York.

In many ways, rural New York appeared to be prime territory for third parties. The region had a history of backing new political movements, from the Anti-Masons, to the Free Soilers, to the Republicans. And if hard times sometimes inspire men to search for political alternatives, in the late nineteenth century, upstate farmers and villagers saw their economic circumstances deteriorate to varying degrees. New York farmers denounced monopolies and railroads with all the fervor of their Western counterparts and blamed government for at least some of their misfortunes. Rural New York nonetheless proved an inhospitable place for two of the period's major third parties, the Greenback and People's parties. When rural men turned away from the Democrats and Republicans, the Prohibition Party received most of the benefits. While troublesome for the Grand Old Party, the Prohibition Party never grew beyond an annoyance.

For men angry with the Democrats and Republicans, the Greenback Party offered a way to strike back. Organized in 1876 in response to the federal government's determination to shrink the amount of currency in circulation and to the severe economic difficulties that decision caused, the party called for a return to the paper money issued during the Civil War to relieve the debt crisis in agriculture and the recession in industry. Greenbackers also called for an end to leasing convict labor to businesses, the end of the importation of Chinese laborers, a reduction in the length of the workday and in the number and salaries of public officials, railroad regulation, and opening Western lands to settlers rather than foreign or domestic speculators. The Greenback program offered policies that appealed to industrial workers as well as to debt-stricken farmers.[55]

In New York State, labor proved the most receptive audience for the Greenback program. The party, whose vote peaked in 1878, did best in the small cities along the state's southern tier. Having weathered a severe economic depression and, in 1877, massive strikes of railroad workers that brought few gains, former Democrats in cities and large villages, such as Corning, Elmira, Jamestown, Hornellsville, and Cortlandville, formed the core of Greenback support.[56] Greenback leaders complained of difficulty in reaching farmers, but they underestimated the Greenback vote in relatively prosperous agricultural townships. In Chautauqua County, for example, the Greenback candidate nearly pulled ahead of the Republican nominee for secretary of state (the top office) in 1877 in the agricultural townships of Kiatone and Harmony, and the Greenback candidate carried Busti. In 1878, the Greenback candidate for judge of the court of appeals gained a plurality in Busti and French Creek, and came close to doing so in Cherry Creek and Kiatone. In central New York, too, Greenbackers won rural votes. In Cortland County, for example, the party carried the townships of Cuyler, Freetown, Harford, Lapeer, and Willet in 1878. Meanwhile, only the Democratic-Greenback fusion candidate for the state assembly managed to win a majority in the townships of Cortlandville, Homer, and Virgil, which contained the county's largest villages. Agricultural towns in the western southern tier (Cattaraugus, Chautauqua, Steuben, Allegany, Schuyler, and Chenango counties) elected Greenbackers for their county supervisors, as did scattered townships along the Great Lakes plain. Rural support for Greenback candidates existed in some of the state's better agricultural areas.[57]

The party declined rapidly everywhere after 1878. But even in its best years, the Greenback Party never gained appreciable rural support outside of the southern tier and some western townships. The party won no votes at all in sparsely populated Hamilton County and found few supporters in the counties surrounding New York City, such as Putnam and Rockland. Greenback candidates also put in poor showings in many of New York's declining townships: less than five percent of the voters of Columbia, Fulton, Montgomery, Otsego, and Schoharie counties, for example, favored those candidates. The party fared just as badly in some prosperous townships, such as those in Wyoming County, but protest of post–Civil War politics was more likely in stable or growing townships than in declining ones.[58] Legislation that aided Western farmers, such as opening public lands to settlers, could worsen the already precarious position of eastern and central New York farmers. Meanwhile, working men's demands met with either hostility or indifference. That a man would want full pay while working fewer hours seemed immoral; that convicts should be spared from labor seemed even worse. Expecting government to do little for them, most rural men evidently turned to self-help or self-blame for solutions to their economic problems or gave up hope that a solution was possible at all.

Despite its thin support, the Greenback Party did well compared to the Populists in the 1890s. Like the Greenback Party, Populists backed paper currency, strict regulation of railroads, equalization of taxes, and the abolition of the leasing of convict labor. They also argued for fundamental changes in the banking system and credit arrangements, governmental action against industrial monopolies, and woman suffrage. Such positions might have appealed to rural New Yorkers, who had groused for years about railroads, unequal taxes, and monopolies. But candidates on the Populist ticket won some votes in the western southern tier, but very few east and north of the Finger Lakes. Drawing its meager backing from rural towns, the People's Party candidates enjoyed their banner year in 1893 when their top candidate garnered 1.7 percent of the votes cast in the state as a whole. Allegany County consistently registered the highest percentages of Populist votes in New York: 8.6 percent in 1892, 8.8 percent in 1893, and 6.1 percent in 1894. The township of Ward in

Allegany was the only township in the state to give a majority to James B. Weaver, the party's presidential candidate in 1892. A number of other rural townships scattered through western and west-central New York indicated relatively strong support for People's Party candidates.[59]

For rural men outside of the southern tier (and for most of those within that area), any solution favored by Southern and Western farmers needed to be eyed with suspicion. Indeed, New Yorkers not infrequently blamed Midwestern and Western farmers—the "foreign competition"— for their troubles. While New Yorkers also wanted to see railroad rates controlled, they sought higher rates for Western farmers, who, they believed, paid less to transport their products to the same markets. Men in declining townships in northern and eastern New York had adjusted to depression decades earlier. For the most part owners of their land, farmers in declining townships ceased to pursue political (or scientific) solutions to their economic problems. And as the difficulties of the Grange in the 1870s and 1880s showed, farmers who practiced mixed agriculture proved difficult to organize for collective buying and selling. Their needs were too diverse and their major source of cash—dairy products—too perishable to hold off of the market. Fruit and vegetable farmers of western New York and hop growers in the central part of the state stood alone as successful operators of rural cooperatives. For most of the state's rural voters, practical differences hampered support for Populist candidates.[60]

Largely opposed to what they knew of the Populist program, New Yorkers remained ignorant and uninterested. In 1891, the Grange of Clymer, New York, intended to discuss the sub-treasury plan, the heart of Populist financial reforms. This Chautauqua County Grange was among the more politically active—it had tested an alliance with the Knights of Labor in the nearby small city of Jamestown the year before and had produced a steady supply of resolutions to county and state lawmakers. The township of Clymer contained a relatively large proportion of Populist voters. But when the members tried to discuss the sub-treasury, "most of them confessed that they were not posted well enough to debate on the subject." The same Grange spent two weeks learning how to avoid buying Western feed grain. Ignorance ensured indifference.[61]

Most rural men who left the fold of the major parties voted for Prohibition candidates. That party largely concerned itself with the moral problem of drink, although its platforms also incorporated denunciations of monopolies and political corruption, and support for woman suffrage. In the state as a whole, the party began to have an impact in the election of 1882, and its peak years were from 1885 to 1888. Prohibitionists drew votes from rural towns everywhere, although, like the Greenbackers and Populists, they could count on their greatest support in the western third of the state.[62]

Prohibitionists and the temperance issue worried state Republican Party managers and divided rural townships. Men who cast a Prohibition ticket doubtless intended to rid the state of liquor and the social and economic menace it posed. But it was also a protest vote in a more general sense. When asked which party he would support in the 1894 election by a Republican canvasser, one Schoharie County man explained that he would vote Populist if the ticket were available, and if not, Prohibitionist. Republican Party leaders rightly felt that the protest was directed against them and that otherwise-Republican votes went to the Prohibitionists. The party was not a problem at the county level—the western part of the state contained the banner Republican counties, and despite the Prohibitionists' relatively good showing, they rarely won seats as county supervisors, much less election to state offices. Republican leaders nonetheless grew alarmed at the Prohibitionists' ability to cut into their state total. The Republican-sponsored Raines Liquor Tax law of 1896, aimed at decreasing the number of saloons, also reduced the Prohibition vote substantially. Afterwards, liquor practically disappeared as a partisan issue.[63]

Few rural men registered displeasure with partisan politics by shifting their allegiance to one of the third parties. Although certain that ordinary politicians lied and worked against their interests, rural men did not find the Greenback, Populist, or Prohibition parties adequate solutions. Regular party politics still had real attractions, despite its drawbacks. As the two major parties portrayed it, partisan politics rewarded character, defended important principles, constructed an important male role, and provided social events for rural towns. By an insistent focus on national issues, even in county elections, the parties paradoxically made their position stronger: the imaginative elements of partisan politics grew more persuasive if they could be separated from squabbles about tax rates. In any event, sticking with the Democrats, or more likely, the Republicans, introduced the least political change, and most rural New Yorkers adopted that course.

But there was a less drastic way to protest government decisions: nonpartisanship. This course did not require men to assume new political allegiances, only to suspend them long enough to examine their best interests. At times, rural men, particularly those involved in agricultural organizations, proclaimed their intention to vote for candidates of whatever affiliation who promised to take the proper positions on issues that farmers cared about. The New York State Grange issued annual injunctions to farmers to vote their interests instead of their parties. Likewise, farmers' clubs, alliances, and local Granges all vowed on various occasions to follow issues rather than partisan loyalty. A speaker at a Farmers' Institute in Steuben County summed up this position: "You can't afford to ignore politics nor can you afford to be chained by party prejudice to the political car or juggernaut, whose relentless wheels are to-day crushing life out of your calling."[64]

In its weakest form, nonpartisanship meant backing farmers for public office rather than the usual band of lawyers. At a meeting of the Central

New York Farmers' Club, one member spoke of the power farmers would gain if they elected their own kind. A lawyer could not be trusted: he was "always honest when honesty best serves his purpose." Unless farmers learned "that in union there is strength, and act upon it, they need expect little consideration or have much influence in public affairs." His talk echoed numerous others in local Grange halls and state conventions, other farmers' meetings, and the agricultural press. If farmers wanted any benefits from government, they had to put partisanship aside, elect men more likely to know and represent their concerns, and learn to work together.[65]

Farmers followed this course intermittently in the late nineteenth century, but nonpartisanship continued to be more a warning to the powers that were, than a description of rural politics. Partisan alignments were reasonably stable through the turn of the century, although a shift toward the Republican direction occurred in the mid-1890s. Split-ticket voting remained rare for state and federal offices. Farmers acknowledged as much. Commenting on a speech promoting nonpartisanship at a Grange picnic in 1898, the secretary wearily noted that "[e]lection will show how many will vote for principle or party." Talks on how farmers must learn to vote their interests at state Grange meetings assumed that they failed to do so. Agricultural groups nonetheless pointed to legislation they secured by making their presence felt in Albany. Indeed, the Grange took credit for seemingly every law that somehow related to rural townships. But the precise role of farmers' organizations in passing these measures remains unclear, while other evidence suggests that at least some farmers actually opposed such legislation.[66]

Whatever its weaknesses at the state level, nonpartisanship became the accepted way to conduct local politics. Township and village offices changed hands very infrequently; any opposition was a newsworthy event. That one party or the other tended to dominate in individual townships accounted for some of the local political peace. Some townships achieved local nonpartisanship by constructing union slates before town meetings. When rival candidacies required the voters' decision, differences were often based on issues rather than party. In addition, partisanship broke down in contests for county offices. When men split their tickets in the late nineteenth century, they usually did so in order to punish or support candidates at the bottom of the ticket. Normally Republican townships not infreqently elected Democrats as county supervisors. Nonpartisanship at the local level stemmed from a number of sources. Local office-holders settled matters of immediate importance. County supervisors determined how the tax burden would be distributed among townships. Assessors assigned property values. Partisanship seemed an inappropriate way of making such decisions. While it was difficult to tell how a tariff would affect upstate New York, the results of taxes could be learned immediately. In some cases, personal friendships or grudges and family ties influenced votes for local men. Rural men applied a different standard to local politicians—one that asked for representation—than they usually did to those running for state and national offices.[67]

Rural men's respect for local government, in fact, helps explain the course they most often took to register their political grievances. When New York men disapproved of a policy, they invariably demanded that the matter be taken "out of politics"; out of the hands of politicians and parties. For late nineteenth-century rural men, ejecting an issue from partisan politics usually meant transferring responsibility to townships or counties. The smaller units of government, rural men felt, were less partisan and more likely to adhere to their wishes. Removing politics from administration and decision-making did not involve putting authority in the hands of nonpartisan commissions. Indeed, rural men denounced the state's "expensive commissions" as loudly as they did the parties. Well-paid commissioners wasted taxpayers' money and served the interests of the politicans who appointed them. Local government, by contrast, seemed cheap, conservative, and accountable.[68]

Road-building was one public expenditure rural men struggled to keep at the local level. Ignoring the advice of the agricultural press and state and national farmers' organizations, New York State farmers sought to maintain local control and funding of roads. A Cortland County Grange pledged its opposition to any measure that would "take from the farmer, the right to make & control their own public highways" in 1897. Cash-poor farmers appreciated the opportunity to pay off their road taxes through labor rather than money, and contended through the turn of the century that good but expensive roads hurt farmers instead of making their efforts more profitable. If designed and maintained by local officials, roads would cost less because townships and counties would choose cheaper materials and would not so easily pad the payrolls with political friends. A speaker at the Central New York Farmers' Club warned that "[w]hen farmers allow the control of their roads to pass out of their hands into a political machine at Albany, they will pay $10 for engineering and superintendents for every ten cents they get in road improvement." Rural men cited the expense and inefficiency of state politicians in arguing for keeping decisions about schools in localities. Schools good enough for rural needs that cost the least money could be had through local administration; state regulations brought waste, change with every new administration, and inappropriate standards. As important community institutions, and, like roads, large local expenditures, schools should be kept free of partisan state control.[69]

If matters that bore on local taxes required nonpartisanship, so did other controversial questions. Injecting matters that seriously divided a community into electoral politics worked against the ability of politics to unite men of different interests. For this reason, a Chautauqua County Grange debated whether they should "use [their] influence to take the temperance question out of politics." Serious community differences were best approached through persuasion that built consensus, not through a process that inflamed and extended disagreements. A newspaper editor regretted that a difficult local issue had found its way into the Otsego town meeting in 1892. Townships chose (partisan) representatives for the county board of supervisors at meetings, and in Otsego, one candidate raised the issue of whether the Cooperstown and Charlotte Valley Railroad should build an extension to Catskill. The stockholders, who included Cooperstown's most prominent citizens, wanted this line, but the railroad's managers did not, and (rumor had it) planned to buy out the stockholders. The Democratic nominee for supervisor from the township of Otsego agreed to run if the matter was not mentioned. The editor concurred that the railroad belonged as "an issue by itself, to the detriment of no man running for a political office." The Democratic nominee won, but by a reduced margin, because, the editor believed, his opponent backed out of an arragement to ignore the railroad question. Divisive national questions also merited discussion outside of the parties. After the trouncing that William Jennings Bryan took in the election of 1896, a Democratic partisan proposed taking the currency issue—the debate about gold, silver, or paper money that had dominated national party politics—"out of politics." Electoral politics excelled at repeating partisan verities and reinforcing standing beliefs about the importance of personal character and virtue. Both partisans and skeptics of party politics doubted its ability to settle differences in a positive way.[70]

Along with attempting to remove controversial matters from electoral politics, rural men struck at government and parties in other ways. Most of all, they sought to reduce the number and salaries of office-holders and to limit government spending in general. This, New York men believed, would make politics work as it was intended to and mitigate their economic problems. Throughout the 1880s and 1890s, Granges passed resolutions "protesting against the injust salaries of public officials." A related complaint involved office-holders' expensive habit of passing legislation. "Each Congress passes about 10,000 bills," a speaker at a farmers' club argued. If congressmen read them all, "they would keep [lawmakers] busy the year round, with only time to sleep, eat and vote." Most of the bills passed by Congress, moreover, "are log-rolling and plundering the public." A reader of the *Freeman's Journal* agreed. "We have come upon a time," he wrote in 1880, when laws "serve little other purpose than to fill tomes at the expense of the people, to the profit of some political speculator, or give to certain professions implements whereby to secure livelihood." Politicians wasted rural men's money by paying themselves lavishly, approving useless projects, and passing a confusing array of laws.[71]

Moving issues "out of politics" acceptably squared partisanship and cynicism about political parties for many rural men in New York State. It enabled them to maintain the imaginative elements of party politics— elections as expressions of friendship, manhood, and character—because it rendered politicians as harmless as possible. Important issues deserved the attention of presumably less partisan local officals, rather than state party hacks. No politician, whatever his party affiliation, could be trusted too far, so salaries should be cut and new initatives curbed. With government thus limited, men could continue to enjoy the social benefits of party politics and to subscribe to the visions of leadership and citizenship political parties sustained. Shrinking the scope of government had advantages over both voting for third parties and nonpartisanship. The last two paths put politicians as untrustworthy as Democrats or Republicans into office and opened the possibility of enlarged government custody of the economy and community morality. The imaginative elements of politics would have to be discarded. Electing third-party candidates would introduce substantial changes in rural life and politics, with unknowable consequences. Voting for major-party candidates demanded the fewest changes in thought and behavior, and meant that rural men retained the benefits and the drawbacks that they knew and believed they could manage.

Taking divisive issues out of politics allowed New Yorkers to pursue a cherished goal of small and economical government. Indeed, this was the rural vision of good government; a powerful one, since it provided a way to retain both partisanship and cynicism. To be sure, progressive types in rural communities—village boosters and leaders of agricultural organizations—fought both the state government and fellow townsmen and farmers in seeking to expand government services for rural people. Farmers, agricultural leaders maintained, would benefit from good roads only the state had the resources to build. Advanced agricultural methods, which the state could teach and support, could make farming more profitable. But farmers remained dubious, as did villagers when told that new projects—waterworks, sidewalks, streetlamps, or whatever—would benefit their town in the long run. Most rural men stuck with the nineteenth-century rule: government ideally remained small and spent as little as possible.[72]

Behind rural men's insistence on small government was a moral vision, as well as the more obvious hatred of taxes. This framework comprised three major convictions: economy, fairness, and the public good. Economy is the most straightforward. Government, ideally, went about its minimal tasks in ways that wasted the smallest amount of the taxpayers' money. But rural men regarded economy as morally good as well as materially beneficial: frugality was a trait to be admired in a legislature as well as in a family. Careful expenditures indicated responsibility, prudence, and foresight.

The goodness of economy derived in large measure from its fairness and service to the public good. Fairness meant that government should not promote the interests of a group or an individual over another without cause. The benefits government had to bestow—from laborers' work to laws—should be parcelled out with regard to character, work, or popular support. Fairness was justice that spread burdens and benefits as equally as possible. Equality, however, had more to do with worthy folks getting their due than with sharing benefits uniformly. Just expenditures rewarded the deserving, and, on a limited scale, helped the unfortunate. Unfairness appeared in the form of taxes levied unequally or without regard for the people's ability to pay. Politicians who voted themselves high salaries when citizens were in need afforded especially grating examples of unfairness. As a Grange petition of 1889 reasoned,

> we recognize the fact that during the period of inflation which our country had passed through many official salaries were doubled and trebled on the grounds that they did not furnish adequate support . . . and if it was justice to increase then it is the justice to retrench now.

When linked to the idea that economy in government was an unadulterated good, fairness prompted real limits on government. Few appointments or programs could be completely fair; all would cost money. When fairness and economy joined limited expectations in a general sense, room for governmental initiatives was slight indeed.[73]

Economy and fairness were desirable because they best served the public good. Like everyone else, rural men argued for certain policies because they would be best for all. At the very least, good policies punished the undeserving who took advantage of taxpayers. With government pared to the absolute minimum, no one would enjoy an advantage, and fairness and the public good would be served. Private benefits, too, could be justified by appealing to either individual merit or the public good. Men asked for favors from politicians by claiming that somehow a broader public would be served. That public might be as small as a family or as large as a labor union or community, but the advantages that would accrue in the larger entity masked the scent of individual self-interest. In the same way, both parties maintained that if their men were elected, all citizens would benefit.

Rural men's expectations of government fitted well with their general social thought. Ideas about work, for example, appeared in rural disdain for politicians, who were usually lawyers, members of a profession that performed no visible useful labor and lived off other people's problems. New Yorkers' understanding of the importance of work also informed their views on numerous issues, such as support for convict labor and opposition to spending for refurbished prisons and poorhouses. The notion that work taught crucial lessons about life's difficulties, together with the conviction that change usually boded ill, produced suspicion of new government initiatives. New programs probably meant that more money would be spent, more lawyers would have work, and yet more laws would join the already too many cluttering the books. Most of all, the idea that prudent men kept their expectations low shaped political opinion: little good could be anticipated either from government or from the men who supposedly represented the people.

Rural men's social thought and political attitudes rested on the same personal characteristics. If a proper social order required that men and women work hard and practice conservatism, a good political system demanded that men exercise related virtues: economy, fairness, friendship, personal loyalty, and devotion to principle and the public good. If both voters and office-holders possessed these traits, a limited government run by the major political parties was possible. Yet rural men's admiration for these six personal characteristics contributed to both their dedication to the political parties and their skepticism about the parties' value. The moral vision of men's politics was not without ambivalence.

Rural voters alternatively felt they were made fools of by crafty politicans and found their values reinforced in partisan politics. By separating national from local politicans, rural men retained the imaginative politics of male virtue while protesting that their interests were badly served by the parties. They settled their grievances about government and politics without harming the standing political order. By striving to limit the government's functions and to keep decisions at the local level, rural men preserved a sense of control, as illusory as it might have been, over public decisions. In New York, the simultaneous existence of partisanship and anti-party politics figured crucially in male politics.

While denigrating politicans and government, New York men were not prepared to abandon the moral high ground. Partisans presented friendship, personal loyalty, and devotion to principle as essential for good citizens and leaders. Yet how could politicians be both partisan heroes and denizens of the dangerous and sordid realm of government? Men (and women) who argued against woman suffrage often highlighted the seamy side of politics in contending that chivalrous men ought to shield unsullied women from political filth. Hardly an honorable calling, much less one that allowed the exercise of public power, politics was merely a dirty job that needed doing. Reducing the reach of government hardly solved this contradiction; by demonstrating men's distrust of politicians it made the inconsistency all the more apparent. Indeed, the discrepancy between men's moral claims about and distrust of politics had no neat resolution in the late nineteenth century. In perhaps the most partisan period of American political history, anti-party (and anti-government) sentiments uneasily sat with grand claims for parties and their leaders. Upper-class men and women were not alone in their hostility toward political parties. Even partisans harbored anti-partisan feeling that merely waited to be tapped.[74]

As contradictory as they were, the claims that government needed careful scrutiny and that politics depended on the existence of certain personal traits in the citizenry were hardly novel ideas. They were among the central tenets of republicanism. Recent students of Populism and labor politics argue that these movements defended particular variants of republicanism against the liberal individualism toward which the nation had veered. They point to such values as personal independence, distrust of luxury, the nobility of labor, devotion to the public good, and the honorable nature of political involvement as surviving strands of classical republicanism in the nineteenth century. Yet it would serve no useful purpose to declare that rural men in New York defended some form of republicanism.[75] By the late nineteenth century—if not sooner—republicanism was a language of opposition that allowed men to criticize the actions of politicians. The criticism that republicanism permitted, however, suggested no particular solutions. While New Yorkers feared power, held that a good polity demanded flawless personal character, and insisted that the public good should be the goal of public policies, they drew very different conclusions from these beliefs than did Populists or the Knights of Labor. If New York partisans agreed with others that the major terms of the republican vocabulary were important but badly served by Gilded Age politicians, they could not concur with the solutions of workers and Southwestern farmers. Republicanism could remind men that civic virtue and the public good were desirable—a lesson few would disagree with—but disputes were certain as soon as men tried to tease specific applications from the flexible vocabulary of republicanism.

In the end, the most important element of the moral basis of rural men's politics was not its connection, or lack thereof, with abstract political traditions. More immediately, the moral framework produced rural men's endorsement of the assumptions of nineteenth-century politics: small government and loyalty to party leaders above the local level. Most of all, the traits demanded for good politics and government were those suspected to exist only in men. Women were thus excluded from participation in electoral politics by a system of values that made such activity by women inconceivable, as well as illegal. Voting and office-holding and the manly virtues they required, however, comprised only half of the political culture of rural New York State. Rural women, especially those who lived in villages, had their own ideas about the role of government and the values that public life ought to reflect. The assumed distinct abilities of men and women created separate public tasks for each, and by exploring both male and female politics we can come closer to understanding their political life as a whole.

CHAPTER 3

The Feminine Virtues and Public Life, 1870–1900

Temperance agitation disturbed the peace of the village of Watkins, New York, in the 1870s. Home to fewer than three thousand people, the Schuyler County town lay at the foot of Seneca Lake. Businessmen had built hotels along the shore to attract summer visitors, and their inns became the center of the temperance debate. Without alcohol, the hotel owners believed, tourists would go elsewhere, darkening the village's seemingly bleak economic future. Temperance advocates, however, remained unmoved. Members of the Sons of Temperance and the St. Mary's Total Abstinence Society encouraged men to give up liquor. Watkins women organized a "praying band" in 1874, which visited the Jefferson House, the largest hotel. "[C]ourteously received and well treated," the women achieved their goal, at least temporarily: while they prayed, the saloon suspended business. Seeking more permanent changes, the women attended a meeting of the village board later that year to ask that all saloons be forced to close earlier than was customary and that no new licenses be granted. Meanwhile, they carried forward their direct efforts to persuade liquor sellers to abandon their trade. In the 1874 village elections, they got their chance to persuade a majority of village men to vote for the temperance slate.[1]

On election day, the ladies fasted and prayed. Despite their earlier efforts to shape village opinion and their present piety, the temperance candidate for the excise board lost by the barest margin—a single vote. By this point, any good humor the pro-license men possessed about temperance had evaporated. Although the temperance movement in Watkins involved a large number of men—nearly half, after all, voted for the temperance slate—women were the special target of the "wets'" ire. In honor of their victory, a group of men fashioned images of the ladies of the praying band, mounted them on poles, and carried them through the village streets. To complete their celebration, the men hanged the temperance women in effigy and then fed a bonfire with the images. Some Watkins women had stepped beyond the line that separated community approval and public hostility.[2]

Despite this display and the narrow electoral defeat, the women persisted. They launched a petition drive to show the new excise board the village's opposition to new liquor licenses and renewals. After gathering 600 names, they presented their petition to the village board in July of 1874. Evidently persuaded, the board voted to deny all licenses except that of the drugstore. After at least a year of work (with more to come in future years) the women had won. Unable to vote themselves or to convince a majority of village men that they should vote for temperance, the women achieved their goal by working outside of electoral politics.[3]

The campaign in Watkins resembled hundreds of incidents of direct action taken against saloons throughout the North.[4] But the experience of the women of Watkins is significant for reasons other than its contribution to the "women's crusade" for temperance. Their actions illuminate women's political involvement and ideas in rural New York. At the most basic level, the Watkins incident demonstrated that rural women, lacking the vote, used more direct means to influence public decisions. Although women's political involvement met with ambivalent reactions from some men, they nonetheless achieved their goals at times, even in divided communities. Their political concerns and activities were a real, and sometimes disturbing, part of rural political life.

Recognizing rural women's political involvement and its impact on their communities is the first step in recovering their political traditions. Theirs was a politics distinguished by exclusion: only a relatively small number of women joined in political action. Material circumstances— economic status, transportation, and communication—shaped the patterns of women's political participation, as did the demands of work in homes and on farms. As rural physical and economic conditions influenced women's political involvement, community constraints of less tangible sorts fashioned its form. While women in rural New York concerned themselves with temperance, charity, and education—issues that also absorbed the energies of urban women—rural action was different from that in cities. As much as rural women's political involvement deviated from their urban counterparts', their political ideas and expectations also differed from rural men's. Like rural men, New York women believed that politics rested on moral convictions—including those concerning the nature of men and of women. Yet, activist women in rural New York disagreed with men on the ways their shared convictions about gender roles, religious teachings, and the value of work should be applied to public life. They also offered different visions of the role government ought to play. While most rural men sought to put limits on government, activist women aimed to have government put limits on citizens' behavior. The conflicts and convergences between the political ideas of men and women helped form the political culture of rural New York.

Nothing like political parties organized the vast majority of women and encouraged them to think about public questions. Rather, some women in rural New York, like those elsewhere, participated in public decisions through their church groups and clubs, which limited women's involvement in public life in a number of ways. Raising money or collecting names on petitions demanded more time than voting for party candidates or marching in an occasional parade, and farm women with heavy domestic responsibilities did not have many moments to spare. Even if a woman found time to take part in a group's work, many organizations eschewed political questions and attended to social or religious projects. Politically active clubs drew their membership selectively: where women lived, their ages and class backgrounds, and the demands of their work, in addition to individual temperament, determined whether or not they would become involved. Rural women's clubs, unlike their urban counterparts, experienced their greatest expansion in the twentieth century. Not until the 1920s did some of the conditions that restricted these women from participation in voluntary organizations significantly fade.[5]

Geography and transportation encouraged village rather than farm women to found and join organizations in late nineteenth-century New York. Villages were more likely to have a sufficient concentration of people to support voluntary societies, and within many villages, women outnumbered men, which was not the case in the open countryside. Village churches drew larger congregations, met more regularly, and supported a wider variety of organizations than country churches did. Transportation facilities made it far more convenient for village women to take part in a group's activities; bad roads posed hurdles for farm women who wanted to attend meetings. If they chose to do so, they probably depended on men to take them to meetings, a step made only when business required a trip to town. Since men usually did the family marketing, women's work did not take them into town as frequently as their husbands'. Too, in some places, mutual suspicion between farmers and villagers made it even less likely that farm women would join village organizations.[6]

Other restrictions curbed women's participation in groups that turned to public activity. Some women could not afford membership dues or balked at joining groups led by elite village women. Teachers and the wives of village lawyers, shopkeepers, businessmen, and the largest farmers dominated women's groups except for Bible study circles and, perhaps, Granges. Women who cared for small children rarely had the time to attend meetings; hence, unmarried women appeared to be more active in women's groups, as were women whose children were grown. Farm women performed a wide variety of time-consuming duties—sewing and mending clothing, cooking and baking, weekly washing, soap-making, cleaning, gardening, churning butter, and caring for chickens—that left little room for club work. In the Finger Lakes area and western New York, women also picked berries and grapes on their farms and those of their neighbors during summers; elsewhere women helped with harvests. As late as 1904, a Grange decided that men and women should "consult each other" when parcelling out work, but their only firm inference was that "the woman should *not* split wood." Although husbands and children often helped with household chores, the hard and extensive work around farms constantly occupied rural women.[7]

Both farm and village women complained about weariness, illness, and loneliness in their diaries. "Done lots of chores," a woman wrote in January of 1884. "My head and eyes and back aches. Am so tired of it all. Don't feel able to do so much all the time, am tired and discouraged. Cried some." Catherine Wood, who worked in neighbors' homes as well as her own, described a typical day: "This morning I got up got my breakfast done up my work went out to Wms come home done my cleaning that is about all . . . oh I feel so lonesome it don't seem as though I could stand it any way." Women may not have been any sicker than men, but they complained more regularly than their husbands of a wide variety of ailments—"about sick" summarized myriad aches and pains, "hard sick" meant "bedridden." Work and illness discouraged farm and even village women from participating in groups that demanded time and sustained attention.[8]

The case of one woman, Jennette Howell Deal Prior, illustrates the limitations that rural life put on women's participation in voluntary societies. While most of her diaries cover the twentieth century (1892–1941), her opportunities and difficulties in taking part in women's groups were little changed from the late nineteenth century. After graduating from a district school, Prior left home to attend a state normal school. While there, and later, as a teacher, she avidly joined a wide variety of church organizations: the Epworth League, Christian Endeavor, prayer groups, the Women's Foreign Missionary Society, and the Home Mission Society. In addition, she taught Sunday school and usually attended two services on Sundays. Prior also went to temperance meetings and lectures and undertook work on the cause's behalf. She replicated her round of activities as she moved to different villages, which she did almost yearly, and maintained most of her memberships when she returned to her family's farm during summers. Unhappy with teaching, the loneliness that came with her frequent moves, and with the work and isolation of the farm, Prior found satisfaction in the moral and spiritual work of the women's groups.[9]

Her routine changed dramatically after her marriage in 1912. She soon became pregnant and cared for her husband's two sons (from a previous marriage) as well. Initially, she insisted on taking charge of all of the work at home. Although her husband helped with housework, she nonetheless had trouble adjusting to her new life. "I don't know what I'll do when I have another to wash for," ran one of her typical protests. She now regarded going to church on Sunday as a welcome achievement; otherwise, she never left the farm at all. After the birth of her daughter, even attending services became a rarity. By 1915, her situation improved somewhat: she and her husband hired a woman to help her, and she gradually eased into a limited version of her earlier involvement in church organizations. By 1918, she attended meetings of a missionary society occasionally. Since she lived some distance from Dundee, the nearest village, her husband or one of her stepsons had to drive her to meetings, so her attendance was sporadic. And she still complained of the difficulty of the work involved in running a farm. "I can never get my work done so I guess I'll just give up," she wrote in 1921. At this point, she helped with the care of a large flock of chickens; picked, cleaned, and packed berries; sewed; churned butter; took care of the garden; preserved food; and with help, saw that the household chores were done. Her activity in women's groups fell short of what it had been before her marriage until later in the 1920s, when Prior took up teaching again and lived away from her home during the week.[10]

If Jennette Prior's situation was at all typical, only with some effort did women who lived on farms and raised children take part in the work of voluntary organizations. Distance and the demands of work discouraged participation, even for a woman who welcomed the spiritual and social rewards of club activities. But the Grange provided a significant exception to farm women's isolation from formal organizations. Indeed, the Grange took pride in its ability to include entire families; Grangers sometimes claimed that the group survived because women joined. Grange women took charge of the socials and dinners that provided an incentive for families to join the Order. The Patrons of Husbandry set aside honorary offices for women that each chapter filled, and in some places, groups elected women to more responsible positions. Within local Granges, however, male and female members argued about meeting times—women favored afternoons, while men wanted evening meetings. Deciding which topics they should discuss also brought conflict, as men complained that Granges spent too little time talking about agriculture while women favored subjects of more general interest—papers on questions such as "Judgment" and the condition of rural life. Women rarely went to meetings unless their husbands joined them, although men often went alone, and men outnumbered women in membership and attendance. But except, perhaps, for Bible study groups, the Grange counted more farm women as members than any women's organization.[11]

While the Grange engaged the interest of some farm wives, voluntary associations remained largely the province of better-off village women. The villagers' relatively light responsibilities—if nothing else, the absence of farm chores—left them with the time to attend meetings and take part in group projects. Since voluntary activities were women's main avenue for participation in politics, only a small fraction of rural women ever became politically active in the late nineteenth century. Women's groups asked for consistent attention that relatively few women had the time or means to give. A public role was not a necessary part of female identity as voting was of male identity. The private occupations of marriage and motherhood anchored traditional female roles.[12] Nonetheless, some women did participate in the public life of their communities and had a significant impact. They expanded the meager efforts to care for the indigent that men sought to limit, attempted to change certain local policies, and offered a vision of government and politics different from that of sparse services provided by partisan officials. Through their attention to both local matters and those that transcended their villages' concerns, politically active rural women fashioned a public role for themselves.

Women's groups in rural New York usually maintained religious connections. Church groups naturally assumed a pious directive, but this was true of ostensibly secular groups as well. Granges featured talks on matters of faith, to which women contributed conspicuously; local chapters of the Daughters of the American Revolution started their meetings with prayer, as did some suffrage groups.[13] That women's groups conceived at least part of their function to be religious was to be expected. Women's role in nineteenth-century society ideally entailed maintaining moral order and community piety; women also filled Protestant churches. Even while sticking closely to their cultural assignment, some women's groups managed to stray from accepted feminine behavior. Two characteristics of womanhood—piety and passivity—came into conflict. Women's groups throughout the nineteenth century, whether organized within a church or not, provided a means for political involvement, and religious imperatives extended the reasons for it. While piety in women was innocuous enough, it also extended an invitation to public activity.[14]

Most women's groups in the late nineteenth century did not take up the invitation and trouble themselves with public questions. Congregations outside of rural New York's usually dominant Methodist and Presbyterian establishment—Baptists, Episcopals, Roman Catholics, and the later fundamentalist and pentecostal groups—rarely supported politically active women's societies. Even in Methodist and Presbyterian churches, Ladies' Aid Societies stayed busy by raising money for expanding pastors' houses, paying their salaries, organizing young people's societies, outfitting better kitchens for church basements, or furnishing churches themselves. The only public function of these societies was supplying entertainment for their communities through running various "socials" to raise money. Church groups thus contributed most of the community entertainment that brought women and men together. While not unimportant, this was their sole public venture.[15] But other groups—chiefly in growing and stable townships and villages—did get involved in questions that troubled their communities and the world outside; especially charity, temperance, and, for some, women's rights.

All organizations that women joined outside of Ladies' Aid Societies and Bible study circles engaged in charitable work to some extent in the late nineteenth century. The narrowest—and commonest—variety of charitable activity took the form of contributions made to members of the organization itself. Thus Granges appointed members (usually women or a married couple) to collect money for members who suffered losses from fires, sent others to visit sick Patrons, and assigned women to arrange for flowers, cards, and visits when Grangers lost family members. Members of Women's Christian Temperance Union (WCTU) chapters likewise came to the aid of members in need. Women's groups within Protestant churches charged committees with greeting newcomers to communities and raised money and gathered food and clothing for struggling or destitute members of congregations. By the late 1880s, women's organizations in larger villages began to apply the lessons of the charity organization movement to their communities. Agreeing with their urban counterparts that charity must be more than random giving to be truly effective, they sent women to determine the worthiness of their potential recipients and to discover their real needs. Women's societies from different congregations discussed how they might avoid duplication of effort. Alleviating the occasional misfortunes of their own members absorbed a good deal of the resources of late nineteenth-century women's groups.[16]

Receiving aid and comfort from one's friends removed the taint of charity while it assured the givers that help would be forthcoming in the event of loss. Letters of thanks attested to the appreciation of this informal insurance. A member of the Presbyterian church in Cazenovia wrote to the women's group expressing his gratitude for their "interest & *Friendship* for one whose lot in life is so destitute of earthly comforts."[17] Helping members of a group expressed friendship, fellowship, and solidarity. It was also a defensive maneuver. When groups grew too ambitious, they risked alienating their members and those in the community they sought to help. Extending aid to people outside of an organization could be construed as unwanted meddling. To pay attention to the needs of a voluntary society's members was a safe alternative to possibly divisive community involvement. Efforts to reach the broader community remained uncommon in the late nineteenth century, and would not really appear until well into the twentieth century.

Neither charity available to any needy villager nor community service was the usual undertaking of women's groups in rural New York. When groups adopted such projects, they often met with disappointment. A women's club in Delaware County twice attempted to establish a reading room in the village of Delhi, and endured public criticism. The first one "went out of existence for the very best of reasons," a newspaper editor noted without further explanation, while a letter to the same weekly asked if the room was "productive of harm." In Madison County, a woman published a letter in a newspaper, which criticized what she saw as unsanitary conditions in the county jail and the custom of incarcerating boys along with men. The sheriff sued the woman, although he dropped the case two years later. Both Granges and women's church societies debated the propriety of giving to families outside of their own groups. And women sometimes worked without success against the prevailing wisdom regarding public spending for the poor. During a meeting of the Cherry Creek Grange, one woman produced a letter written by an inmate at the Chautauqua County poorhouse. With this evidence, she hoped to "correct the wrong impression that it cost too much to keep the inmates of the county house." The secretary left no record of the Patrons' immediate response, but the Grange, which often moved quickly to urge spending cuts, took no action.[18]

While charitable activity fell squarely into the sphere of women's natural concerns, projects aimed at the entire community did not. Villages, it seems, did not welcome the rare occasions when women's groups proposed to raise money for local improvements—sidewalks, parks, reading rooms, and the like. Ideas about charity and about women confined female efforts, and so did economic constraints. Women's groups avoided overstepping their boundaries by extending aid to those outside of their club or church. Voluntary societies lacked the resources to sustain elaborate community projects. Local campaigns for public improvements thus remained largely the responsibility of village businessmen.

It is not clear, however, that organized women would have reached out consistently to the rural poor even if money were not a problem. Both men and women derided fellow townspeople who lived in ramshackle houses and avoided the ministrations of churches, with locally coined names like "floodwood" (in Schoharie County). With many New York farm families themselves suffering hard times, Granges could only muster support for the obvious cases of the worthy poor: hardworking families that suffered the misfortunes of fires. Those outside of respectable society remained invisible except when blamed for trouble: when Indians were arrested, when Italian peddlers did not act with sufficient deference, when people who lived in the hills got drunk in town. Help for the poorest villagers—farm laborers out of work for a season, the elderly without families to provide for them, and in some places, orphans and the insane, continued to be the duty of local office-holders for whom parsimony measured success.

Largely steering clear of struggles with local problems, women's groups turned to national or international projects. Indeed, supporting urban hospitals and orphanages and foreign missionaries engaged the best efforts of women's organizations in rural New York. The work of the Torry Mission Band in Cazenovia was typical. The women chose projects at the beginning of the year and spent most of their time on those tasks. Thus, in 1881, they decided raise money for an African mission as their foreign project and chose the Whitehall Seminary in North Carolina for their "home" work. Through the late nineteenth century, they devoted some effort to community projects—sewing for the "young girls" of the Brooks family in Cuyler in 1882 and sending five dollars to a "burnt out family" in their village in 1884, for example. But most of their work focused on funding schools in the South, and missionaries in the American West, China, Japan, Central America, and Africa.[19]

The major feature of their meetings, like those of other groups, was reading the letters they received from their beneficiaries. Letters from missionaries in India or China furnished upstate women with interesting and curious tales about exotic places. These letters also confirmed that the recipients needed their gifts and, more important, appreciated them. When the women of the Presbyterian Ladies' Missionary Society of Cooperstown furnished a room at the Ingleside Seminary in Amelia Court House, Virginia, they received letters of thanks, both from the teachers, who described the items sent and the uses the gifts would be put to, and from the girls who occupied the room. One girl described the seriousness of the poverty in that part of the state; another pledged to the Cooperstown ladies that "I appreciate and will keep things as nice as I know how." Such letters connected rural women with their far-flung beneficiaries, who assured the women that their gifts were valuable and that young girls in Virginia and missionaries in India honored the same values as the upright people in New York villages. Insofar as it guaranteed praise and fascinating stories, charitable work outside of rural townships and villages promised greater satisfaction than working with local people, who were neither exotic nor far enough away to inspire pity.[20]

Along with gaining psychological comfort, women in New York villages learned of problems that remained invisible in their own communities through their contacts with state or national parent organizations. Women's groups contributed to orphanages and homes run by voluntary organizations that supplied alternatives to state institutions. They also supported hospitals for women and benevolent societies in nearby cities. Grange women collected money for orphanages and food for urban charities. Local chapters of the WCTU made yearly donations to the home for unwed mothers run by the New York Union and sometimes sent local girls to it. Some church groups resented parent organizations that attempted to determine which institutions deserved aid. When the parent organization of one church group insisted that locals limit their activity to sending cash to the regional office, the local balked. It continued to pick its own projects and most often directly sent clothing and furniture to missionaries rather than money. But for the most part, locals gladly cooperated with larger organizations that gave them roundabout ways to address problems they could or would not touch at home.[21]

Temperance, unlike benevolence or community service, inspired local action. Poverty and godlessness might have been urban or foreign problems, but organized women saw liquor as both a national and a local concern that required persistent attention in their own villages. In this, they received the support of some men. If strict economy stood as the most inspiring goal for government that many rural men could devise, crushing intemperance commanded equally sustained attention from activist women.

Organized rural women moved at both the local and state levels to combat intemperance. They tried to persuade saloon owners to close their doors. Until 1896, towns elected excise boards that had the power to grant licenses, and women urged men to vote for representatives who promised to reject all applications for liquor licenses. Failing that (or in addition to it), women's groups and Granges petitioned state legislators to pass temperance legislation. Such laws included both prohibition measures and laws mandating temperance education in all public schools. Some women's groups worked to enforce what temperance legislation was in effect. Together, these endeavors on behalf of temperance made organized women a political presence in New York villages.

Direct persuasion reached its greatest popularity as a political tactic in the temperance campaigns of the 1870s. In small and large villages throughout the state, but especially in the southern tier and the Finger Lakes district, women prayed, sang hymns, and petitioned saloonkeepers to persuade them to shut down. In 1871, the "Mothers, Wives, and Sisters" of Cortland Village petitioned their excise board to cease granting licenses because of liquor's "blasting and withering effects" and its ability to destroy "Human Character, and the destiny of undying souls." Women's groups, such as the Band of Hope in Cortland County, sponsored temperance workers, who (with luck) worked with local ministers to persuade men to give up liquor. Church societies brought male and female temperance lecturers to their towns to bolster the convictions of the "drys" and to win new converts. Some WCTU chapters provided alternatives to saloons. An Allegany County Union operated a restaurant, and others served meals on court and election days. Women's groups commonly gathered on election days to fast and to pray that the men would vote the town dry.[22]

At times, they moved their prayer meetings to polling places. In 1887, women in Almond—mostly members of the WCTU—arranged to serve meals during the town elections from a room near the polling place. According to a newspaper sympathetic to temperance, a group of "whiskeyites" flung parts of a dismembered skunk into the lunchroom. "The ladies were indignant," the article reported, "and providing themselves with no-license ballots, went to the polls and used every influence to secure votes for the no-license candidate." From that point, the women's presence changed the course of the election, though their troubles were not yet over. "Several rowdies . . . spi[t] at the ladies, and us[ed] all kinds of language." When the votes were counted, the no-license commissioner had won; due, in part, the newspaper correspondent believed, to the unruly behavior of some of the men. In Almond, some men detected (rightly) a temperance agenda even in such a tame expression of women's political interest as serving meals during town meetings, and the "wets'" disapproval, in turn, brought more direct political action and the support of other men.[23]

As such events suggest, the women's temperance activities brought conflict to their villages. While rural newspapers tended to play down community disagreements—discord was thought to reflect badly on a village—some cases, such as that in Watkins, received coverage in country weeklies. The WCTU of Long Eddy, Sullivan County, sought to make Monticello, then a Catskill resort village, no-license. As in Watkins, hotel owners led the opposition because they saw liquor licenses as a necessity for winning the tourist trade. Acknowledging the rancor their campaign caused, the WCTU nevertheless persisted. "Is Sullivan County . . . to be turned into a great pasture in which the beer-drinking herd of New York city are to be turned out to grass every summer?" they asked. Despite what they described as the growing sympathy for the WCTU and its goals in the village, the local excise board continued to grant licenses in Monticello.[24]

Accounts of obvious conflicts between pro- and anti-license forces remained outside of the mission of most rural weeklies, but attempts to discredit temperance workers appeared frequently. Most of all, newspapers tried to dismiss them as hypocrites and their allies as naïve. In Preble, temperance workers inspired irate letters to the local newspaper. A writer to the weekly claimed that a male temperance worker tarried in barrooms "lounging and loafing with that reckless abandon which characterizes a constant habitue of such a place." The temperance worker's zealousness caused needless community divisions: he claimed that Preble's hotels were brothels and their owners should be ostracized by the community. Defenders of the temperance workers, meanwhile, maintained that the charges against the temperance workers were false and that Preble's ministers, fearing for their places, remained silent despite widespread intemperance in their congregations. The controversy continued in Preble, and similar ones appeared in other New York townships. Defending abstract freedoms as well as their livelihoods, some community members painted temperance agitators as troublemakers who sought converts to the Prohibition party at the expense of the Republicans. Male temperance workers, as outsiders, and local women, as meddlers in local politics, posed the easiest targets for pro-license criticism.[25]

While partisans may have feared that temperance agitation would generate defections to the Prohibition Party, temperance advocates in the 1870s usually tried to reform the habits of individual men, not gain uniform legislation. This tactic worked best in places where there was already substantial agreement among men and women about the evils of strong drink. The Oaksville Christian Temperance Union for the Advancement of the Cause of Temperance provides a good example. Residents of the hamlet of Oaksville—virtually all of them—formed the club in 1878. During the first two years of its existence, the Oaksville club recruited new members and occasionally disciplined those who violated their pledge to "shield [themselves] from the evils of intemperance." Unlike most voluntary organizations, this group's vigilance committee reported trangressions during their meetings and suggested punishments. Public scrutiny could work in Oaksville: it was a tiny hamlet and the club signed up 189 men and women by the second meeting. Anyone who favored granting liquor licenses would have found few allies.[26]

Even in Oaksville, sterner measures followed. Their town safely dry, club members turned to the neighboring hamlet of Fly Creek, where hotels served alcohol, one even without a license. Club members sent a committee to Fly Creek and threatened prosecution. By 1880 they saw themselves as informal enforcers of the excise laws. In addition, they sponsored rallies for the Prohibition Party and engaged some of its candidates as speakers. The club also acted as a social center for the community: it held dances and hired lecturers for the community's entertainment and as a way to raise money. Having suitably reformed the habits of the townspeople, the Oaksville Temperance Union tackled broader matters.[27]

Indeed, the Oaksville pattern reflected temperance trends in the state as a whole. Direct action persisted throughout the nineteenth century: women worked to induce men to vote for no-license candidates, held prayer meetings on election days, and invited temperance speakers and workers who sought to convince men they should give up liquor. Men and women still joined groups dedicated to persuading individuals to keep on the straight and narrow. But by the 1880s, the focus moved away from these methods towards attempts to change legislation. A number of reasons dictated such a shift. Temperance victories that counted on the reform of individual men remained fleeting—conversion hardly prevented backsliding. Few towns remained dry on the basis of moral suasion alone. And even towns that voted no-license (282 by 1895, the last year of the local excise board system) found their decisions subverted: saloonkeepers shifted their businesses to locations just outside of village boundaries or simply operated in a less public fashion.[28]

The WCTU also helped redirect rural women's attention to questions of state legislation. Unable to depend on good intentions, temperance groups sought to have their gains codified as law. Female temperance advocates looked to the state for help in keeping their husbands and sons away from liquor. The WCTU, along with other temperance organizations, church groups, and Granges, could be counted on to support any and all measures that restricted the sale of liquor in New York. Male and female members sponsored such laws. The threat posed by the Prohibition Party to the Republican vote in upstate New York encouraged the G.O.P. to back the efforts of temperance advocates. But few Republican leaders wanted to see total prohibition become state law, and they carefully defined their position as promoting high license fees for liquor dealers. Prohibition or even stricter regulation of alcohol would have posed a political danger, as such laws were hardly goals of all Republican voters. Seeing that prohibition had produced violence in Iowa, many thought community peace might be threatened as well. Thus through the 1880s and 1890s, Republicans backed various high-license plans, hoping to mollify some of their constituents. While disappointed, temperance advocates at the local level generally supported high-license laws.[29]

While temperance men could vote for Prohibition candidates, women could only petition office-holders and exercise moral pressure. When Republicans in the state assembly passed a high-license bill in 1888, temperance groups flooded Governor David Bennet Hill with petitions and letters asking him to sign it. Petitions collected by WCTU members across the state appeared in Hill's mail. Urban and rural women also sent personal letters. "If you can do any thing to Promote High License for Gods Sake do it and you will Confer a Lasting favor upon the Citizens of East Syracuse . . . there is more money spent for Beer & Whiskey here than would buy Shoes for Every man woman & Child," one woman pleaded. An equally large number of letters came in opposing the bill. A man from Watkins wrote that "most all republicans & Democrats [were] most Bitterly opposed to it." He owned a saloon and believed that people had a right to drink as they chose; "That is if we live in A Free Country." Hill vetoed the bill, which occasioned another flurry of angry letters, as well as those congratulating him for his "manly stand." A "Citizen of Brownville" wrote that "I take you to be a *first class bar-room loafer.* You have taken the shoes from the feet and bread from the mouths of the drunkards' wife and children and have given them to the rumseller."[30]

Each high-license bill spurred temperance forces to demonstrate to lawmakers the support for and moral righteousness of the cause. The state WCTU reminded locals to send petitions to their representatives. The Grange did the same, and often left the work of gathering signatures to female Patrons. The WCTU sponsored legislation that required public schools to teach "scientific temperance." Since temperance laws still allowed voters to determine indirectly whether to license the sale of liquor in their towns, petition drives at the local level continued. The WCTU sent members door-to-door with petitions for local and state legislation to limit or prohibit the sale of alcoholic beverages. Throughout, women's organizations continued their prayer meetings and fasts on election days when temperance questions were to be decided.[31]

Thus organized women in New York and their male allies worked for temperance legislation in a number of ways. Throughout the late nineteenth century, temperance women petitioned their village governments to put a stop to local liquor traffic. Using visible demonstrations of female piety, women's groups also tried to dissuade saloonkeepers from practicing their evil trade. As late as 1910, one WCTU chapter visited village businesses regarding Sunday closings and ran petition drives to shut down saloons. At the state level, the WCTU orchestrated petition campaigns, directing locals to gather signatures in their villages on pending temperance legislation. These attempts to apply direct pressure to local and state lawmakers sometimes brought results, even though women could not vote. Towns exercised their option to enact local prohibition; the Republican Party supported high-license legislation in Albany; and in the 1880s, temperance became one of the subjects taught in public schools. The WCTU claimed more than its share of the credit— their "invincible petitions" certainly required the cooperation of male temperance advocates to push measures through the state assembly. But women's groups helped keep temperance a visible issue in local and state politics.[32]

Organized women's participation in politics regarding the temperance issue, however, did not stop with attempting to get temperance laws passed by state and local governments. Women's groups also helped enforce legislation once it was on the books. They encouraged the work of Law and Order Societies, which appeared when towns voted no-license, and gathered evidence and arranged for the prosecution of illegal liquor-dealers.

The actual work of the many Law and Order Societies formed in small towns throughout New York State remains shadowy. None left records of meetings. Rather, the Societies can be traced in Grange resolutions to join in the work of the Societies in enforcing dry legislation, and in newspaper articles that announced the creation of local groups. Law and Order Societies seem to have included only male members, and they attempted to prosecute violators of dry statutes. Thus the Law and Order Society of Cuba in 1893 organized to "see that the existing laws for the suppression of vice were ENFORCED in our town." If members noticed that unlicensed operations sold liquor, they initiated proceedings to fine the offenders and close their shops. In addition, they urged their fellow townsmen to vote for no-license commissioners.[33]

Women's organizations, such as the WCTU, supported local Law and Order Societies by helping to marshall the evidence needed for prosecution. When members determined that the Societies moved too slowly in bringing illegal liquor dealers to justice, they initiated their own prosecutions. In 1887, the president of the Ontario WCTU wrote to a lawyer who specialized in prohibition violations for advice on how bring charges against liquor sellers and poolroom operators. The Law and Order League in Ontario, the WCTU believed, had failed to provide the necessary level of enforcement. Local government was worse: "Formerly our prosecutions have been conducted through the Town Officers, but this is unsatisfactory to say the least, and so many things can occur to hinder the work." Other WCTU members wrote to discover the "quality of evidence" needed for prosecutions, to have the attorney represent them, and to learn what kinds of businesses could be closed through the standing excise laws. Dissatisfied with their township governments, which often seemed to leave local limitations on liquor sales unenforced, women's groups attempted to make township regulations work.[34]

WCTU chapters in rural New York also tried to insure that temperance sentiment remained in local political debate. On election days, along with serving meals, women acted as poll watchers to guard against possible fraud. In the early twentieth century, others checked periodically on village saloons to guarantee that they remained closed on election days. Larger Unions commonly taught temperance in Sunday schools during the early 1880s. When the state passed legislation in 1884 mandating that "scientific temperance" be taught in the public schools, the members of one Union sat in on the classes to make certain that "the hands of little children are being taught to uplift the white banner of temperance." In places where local decisions had not brought prohibition, women continued to work toward closing local saloons. And women's organizations worked to crush other manifestations of village vice: pool halls, gambling establishments, and tobacco.[35]

Through agitation and enforcement by women's groups on both the state and local levels, temperance became the cause that most visibly absorbed rural women in public life. Indeed, although rural men also sought to put temperance laws on the books, the issue became identified as a woman's concern. When local Granges formed "Women's Work" divisions in 1889, these committees took over any temperance activity the organization engaged in. One Grange concluded that if "our women" worked hard, "[t]emperance would win" in New York. Both rural men and women agreed that the suppression of drink was part of woman's sphere, even if disputes erupted over what tactics women should employ. Rural women, like their urban counterparts, saw alcohol as a threat to women, children, and the home. Liquor "makes our husbands demons, our boys drunkards, and . . . constantly jeopardizes . . . all that makes life desirable," claimed a women's group in central New York. The seriousness of the danger that intemperance posed made public action necessary. Temperance men found women's groups useful allies, and men who considered the Prohibition Party an unwelcome nuisance encouraged women's groups to continue their efforts to change the moral climate of communities. A condescending Watkins newspaper editor thought a Prohibition Party "very ultra and untenable," but believed that if a woman

> act[ed] discreetly, meekly, and lady-like, as behooves women and true womanhood . . . she may be the means of winning, by her prayers and entreaties, her kind and gentle influences, and her deep solicitude, whole communities from the errors into which they have fallen and banish liquor traffic from our land.[36]

Rural women's groups soon learned, however, that prayer and moral influence fell short of drying up villages. When towns elected no-license commissioners, or, later, voted for local prohibition, the task of enforcement remained. Moral suasion was at best a protracted process and at worst an ineffectual one. Thus, while continuing to press their concerns at the local level, women's groups also sought state legislation that would end intemperance. Toward this end, they received the guidance of the state WCTU, which informed local chapters of wider efforts and enlisted their support. Aside from bringing local women's groups into contact with state and national questions, the WCTU encouraged their members to ponder broader problems, such as education, and, most of all, woman suffrage. Taking women's interest in temperance as a starting point, the WCTU inpsired at least some rural women to support woman suffrage.

Existing temperance societies formed the Women's Christian Temperance Union as the crusades of the 1870s abated. Throughout its history, the WCTU worked to gain local or state prohibition, high license fees, and other anti-liquor legislation. But under the leadership of Frances Willard, the WCTU argued for more general reforms. Willard tested alliances with the Knights of Labor, the Populist Party, and the Prohibition Party, and encouraged local Unions to do the same. She suggested projects for them and provided a structure of "departments" concerned with matters as diverse as labor, health, social purity, peace, and education. Locals nonetheless retained the final word on what projects they would take on: this was Willard's "Do Everything" policy, which admitted both national direction and local control. A flexible structure, as well as female anger at intemperance, made the WCTU the largest single women's organization of the nineteenth century.[37]

Although Willard was extremely popular among the WCTU's vast membership—decades after her death, locals in rural New York continued to read her writings and celebrate her birthday—her support for woman suffrage nearly split the organization. For many members of the WCTU, woman suffrage remained a drastic, unnatural step: in a proper social order, women devoted themselves to the home and family, while men took part in the somewhat sordid and corrupt sphere of politics. Attempting to induce men to vote for temperance candidates was one thing, but voting themselves struck many rural as well as urban women as a far-too-complete break with the familiar world of separate spheres. Nonetheless, the WCTU managed to take women's interest in temperance and turn it into support for woman suffrage. Women should have the vote, according to the WCTU, because American politics badly needed the benefit of women's moral nature. Temperance women, in turn, ought to recognize their responsibility to the cause and work for woman suffrage: "Great evils can never be uprooted by kindly condoning them," a speaker at the 1889 state WCTU convention admonished. The WCTU combined ideas about woman's sphere with suffrage under the rubric of "Home Protection," an argument that implied that female values merited a regular presence in electoral politics. While taking traditional domestic concerns seriously, the WCTU taught women how to expand them into wider social concerns and political action.[38]

A number of local Unions in New York villages followed the reasoning of the national WCTU and began work for woman suffrage in the 1880s. WCTUs erected booths at county fairs and handed out pro-suffrage literature along with temperance tracts. Individual women attended suffrage meetings and reported the proceedings at WCTU meetings. Local chapters sent petitions to Albany when the state assembly considered bills regarding school, municipal, and general suffrage. To be sure, the main concerns of local Unions continued to be the suppression of liquor and related vices. Some, however, began to heed the national organization in thinking about how alcohol related to other social problems and what women could do to solve them. "The idea that temperance work has to do only with liquor-making and liquor-drinking is a mistaken one," one local declared in its newspaper column in 1887. "Efforts directed exclusively to those two parts will fail of accomplishing permanent results." To attack both intemperance and other social problems, women needed the vote.[39]

WCTU members in rural New York, as elsewhere, argued the cause of woman suffrage by noting the good that would result from placing ballots in the hands of moral and pious women. Not only would women bring their sorely needed feminine values to bear on electoral politics, but they would exercise the franchise on a different basis than men. Gone would be the drinking and rowdiness that some women's groups claimed went along with election days. According to one WCTU member and newspaper editor, women would as a first step see to it that "no whiskey brains or beer puffed body would receive our support." Women, she believed, would also vote from principle rather than party. Indeed, if all voters put principle first, she claimed, "morals would be purer; strikes would be less; bank failures few and far between; honor and respect for men would be more general and our country would be fulfilling the designs of our forefathers,—a land of peace and plenty, of wealth, honor, and of christianity." When men and women moved principles— chiefly moral ones—to the center of politics, WCTU members claimed, American government and society would vastly improve.[40]

The Grange and suffrage clubs joined the WCTU in putting forward such arguments and supporting woman suffrage in rural New York. The national Patrons of Husbandry went on record early in their support for woman suffrage, and the New York State Grange followed. Woman suffrage fit closely with the Grange's official nonpartisan and anti-corruption approach to politics. Nevertheless, women members protested their lack of representation on important committees and in votes on resolutions within the state organization in the 1870s. This situation did not improve until the mid-1880s, when committees made up of women took charge of the Grange's statements on women's rights and temperance. By 1883 the state Grange unfailingly sent petitions to Albany stating its support for all proposed legislation extending the vote to women; it sent sample petitions to local Granges to sign and mail in as well. Taking pride in what they considered an "advanced" position, the leadership of the state Grange was a dependable ally of woman suffrage.[41]

The state Grange cited both justice and pragmatism as reasons why farmers should favor woman suffrage. As Worthy Master W. A. Armstrong argued in 1883, women earned the right to vote through their work on farms and deserved it because of their concerns about the health of the home. "In every field of human achievement she has had her part, as the symmetrical half of a creation to which was given domination over the earth and sea," he contended in his annual address. "[A]rbitrary edicts brought from the dark night of barbarism" presently denied women the right to vote. Three years later, a woman speaker at a state Grange meeting elaborated on these themes. "Natural rights" dictated that women should be granted the vote, and so did women's special insights. Men could not represent women because male "interests and occupations are different. Men specially represent material interests; women will specially represent the interests of the home." She predicted that when women voted, equal pay for equal work (especially in teaching) would follow, as would meaningful temperance laws.[42]

The state Grange reliably sent suffrage resolutions to Albany, but the attitudes and actions of local Granges were much less predictable. One Grange in Scriba pondered woman suffrage in 1881, and "the gentlemen seemed to carry the idea that it was right." During the next year, a male Granger offered lectures to the women on government in anticipation of their future exercise of the franchise. In 1894, that Grange decided that "some of the evils of the land would be eradicated" if women could vote, and throughout, they sent pro-suffrage petitions to their representatives. But other Granges harbored mixed opinions. The Clymer Grange received suffrage petitions from the state Grange in 1891, with "some being in favor and some against." The entire group could not endorse the petition, so they took a recess "for those to sign the petition that would." Other Granges concluded that women should not have the vote. Despite the consistent position of the state organization, members of local Granges remained uncertain about woman suffrage.[43]

While the WCTU gradually came to favor woman suffrage and local Granges debated its propriety, members of Political Equality Clubs in rural New York kept up agitation for suffrage. The large villages and cities sustained the most active clubs, most of which were formed in the 1890s. Members of Political Equality Clubs sponsored lectures and gathered petitions to persuade legislators to allow women the franchise. They also aimed to educate their members on the workings of American government. Toward that end, the groups read John Fiskes' *Civil Government,* held drills on parliamentary procedure, and practiced voting. Club women discussed current issues and pending legislation on a variety of issues in national and state legislatures. Aside from their natural emphasis on the question of voting rights, the work of Political Equality Clubs differed little from that of WCTU chapters. Political Equality Clubs, too, carried on campaigns against vices like tobacco. One fought to have a curfew put into effect in the small city of Oneida. The Cattaraugus County organization read selections from the Scriptures before their meetings. In many towns and villages of rural New York, both WCTU chapters and Political Equality Clubs pursued moral reform as well as political rights.[44]

Whatever successes members of Political Equality Clubs saw in their reform projects, they and suffragists generally could take comfort in few victories in the late nineteenth century. Their petitions to the legislature to remove the word "male" from the state constitution failed to sway many lawmakers; suffragists' efforts to amend the document during the 1894 constitutional convention also fell short. They did not gain the chance to bring the issue directly before the voters until 1915. Even partial suffrage in the form of allowing women taxpayers to vote on municipal questions failed in the state legislature. In New York, as in other states, the last two decades of the nineteenth century were slow and stormy years for the suffrage cause, punctuated by a string of defeats and divided leadership that made the issue of woman suffrage a less visible one in public debate.[45]

But suffragists in New York could remind themselves of some gains achieved in the late nineteenth century. The most prominent of these was the right of some women in the state to vote for school officials. As was the case in many states outside the South in the 1880s and 1890s, the New York legislature amended suffrage requirements to allow women to vote in the elections of school officers. In New York, this legislation had a tangled history. The first act, passed in 1880, allowed women who raised children or paid taxes to vote for members of some urban school boards or, in rural areas, school district officials, including trustees. This legislation also enabled women to run for these offices. In 1892, a new statute gave women the vote for county school supervisors, who were chosen during the November elections, and allowed them to run for those offices themselves. In 1894 the Court of Appeals ruled that female voting for school supervisors violated the state constitution's suffrage clause, although women could still run for the office and participate in school district contests. Thus New York women voted for school commissioners only in the election of 1893. In 1901, the legislature expanded partial woman suffrage to some township and village elections. Women who paid taxes could vote in local elections that decided questions of taxation. Women in certain parts of New York who met the legislative requirements could exercise the franchise in a small number of elections by the turn of the century.[46]

Members of Political Equality Clubs, joined by women of the WCTU, sought to take advantage of women's partial enfranchisement. The Political Equality Club of Cattaraugus County resolved that "the best interests of our Common Schools demand that all voters male and female feel and show an interest in the Schools, and the interests of P.E. also demand that women exercise the rights of Sufferage conceded to them." They, with other clubs, sought to "induce women to vote in school meetings, and for School Commissioner." This club also worked for the nomination of a female candidate by the Republican Party in 1893, and then helped in her campaign. The Madison County club suspected that inspectors of election deliberately threw out women's votes in the 1898 election, and they appointed a committee to investigate the matter. Meanwhile, a WCTU chapter resolved that it would "take up the duty growing out of the right conferred upon us to take equal privileges with the men in our school meetings." WCTUs reported work done on behalf of female candidates during their state conventions.[47]

District school elections rarely generated much interest from either male or female voters. A brief flash of heat attended the elections in the early 1880s when women first gained the right to vote for district school officials. Suffragists, female professionals, and wives of male professionals ran for school district positions and encouraged women to vote for them, and the novelty of women candidates and voters inspired newspaper coverage and relatively high voter turnout. But while a large "woman vote" helped elect women candidates in Perry, Wellsville, and other places, school meetings soon returned to normal: routine, poorly attended events stirred to life occasionally by bitter, even violent, quarrels over spending, taxes, and (less frequently) religion. The same officers generally won reappointment year after year, with, at best, some attempt to rotate the available offices among the usual group of officeholders. Neither men nor women took much interest in winning a position that had as its major responsibility, after signing on a teacher, determining who would get the contract to provide the school with wood for the winter. Even suffragists and temperance activists had trouble mustering interest in school district elections.[48]

The 1893 election of school supervisors offered a new opportunity for woman suffragists. Political Equality Clubs sought to show doubting legislators that women would vote if given the opportunity and took pains to register women, get them to the polls, and sponsor candidates. The Warsaw Political Equality Club canvassed the women of the village in September and persuaded 650 of them to register. The clubwomen worked for the nomination of a male supporter of woman suffrage for the Republican nomination; when he lost, they backed the female candidate, Ella K. Avery, who ran as a Prohibitionist and Populist. On election day, club members stationed themselves at the polls, "though the places were all dirty and uncomfortable as in a barn," to guard against attempts to intimidate or otherwise restrict women's right to the franchise. According to reports of both the club and a village newspaper, 279 village women voted; a majority, the club claimed, for the woman candidate. She came in a distant third in this election, however, behind the victorious Republican nominee and the Democratic candidate.[49]

Female nominees ran—and lost—in virtually every school commission district; most, like Avery, as candidates of minority parties. But four women, all nominees of majority parties, won positions as school commissioners in 1893. In the second school commission district of Cattaraugus County, Martha Van Rensselaer, a teacher who received endorsements from the county Political Equality Club, outlasted her male opponents through forty-two ballots to gain the Republican nomination. In support of her candidacy, Republican men cited Van Rensselaer's expertise softened by her femininity. After applauding her "graceful remarks" upon winning the nomination, a party newspaper described her "successful experience as a teacher" to assure voters that "the duties of the office will be faithfully and conscientiously discharged" if Van Rensselaer won. While solidly in support of her candidacy, the newspaper sent mixed messages about women voters. One column encouraged Cattaraugus women to "show their appreciation of this compliment paid to their sex in this nomination" by voting for Van Rensselaer; another called her Democratic opponent who questioned the constitutionality of female votes a cheat and a bad sport. Yet a local column claimed—with something less than crystalline logic—that women "don't want to vote, but only think they want to," so only an "exceedingly small" number of the 220 Franklinville women who had registered would actually show up at the polls. On election day, Martha Van Rensselaer and the entire Republican ticket coasted, as usual, to victory.[50]

Most female candidates elsewhere in the state were not so fortunate. In Schoharie County, a Democratic stronghold, a woman ran for one of the county school commissioner positions as a Republican in 1893. A Republican newspaper mentioned female freedom from partisan ties along with expertise on educational matters as reasons to vote for a woman. To elect a woman would be to "take the public schools out of the hands of partisan politicians and insur[e] the services of a class who, as a rule, discharge their duties with an eye to the cause of popular education." A man wrote to the newspaper to offer his opinion that minority parties did well to nominate women, since in some places that tactic brought otherwise rare victories. That result did not occur in Schoharie. Lena Sias lost, as did the other Republican candidates. Women's votes, or the general desire to reward "expertise" and remove "politics" from the schools, were inadequate to break the county's normal Democratic majority.[51]

At least one commentator blamed Sias' defeat on the women of Schoharie. In one town, a newspaper account claimed, only eight women bothered to vote, and they divided equally between the male and female candidates. "If all the women in the town had voted," the writer explained, "Mr. Alverson's majority would probably have been greater, as most of the women in Conesville believe that a woman is out of her sphere when running for office." That opinion was a controversial one, but it did point to some of the problems women candidates encountered, especially if they relied on the support of other women. Few women—probably well under half of the 200,000 reported to have registered—made their way to the polls to vote for a single office, even when female candidates ran for it. To begin with, a good deal of confusion remained about whether women could indeed vote in such elections. Granges appointed committees to discover whether women had that right. Some partisan newspapers suggested that women voters would be challenged. One editor claimed that it was "unquestionably very doubtful at least, whether any body but a male citizen is eligible to the office of school commissioner," and asserted that a supervisor of federal elections said laws that enfranchised women for school elections were unconstitutional.[52]

In late October, those who suspected female votes would be illegal gained support from Superior Court justice Pardon Williams, who determined in a case that arose in Onondaga and Oneida counties that the 1892 law violated the state constitution's suffrage clause. His decision did not settle the question—suffragists immediately appealed his ruling, which in any event applied to only two counties. Williams' opinion, however, apparently persuaded some women to stay home on election day: suffragists reported that in one village, "all but nine" of the 102 women who registered "were intimidated by Justice Williams' decision and did not go to the polls." For the women who learned that they could vote and wanted to make use of that right, other obstacles remained. For farm women, getting to the polls could prove difficult. If a woman took that trouble, casting a ballot could have been an intimidating experience. Elections remained male events; held in male enclaves and, with men milling about and the noise and confusion, perhaps inhospitable to women. Thus WCTU chapters and suffrage clubs devoted time to convincing their own members (presumably favorable to the enfranchisement of women) that they should turn out for school elections. A good number of rural women doubtless lacked sufficient interest in schools or suffrage to compel them to vote, while others opposed the whole notion of woman suffrage.[53]

That said, it unfortunately remains impossible to determine systematically how many women voted in school elections and for whom they voted. In some places, however, a substantial number of women voted; and fearing that female votes would be challenged, election officials counted their ballots separately from the men's. The cases of these counties provide some intriguing evidence that women tended to support women candidates. Martha Van Rensselaer, for example, received 68 percent of the total vote but fully 90 percent of women's votes. In the largest village in the second district, women voted as a bloc: virtually all of the more than 200 women voters support Van Rensselaer. In the first district of Cattaraugus County, the male Republican candidate won with 42 percent of the combined votes of men and women, while the male Democrat trailed with 36 percent, and Phoebe Wood, the Prohibition candidate, gained 22 percent. Yet Wood received two-thirds of the 828 women's ballots, with the remaining third divided nearly equally between the Republican and Democrat. Returns from other areas did not show such stark differences between male and female voters. In Washington County, for example, women in some townships and election districts were more likely to vote for Republican Roxie Tuttle than men were. But in one urban election district, nearly all of the men—like nearly all of the women—voted for her Democratic rival. Women's voting patterns, however, were distinctive enough to suggest a hypothesis: late nineteenth-century women voters, to a greater extent than those in the twentieth century, tended to support women candidates.[54]

Research into partial woman suffrage in other places could confirm or negate this supposition. New York women lost the right to vote for school commissioners in 1894, when the Court of Appeals upheld Justice Williams' decision. Yet women continued to run for positions as school commissioners—and to win even without female votes. The 1894 decision also did not affect women's ability to vote in school board elections in small cities and villages and in school district contests in rural townships. Women candidates continued to revive interest in the elections they ran in. In Jamestown, the 1889 election featured two women who campaigned for positions on the school board. One newspaper described it as a "hot fight," although "the best of humor prevailed during the afternoon, and many were the jokes cracked between the men and women workers." Turnout for this election was unusually high, and the women candidates defeated their male rivals: they won 708 and 700 votes, to the men's 357 and 354. The interest in this election—and the mobilization of women in Jamestown—had to do with dissatisfaction with the sitting school board, which had ruled that female teachers who married automatically lost their jobs. Given a compelling issue, women did participate in school elections, and their votes could determine the results of those canvasses.[55]

As late as 1915, the interest that women candidates created in local elections also took negative turns. A school election in Delhi brought results very different from those in Jamestown. Two women held positions on the village school board they had won in a special election the previous year. As the 1915 election neared, no sign of conflict appeared. This school election seemed to proceed like all others: incumbents rarely faced challenges and little excitement attended the selection of trustees. But less than a week before the election, a "men's ticket" appeared. Indeed, newspapers failed to mention that ticket until they reported the election results. In Delhi, despite the efforts of the village suffrage club, which "worked the polls very hard," the "women's ticket" lost by a vote of 156 to 144. Hostility to women candidates could be strong enough to break the usual patterns of local politics; in this case, the usually reflexive re-election to trusteeships few citizens paid much attention to.[56]

The experiences of the female would-be office-holders in Jamestown and Delhi, and the course of school suffrage generally, illustrate that for many rural men and women, woman suffrage seemed too drastic a change to earn support. Temperance campaigns and other activities that brought women into public life were potentially divisive, but suffrage, by moving women into the male world of partisan politics, was a direct threat to the doctrine of separate spheres. By challenging ideas about woman's place and suggesting that wives might dissent from their husbands' opinions, woman suffrage remained a radical demand through the turn of the century in urban as well as rural places. Insofar as some men believed that participation in electoral politics demanded a specific kind of character—one composed of a set of traits collectively called "manhood"—the prospect of women's voting and holding office appeared ridiculous. Women, they argued, would be at a loss to know how to function in electoral politics. The traits of character women were to aspire to were not those demanded by partisan politics. Women's participation would thus threaten the functioning of electoral politics as it was. Worse, opponents of suffrage claimed, women would lose their womanly traits if they cast ballots once a year. Woman suffrage would therefore both put the home in danger and disrupt the normal practice of partisan politics. These risks seemed too extreme to many men and women: the individual's rights mattered less than a stable social order.[57]

School suffrage was an unhappy compromise between pro- and anti-suffrage views. Many suffragists regarded it as a galling halfway measure that granted women no political power, while opponents of suffrage could see the beginnings of the disaster they predicted in the conduct of school elections and the spectacle of women's running for office. But it was the major concession to suffragists' demands in the late nineteenth century. If a compromise had to be made, school suffrage was a sensible one for anti-suffragists. Women, by virtue of their work in the home, commanded certain kinds of expertise, and the care of children was one of those areas. In rural New York, women had been involved in school politics in other ways. The Grange sent committees consisting of women or married couples to discover if obedience and respect were properly taught and to learn if better-trained and -paid teachers might improve the schools. Because of their roles as mothers, and in some cases, as teachers, women presumably knew more about children than men did, and had a greater stake in how schools were run. At the same time, especially in regard to school district elections, the electorate's lack of interest mitigated any harm that women might cause.[58]

Participation in school elections thus was one limited way women could become directly involved in partisan politics. Yet that involvement labored under the same limitations that women's voluntary work did. Involvement in, or creation of, local controversies held few rewards for women's groups. School board policies mobilized women in the small city of Jamestown. But in smaller villages and towns, women's associations encountered more determined opposition. Change in policies that might increase the cost of government came slowly and grudgingly to rural townships and villages, especially those experiencing decline. Faced with a situation that left little room for local political action of any sort, women's groups in such places looked outward to involvement in national or state organizations and issues.[59]

To the extent that rural women's groups avoided community involvement, they diverged from the pattern of female organizations in urban areas. Throughout the early twentieth century, women's clubs carried on a tradition of municipal involvement begun in the early nineteenth century. These clubs founded and operated hospitals and orphanages, employment services for women, and libraries. Urban women's organizations built parks and playgrounds and worked to guarantee untainted supplies of water and milk. Rural women, by contrast, did not undertake similar community projects until the late 1910s and 1920s. A practical difficulty precluded such involvement in their communities: rural women's groups simply could not raise the money to sustain long-term community projects. A WCTU chapter in Angelica explained its problems when it placed stands containing temperance literature in the village's railroad depot. "These little duties," its secretary wrote, "which can be so easily performed are just as necessary as larger ones, and Unions that are not able to spend money in other work will find something of this kind effectual, and stepping stones to higher places." With meager resources, women's groups in villages and rural towns took on extremely limited community projects, if they sought out such tasks at all.[60]

But as the case of the school election in Delhi suggests, women's organizations at times faced problems on top of limited money. Some rural communities were simply not receptive to women's public action. Even such seemingly innocuous events as election-day dinners sometimes angered some men if they suspected that the women had a larger political agenda. Pressure on women's organizations to curtail certain public activities could have great effect in small and declining communities, where men who sought changes also found frustration.[61]

Thus, unlike urban groups, rural women's groups often leapt over their communities when they decided to engage in political activities. Activist women in rural areas learned to look beyond their towns if they desired to address social problems; and, perhaps more important for rural politics, they developed the habit of considering the state government as a crucial possible ally. The state provided the legal context for local liquor policies, and any changes that women's groups wanted made in that legislation had to be accomplished with statewide organization. Even the largest villages could not sustain the construction and operation of hospitals, but local groups could participate in extensive charitable work by supporting urban efforts. Since many of the women's organizations of the late nineteenth century were part of state or nationwide groups, rural women came into contact with a wider array of projects than they would have if they had engaged only in local affairs. For activist rural women, there was an important lesson: women's groups could accomplish little without the help of the state, either because of the intransigence of local communities or because of the nature of the problems they chose to attack.

To the extent that women's groups perceived the state government as a potential ally, their members differed from their husbands and fathers. Most men in late nineteenth-century rural New York saw state government as overly partisan and expensive and as the source of policies that benefited only rich urban men. Activist women's ideas about the possibilities of state government were not the only areas in which their political expectations deviated from those of men. Rural women and men agreed that politics ideally reflected certain moral and Christian values, but that consensus dissolved when it became necessary to decide how and to what extent such values should be applied. In part because of their distance from the rituals that surrounded partisan politics, women's connections to the political parties were weaker, and their views of the parties' usefulness in government less positive, than those of even the most cynical man. As a result of their exclusion from formal politics, rural women maintained an awkward understanding of how public power operated and what they could ask of office-holders. But in the twentieth century, more men drew closer to women's ideas about politics and their methods of political participation.

Two traditions—Christianity and domesticity—shared in some measure by both rural men and women, formed the background of women's political ideas. Women filled their diaries with expressions of piety on a more regular basis than men. Rural women, along with men, also wrote of their belief in the literal existence of heaven and hell, of the revealed truth of the Bible as a guide to everyday life, and of Jesus as a constant source of support through great and small trials. For some Protestants such understandings of God's will encouraged some public action. For rural women, this meant, at the very least, attending church services whenever possible and further study of the Bible, with or without the fellowship of a group dedicated to that purpose. Some New Yorkers participated more extensively. They understood supporting missionaries and charities as part of Christian duty, along with engaging in some charitable work within their congregations and communities. The suppression of sin, especially drink, was considered proper behavior for Christian women.[62]

Protestant principles could demand political expression, and such public action remained compatible with nineteenth-century ideas about domesticity. Piety was part of woman's nature, according to this view; along with devotion to home and children, sentimentality, a tendency to follow emotion rather than reason, and selflessness. While not traits suited for electoral politics as men had constructed it, women's interest in questions that related to the home, children, or moral standards was understandable. If the participation of women in public debates required an explanation—and both rural men and women acted as though it did—Christianity and domesticity granted adequate cause for women to organize, circulate and sign petitions, take part in public demonstrations, and otherwise try to bring community opinion around to their position. God and womanhood, according to one WCTU, dictated their actions: "women who in the firm belief that God has called womanhood to aid Him in the redemption of humanity from the rum-curse and its attendant evils" made up the WCTU. Christianity and domesticity set constraints on public action, however, even while advancing reasons for it.[63]

Christian and domestic values implied a critique of late nineteenth-

century partisan politics and of the normal run of office-holders. Politically minded women applied a different standard to voters and politicians than did male partisans. Temperance advocate, suffragist, and
newspaper editor Mrs. M. L. Rumpff criticized the conduct of men in
Angelica during the village caucuses. "[I]t is a pity and a shame that
human beings are not capable of making selections of officials without
using liquor," she asserted. Along with belittling some election-day traditions, she recommended candidates for reasons different from those
offered in partisan newspapers. She outlined the qualifications of her
choice for assemblyman in 1887: A. B. Cottrell was a former school-
teacher, soldier, state representative, and "with all a solid temperance
man." She stressed that she knew him personally, and could attest to his
"excellent principles" and ability to represent the district. Devotion to
certain principles, rather than character, mattered in politics, in her
view; as did experience. Personal friendship, rather than the political
variety, was the means of judging a man's worth. Since as a woman in
"this free and glorious country,—we cannot vote, consequently have no
politics," she endorsed Republicans, Democrats, and Prohibitionists for
different offices. In every case, she commented on the man's moral
worth and (if known) his position on and practice of temperance. The
differences between her views and those of her partisan colleagues
became clear in the extensive criticism she received from male newspaper editors. One Republican editor accused Mrs. Rumpff of taking
bribes in exchange for her newspaper's support. She claimed that other
editors called her newspaper " 'insignificant,' 'vindictive,' 'irresponsible,'
'ignoble,' 'anti-republican,' 'anti-christian,' 'anti-decent.' " That a woman
would take political positions at all earned her the wrath of the partisan
editors; that she failed to follow a party line made her naïve or somehow corrupt.[64]

By employing standards of moral righteousness and correctness to
certain issues, women concerned with partisan politics found it difficult
to identify with the major political parties. As coalitions of men with
different interests, the Democratic and Republican parties stressed the
features that all their supporters shared: chiefly, their traditions and
positions on the tariff. The Republican Party came closest to meeting the
criterion of temperance support, but its commitment to the cause remained guarded and limited to advancing high-license plans. Meanwhile, the male rituals so conspicuous in late nineteenth-century electoral
politics—the martial rhetoric, parades, and masculine values—gained
power from their exclusion of women. Given women's distance from the
traditions and practices of electoral politics, nonpartisanship of the sort
that Mrs. Rumpff practiced was one way that they could relate to electoral politics. By refusing to identify with any party, women could pick
and choose among the candidates on the basis on their positions on issues
and personal moral standing. This was the position of the WCTU and
suffrage clubs, both at the state and local levels. It was a form of single-

issue politics, in which women chose to support in whatever way they could candidates who agreed with their views, or failing that, worked to persuade public officials to vote their way.

In addition to providing a way to express political preferences while avoiding what were for rural women meaningless labels, nonpartisanship fit with a broader conception of how politics ideally worked—one that ran against the grain of traditional feminine traits. Women might have learned about the parties through newspapers and male kin. When they wanted to learn about politics, however, they turned to textbooks. Their vision of politics thus idealized the independent, public-spirited citizen of the civics books, not the partisan. It was a rational rather than an emotional ideal: intelligence, attention to the public good, and Christian values were the attributes of dutiful citizens and legislators. Suffrage clubs and other women's organizations that considered political matters deemed politics a subject that required serious study if one aimed to gain the desired political traits. Members of suffrage clubs researched the duties of local and state office-holders, which they considered preparation for their eventual enfranchisement and important knowledge for all citizens. "The subject was somewhat bewildering to us women," the secretary reported, "and we came to the conclusion that few men knew the subject as they should." In a speech given at a Political Equality Club banquet, one woman claimed that

> [t]he bane of political life to day is the struggle for office and the sacrifice of principle to obtain it . . . . If women want to obtain power politically which will tell for the future of this country, and make us proud to call it ours, we must hold a righteous cause above political preferment. We must recognize the whole as greater than a fraction, though that fraction be ourselves.

As a practical application of this principle, club members decided that when they voted for school commissioners, they would pay closest attention to qualifications and keep in mind what was good for the schools. A woman candidate would only be preferred if her opponent was of lesser or equal "moral worth and intellectual power."[65]

Education for proper political participation involved more than learning about the structure of the political system and minding the public good. It also meant scrutinizing candidates and parties and sharing their knowledge about the nation's fundamental political principles. One woman urged the people of her village to go out and hear all the political speeches given in the campaign of 1887. "It is no evidence of fidelity to party to purposely stay away from an opposition speech, but rather shows a desire to remain in willful ignorance and bigotry." Rather than occasions of partisan celebration, speeches provided an opportunity to learn: if men and women went to all of them, they would be "posted on all sides, able to talk and vote with reason." the Warsaw Political Equality Club gave 1894 and 1895 over to the study of past and present American political parties, an endeavor its members considered a success because it "broadened us and made us realize the good points in each of their phases of thought." The Alfred WCTU directed its Reform Department in 1884 to speak to groups in the town on "the Duties of American citizens treating especially upon our obligations to the government, making ourselves . . . acquainted with true politics." The male ideals of friendship and loyalty had no place in this vision of government; reason and Christian principle ought to guide political behavior.[66]

Despite the disparity between these women's political views and those of partisan men, other rural women identified with the parties and sometimes joined party organizations. Individual women, even without the vote, considered which party they should claim as theirs. After attending temperance lectures and a Republican campaign meeting in 1892, Jennette Howell Deal Prior wrote in her diary that while the Republican "lecturers" were good, "I think I am still *almost* a Prohibitionist." Some women joined chapters of the Women's Republican Association in the 1880s and 1890s. Such clubs were probably not numerous or large, although systematic records are not available to determine how many women belonged. Records for two upstate New York clubs exist: one set of minute books for the chapter in Alfred and newspaper accounts of the meetings of the group in Cuba, both in Allegany County. The Alfred chapter enrolled about forty members, many of them wives of men prominent in the county Republican Party. The Carrie Harrison Club of Cuba claimed 112 members in 1888.[67]

Significantly, both clubs were located in a part of the state where the Prohibition Party remained a political presence despite secure Republican majorities. The clubs saw part of their purpose as warning women away from the Prohibition Party. The Carrie Harrison club heard Mrs. J. Ellen Foster, president of the national Women's Republican Association and temperance worker, advise women to ignore the lures of total prohibition in general and the Prohibition Party in particular. To demand prohibition would be to insist on an unreasonably high standard of purity that would lead to anarchy. The Prohibition Party

> appropriates [woman's] work and her influence to its own purposes and pays a fulsome flatteries; it gives to women seats in conventions, and places their names on meaningless committees and tickets impossible of success. . . . The pity of it is that women, gentle and refined, and sometimes strong, should be vain enough to be thus cajoled and their God given powers thus mortgaged.

Women's proper rules in electoral politics were to do whatever they could to see Republicans elected, to raise Republican sons, and to work to change public opinion in favor of temperance. Only laws that trailed changes in public habits and attitudes stood a chance of having any value.[68]

While the women of the Republican clubs followed Foster in treating temperance as a goal to be approximated rather than fully achieved, they shared with members of Political Equality Clubs an interest in woman suffrage and a rational approach to politics. The Women's Republican Association of Alfred examined the platforms of all of the parties in 1892, discussed current issues and recent congressional speeches, boned up on parliamentary procedure, practiced voting, and when women gained the right to vote in school elections, canvassed "all Republican women" in their village. Both the Alfred and the Cuba clubs supported woman suffrage. In Alfred, the women sent a delegate to a woman-suffrage convention and petitions to their state representatives. The correspondent for the Cuba group did not mention any specific action, but described pro-suffrage—and nativist—sentiment.

> As we noted the intelligent enthusiasm with which women voiced their political preferences, we thought surely the right of electoral franchise would be as safe in the hands of these as in those of some naturalized democratic voters . . . who we are credibly informed were not aware of the existence of a public debt, and we concluded that among the few mistakes made by the republican party when in power was that of not enfranchising women.

While partisan, these women believed that their connections to the Republican Party grew out of their careful consideration of issues and the positions of the parties. The Republican women's loyalty rested on a different foundation from that of the men.[69]

Most women in upstate New York, however, apparently gave little thought to the political parties. At best the parties and electoral politics deserved minimal notice: participation in politics was a vaguely squalid undertaking of their husbands or fathers. Men habitually complained about politics and politicians, yet did little to try to change the deficient conditions. After listening to another round of objections about politicians in her Grange in 1882, one woman remarked " '[t]hat they could express themselves here as being independent but when they come to vote it would be the *same old Ticket.*' " But silence was commoner than cynical words about politicians or voters. The female professionals and wives of male professionals who formed suffrage clubs in villages advanced a civics-book understanding of government and politics; farm women expressed a weary cynicism about the topics; but unless involved in organizations other than narrowly religious ones, rural women either paid scant attention to politics or failed to record their ideas. They left politics to men, however well or poorly they believed men conducted it.[70]

In one important respect, it made no difference whether rural women adopted the rational and moral approach to politics or ignored such questions completely. Both ways of thinking about politics fostered an uneasy relationship to public power. Once outside of their own groups, rural women seemed uncertain about how to ask favors of politicians and about what kinds of requests they could legitimately make. Male traditions of friendship and reciprocity did not govern women's relationships to political figures, nor did any of the rules of discourse that men followed. This was the case if only because women had nothing to trade: they could not assert their support in the past or promise future votes and those of their friends. At best, women could offer prayers in return for a favor done, or claim, as one woman did, that if she could vote she would support the politician's career. But along with indicating the limits of women's political influence, women's letters to politicians illustrate the ways they attempted to gain public favors before they were granted the ballot. These letters provide insights into what some rural women believed politics was for, the kinds of favors one could expect from those who held political power, and how some women understood public power before enfranchisement.

It is easy to find women's letters among those collected in the papers of late nineteenth-century politicians. Theirs were invariably the longest, composed on plain stationery. That few women, aside from officers of women's clubs, would have cause to use official stationery accounts for the latter fact. The amount of space rural women needed to apologize for making a request explains the length. Before asking S. Fred Nixon's help in finding a job, one woman wrote:

> You will doubtless be surprised at the receipt of this letter but I know of no one else to whom I would rather relate the contents of this epistle. At the same time I suppose I ought to feel like a trespasser to ask a favor of one so busy as I know you always are; but I must come to the point or you will not be at liberty long enough to read what I am about to write.

Such apologies for taking the time of the reader, for imposing, for possibly inappropriate behavior—virtually absent in men's letters—were extended by nearly all women writers, from the politically sophisticated to the most desperate job-seeker. With nothing to promise in return, women tried to make amends by asking for sympathy.[71]

Just as women apologized for their transgressions of the boundaries of male prerogatives, they also often claimed that the favors they asked would benefit others. In the case of Mrs. L. P. Austin of Silver Creek, this was clearly true in that she wrote on behalf of her husband. "Excuse the liberty I take in writing to you," she began her letter to S. Fred Nixon, "but my husband . . . applied to you some time ago for a position there at Albany this winter . . . and I determined to write this unbeknown to him." Other Chautauqua County physicians had filled the job in the past, and she felt that her husband's turn had justly come. Moreover, "he has struggled along in this little place," but circumstances had conspired against him. Without ever mentioning herself, Austin asked for Nixon's support.[72]

When women wrote to ask for jobs or consideration of particular laws, they strove to make sure the recipient understood their unselfishness or dire need. A Mrs. Harper, who sought a job in Albany, stressed the seriousness of her economic plight: "I shall lose my old home, and find one in the Old Ladies," if Nixon failed to help her. A former New Yorker who found work as a clerk in the Treasury Department in Washington employed flattery and feminine helplessness in asking David Bennet Hill for assistance in keeping her job. "Please use your unbounded influence, dear Mr. Hill," she asked, "to keep me where I am for whom should I go if not to my own Senator for protection." Annette Rose wrote to Nixon to enlist his support for legislation to regulate the nursing profession. She justified writing to him by noting that she was from Westfield, Nixon's hometown, and that while she felt "very keenly the liberty I am taking in writing to you . . . Mr. Rose suggested that I should." When another woman requested Nixon's help in getting money from the state for the school in her district, she described the able work she, with "the intelligent portion of our people," was already doing and the good that would come to the children. Female correspondents took great pains to point out that they made their personal or legislative requests only with ample justification, in response to prodding from others, or for the benefit of their communities.[73]

New York women understood that one way to find or keep a job or to gain some influence over legislation was to write their representatives. It was the tone, not the subject matter, that distinguished men's and women's letters. This difference reflected men's and women's perceptions of their proper gender roles. Both men and women understood that their representation of the traits required of their sex would earn them consideration for public reward. Just as men assured their would-be patrons that they possessed the relevant attributes of manhood, women listed their feminine virtues. They made clear their meekness, piety, and need of masculine protection. Neither men nor women could be assured that their requests would be granted, and thus they provided justifications. They chose faithful maintenance of gender roles as the behavior that made them worthy. In so doing, rural New Yorkers followed the lead of the politicians they wrote to—men who stressed their "manliness" in their campaigns. The letters of rural men and women and the recommendations of politicians on the stump illustrate the extent to which late nineteenth-century politics drew upon—and reinforced—ideas about proper gender roles.

More than a confirmation of the writers' femininity, the apologetic tone of women's letters showed that women negotiated for politicians' favors from a position of weakness. This perception of powerlessness also gripped men caught in desperate economic positions, and when writers literally begged for gifts or loans, differences between the sexes disappeared. Men and women alike detailed their economic woes and swore that uncontrollable circumstances, not character defects, forced them to stoop to making embarrassing requests for help from strangers. Roswell P. Flower, a rich Democratic politician reputed to have a philanthropic bent, received scores of pleas, especially from his native Jefferson County. A. F. Dean of Richville assured Flower that he had never before been driven to "plead poverty" and promised that a gift would "not be squandered by us for I am a temperate man." "It is with humble submission to my coushdoisn that I write you these few lines in my behalf hopping that I could interest you in the same," began another man who wanted a loan. These men's entreaties closely resembled those of women like Kate M. Ball. She thanked Flower for fifty dollars he had sent to help her recover from her "long and painful Sickness from *overwork*" and hoped "it may never be necessary for any one to beg for me again." Despite the indignity felt by these petitioners, those less fortunate than Ball nonetheless persisted after being turned down. Adda E. Boole asked Flower for $250 to save her family's farm. "When I received your letter my heart bounded with joy I almost shouted We are saved but a las when I opened it I had to shed tears," she wrote. She urged him to rethink the matter and pledged, "if I had it I could work with all the light heartedness in the world." Men dropped claims of partisan friendship and reciprocity when faced with trying circumstances and, along with women, stressed traits like hard work and unselfishness, admired in both sexes.[74]

If bleak prospects forced men to abandon the usual form of request, not all mail that women sent to politicians exaggerated the writers' femininity. Form letters and petitions regarding specific issues departed from this pattern, as did the letters from leaders of the state woman suffrage movement. While polite, such letters stuck to the business at hand. Expressions of anger at new legislation—in New York, usually temperance, but also turn-of-the-century laws that regulated the medical profession— contained religious overtones, but otherwise few appeals to femininity. Finally, other letters kept the form of feminine appeals, but departed from the normal subject matter of political correspondence. One twenty-seven-year-old woman, for example, wrote to David Bennett Hill to ask whether or not she should become a nun. While she would "rather be a nun than Queen Victoria," her parents objected. She called on his "unerring judgment" to settle the matter, promised to abide by his decision, and sent him ten dollars for his trouble. While unusual, her letter stands as an illustration of rural women's uneasy relationship to electoral politics, in which both culture and law left them ill-suited to operate and dependent on the kind assistance of men.[75]

Despite their exclusion from electoral politics, activist women in rural New York carved a place for themselves in the public life of their communities. Working through their organizations, they contributed some limited social services and kept the temperance issue in public debate. Turning away from their own communities, rural women learned to consider state-level projects outlets for their energies and to look to state government for assistance. At a time when urban women engaged in community projects, rural women in New York directed most of their attention to needs outside of their villages, and would avoid local involvement until the twentieth century. While the structure of rural communities strengthened the style of electoral politics practiced by men, it hindered women's activities.

The forms of women's political participation—petitioning, letter-writing, and membership in organizations—excluded many rural women from public life. Only the reasonably well-off who lived in villages and had the time to attend meetings could consider joining in. Women who participated articulated views of government and politics different from those of rural men. As matters stood, politics was a somewhat shady endeavor that men enjoyed, but "true" politics would engage rational and moral men and women who studied issues and the structure of government and acted in ways that would benefit all citizens. The personal motives of friendship and loyalty had no proper place in politics. The state government, providing resources and expertise, could be a valuable ally; the tendency of local government to search for the cheapest solutions needed to be curbed. Ultimately, neither rural men nor women had much control over what was happening to their communities. But women's approaches to politics—both the rational and moral and the alienated—became the dominant ones in the twentieth century, although women would fail to profit from that change.

Modifications in rural men's and women's political ideas and behavior would come when the importance of gender roles in public life abated. At the very least, the twentieth-century system less strictly demanded that men and women display their adherence to their private roles in order to gain public approval. But in the nineteenth century, rural political traditions were based on popular understandings of the roles of men and women. This was obviously manifested in who could vote and in the distinct styles of political participation and the differing understandings of the purpose of politics that men and women held. The connections between gender and politics also appeared in the weight that ordinary men and women and politicians alike gave to the fulfillment of their gender roles as reasons to merit election to office or appointment to government jobs. By the turn of the century, changes in local and state government, and in rural life in general, encouraged New Yorkers to rethink the symmetry between private values and public life.

CHAPTER 4

Economy and Harmony: The Goals of Local Government in the Late Nineteenth Century

The male vision of government that valued the lowest expenditures and slightest presence possible attained clear expression in the operation of township and county governments. Local lawmakers argued about whether they should pay for the coal county clerks burned in their offices and how counties could pay less for poorhouses and prisons. Any expansion in the ways towns and counties defined and delivered public services—providing water, caring for the poor and insane, installing sidewalks and streetlamps—encountered steady and often successful resistance in many communities. Local governments, meanwhile, sought to make decisions about expenditures and services in ways that suggested there was a cheerful unanimity among all citizens. Agreement on the goal of economy hardly brought consensus on how it was to be effected. Office-holders in rural New York set themselves difficult tasks in the late nineteenth century: maintaining minimal spending with the appearance both of local prosperity and of the assent of nearly all citizens with the lawmakers' decisions.[1]

In many rural townships, the result of these often-conflicting goals was immobility, an unusual object of scholarly scrutiny.[2] Some towns and counties took on new projects only when forced to do so and otherwise carried out the minimal tasks set decades earlier in the most frugal manner possible. That local governments moved so slowly was due in part to deep disagreements over the details of tax schedules and funds for roads, poorhouses and county buildings. Changes came hard. However assiduously local officials courted satisfying compromises, they could nonetheless look forward to legal challenges from irate citizens when they called for new spending. Fights erupted in meetings called to determine whether new schools should be built. Local officials grew frustrated as they were pulled by calls for low taxes and pushed both by state rules that expanded throughout the end of the century and by demands for better services.

By the end of the century, the men who ran local governments began to waver in their commitment to inexpensive government run at the local level. The producers of partisan rhetoric for state and national elections—the newspapermen, lawyers, and local elected officials—found that economy and harmony were in fact incompatible goals. As they searched for procedures or compromises, the state government claimed greater responsibility for how taxes were levied, schools were run, roads were built, and liquor was regulated. Local lawmakers increasingly looked to the formerly suspect state government for solutions to both traditional and newly created difficulties. By their willingness to invite state support, local party spokesmen began to lead rural men away from the party loyalty that had defined male politics.

Proponents of new projects in rural towns learned the virtue of patience. Convincing skeptical townsmen required time and an extensive fund of arguments and invective. But victory brought lasting rewards, since, if an initiative won, it quickly became the new orthodoxy, budged only with great effort. The circumstances that surrounded the decision to build waterworks—gravity-driven pipelines—in Cuba, a western–New York village, were typical of the difficulties that champions of "progress" faced in rural towns and villages. This particular issue divided many communities in the state in the late nineteenth century. Villages needed stable sources of water to grow and attract industries. Even in stable or prosperous towns, departures from established practices raised suspicions and generally required time and negotiation.

In January and February of 1888, the debate over whether or not the village of Cuba should bond itself to pay for a waterworks project began in anticipation of the spring elections. A proposal to hold a referendum on the subject had slowly gained the approval of the village trustees. For the boosters of the project, the choice was one of progress or admission of Cuba's fate as a declining village. Men skeptical of the plan, however, voiced their concerns about putting the village into debt for a dubious cause. Not only would Cuba be faced with paying off the bonds, according to one opponent, but the village would be doing it for "the very few who have neglected to provide themselves with water by the usual methods, or who wish to indulge in the luxury of sprinkling their lawns or flower beds with a hose . . . at the expense of the taxpayers." Both fear of debt and contempt for the idle rich and lazy argued against the water works bond.[3]

As the election neared, the proposal's boosters marshaled their arguments. The editor of the Cuba newspaper saw the waterworks as crucial to the village's future, and he published the opinions of engineers on the quality of the project's design and the testimonies of presidents of villages that already had water systems in place. He claimed that in fact the

waterworks would cost the village no money at all, and referred to those
who opposed the plan as "chronic kickers," and "salt box orators." He
described a meeting held in the village at which townspeople discussed
the measure and took special notice of the attendance of "[m]any ladies,"
which he considered a good omen. When the election came in March,
villagers voted down the bonding proposal by 94 to 70. "Thus ends for
the time the grandest effort ever made by our village in its own behalf,"
he concluded. But he promised that the effort would go on, and blamed
the defeat on certain men's personal greed.[4]

During the following weeks, the editor kept the waterworks plan in the
news. He noted installations in other villages and lamented that Cuba
was needlessly lagging behind. On December 22, 1888, the village held
another election, and this time voters approved the bond proposal by
109 to 79. The editor celebrated. "The Sun Is Shining on Cuba. Another
Campaign of Intellect," his headline ran, surrounded by woodcuts of
crowing roosters. Those who believed that "Cuba had lived and grown
for a half century without water works" and could therefore do without
them now—the "stage coach obstructionists"—had been defeated after
more than one year's work. The editor's efforts in keeping the issue
before the villagers, and before that, in getting the proposal before the
voters, had finally paid off. After but one failed attempt, the bonding
proposal passed, leaving the long task of completing the project to be
carried out with barely an additional word in the local newspaper.[5]

In rural towns and villages, numerous issues engendered the same sort
of opposition and support as the Cuba water project. Efforts to institute
graded schools typically unleashed boosterism and homilies on progress.
The editor of the *Ballston Journal* portrayed the debate there as involving
"the forces of evil and good," and urged voters to "testify to the world
that Ballston Spa has a public spirit commensurate with the demands of
the age in which we live." A reader, meanwhile, suggested that graded
schools were necessary if the village meant to remain stable. "Something
must be done to keep even those who are here," the more restrained
reader claimed. In Westfield, a newspaper editor blamed the loss of a
woolen mill on voters' obdurate refusal to approve money for a new
bridge. A more farsighted neighboring town got the mill, and Westfield,
according to the editor, could slip further behind if the villagers refused
to take action.[6]

In each of these cases, similar patterns held. Newspapermen, as self-
conscious agents of progress and representatives of local merchants,
took the lead in arguing for new projects. Although they usually stressed
that economy should be heeded at all times, they minimized financial
risks. Editors painted the debates as quarrels between proponents of
progress and those of economy—or foolish spenders against myopic
"kickers," as they otherwise described the sides. The supporters of progress and of economy accused each other of endangering the towns' futures, either through saddling an impossible burden of debt on genera-

tions to come, or through failing to provide amenities necessary to modern life. These debates were divisive, and close votes on questions that required voters' approval were common. Putting plans before the voters took time, since that step required the assent of the town or county legislature, and sometimes both. Few projects that demanded public spending sailed past any town's trustees and voters.

Getting beneath the name-calling to gauge whether certain groups consistently opposed new spending is complicated. Numerous resolutions of local Granges suggest that farmers usually took up the cause of economy. The voices of laborers were less regularly heard (or at least recorded), although workers, together with businessmen, supported additional spending for a school in one village while farmers balked at new taxes. But many rural New Yorkers had good reasons to approach new plans with caution. The chastening experience with railroads that many towns had endured reminded men of how "progress" could backfire. During the 1860s and 1870s, some rural towns collected private contributions from local businessmen and issued bonds to induce railroads to connect them to a branch line. Some of these railroads were never built; few ever turned profits. Towns found themselves forced to sue railroads, some of which declared bankruptcy. Anxious to secure growth and prosperity during the economically good years, some towns instead faced paying off bonds, long after the boom times had passed, for nonexistent or marginal services.[7]

Farmers had additional cause to appraise new programs with skepticism. For farmers in most parts of the state, times were lean during the late nineteenth century. Any amount of taxation above current levels seemed to many of them the final step to the poorhouse. The financial demands of the state and of the counties were indeed high in the 1870s and 1880s, and real property bore the brunt of those taxes. Projects that could be put forward as beneficial to farmers—better roads, for example—met with farmers' opposition; projects that less clearly addressed their needs, such as improved schools, seemed like especially useless luxuries. Farmers who might have abstractly appreciated the good of such proposals put pocketbook considerations first.[8]

The task of persuading rural men to pay for new projects became even more difficult when additional issues complicated the picture. Rivalries among towns or villages, for example, frequently confused local spending questions. Proposals to refurbish county buildings—jails, clerks' offices, courts, and poorhouses—invariably raised the questions of whether counties should build new structures and if the offices should be placed in another village. Because county seats were sources of local pride and, more important, of income that could mean the difference between stability and decline, attempts to move these buildings were always contentious. And because counties needed to rebuild the standard structures of county government periodically, most of them experienced at least one of these battles in the late nineteenth century.

Country editors saved their finest invective for attempts to move county seats and change boundaries. In 1888, some residents of Steuben County advanced a plan to take parts of that county and Allegany to form a new one. An Allegany editor howled his indignation at the "swinish ambition" involved in this "plunder." He offered his hope that Allegany County, "with its history of patriotism, of legality, and Republicanism, pure and undefiled, in the shape it was, and is, and ever shall be," would stand. Both the supporters and the opponents of county-seat changes accused each other of putting personal greed above the greater good of economy. Even without a compelling issue, battles between towns went on. Newspapermen typically chose a nearby town of roughly the same size as their towns' chief rival, and carried on long-running quarrels in print with the rival villages' editors. In the twentieth century, such rivalries also found expression in contests between baseball and basketball teams. Whether these disputes reflected abiding bitterness connected with an otherwise forgotten slight, or a bid to maintain readers' interest through sham battles, they graced the pages of most rural weeklies.[9]

Editors' denunciations of other towns and depictions of their citizens' failings contrasted sharply with how newspapermen portrayed their own villages. There, people visited neighbors, had children, fell ill, and died. Church groups held socials, farmers repaired their buildings and harvested crops, and merchants expanded their lines of merchandise. Occasionally families moved away. Men waged partisan campaigns from year to year, which occasioned extensive criticism of the opposition party but rarely of fellow townsmen. Editors made no space for the numerous conflicts that occupied justices of the peace—for the men who sued each other for borrowing harrows, who got into fistfights, and who spread tales about other men's drinking habits. In other villages, meanwhile, greedy men schemed, people disagreed, and strikes broke out in small factories. In all but the largest and most prosperous villages, news of conflicts among townspeople failed to make the weekly paper. Newspaper editors sought to leave their readers with the impression of their towns as places of quiet and steady prosperity.[10]

Rivalries between towns, the conservative tendencies of local governments, and the values of economy and fairness were important themes in discussions of two issues that unfailingly commanded the attention of rural men: taxes and roads. Both questions involved the state as well as local governments in determining and administering policies. State regulations drew the boundaries within which local officials made decisions, and state agencies acted as the final court of appeal for rural citizens dissatisfied with local rulings. The decisions that had the most immediate impact on rural New Yorkers—how much tax they would have to pay in a given year—were in the hands of local officials. These men gradually turned to the state government for relief from the frustrations of local politics.

A combination of state guidelines and local decisions determined the amount of taxes that rural New Yorkers paid in the late nineteenth century. Before 1880, the state collected virtually all of its revenues through property taxes. The state legislature decreed the amount of money each county raised, and local assessors, with some guidelines, arrived at the values of real and personal property in their towns and counties. The county boards of equalization, made up of county supervisors, wrote tables that laid out what they considered the fairest distribution among the townships of the taxes required by the state and county. Assessors determined the value of personal property largely on the basis of their impressions. Citizens brought their complaints about their assessments to their board of supervisors through petitions. If residents believed their entire town's equalization was too high, they had their supervisor bring their grievances to the board; if that appeal failed, they could take their disagreements to the State Board of Assessors.[11]

This system satisfied few rural New Yorkers. As long as taxes remained low, few men grumbled. But when the state's demand for revenue grew during and after the Civil War (reaching a new high in 1872), accompanied by similar increases at the town and county levels, defects in this system seemed apparent. Farmers rightfully complained of the injustice of relying on property taxes alone for revenue, especially when New York's industrial and commercial concerns grew and the amount of acreage under cultivation declined. Other groups joined them in citing the unfairness of the state's lack of a corporate tax and haphazard assessments of personal property. Even the state assessors denounced the tax system in 1879: if "the Legislature gives no heed to injustice so flagrant, then indeed our labors are in vain; and the people must continue to put up with wrongs sufficient, in some countries, where obedience to law is not a virtue, to provoke rebellion from such an established order of things."[12]

A state commission appointed in 1871 had recommended a series of changes in New York's tax laws, but the legislature's only response was to increase assessments on real property. A fuller revision of the codes waited until 1880. Then New York began to collect some of its funds through taxes on corporations and inheritances. The new laws also required localities to keep separate records of the portions of property taxes that went to the state and those that remained for local purposes. Local assessors retained their authority to set property values until 1896, when a new State Board of Tax Commissioners formulated firmer guidelines for how counties determined assessments and equalization. That same year a liquor tax added to New York's revenues. The revisions of the 1880s and 1890s hardly remedied all of the problems that rural (and other) New Yorkers had with local and state tax codes. Farmers still protested the proportion of the tax burden that remained on real property. The amount of taxes that corporations had to pay seemed unfairly meager. But the diversity of revenue sources in the new tax codes paved the way for a short period in the early twentieth century when the legislature eliminated all property taxes for state purposes.[13]

Before the more explicit assessment rules of 1896, the tax laws left abundant room for disputes between towns over equalization. The county boards of equalization thought themselves overburdened, and not without cause. Equalization occupied the greatest portion by far of the yearly meetings of county boards of supervisors. The assessors' power also encouraged local grievances. State officials, for reasons of their own, sought greater centralization in tax policy by the 1890s. Local officials encouraged this trend, which would work changes in rural men's political ideas.

The usual quarrels dominated the meetings of the Otsego county supervisors in 1880. The representatives of the twenty-four townships debated special resolutions, such as one declaring that the city of Oneonta had illegally charged the county $500 for the care of victims of a smallpox epidemic. Above all, the board discussed tax assessments. With the tax law of 1880, the supervisors' tasks grew more complicated and the assessors' work more demanding. Most of the Otsego supervisors were dissatisfied with the report the equalization committee turned in. The representative of the rural township of Pittsfield felt its landowners would be grossly overtaxed, and, along with the supervisors of five other towns, believed the assessors' reports contained so many errors that the equalization tables based on those findings were useless. The committee produced a second, equally unpopular, draft. Retaining local authority in taxation while rates rose added protests to the standard disagreements about how best to cut costs and how some townships received favors denied others.[14]

Recognizing the problems with the assessments and equalization tables, the supervisors chose to change the structure of the equalization committee. Democrats accused Republicans of partisanship in determining property values, and the supervisors of rural townships suspected that the villages got off too lightly. Changing the structure of the board proved no easier than approving an assessment schedule. One member of the board proposed to increase the number of supervisors on the committee to ten: five Democrats and five Republicans who represented different sections of the county. Another supervisor moved to table this proposal, which lost by one vote. A third supervisor suggested that three men who were not members of the board be placed on the committee. Unable to settle this question, the supervisors continued to discuss the tax burdens of the various townships. Pittsfield residents presented a petition signed by 112 taxpayers protesting their assessments; the assessor claimed the petition was a fraud. By the end of their meetings, the supervisors simply gave up: acknowledging imperfections in their rewritten equalization table, they let it stand with the hope that the next board would make suitable corrections. Sympathetic to the board's plight, a newspaper editor proposed to lengthen their annual session, rather than shorten it as some of his unhappy townsmen had asked. In Otsego County, the new tax laws had exacerbated disagreements about assessments. These were quarrels that county governments could not easily settle.[15]

Interest in economy, contests between towns, and the resulting protracted debates engaged county and township governments throughout rural New York. In the 1880s and early 1890s, boards of equalization sometimes presented majority and minority reports, and left it to the supervisors to make adjustments. At the meeting of the supervisors of St. Lawrence County in 1885, the two tables, minority and majority, differed in their equalized value of property in every township. In cases like that, the supervisors sought to adopt the report that showed the lowest value for their townships. Meanwhile, as a matter of ordinary practice, supervisors found reasons for lowering the assessed valuations in their townships. In Otsego County, the supervisor of the agricultural township of Decatur acquired some local fame for his "battles for the lowest taxes for his constituents," which involved "showing the committee on equalization how poor and unproductive the land in general in his town is." The supervisors of three townships in Lewis County believed their townships unfairly equalized in 1885, and voted against adopting the table prepared by the equalization committee. When the board accepted the committee's report, the supervisors of those townships promptly appealed their case to Albany. These attempts to gain advantages for particular townships and to find settlements on equalization compounded the usual disputes regarding errors in assessments presented by individual residents.[16]

One way to curb conflicts over taxes was to seek ways to lower the rates for all of the townships in a county. Thus, while engaging in their yearly struggle to calculate the tax property owners would pay, county supervisors sought ways to reduce spending in general. Supervisors from rural counties voted on a petition circulated by the board in Seneca County that urged a reduction in real-estate taxes in 1880. In a measure supported by the state and local Granges, county boards sought approval in Albany for making the office of sheriff a salaried one in the 1880s. Traditionally paid on the basis of fees charged the counties for each prisoner held, rural residents suspected that sheriffs incarcerated tramps longer than necessary and needlessly ran up their fees. County supervisors aimed to replace individual decisions about some expenses with uniform regulations enforced by the state as a means of bringing down the cost of local government.[17]

In addition to waiting for state action, counties tried to minimize their own expenditures. A supervisor of Lewis County noticed in 1885 that Lewis spent an average of $1.65 per week for each person in the county poorhouse, whereas neighboring Jefferson County spent only $1.17. He presented a resolution—which passed—requiring itemized lists of all purchases made for the poorhouse, directing the superintendent of the

poor to buy wholesale whenever possible, and instructing the superintendent to bring down the weekly cost per person to $1.25. Other boards
sought to make certain that county office-holders restrained spending:
Otsego County, like others, set limits on how much the sheriff could
spend on housing prisoners and left him to hire any necessary help out
of his own pocket. County governments attempted to minimize the
amount of money they spent by reducing the costs of administration and
of the care of those in no position to protest—inmates of the county
prisons and poorhouses.[18]

Counties achieved some success in these tasks, depending on how one
chooses to measure taxes and expenditures. The amount of money the
state asked of the counties peaked in 1872, and aside from a few exceptional years, slowly declined thereafter, even disappearing from 1906 to
1910. County spending rose slightly overall through the late nineteenth
century, although thanks to the state's diminished demands, tax rates
and expenditures remained fairly stable. Modifications made by the state
assessors sometimes created pronounced variations in the equalized valuations of a county, which changed the share of the state tax that county
owed. And sharp variations existed both between townships and within
the same townships over time. Township officials could predict most
year-to-year expenses—renting buildings for elections, contributing to
the costs of housing the local poor or infirm at the county home or a state
facility, and hiring constables. Outlays for roads, bridges, and, in better-
off places, town buildings, however, entailed large expenditures. Thus
town meetings carefully considered such spending before making a decision. No matter how necessary an undertaking might seem—grading a
road, installing village sidewalks, or building a water system—critics of
increased taxes and spending stood ready to block such proposals, or to
find ways to make individual citizens responsible for the costs.[19]

Such attitudes were understandable. Although the revised tax codes
had reduced New York's reliance on real estate taxes, counties, townships, and school districts still counted on property taxes alone. Some
relief came in 1896, when local governments began to share with the
state the money raised with the liquor tax. New York expanded such
divisions of revenue in the early twentieth century to include funds from
the mortgage tax and automobile registrations. Nonetheless, local governments expected property taxes to provide the largest part of their
budgets, and as late as 1930, ninety percent of property taxes fell on real
estate. Thus, especially in the late nineteenth century, when prices for
the state's staple crops—dairy products and hay—remained flat, farmers
in poorer towns saw any increase in taxes as a serious threat to their
standard of living. Their situation worsened as population declined,
since fewer people increasingly bore a larger share of a township's tax
load. The predicament of marginal farmers brightened somewhat in the
early twentieth century as prices improved. But unproductive lands endured, and farmers continued to abandon the poorest parts of the state,

leaving those who stayed in declining townships even worse off when prices collapsed again after World War I.[20]

The preferred solution of rural men in New York to the problem of taxes and their related economic woes was to move important public decisions to the local level. They believed with justification that towns and counties would administer services more cheaply and in a less partisan fashion than the state would. County supervisors ran with party labels at town meetings. But an examination of county supervisors' reports indicates that sectional disagreements within counties were far more common than partisan ones. County supervisors' meetings brought out differences between towns—some sought lower assessments, which meant increasing those of others; or county funding for special projects. The supervisors tended to be arrayed against each other in geographical patterns. Certain issues, including taxation, produced economically based alignments—agricultural townships against villages. Indeed, farmers and leaders of agricultural townships suggested at a number of points that propertyless men—primarily village and small city laborers—should be denied the right to vote on bond issues. Economizing thus involved some class and ethnic tensions, but not often partisan ones.[21]

Party affiliation, however, was not entirely absent. It entered into decisions about which newspapers would receive the county printing, the appointments of board clerks, and on occasions when a board had to fill a vacancy in one of the elected county offices. These debates could be spirited: the St. Lawrence County Board of Supervisors took two days and seventeen formal ballots to fill the position of Superintendent of the Poor. Another board spent a morning settling on a clerk. More often, however, county supervisors settled on arrangements, such as rotating patronage, that muted partisanship in making appointments. Otherwise, both citizens and supervisors carefully watched for signs that assessors were making decisions in a partisan fashion, which both Republicans and Democrats agreed was wrong. Thus, in those areas that occupied most of the supervisors' time—taxes and favors granted to particular townships—disagreements were largely based on section, not party.[22]

Partisanship had even less of a place in town meetings. Town officers (except supervisors) often ran with special designations—on a "Citizens" ticket, for example, indicating the candidates who supported enforcement of liquor regulations. "Union" tickets were composed of candidates with various political views arranged before town meetings both obviated the need for an election and discouraged any potential contests. But town elections were normally sleepy affairs, even without the precautionary effort of constructing a "Union" slate. The usually small number of men who attended these meetings elected the same village and town trustees year after year. In some cases, officials claimed they wanted to leave office, but could not because no one else wanted the position. Described as "thankless" jobs, town offices offered none of the partisan romance that newspapermen extended even to county coroners. These officials settled boundary disputes, kept the local peace, and determined property values—none of which rural men saw as partisan tasks. Temperance and new bond issues ignited rarely seen interest and participation in town politics.[23]

While retaining decision-making at the local level might have encouraged economy and nonpartisanship, it also ignited discord. When town meetings did not enjoy early compromises, feelings at these elections ran higher than at partisan contests, which were bathed in friendship and loyalty. "Very hard going. Hardly ever saw it worse," reported Edward Filkins in 1872. At the Berne town meeting, "[a]s high as $36 has been paid" for votes, he lamented. "I regret that we cannot have a quiet, peaceful Election and are allowed to conduct ourselves like men." The meetings of county boards of supervisors grew longer and more contentious in the 1880s. Before 1896, rural towns and counties largely footed their own bills for roads, schools, and public improvements, in addition to providing their portion of the state tax. In places where population declined, shrinking tax bases encouraged local officials to redouble their efforts to reduce expenses. The combined forces of the need or desire for new services, lower taxes, and fewer taxpayers compelled county office-holders to search for compromises—and state support.[24]

Determining how county governments settled their differences is an elusive task. Despite the friction, leaders of rural townships wanted to maintain the appearance of harmony. Local disputes rarely found their way into village newspapers. The published reports of county supervisors' meetings failed to record debates. Adding to the quiet, supervisors struck formal or informal agreements on how to deal with certain questions that minimized public bickering. To forestall one conflict, for example, county boards carefully rotated their printing contracts through as many newspapers as they could. Sharing this important source of local patronage meant maintaining a partisan balance and recognizing newspapers from different parts of the county. On occasions when county boards departed from their usual procedure, newspapermen complained bitterly about losing their "turn." In a similar attempt to lessen (or transfer) conflict, some county boards put as many as half of their members on equalization committees. Formal and informal arrangements saved time and eliminated public quarrels, but they make tracking the process of local decision-making difficult.[25]

Some county boards realized greater success than others at quietly settling conflicts: some boards spent full days debating issues like taxes and local patronage, which supervisors elsewhere dispatched with unanimous voice votes. A good number of the compromises that county governments built were procedural. In some counties, county boards passed all projects that town supervisors wanted; in poorer counties, few or none passed. In rapidly declining Schoharie County, for example, new projects had little hope of success. The virtual absence of industry, combined with some of the poorest farming conditions in the state, meant that few innovations would be heard out, or ever introduced. By approving all requests or none of them, governments in different kinds of rural places determined how to spend their money.[26]

Township and school district boards confronted divisive issues in much the same way that counties did. These office-holders carried out routine tasks—ones probably also governed by informal rules—with a minimum of fuss. Township highway supervisors assigned taxpayers the work they would perform or money they would pay for road maintenance; health officers recorded births and deaths, occasionally cited citizens for public health violations, and collected fees for each service performed; school trustees made their yearly purchase of wood. Voters determined how townships would respond to more difficult issues, such as whether to undertake expensive projects like water systems. Townships required the approval of the county supervisors to float bonds for road and bridge improvements. Trustees also called meetings so voters could settle whether they should continue to pay off debts contracted for railroads that were never built.[27]

Some of these decisions could be made with speed, but others took years to resolve. Trustees searched for agreement before taking action, at least in small villages and towns; and finding it took time. Newspapermen, usually the noisiest village boosters, labored for months in advance of town meetings to persuade men to accept new projects. Meanwhile, township office-holders constructed compromises that put off choices. The Board of Health of Truxton posted notices of violations, but never forced compliance or provided money to relieve the problems. Another compromise involved changing decisions from year to year. The Cortland village trustees forbade their fire company to attend a competition in neighboring Marathon on July 4, 1870, because they believed fires were likely to occur on that day. But faced with angry firemen, they reversed their decision the following year, and thereafter tried to have the competition held in Cortland. In a similar way, townships established and then rescinded fishing restrictions on lakes, and finally threw the decision to counties, the state legislature, or to the courts if the issue remained controversial.[28]

School districts showed the same tendency to forestall or duck difficult choices. Each school district held a yearly meeting at which the officers mandated the length of the school year (until state regulations decided that for them), elected officers, and hired teachers. Trustees generally moved forward on these matters without discussion. Few men or women attended these meetings; those who did, rotated the available offices among themselves, usually without need for a formal vote. But again, less-routine issues could not be resolved in the normal fashion. Plans for new buildings aroused community concern. To arrange for a new school building typically required two years: during the first, those who attended the meeting voted to appropriate the money; and those at the

next meeting, one year later, voted to reconsider the initial decision. If
the mandate still stood, the trustees made arrangements with contrac-
tors. Even at that point problems remained. Those who attended a
school meeting in Hartwick in 1872 directed the trustee to meet with a
builder. "[I]f they don't agree shall choose two disinterested men out of
the District if they cant agree choose the third man." Planning and
building new schools demanded substantial agreement and assurances of
economy before the trustees would act.[29]

Indeed, because of their small numbers, participants in district meetings needed a majority just short of full agreement for a decision to stick.
Large, though not absolute, majorities were enough to take no action,
such as deciding not to hire a certain teacher in one district. Bare majorities, however, apparently suggested to school officers that the time to
push an issue had not yet arrived. A tie vote in one district on whether to
expand their building suggested to the participants that they should
drop the matter; a 10 to 11 vote on whether to cut the weeds around one
school in 1887 brought an early end to the meeting in another district.
Patiently waiting for consensus was one way that school districts medi-
ated between those who wanted improvements and those who sought
economy.[30]

Discord was the price of impatience. "Riotous conduct" marred an 1888
meeting in Scott, in Cortland County, called to determine whether to
merge two small districts. After rumors spread that the floor was about to
collapse, constables arrived and arrested two men. An 1896 contest between two factions in Saratoga County broke down in "confusion and
disorder . . . increasing in volume and virulence; vile epithets were applied to some of the persons and the chairman; several persons rushed
upon the platform . . . shaking their fists in the face of the chairman, and
threatening two members of the board of education with personal violence." In countless other instances, belligerent groups stopped short of
disrupting meetings. When rival factions vied for power or citizens objected to decisions about new buildings or spending, appeals to the State
Superintendent of Public Instruction followed angry meetings.[31]

Fiscal questions—those of taxes and expenditures—generally demanded a search for compromises in meetings of county, township and
school district leaders. Office-holders at all three levels of local government tried to meet their constituents' demands by holding expenditures
to the lowest possible levels, while also slowly introducing new public
projects. And they went about this work in a nonpartisan way, with few
exceptions. Local government in the late nineteenth century, then, fulfilled rural men's wishes: it was cheap and largely oblivious to party
ties. In taking this cautious direction, however, local governments created new conflicts while failing to face older ones. Township residents
still wanted special projects; county buildings decayed and needed replacement; the number of county poor increased, while the tax base
eroded in rural towns, suggesting the need for further cuts in taxes and

spending. Farmers and businessmen who furnished supplies to poor-houses and prisons would also have second thoughts about cutting costs or making such institutions self-supporting. As a result, harmony was endangered. Local governments sought ways to square new demands with an insistence on economy: they passed laws that went unenforced, cut back on services to those least able to protest, waited for agreement to form, or depended on procedures. Local officials worked out compromises as best they could, but as rural New York slid further into economic decline, fiscal problems worsened.

One way out of the contest between economy and harmony was to ask the state's help in paying for local services. This solution had its advocates, both male and female, in rural communities. Convinced that excessive partisanship and expense characterized state government, however, most rural men remained suspicious of this solution. Rural officials did gradually resign themselves to dependence on the state as community conflicts and expenses swelled. In the meantime, rural men fought possible encroachments of state power upon local decisions. The issue of rural roads illustrates initial rural resistance to state support—and their later welcoming acceptance of it. Temperance legislation, which combined moral, economic, and gender-related concerns, illuminates both community conflicts and the changing relationship between the state and local governments. Made to choose between inexpensive government and peaceful communities, rural leaders increasingly opted for the latter, but hoped that they could control the state's actions and ultimately get both.

If diarists' descriptions were true, roads in rural New York in the late nineteenth century had improved little since the arrival of white settlers. For those who lived in the open country, winter brought the best conditions for travel. After the ground froze, rural roads supplied uncomfortable but certain passage; winter snows allowed rural people to pull out their sleighs, prized for speed and its attendant pleasures. Road conditions were mixed in autumn. Spring meant mud, and summer both dust and mud. Farm families carefully planned their trips to town for good reasons.[32]

All rural men who lived outside of the villages—and some women—had a more direct relationship with their local roads than that of cursing at the mud. Until the 1890s—and in some places later than that—townships required all men over the age of twenty-one to work on the roads. In addition, everyone else who paid taxes on real or personal property had to help maintain the roads as well. Unless property owners paid a specified amount of money to their district's overseer of highways, they reported to work at a specified time with a team or whatever other equipment was needed. This system made elected highway supervisors responsible for all of their townships' roads. They in turn divided their townships into districts and appointed a man in each one to assign work and collect fees. Building new roads and bridges required county approval as well as additional help in design and construction. But rural people performed the routine maintenance on the roads they normally traveled.[33]

The township road system—including local responsibility and the option of "working off" one's obligations—had its detractors as well as supporters. For "progressive" farmers, it meant that untrained local men maintained the roads and rounded up equally unsuitable help. Members of county agricultural societies, for example, declared the often abysmal conditions of the roads—the mud, ruts, steep ungraded ascents, and weeds—made marketing crops far more expensive and time-consuming than it ought to be. If farmers were to sell a perishable product, such as fluid milk, they would need more reliable transportation. These critics thus suggested that townships follow the same rules as villages did. There, property owners paid a specified amount of money each year, and while the overseer was not likely to be any better trained than his country counterpart, the work was at least completed in a more regular fashion. The "money tax" would not provide the unified highway system that agricultural spokesmen wanted, but it would be a good first step.[34]

Other farmers remained unconvinced that a new system's benefits would outweigh the costs. Diaries of country people treated bad roads the same way they did the weather—as a notable but inevitable fact of daily life. Providing labor seemed less of a tax than paying cash, and for many New York farmers in the 1870s and 1880s, money was in short supply. Dissatisfied with the condition of rural roads, one local Grange believed that more money would not provide a solution. Instead, present taxes, "if judiciously expended," could provide adequate roads, if "practiced road builders" were put in charge and townships allowed citizens to work off their taxes. Given the chance to vote on the measure at their town meetings, agricultural townships registered mixed returns. Some quickly adopted the money system; others declined; and still others vacillated. Increasingly important to profitable farming but requiring substantial outlays of scarce township money, "good roads" remained an idea touted by proponents of scientific agriculture and members of bicycle clubs.[35]

But pressure from those groups, along with the state Grange, brought some changes in the state road regulations in the 1890s. In 1893, Governor Roswell P. Flower signed a bill that offered townships the opportunity to adopt a "county road system." This legislation, which the Governor heralded as the "golden mean" between the "extravagance in State expenditures and stinginess in local expenditures for local improvements," allowed counties to designate certain rural highways as county roads. Townships, in turn, had to abandon the labor system of taxation before their supervisors could go before their boards with petitions for county road status. If the board approved, the county, rather than the township, would maintain the road. Some townships found this option attractive. Township taxpayers could naturally be expected to appreciate the chance to spread the cost of their roads over a larger group of citizens. But this system introduced new problems for county supervisors, who had to find the money. Advocates of "good roads" had additional criticisms. This system was no system at all, they believed, in that it established no network of market roads. The new laws succeeded in sharing out some of the costs of rural roads but failed to institute any further changes.[36]

New state legislation later in the decade promised to address such objections. Assemblymen advanced various plans that would divide the costs of new roads and the maintenance of existing ones between the state, counties, and townships. Different proposals apportioned the shares in different ways. Along with state funding, local governments would receive guidance from Albany. Engineers would design and oversee the construction of new roads, and a state commission would make certain that rebuilt highways contributed to a system of market roads of uniform quality. Plans for state support for highways became a reality in 1898, when the legislature passed the Highbee-Armstrong bill. In the final version, it provided that the state would pay half of the costs connected with highways, while the counties would pay thirty-five percent and the townships fifteen percent. State engineers bore full responsibility for building the expensive macadam roads that Albany favored. Meanwhile, townships received direct aid if they accepted money rather than labor as payment of their taxes. This legislation was a step toward a system of state, county, and township roads. Rural townships were on their way to becoming consumers rather than producers of state tax money.[37]

Such legislation had long been the goal of organized advocates of "good roads," who lobbied for state-supported highways, published a magazine, provided copy for newspapers, and chartered clubs across New York. Enlisting chiefly urban support, the cause of good roads became something of a movement by the late 1890s. Good Roads Clubs sponsored conventions, at which speakers aimed to win the support of county and state lawmakers. Promoters of the state system cited statistics to prove that state-built quality highways would actually cost less than local roads. And farmers, they claimed, would benefit, since properly built roads would increase both the lives of their teams and the loads their horses could haul. Agricultural organizations—first, county and regional farmers' clubs, and later and more reluctantly, the state Grange—joined in the agitation. For state assemblymen and senators, it could well have appeared that the condition of roads was a central concern to rural voters.[38]

But rural men seemed less impressed with the issue than the boosters of state-supported highways allowed. I. B. Potter, secretary of the Road Improvement Association, admitted as much. Most farmers, he asserted, had "never seen a really good country road," and therefore "will not of their own motion supply themselves with better roads." Rural men voiced misgivings about a state highway system. At local Grange meetings, they argued that such a system would be far too expensive for rural taxpayers, even with state aid. Well-made dirt roads, some farmers suggested, were good enough. Gravel roads would be better still, especially if prisoners in county jails were forced to crush the stones. A newspaper editor suggested another answer: forget "impractable" solutions and prosecute highway commissioners if road work was not up to par.[39]

Not only were the methods and materials that Albany proposed for roadbuilding prohibitively expensive, but the introduction of politics that any state program entailed would drive up the cost further. Some Grangers suggested that if the state government became active in making roads, New York's highways would come to resemble the Erie Canal—a place where party hacks could find money for handsome contracts to reward campaign contributors and jobs for their cronies. Their objections to state-funded roads echoed those of Governor Flower in 1893: whatever the legislators' intentions, the system would "lead to extravagance in cost and favoritism in the location of public highways." Locally controlled roads had their drawbacks, but rural residents believed them to be inexpensive and free of politics.[40]

If local discussions of county roads escaped partisan wrangling, those roads added to the normal run of sectional quarrels. County boards of supervisors now had to determine the merit of petitions for improved roads. The relatively small number of requests supervisors heard typically produced votes split on geographic lines. Unless supervisors granted all petitions—and increased taxes—they had to make difficult choices. Rather than puzzle over the problem of merit, the supervisors of St. Lawrence County took direct action. After rejecting one township's request for a county road, they prepared a petition for their state senator that asked that the legislature amend the 1893 law to make individual townships responsible for county roads. While counties would oversee maintenance and construction, thus encouraging uniform road conditions, individual townships would still have to raise the money themselves. Such a plan, the supervisors believed, would best relieve agricultural counties of expenses they could ill afford.[41]

Rather than pursue this option, rural supervisors began to pay closer attention to legislation that shifted a larger share of road improvement to the state. Even in the late 1890s, the idea of state support was not uniformly popular among supervisors of rural towns. Macadam roads, even ones the state helped finance, still cost more than roads made of crushed stone. Some boards of supervisors were reluctant to allow their members to attend Good Roads Conventions. But confronted with the choice of either increasing county spending and taxes or judging the merits of township projects, they instead opted for state aid as a way out of their quandary. Rural roads were no longer economical and uncontested projects carried out by the townships.[42]

No county supervisor left an explicit account of how the boards came to accept passing the responsibility for rural roads to the state. But one committee from Cortland County attended a Good Roads Convention in

Albany and described their new enthusiasm for state roads and reasons they deserved support. As residents of a largely agricultural county, part of their interest in state support sprang from their conviction that farmers could finally get their share of the state's largesse.

> When we think of the miserable condition of our country roads and of the small expenditure that is being made for their improvement, and then think of the millions of dollars that has been expended . . . for the opening and enlarging a ditch across the State . . . your Committee believe that the millions that use the country roads have a right, yea, are in duty bound to clamor for State aid in road improvement, and that in such a way as not to overburden the small tax-payer in the country districts.

State aid for country roads, whatever the cost, represented justice for long-suffering rural people. Other Northeastern states, they said, had already surpassed New York in their efforts to improve rural roads. They suggested that the state float a bond for one million dollars for a fund for road impovement. Whether or not the luxury of macadam roads was necessary, rural people deserved them because of their past sacrifices.[43]

Turning to the state allowed some reduction in costs, county lawmakers came to believe, and would also contribute to better roads. Meanwhile, they avoided the hard choices inherent in passing or rejecting townships requests. Any hope that state funding would decrease the amount of money townships and counties spent on roads was soon disappointed. The 1898 road law instead increased local spending. Just as critics claimed, one-half of a macadam road cost more than an entire dirt or stone road. As late as 1906, some rural New Yorkers complained of the cost of state roads. "Few taxpayers," an editor predicted, "will favor mortgaging future generations for the sake of securing 'aid' from the state to make extravagantly constructed roads" that provided a living for "numerous engineers, inspectors and others holding political jobs." Hence, some townships continued to build and maintain dirt roads. And 283 rural townships stuck with the labor system until 1908, when the state forced all townships to collect money taxes.[44]

Rural residents who had committed themselves to state help worked to make that aid less costly. Some called for full state responsibility. Others wrote to their representatives in favor of the million-dollar road fund to be raised by all of New York's taxpayers. Unlike earlier proposals, this measure enjoyed wide support from both state and local farmers' organizations. In addition, representatives of rural areas argued for legislation (eventually passed) that gave a larger portion of the cost to the state and eliminated the townships' share. Having passed a formerly local responsibility to the state, rural representatives meant to retain control, which they achieved to a large extent in this case.[45]

Thus, by the turn of the century, both county legislators, and to a lesser degree, ordinary rural men, had chosen to give up local control of highways for state aid. While not providing the savings advocates initially envisioned, state support worked in favor of rural townships as time went on. New York picked up a larger part of the tab for rural roads in later years. That rural areas of the state remained overrepresented in Albany helped toward this end, although rural voters hardly admitted that an imbalance existed. The new road laws of the turn of the century meant that all rural townships could benefit from state aid, formerly a luxury granted only to those lucky villages that won state institutions.

State funding for roads was a curious victory for rural New Yorkers. Farmers, the presumed beneficiaries, paid relatively little attention to the issue. Good Roads organizations, not ordinary citizens, deserved and received the credit for the 1898 legislation and what followed. Only later, when automobiles came into common use, did rural voters work for improved roads. Then they badgered their assemblymen, not their town supervisors. The habit of looking to the state for assistance in solving local problems took time to develop in rural New York. During the 1890s, local governments, more than rural voters, seemed anxious to introduce state support. In the case of rural roads, the leaders of counties and townships moved ahead of their constituents to gain state aid, an act that promised escape from both high taxes and local strife.[46]

In ascertaining the best way to deal with liquor, too, rural people remained ambivalent about what role the state ought to play. And just as much as (or even more than) issues that entailed substantial spending, temperance divided rural communities. But liquor laws proved even more complicated for townships and villages to sort out than taxes or highways. Settling on a policy involved both partisan and moral considerations, engaged usually silent members of the community in the debate, and potentially provided a town with badly needed revenue. While the temperance issue waxed and waned in importance at the state level, it persisted as a source of discord in rural communities.

Ambitious attempts to prevent the sale and consumption of alcohol seemed a thing of the past in rural New York in 1870. With the failure of statewide prohibition in 1855, the temperance movement had settled back into personal resolutions to avoid drink. Ministers, temperance societies, and church groups gathered the dry together. Beginning in 1870, elected township excise commissions collected fees for liquor licenses, or in some cases, refused to grant them. But by and large, temperance failed to produce divisive, newsworthy events to trouble either local governments or their rural constituents.[47]

This quietude, of course, was not to last. In the early 1870s, groups of village women set out to persuade rum-sellers to close and their townsmen to elect excise commissioners who promised to grant no licenses. Temperance activity brought a new group into public debate—women, whom men had seen as nonpolitical—and new ways of making demands that ignored partisan politics. The Prohibition Party represented a different kind of threat to the major political parties' hold on rural men's imaginations. Prohibitionists nibbled at the normally commanding Republican majorities in rural New York, endangering the party's ability to compete for state offices in the 1880s. The temperance issue thus disrupted the normal course of partisan politics by introducing both new political actors and tactics and a political party capable of disturbing the usual partisan balance.[48]

While Republican Party leaders worried about how to defuse the appeal of the Prohibitionists, residents of rural townships faced their own immediate problems. From 1870 to 1896, every rural township elected excise commissioners at town meetings. This board collected license fees and determined which, if any, potential liquor dealers ought to be granted licenses. Filling the places on township and village excise boards introduced political conflicts in some places. After an extremely close election, two rival excise commissions in Glens Falls claimed legitimacy in the late 1880s. Their struggle left the village without any policy on licensing and was one of the more extreme examples of how hard-fought excise elections could be. Unlike in most Allegany County townships, which quickly voted "no-license," the question lingered for years in Cuba. In 1888, a record 616 voters turned out for the town meeting and voted for a pro-license commissioner by a single vote. Next year, however, the no-license supporters put one of their own on the three-man board, and at the following spring meeting, they elected another anti-liquor commissioner. This election broke the 1888 turnout record, and according to a pro-license editor, was hotly contested. "The license men fought the battle for all they were worth," he concluded, "but the opposition to them was very bitter." As was shown either by the direct harassment of women who campaigned for no-license or by extremely close elections, the temperance issue created divisions in rural townships.[49]

Whatever conflicts attended town elections, by 1895, 282 upstate townships had elected no-license excise boards. How those dry townships enforced no-license rulings remains uncertain. No fully satisfactory solution appeared, except in towns where temperance sentiment was virtually unanimous. WCTU chapters and Law and Order Leagues tried to turn their electoral victories into laws their fellow townspeople would observe, by hiring lawyers to prosecute liquor dealers. Such groups acted out of impatience with their excise boards, which struck them as laggard in enforcing the law. Meanwhile, newspapers on both sides of the license issue complained about the persistence of drunkenness. The truth of the matter is hard to determine: both sides believed they gained advantages by pointing out flaws in the operation of current liquor legislation. Drys hoped to see, ideally, statewide prohibition; or, less ambitiously, local option and sterner measures taken against illegal liquor dealers. Therefore, they depicted violations of no-license rulings and personal tragedies that liquor caused in license towns. Those who supported partial or full licensing pointed out the peacefulness of towns with licenses and the continued drunkenness in presumably dry communities. To return to the case of Cuba: the editor who lamented the no-license victory spent the next year describing drunken brawls and other infractions of the law in the village. The remaining records on local enforcement provide little help in determining how local option worked in rural townships.[50]

A few speculations, however, seem reasonable. Residents of no-license townships probably struck some set of compromises after voting against saloons. Both sides of the license question, each for its own reasons, reported that the problems of drunkenness were far from solved. Both sides may well have been correct. Men and women made and consumed their own brew; doctors distributed far more liquor than any illness warranted; and villagers frequented the saloons just over their township line. By passing over such behavior, excise boards satisfied neither the license nor the no-license forces, but they did find reasonable compromises for divided communities. Indeed, after initial close votes, "no-license" became much less of an issue in local elections: fewer voters turned out to reject halfhearted challenges. While maddening to both the true believers in the sinfulness and social costs of drink and those who resented the loss of license fees, such bending of the rules doubtless kept the local peace.[51]

Even if townships resolved the liquor question, local Republican politicians had to confront a slightly different dilemma. State party leaders attempted to avoid taking direct action on temperance while persuading their dry followers to shun the lures of the Prohibition Party. Republicans put forward statewide prohibition amendments, which they extended no real support to in the 1880s, and finally settled on high license fees as their solution to controlling saloons. This stance hardly eliminated the threat posed by the Prohibitionists to the G.O.P. and proved even less satisfactory at the local level. Partisan newspapermen felt most keenly the conflict between support for temperance in the abstract and opposition to local option. Editors of Republican newspapers denounced liquor and its effects on men and their families but argued that local or state prohibition would worsen drunkenness and the crimes it caused. When boosting their villages, they described the peaceful, sober people who lived there; when rebutting those who wanted no licenses, they noted drunks fighting in the streets of dry towns. Rural editors generally sought a middle ground. Deciding that saloons, rather than alcohol itself, produced problems, the editor of the Republican newspaper in Westfield argued for the abolition of bars while permitting sales in hotels and drugstores. Hoping strident rhetoric would mask the mildness of his position, he made this claim as if it were an extreme prohibition stance. Other editors supported higher license fees as the best way to reach what they portrayed as the common goal of curbing liquor sales. This position, they claimed, would reduce the number of saloons and also keep the peace in rural towns.[52]

The Raines Law of 1896 both furnished clearer guidance for local

Republican leaders and effectively ended the encroachment of the Prohibition Party on Republican majorities. This legislation, shepherded through the assembly and senate by the Republican leadership, abolished local excise boards and replaced them with a state board of excise. It increased license fees everywhere, but especially in New York's largest cities. The state and local governments divided the proceeds from the licenses. Despite state regulation, the law strengthened local option: now voters in townships and villages could vote directly on whether or not to allow liquor sales. In a provision that upset temperance advocates, this legislation allowed Sunday sales in hotels where voters had approved licenses.[53]

By winning moderate temperance advocates back to the Republican Party, the Raines law was a political success. And it won the support of the most consistent friends of temperance in rural townships. Despite their objections to Sunday sales, WCTU chapters gathered petitions in favor of the law. In time, they mobilized as well for revisions that would force Sunday closings. Grangers also studied the Raines law, and the subordinate Granges that still took an active interest in politics responded favorably. Democratic newspapers decried the end of home rule and the encroachment of state power; Republican editors hailed the law's wisdom. The New York Republican Party had found legislation that took a tough enough stand on liquor to satisfy all but the most extreme temperance advocates, made concessions to urban voters, and, as a bonus, raised new income for the state.[54]

In practice, however, the Raines law proved as difficult to enforce as the earlier regulations. For the townships that voted dry—262 townships forbade all sales, while 321 allowed licenses for hotels and drugstores during the first year of the Raines law—the same complaints about lax enforcement and public drunkenness remained, although Republican newspapers less commonly spread tales of local violations. New York now provided inspectors charged with tracking down lawbreakers. But as one Chautauqua County man explained, those officers were all but useless in rural townships. As strangers, he pointed out, the inspectors attracted immediate attention; and as a rule, illegal liquor sellers sold only to those they knew. WCTU chapters, meanwhile, tried to bring charges against known violators and worked to persuade men in license towns to vote against liquor. Under the new law, citizens directly decided the question of liquor in their towns, with the same mixed results as electing representatives under the earlier rules.[55]

For those who wanted total prohibition, the Raines law was obviously insufficient. Local prohibition proved daunting to enforce whether it was instituted directly by voters or by town excise commissions. In 1899, the Anti-Saloon League presented a strategy and organization for those who believed that state- or nationwide prohibition was the only possible response to the evils of liquor. Led by men, but copying the structure of the WCTU, the League lent its support to local-option campaigns as a steppingstone to state prohibition. In rural New York, League speakers visited Grange halls and Protestant churches in order to maintain interest in the liquor question, raise money, and provide direction to local temperance campaigns. While courting the rank and file, the Anti-Saloon League proposed an ambitious legislative program. Like the WCTU, the League organized letter-writing campaigns for bills related to alcohol; discarding the idea of forming a separate political party, the League's leaders determined the positions of assembly candidates on prohibition and advised voters accordingly. In so scrutinizing parties' nominees, the League went farther than the WCTU; in limiting its attention to liquor, it remained far more focused than the women's group. Its skillful use of existing temperance organizations, ability to generate publicity, and innovative political tactics made the Anti-Saloon League a forerunner of publicity-based pressure-group politics. Turning sharply away from the standard political practices of nineteenth-century men, members of the League appraised the candidates of the major parties instead of forming an alliance or a new party. Their choice of tactics forecast changes in the place of the party in twentieth-century politics.[56]

The Anti-Saloon League's day would come in the 1910s. Its appeal to temperance advocates in rural New York, however, suggests some of the limits of local government in the late nineteenth century. The men and women who worked for temperance sought initially to control liquor in their own towns. Dissatisfied with the operation of local excise boards, they then supported local option. Voting directly on licenses, however, worked as badly as the excise boards for those who sought prohibition. Townspeople continued to look the other way when they knew of violations, and the law remained difficult to enforce. Given the divisiveness of the temperance issue, townships and villages proceeded in their usual fashion: groping through to some sort of compromise that maintained a semblance of peace and quiet. For prohibitionists, however, crushing the evil in their midst deserved more attention than maintaining local calm.

Saddled with an unenforceable law, temperance workers looked to statewide prohibition to solve the liquor question once and for all. Thus, as in the cases of roads and taxes, a function once of local concern came to rest with the state. With temperance, however, the shift to the state level came for different reasons. The normal techniques of local compromise broke down when forced to deal with demands for new roads and other services, and state support relieved townships of issues that had become too divisive. Conversely, local compromise apparently worked for the temperance question: township and village governments settled into routines that gave temperance people no-license and provided those who wanted whiskey a place to drink. For temperance advocates, such local compromises proved the need for statewide prohibition. That course would not only break the power of the "whiskey trust" and cure cities of their evils, but would also encourage towns to enforce the laws already on the books.

In the cases of roads, taxes, and liquor, then, the state government came to play an increasingly important role in what had been jealously guarded local decisions. Local rural politicians had good grounds for passing decisions and responsibilities on to the state. While rural men rightly believed that local governments would be more frugal and less partisan than the state, they underestimated the conflicts that placing decisions in local hands would bring to their townships and counties, especially as costs and demands escalated. Officials of the state government had their own reasons to pick up local responsibilities. Late nineteenth-century state and federal departments were not known for their capacity to administer programs or regulate economic behavior or social institutions. But after the Civil War, state agencies nonetheless had grown in number and gathered authority in areas like agriculture, charity, prisons, and schools. Functioning both as a way to rationalize and systematize scattered local efforts and as sources of patronage, state departments took hesitant steps toward centralizing administration in the late nineteenth century. In so doing, they restricted the ability of local governments to make their own fundamental decisions.[57]

In some instances, local officials proved anxious to please state agencies. Expanded state control offered something to both state and local politicians. In the late nineteenth century, however, some village and township office-holders strove to retain their control over local institutions. The case of the Cortland Normal School in the 1880s points out the tensions as well as the mutually satisfying agreements between state and local governments.

Cortland Normal, a training school for teachers, began as a private academy, like most such institutions in New York. In 1866, the state legislature recommended chartering four new normal schools to relieve the burden carried by the two in existence. These schools would receive $12,000 per year in state aid, although the cities or villages would remain responsible for buildings and equipment. Through hard work by local politicians and money raised by villagers, Cortland won a charter. The village contributed the buildings and $75,000. The state agreed to keep an academic department at the school, which offered standard high school subjects not normally part of teacher training. Villages coveted institutions like normal schools, which were sources both of local pride and state aid. Cortland residents willingly spent a total of $100,000, much of it raised by bonds, to reap what they hoped would be the long-term benefits of the school.[58]

Just as the new school derived funding from both the state and the village, the local board and the State Superintendent of Public Instruction split authority over important decisions. Throughout the nineteenth century, the local board hired teachers and fixed their salaries, designed the curriculum, and recommended replacements when vacancies appeared on the board. Technically, such decisions required the approval of the New York Superintendent of Public Instruction; in practice, local boards exercised much of the power. Superintendents rarely challenged local board actions; they controlled matters pertaining to the composition of the student body and requirements for certification and graduation. In Cortland, prominent village men sat on the local board, a number of them active in Republican Party affairs. Considering the school important to Cortland's future, board members took their duties seriously. They attended to questions as diverse as the moral conduct of the janitor and the appointment of new faculty members. Given the investment Cortland had made in the school, the board sought to maintain control over great and small decisions.[59]

The Cortland Normal School had been the site of small controversies. County Democrats, for example, accused both the faculty and the local board of wrongly mixing politics with education. More seriously, the Superintendent of Public Instruction tried to eliminate the academic department at Cortland in 1877, an action the local board successfully fought. But the division of power between the local board and the superintendent laid the groundwork for a clash serious enough to threaten the school's existence in the early 1880s. This case tested the rival claims of local and state authorities and exemplified the difficulties the state encountered in centralizing formerly local matters.[60]

The source of the Cortland controversy was the bid by the State Superintendent of Public Instruction, Neil Gilmour, to remove the principal of the Normal School, James H. Hoose, in the summer of 1880. According to Gilmour, Hoose, who had been approved by Gilmour's predecessor, was incompetent, wrote "almost incoherent" reports, and went away on speaking engagements far too frequently to do an adequate job as principal. Hoose, who had written well-known textbooks and was widely known among educators, replied that Gilmour's wrath was politically motivated. Hoose had argued for a centralized educational system for New York that would have done away with Gilmour's job and had opposed Gilmour's appointment. Both men's charges contained truth as well as exaggeration. Hoose's travels required numerous absences from Cortland, but he had more than sufficient qualifications for his position. And Gilmour apparently did harbor grudges against Hoose. Both men were stubborn and vindictive, according to contemporaries, which encouraged a confrontation.[61]

But a conflict would have been unlikely had it not been for the local board. By majority vote, the board decided to back Hoose by claiming that Gilmour could not fire him and name a replacement without its approval. Gilmour cited the opinion of the state attorney general to prove the legal basis for his action, but the local board stuck to its position. The issue expanded from a personal conflict between two men to a debate about whether the school was a state or local institution.[62]

As September neared, the controversy moved no closer to resolution. In August, Gilmour appointed J. M. Cassety, vice-principal of the normal school at Fredonia, to Cortland and warned he would sever the state's connection with Cortland Normal if the local board refused to recognize the new principal. The board repeated its intention to keep Hoose and posted a sign on the school building indicating that the school would open as usual. Gilmour responded by threatening to fire any teacher who sided with the board and offered to place Cortland students in other normal schools. When Cassety arrived, the board refused him entrance to the guarded school building. The local board also informed the teachers that the school would open and hired substitutes for those who failed to report. When the school year began, both Hoose and Cassety claimed to be the principal. With no resolution in sight, both sides resigned themselves to letting the courts sort out the conflict.[63]

Cortland newspaper editors hoped for a quick settlement and feared for the future of the school. The village had not yet paid off the bond, and without an agreement, they believed, it might lose the school. William H. Clark, editor of the *Cortland Standard,* had been a steady supporter of Gilmour, beginning with his nomination as superintendent, and did not desert him in 1880. Clark, later a member of the local board, tried to convince his newspaper's readers of the importance of state funding and the threat to the school posed by the pompous Hoose. The *Cortland Democrat* at first simply reprinted letters and public documents relating to the controversy without comment. Later, the editor lost patience, but retained some sympathy for Hoose. "Selfish interests and improper or revengeful motives ought not to control," he declared. "The school is paramount to all other interests. Let us save the school even if good men fall."[64]

The editors of the two Cortland newspapers laid the blame on Hoose and Gilmour, both outsiders, rather than on the local board. The *Democrat* was most specific on this point. The local board had "always enjoyed the confidence and respect of the people . . . and we have seen nothing so far to shake the confidence of the people in their integrity or desire for the public good." Forgetting earlier charges of partisanship, even the Democratic editor presented the controversy as one between two men; their struggle involved the village's interests but did not reflect badly on Cortland or its citizens who sat on the board. For the editor of the *Democrat,* the issue could be resolved if it remained nonpolitical. Indeed, if the Normal School question became a political rather than a personal one, "disaster" would befall the school. Keeping the conflict nonpartisan also improved the village's chances for a peaceful settlement. "There has been too much anger displayed on that subject and a little spell of quiet is to be deserved," he declared.[65]

On January 4, 1881, the court's decision came down in favor of the superintendent. While the local boards could rightfully recommend teachers and principals, the superintendent had the final say. Both newspapers celebrated the decision and hoped for calm. But Hoose, who took a temporary position in Binghamton, appealed the decision to the State

Supreme Court. Again he lost, in January of 1882. Convinced of the justice of his claim, he took his case to the Court of Appeals. This time Hoose won. The judge ruled that a teacher could be removed only if both the local board and the superintendent agreed. Local control, the judge claimed, was essential for a normal school's success. The *Standard* saw the ruling as a dangerous precedent that might mean the eventual end of state aid. The *Democrat* expressed some relief to see the overbearing Gilmour defeated, but called for Hoose to resign to keep the peace. A petition signed by more than eight hundred villagers suggested the same. Hoose spurned this advice; he stayed on until 1891, when a reconstituted local board, including editor Clark of the *Standard*, asked for his dismissal. The new Superintendent of Public Instruction, Andrew S. Draper, hesitated for a number of months, but finally agreed with the local board. Hoose left for a position at the University of Southern California.[66]

In the years following Hoose's dismissal, the state superintendent moved to ensure that normal schools were "not local but state institutions." In 1891, New York consolidated its various agencies that dealt with education under the Commissioner of Education. The commissioner now had greater control over the composition of local boards and had the final word on all matters save those connected with buildings. Local control diminished further with new regulations in 1921, which deprived the boards of the power to recommend teachers without faculty approval. By 1926, the boards' only rightful function was visiting the schools; all decisions were left to faculties or the commissioner. A conflict like Cortland's of the 1880s was no longer possible.[67]

Beginning in the 1890s, local authority over education generally decreased. In 1893, the state set 160 days as the minimum length for the school year in public schools. Rural schools had long received some state aid, which they supplemented with local taxes. If a school district failed to comply with the new rule, it would lose that help. One year later a compulsory education law required all children between the ages of eight and sixteen to attend school and made parents responsible for young truants. In 1895, the state superintendent took the first steps toward designing a standard course of study for state-supported grammar schools. At the same time, rules regarding teacher certification, long the province of county authorities, grew more stringent and less variable from county to county. A notable failure in the centralization of rural schools occurred in the late 1910s, when the state legislature, bowing to adverse rural reaction, cancelled an order to consolidate small rural district schools. Except when district schools joined voluntarily, they remained independent until 1938. But by the 1920s, curricula, teacher education and certification, and student requirements were firmly in the hands of state authorities.[68]

As the case of the Cortland Normal School suggests, rural residents disagreed about the wisdom of state authority. For the citizens of Cortland, the school issue brought conflict between two desirable ends: local authority and state money. Finding the conflict distasteful, both commentators and local officials sought solutions that would let them keep both. For the local board, this meant turning the matter over to the courts. For the village newspapers, it entailed blaming two willful men, neither of whom was a village native, while downplaying the pivotal role of the local board. No one expressed any desire to see the issue enmeshed in the contention of partisan politics. All sides wished for peace, and voiced frustration when Hoose chose to return to Cortland. Eventually, a new local board, finding state support far more vital than the power to make certain decisions, achieved revenge on Hoose and their wish to see the school considered strictly a state institution. Local control would have been a hollow victory for them if it meant that the state could withdraw support for an important village institution.

The Cortland Local Board, like the county supervisors who dealt with requests for new roads and lower assessments, discovered that the goal of economy might best be met through courting state support. In part because of rising expectations for services, but more immediately because of state regulations, local governments found themselves spending more. Depressed agricultural areas refused as long as possible to provide additional services or to make improvements. Even better-off townships and counties spent with hesitation. At least one rural man wondered how it could be that taxes had risen substantially while his county's population—and presumably, demands for services—had declined. To put off such questions, to avoid difficult choices about the worth of competing projects, and to maintain the sense of marching with progress while holding down local taxes, local governments, with enthusiasm or reluctance, solicited state help. By the 1910s local office-holders administered programs funded by a variety of sources outside their communities. Townships and counties gradually lost the authority to make many basic decisions, but they achieved relative economy and avoided bitter local conflicts.[69]

In the cases of taxes, roads, and schools, local and state legislators, not rural voters, resolved to increase New York's role in township and county government. Indeed, rural men, even Grangers, remained skeptical about the savings that might be achieved by accepting state support. By taking state money, local governments invited partisan control. The goal of limited government had to be abandoned. Partisanship and grandiose plans would combine to erase any reduction in local taxes. While some rural men hesitated, rural women expressed a greater willingness to seek state help; especially with prohibition, but also with schools. Village boosters, meanwhile, particularly newspapermen, steadily advocated "progressive" measures that separated "wide-awake" villages from declining ones. But in the end, the local notables had the final say.

The male vision of good government—one that involved important decisions made locally and that honored conservative and inexpensive solutions—was to a large extent the reality in the late nineteenth century.

But even then, that reality was being slowly transformed by growing state control of local services. More dramatic changes in state and local relations waited until the twentieth century, when laws prevented successful challenges like that of the Cortland local board, and rural communities received far more state money than they paid in taxes.[70]

Rural men slowly undertook to avail themselves of New York's generosity. By the early twentieth century, farmers in particular tried to win what concessions they could from the state, and for a short time seemed to believe that they could control how state regulations affected them. With some bitterness they would encounter the boundaries of their influence, even as they adopted the pressure-group tactics formerly utilized by women. Rural men's awakening would be much like that of New York women, who learned that the vote alone would not bring lasting political gains for them. Both rural women and men first expected substantial political benefits and then, in the early twentieth century, realized the limits of their public influence. As the state accomplished some of the vital tasks formerly carried out by nonpartisan local officials, men increasingly saw value in reducing partisanship in state government. State policies helped change rural political attitudes and behavior.

1. *Campaign for Frank Straub for Superindent of the Poor, Schoharie County, 1910, in front of Straub's store. (Middleburgh Public Library)*

2. *Men, women, and children listening to Charles Evans Hughes speak, Middleburgh, undated. (Middleburgh Public Library)*

3. *Men near Fillmore knocking off from work, undated. (Wide Awake Club Library)*

4. *Mother's Day, Middleburgh, 1909. (In possession of Helene Farrell)*

5. *Old Home Week, Middleburgh, 1912. (In possession of Helene Farrell)*

6. *Cuba, 1985. (In author's possession)*

7. *Pleasant Brook, 1985. (In author's possession)*

Photos 8 through 15 were taken by researchers from the College of Agriculture between (roughly) the 1910s and the 1930s. The photographs and the accompanying commentary suggest insights into both rural communities and the expectations of rural reformers.

8. These are children attending a country school in Rodman township, Jefferson County, "a region of miserable squalid homes. A daintily dressed teacher can not but exert a strong influence on the young boys and girls." September 1911. (Cornell University, Farm Management Photographs, #1201)

9. Farm labor: The farmer "handles the day labor question in potato picking, and crop hand hoeing by building a shack in his orchard and hiring gangs of 1–5 Italians. He finds it very satisfactory. Wages $1.75 per 10 hours work. Board themselves." East Bloomfield, 1912. (Cornell University, Farm Management Photographs, #1574)

10. Farm labor: "Caldwell [a tenant] and . . . hired men—hired boy and dog. The wife is not shown. She is the other one. . . . He gets up about 5:00, goes to breakfast about 7, wagon ready to go to milk station about 8, ready for field or other work at about 9, has dinner from 12–1 or 1:30, then starts field work, begins milking at 5, about 7 to 7:15 he goes in for supper." April 1919. (Cornell University, Farm Management Photographs, #2693)

11. *Women's work: "Mrs. Caldwell out with her rubber boots feeding the hens. She keeps 200–300 hens, washes and packs the eggs, takes care of the chickens, cooks for the hired boy and herself and husband, washes the milk pails and strainers, takes care of the lanterns, etc. etc." April 1919. (Cornell University, Farm Management Photographs, #2696)*

12. A rural reformer notes: "Farmer says he doesn't know why some farmers are prosperous and he is not when he works just as hard as they do. This picture illustrates one reason why." Tompkins County, September 1918. (Cornell University, Farm Management Photographs, #417)

13. The house of a relatively prosperous farmer, a "[m]an who keeps no cows at all." April 1919. (Cornell University, Farm Management Photographs, #2676)

14. *Rural poverty: "Unpainted house characteristic of poor region." Undated. (Cornell University, Farm Management Photographs, #3006)*

15. *"Three Ithaca residences. [N]ot abandoned." August 1908. (Cornell University, Farm Management Photographs, #332)*

16. Former farms: Madison County and Schoharie County, 1985. (In author's possession)

The Intelligent Farmer and His Intelligent Wife: Political and Social Change, 1900–1919

Rural New Yorkers recognized the beginning of the new century as a milestone of sorts. First they tried to get their facts straight: Did the twentieth century begin in 1900 or 1901? the Grangers asked. Whatever their answers, they spent an increasing amount of their time pondering historical questions. In one local, Patrons entertained themselves by bringing "relics" to their meetings—objects more than fifty years old. Others were content with debates. What had changed in the past fifty years? Had farm women's lot improved? What were the most important inventions? Who were the great men of the nineteenth century? Their answers reflected uncertainties. In 1910, members of the Manchester Grange judged that farmers were better off forty years ago, as "things are too complicated now-a-days for real enjoyment." Yet they appreciated some of the changes that had made rural life harder to understand. They talked about how they lived "in a very inventive age," and imagined a time to come when farmers would no longer work since gasoline engines would run everything. Such speculations about the history of rural life signaled that an era had passed, and the new one was exciting but disturbing.[1]

The Grangers' wistfulness stood in contrast to the outrage and political ferment that historians tell us marked the "Progressive Era." Everywhere, or so it seemed to some turn-of-the-century Americans, rapid industrialization and population growth had strewn dangerous problems in their path. Deepening divisions between the rich and the poor put democracy in peril, and powerful businessmen abused their wealth by exploiting workers and consumers. Immigrants who spoke strange languages and practiced foreign religions crowded into cities where disease and hard work enfeebled and killed men, women, and children. City and state political machines bought immigrant votes, some charged, and further desecrated the ideals of democracy by accepting the bribes of businessmen. For some Americans, the nation's Christian and republican heritage appeared endangered, and they called for spiritual renewal and political reform.[2]

This perception of danger inspired a creative period in American politics. Fundamental changes seemed possible: the Socialist Party gained its greatest following, and its candidates won local and state offices. A diverse assortment of men and women—businessmen, union leaders, politicians, clubwomen, social scientists, and ministers—worked to enlarge the scope of government, especially its role in the economy. The results of all of the plans for social justice and a new democracy were less than many reformers would have hoped for, but American politics was reshaped nonetheless. Building on gains made in the 1890s, state government continued to exercise greater authority over what had once been local matters. At the state and national levels, new agencies regulated economic behavior and social institutions formerly left to market forces or individual discretion. Partisanship, according to reformers, was an evil remnant of earlier times; rational deliberation, rather than habitual loyalty, better suited modern politics. Thus they aimed to remodel electoral politics: primaries supplanted party caucuses; voters, not legislators, elected United States senators; state-printed ballots replaced party tickets; and registration laws grew sterner. Men still voted for candidates identified with one of the parties, but those candidates probably described themselves as anything but party men. Voters—both male, and after 1920 (1917 in New York), female—were less likely to turn out for an election than nineteenth-century men, and some supplemented voting with interest-group politics.

But what of the Grangers? Rural New Yorkers, like most Americans at most times, did not involve themselves in the political upheaval in ways more direct than voting for candidates. When Progressivism arrived, government action, not a popular movement, acted as the catalyst. State departments like the Department of Farms and Markets and quasi-public agencies like the Farm Bureau sought to help farm families adopt new marketing and farming practices and standards of housekeeping. The same agencies, meanwhile, tried to cultivate enthusiasm for community betterment projects of the sort that spearheaded urban Progressive reform. In a similar way, rural men's demands on government came in the wake of the transformation in the state's activities. New state regulations inadvertently created interest-group politics as farmers organized in part to oppose state policies. In rural New York, the state had a large hand in forming the patterns of political organization and community involvement that preceded Progressivism elsewhere. Progressivism came later to rural New York; governmental action, especially the burst during World War I, marked the route. Government, in the guise of rural reform, agricultural policies, the Farm and Home Bureaus, and woman suffrage, was the shaping hand in the creation of a new balance between public and private life.

Rural New Yorkers found much to admire in the Progressive campaigns of the first decade of the twentieth century. Grangers cheerfully joined in denunciations of trusts and monopolies: one in 1900 expressed his thanks that "the Trusts have not a monopoly on pure air." Another Grange resolved against "Bossism." Granges that retained an interest in politics fired off petitions to congressmen and senators in favor of railroad regulation; Grangers also supported the direct election of United States senators and primary elections. Rural newspapermen responded swiftly. They referred to their favorite candidates as "progressive," as if it were a synonym for "good," and dwelled on the evil bosses and scandals that cursed the opposition party. Women's groups, too, followed the wrongdoings of powerful politicians. For suffrage clubs, such incidents constituted arguments in favor of allowing untainted women the vote; for temperance advocates, the machinations of the "Whiskey Trust" suggested the need for state or national prohibition. Progressive reform seemingly offered something to every group in rural New York State.[3]

The revelations of muckraking journalists about political corruption and those of settlement workers about the squalor of city life scarcely disturbed rural men's and women's political convictions. Such exposés confirmed what rural people already knew about politicians and cities. For men and women who had long harbored a distrust of politicians and cynicism about party politics, tales of stolen elections, bribes, and kickbacks hardly raised an eyebrow. For people growing more and more hostile to cities, news of disease, danger, and appalling working conditions were a positive comfort. Those who had decided to remain in rural townships found that choice vindicated and their political views confirmed.[4]

Even for partisan newspapermen, Progressive denunciations of party politics were not necessarily hazardous. Republican editors took pride in Theodore Roosevelt's image as a reformer independent of would-be party bosses. Roosevelt was both Progressive and safe, unlike "demagogues" like William Randolph Hearst who needlessly inflamed class antagonisms. Democratic newspapermen, meanwhile, emphasized the misdeeds of state Republican leaders while quietly distancing themselves from Tammany Hall. In the end, Progressive campaigns may have made partisanship easier for rural editors. With the bosses driven from their ill-gotten seats of power, the parties deserved men's loyalty more than ever. With politics thus purified, no gap need remain between party politics in imagination and in reality.[5]

While enjoying these psychic comforts, rural New Yorkers had more immediate reasons to rest content. Agricultural prices improved generally in the early twentieth century, and New Yorkers shared some of the rewards. Dairy farmers got better prices than they had in years. Those with easy rail access to New York City had the additional advantage of being able to ship fluid milk to the city, where it commanded higher prices than milk sold locally or processed into cheese or butter. Vegetable

growers in townships near the Great Lakes and the Genesee Valley pa-
tronized canning factories that offered new markets for their peas,
beans, and fruits. But the relative prosperity of the early twentieth century was hardly equally shared. Inconvenient travel to railroad stations
locked some farmers out of markets. Those trying to make a living on
poor land endured additional problems: their farms produced low yields
of feed grains, which forced them to buy high-priced feed. Farmers
across the state complained of the high wages demanded by hired help,
if they could find help at all. And rural men and women continued to
leave the state's farms for the villages and cities. Nonetheless, the early
twentieth century was a much less grim time for New York farmers than
the late nineteenth century had been. Some of the large, once-fine frame
farmhouses still common in the New York countryside date from these
years, as do the even grander homes and business blocks in villages.[6]

Not all rural New Yorkers, however, were sanguine about their prospects. Some farmers worried that they were slipping behind Western
rivals, even as the economy improved. Good times afforded the time and
resources to secure benefits rather than coasting until disaster again
struck. Deserting time-honored attacks on government spending and
services, some rural men turned to the state for help. The attempts of
Lake Erie fruit growers to enlist state aid in battling insects and improving productivity provides one example of how some farmers imagined
new uses for government. In Madison County, meanwhile, a series of
local crises moved one rural newspaper editor from traditional partisanship, advocacy of economy, and amusement with scientific agriculture, to
independent politics, new expectations of state government, and support
for science on the farm and at home. Here, then, are two exceptions:
places where Progressive politics and values arrived on time.

Chautauqua and Erie County fruit- and grape-growers stood apart from
most farmers in New York State. They were the first to organize active
cooperatives. The Chautauqua and Lake Erie Grape Union pooled its
members' grapes; graded, marketed, and placed advertisements for the
fruit; and bought supplies in bulk during the 1890s. A local newspaper
devoted to grape-growers' concerns opened shop in 1893. While not
ignoring divisions within the union, the newspaper's editor reminded his
readers of the benefits of cooperation. "Most thoughtful growers admit
that intelligent cooperation is the only salvation for our great industry,"
he claimed, arguing that lasting prosperity would come only when growers mimicked the organization of corporations. Cooperation, however,
would not bring growers' "salvation" unless they also attended to scientific agricultural practices. Organized grape-growers followed the findings of agricultural scientists long before other farmers in New York
heeded those results. Modern, businesslike farming, they believed, demanded increased productivity and lower costs through the use of new
fertilizers, methods, and strains. The lake-area farmers' careful cultiva-

tion of a single crop and successful efforts to organize made them unique among New York's mostly diversified, independent farmers.[7]

As early as the 1890s, the grape-growers detected possibilities in the state government and sought to use it rather than weaken it. In 1894, they helped persuade state lawmakers to fund agricultural education and research in the grape-growing towns. The work done by New York's Agricultural Experiment Station in Geneva, the growers noted, was valuable but inadequate. Research conducted in central New York had little relevance for the western part of the state. The grape-growers did not labor alone in lobbying for state aid. Their allies included the Grange and representatives of the College of Agriculture at Cornell University, which acquired the money to do the research and worked hard for the appropriation. Sponsored by Chautauqua County assemblyman S. Fred Nixon, the bill passed in 1894, and work commenced in 1895. Thus began a long alliance between the College of Agriculture, the state and specialized farmers—one that offered additional funds to the college, free advice to farmers, and the promise of rural votes to office-holders. The Nixon Act inaugurated a full-fledged agricultural extension service. As that developed, grape-growers brought other problems to the state's attention. In 1902, insects endangered their crops, and they again approached the state for help through the College of Agriculture. Jacob G. Schurman, president of Cornell, offered to "bring science to bear directly upon this problem and save the district from devastation" in return for a larger appropriation for the agricultural school. Lake Erie–area farmers received the aid the college was anxious to contribute.[8]

Grape- and fruit-growers did not always get what they wanted. In 1900 and 1901, fruit-growers in the Lake Erie townships found their orchards infested with the San Jose Scale, an insect that endangered the lives of their trees. The Experiment Station discovered what kinds of pesticides would kill the insect. Spraying orchards, however, did not eliminate the problem. When farmers planted new trees, the scale reappeared: nurseries sold infested trees, and the insect again spread through orchards. Angry at having to pay for spraying when new trees carried the pest, orchardists asked the state to require all New York nurseries to spray trees before selling them to unsuspecting farmers. The nurserymen objected. They offered to regulate their own nurseries, to encourage growers to buy only from New York nurseries, and if the scale reappeared, to support a spraying program at state expense. Nurserymen claimed that the fault was not theirs. "The nurserymen *must* and *will* see that their own stock is kept entirely clean, for their reputation and trade demands it, and they recognize that their interests and those of the fruit growers are mutual," one averred. Orchardists responded that the opponents of legislation mandating the spraying of nursery trees were "*not nurseryman at all*—only *scalpers*," who bought their trees "wherever they can *obtain it* most cheaply, which, as a rule, is *outside* this state." The growers lost this round; nurserymen secured a reprieve from spraying their stock. Both the nurserymen and the growers, however, got help from the ever-willing College of Agriculture. In the end, both sides received state assistance.[9]

Great Lakes–area farmers learned early the benefits of state government. Organized farmers' demands on the state also brought different attitudes toward the parties and the proper function of government. In 1893, the *Grape Belt,* the fruit-growers' newspaper, announced its editorial policy. "[A] publication worthy of the name of a newspaper is not primarily a vehicle for the expression of the ideas of any one man nor any set of men," the editor proclaimed. The newspaper would be nonpartisan, "open to the hospitable reception of all shades of opinion provided only that utterances are prompted by an intelligent desire for the common welfare, [and] are expressed in courteous language avoiding personalities." Men's "common interests" were more important than partisan differences. The newspaper's pages were full of support for village and township improvement projects, agricultural advice, and news of the Grape Union. Chautauqua County, meanwhile, remained a Republican stronghold; but for at least one resident, party loyalty rested on the party's reformist traditions. "[R]eform and relief must come through the Republican party," he wrote in 1903. "Must the party be put to the test and meet with rebuff or defeat before it will hold to the traditions of the past?" Chautauqua men were among the first in the state to register a rejection of nineteenth-century partisanship: turnout declined earlier and more precipitously than in other upstate counties. A rethinking of partisanship took place as men wanted more from government than minimal services and more from its officials than recitations of cultural verities.[10]

In Madison County, too, nonpartisanship and support for expanded state services sprang from the inability of local men to solve novel problems. For one man, John Broad, a series of threats to his village's existence suggested the need to reconsider party loyalty, the uses of state government, and the value of science in agriculture. As the editor of the *Madison County Leader* of Morrisville, the county seat, he produced a typical Republican newspaper in the 1890s, which exalted men who stayed true to the party. He described the Republican nominee for County Treasurer in 1901 as a man who "has by diligence and close application to his chosen profession risen step by step to the exalted position he now occupies in the legal profession of this county." While as village booster Broad backed better schools and roads, he remained a steadfast friend of economical government. He also made space to chide those too devoted to scientific agriculture. In 1907, for example, he told the story of a Schoharie County man who "made himself poor by exercising too much system in care of his stock." Broad thus repeated nineteenth-century truths: partisanship in politics, economy in government, and common sense in farming.[11]

Broad faced a test of his political faith in 1906, when the city of Oneida attempted to move the county seat from Morrisville to Oneida. Mocking the pretensions of the "Lilliputian city," Broad dismissed this action. Events vindicated his disdain: while both Oneida and the nearby village of Canastota wanted the county seat moved to the northern part of the county, the representatives of the townships could not agree on where to put it. Both places wanted the county buildings, and their supervisors defeated each others' efforts. Town rivalries frustrated this attempt to move the county seat.[12]

But this was not the end of Broad's troubles. Madison and Oswego counties shared a state senator, and the delegates at the 1906 Republican Senatorial Convention disagreed about which county should be represented. Madison men contended that a deal struck a decade ago obliged the two counties to rotate the honor, but the Oswego delegates favored majority rule over old agreements. When the convention nominated Thomas D. Lewis of Oswego by a 12 to 9 vote, friends of Francis H. Gates, a Madison County man, prepared to wage an independent campaign. Broad thus had to decide between a local man and party loyalty. He chose the party, with misgivings. While criticizing the bid of the "Sullivan millionaire," he also defended Gates' character. Broad also understood why Madison men might vote for Gates, "inspired from what they consider to be principle, or from local loyalty or friendship." Gathering the votes of Madison men and Oswego Democrats, Gates, candidate of the Square Deal and Democratic parties, won the election. Party loyalty alone proved too weak to carry Lewis' candidacy.[13]

Soon after the election, supervisors of the northern townships returned to the question of the county seat. Madison County supervisors resolved in 1907 to let voters decide whether to move the county seat to the hamlet of Wampsville, located between Canastota and Oneida. Proponents of removal argued that the buildings in Morrisville had fallen into decay and needed to be replaced; it was better to construct new buildings in a more convenient location. Broad, meanwhile, professed confidence in the frugal people of Madison County: surely they would choose to make minimal repairs on the standing buildings. But his alarm grew. He suggested that the laborers of Oneida could be bought and were indifferent to property taxes and therefore should be denied the right to vote on the county seat question. Through the Businessmen's Association of Morrisville, he raised money for a proper campaign that resembled a partisan contest. He wrote stories highlighting the base motives and outright lies of the supporters of the Wampsville site. Bands and glee clubs entertained at anti-removal rallies held in various towns. But the campaign involved far more than diversion. For a village distant from a railroad station, like Morrisville, county buildings made the difference between a stable future and none at all.[14]

Despite the efforts of Morrisville people, Madison County voters endorsed moving the county buildings to Wampsville.[15] The combination of this defeat and the 1906 state senate campaign suggested to Broad that the time had arrived to abandon his nineteenth-century vision of politics. To be sure, urban men, for different reasons, came to similar conclusions about partisan politics. In rural New York, local problems pushed some men to reconsider partisanship, especially when the state government might be called upon for rescue. Broad and the Businessmen's Association quickly approached Gates and other state office-holders. Morrisville offered to donate the former county seat buildings to New York for a state-funded agricultural school. As with the county seat campaign, Broad took help where he could find it—partisanship had little place in this effort. Support for the agricultural school became his chief means of measuring the fitness of potential state office-holders. "The Leader is more interested in the welfare of its home town and that of its patrons" than with any man's "political ambitions," he explained. The measure granting aid passed the senate and assembly and waited on Republican governor Charles Evans Hughes' desk. Broad warned that Hughes would have to cancel any ambitions for the Presidency if he vetoed the bill, but Hughes spared himself that test and signed it in 1908. Broad judged the trade of a county seat for an agricultural school to be a "bargain" and returned to boosting his town.[16]

His newspaper changed noticeably, beginning with the 1906 county seat campaign. Broad's nonpartisanship went farther than measuring all candidates against a standard of support for the new agricultural school. He began to target Republicans for criticism even more than Democrats, sparing only the firmest friends of the school. He accused one assembly candidate of mouthing Progressive principles only because they were popular. He backed village and town improvements, such as better roads, because they were modern, and he never mentioned the cost. And Broad became an enthusiastic advocate of scientific agriculture. Northeastern agriculture had fallen behind the West, he alleged, because Northern farmers greeted new techniques with "hoots and jeers." Western farmers sent their sons and daughters to agricultural schools, and when they graduated, they taught their parents. Now that agricultural education was Morrisville's, Broad promoted it tirelessly.[17]

Faced with a serious local crisis, John Broad had converted his paper from a traditional party organ to one far more attuned to his village's issues and needs. Partisanship was an expendable luxury when Morrisville's future seemed at stake. Like the organized farmers of the Great Lakes area, he and village businessmen quickly learned the positive role government could play when local people encountered problems they could no longer solve or put off. In both places, Progressive political attitudes followed on the heels of local crises when people discovered the benefits of state support. Nineteenth-century insistence on small government, local control, and firm partisanship no longer met either psychological or material needs. Progressive principles—nonpartisanship, "efficient" government, and a "scientific" temperament—received wide publicity in New York in the first decade of the twentieth century, and perhaps suggested a course of action to rural men confronting new problems. Local distress, however, transformed Progressive ideas from words to plans for solutions.[18]

Such transitions were slow in coming to other parts of the state. This was not for want of trying. Teachers and other representatives of the College of Agriculture and New York's Experiment Station fanned out into the countryside. They tried to show other New Yorkers what the Great Lakes farmers already believed: scientific agriculture was the surest route to efficient farming, and organization and cooperation meant profits. Initially, those who prescribed rural uplift faced polite but less than cooperative audiences. Their ideas became relevant only when farmers were faced with new economic difficulties. Eventually, organizations like the Dairymen's League and the Farm Bureau contributed to leading rural men toward different methods of political participation. Rural reformers sought out farm women as well, and tried to demonstrate the advantages of modern technology for the home and the useful pleasure that could come from providing physical and civic improvements for villages. In time they organized farm wives who had been shut out of earlier women's groups. Suffrage groups, meanwhile, finally succeeded in persuading men to grant women the ballot. The work of the state government, together with the demands of reformers and some rural residents, slowly persuaded upstate men and women to rethink what they might ask from government and how they might behave politically.

Contemporaries perceived efforts to change the ways of rural Americans in the twentieth century as broad and important enough to be termed a movement. The "country life movement" combined the energies of educators, ministers, and journalists, along with those of the leaders of some agricultural organizations. It emerged in the 1880s with the appearance of books and articles decrying the alarming decline in the quantity and quality of people in the Northeastern countryside. By the turn of the century, rural reformers still spun harrowing tales of rural decadence, but they also put forward fresh solutions to the problems of life on the farms. The farm-reared men and women of the twentieth-century country life movement sought to create "intelligent" farmers and wives, people versed in science, alert to their lack of knowledge (and therefore willing to seek "experts' " help) and able to manipulate modern government agencies.[19]

In New York, agricultural reform scored its greatest success in gaining the ear of the state government. Federal legislation in 1862 had created state agricultural colleges; New York's went to Cornell University. The state supported agricultural research conducted in Geneva, New York, beginning in 1880, and in 1887, federal money became available for the Experiment Station. Until the late 1890s, both institutions floundered. While stronger than the agricultural colleges in other states, New York's school attracted few students. It also had no clear purpose: its program was too long and technical to lure farmers, and no certain place existed for graduates of agricultural colleges. The Experiment Station had a somewhat clearer goal, but its scientists were caught between serving the commercial needs of farmers and "pure" science. Both the school and the station regrouped in the 1890s. The college's leaders lobbied in Albany for additional appropriations, and they came away with new buildings, more money for staff and facilities, and additional responsibilities. Cornell's success excited the envy of the presidents of other New York colleges, who believed that Cornell had garnered far more than its share because of its supporters' political connections.[20]

While Cornell's links to the state government helped the school gain new funding, its leaders also constructed a convincing set of arguments to offer assemblymen and senators. Farmers needed and wanted an expanded program of agricultural education, which the college and Experiment Station could not presently supply. A separate agricultural extension system, they argued, should serve New York farmers. This system took shape at the turn of the century. The College of Agriculture published articles on specific farming problems and offered "short courses" in the winter when farmers might have time to attend. The college also designed a reading course for farmers. Men subscribed; or, better yet, they formed clubs at which they discussed the assigned material, took quizzes, and mailed the results back to Cornell. A reading course for farmers' wives soon followed, as did an effort to organize rural children. With the cooperation of the Department of Public Instruction, the college supplied lecturers on nature study for teachers' institutes, and eventually made that subject part of the rural school curriculum. New York farmers needed scientific knowledge if they were to remain competitive, the scientists and their allies believed. Rural politicians went along, and at election time, pointed to their backing of agricultural measures as a sign of faithful service to their districts, if anyone asked.[21]

As institutions devoted to agricultural science grew, so did popular attention to the problems of life on farms and villages. The "country life problem" was the subject of an increasing number of books and articles in the first two decades of the twentieth century. Theodore Roosevelt's Country Life Commission, formed in 1908, found much amiss in rural America: substandard roads, schools, homes, and churches; meager social opportunities; and few efforts to reap the benefits of cooperative farming. The commission suggested greater governmental involvement in agriculture, especially support for education. Country lifers usually admitted that rural problems would be difficult to cure, as they were at once psychological, social, and economic. Traditional country virtues, especially independence and hard work, hurt farmers in organized, industrialized America. A new way of thinking, grounded in scientific attitudes, had to replace rural people's lethargic devotion to tradition. Rural social institutions, such as schools and churches, had failed to keep pace with urban ones, and reaffirmed outmoded values. Farmers in different parts of the country confronted particular problems—sharecropping in the South, declining soil fertility in the North, and scarce water in the West—but most shared an ignorance of new methods. Members of the Country Life Commission, like others interested in rural problems, held out the hope that science and education could come to the rescue.[22]

Without much support in Congress, the commission's recommendations remained suggestions. But social scientists, mostly based in agricultural colleges, produced studies of rural communities and stood behind state initiatives. The social scientists scrutinized country schools and found them hopelessly outdated and inadequate for the task of creating better rural citizens. Together with some rural residents, they called for the replacement of one-room district schools in New York with township schools that could provide better facilities and teachers. Such schools could offer courses in scientific agriculture and homemaking, which would improve farming and encourage good students to remain in their townships. Churches, too, would benefit from consolidation. As matters stood, reformers believed, villages suffered from "overchurching"—the existence of more churches than a community could support. Narrow and sectarian, country churches had not yet gotten the word on the social gospel; instead, they persisted in preaching the rewards of heaven and the pains of hell. Both schools and churches squandered opportunities to uplift and unite their communities. Farm homes, meanwhile, lacked modern conveniences, required too much hard and inefficient labor from farm wives, and looked ugly. Farm women thus needed retraining; as did their husbands, who remained ignorant of soil chemistry, proper care of animals, and the control of damaging insects. Having convinced lawmakers, country lifers set out to demonstrate to farm families the bonuses offered by scientific thought and practice.[23]

Rural people proved to be a more difficult audience than assemblymen. County farmers' clubs and agricultural societies, dedicated to furthering agricultural knowledge, did find much to admire in plans to bring Progressivism to the countryside. A visit to the college by the New York State Grange in 1877 persuaded doubting Patrons of its usefulness; thereafter it faithfully sent petitions to Albany in favor of all increases in Cornell's funding. Members of local Granges, however, seemed more ambivalent. Some adopted the Cornell Reading Course and steadfastly stuck to agricultural topics, although farmers resented being quizzed by the college men. More commonly, however, Grangers discussed questions about scientific agriculture and homemaking—and even rural uplift—for a time and then let matters drop in favor of social hours, poetry readings, and talks on topics like "how to manage a husband" and cutting government spending. In other Granges, agricultural and homemaking topics disappeared until the 1910s and resurfaced only with the prodding of Farm and Home Bureau agents. Without direct encouragement, Grange members used their organization as something other than a school for the advancement of science. Most New York farmers seemed satisfied to wait and see whether scientific farming would pay and gathered information on their own, not through the Grange.[24]

New Yorkers also had mixed feelings about the Country Life Commission and the whole idea of rural uplift. Letters sent to Liberty Hyde Bailey, chairman of the commission, and to Theodore Roosevelt expressed a wide range of responses. A Tompkins County farmer cheered the commission and complained about the backwardness common among farmers. His uncle, he wrote, was typical of farmers in his area: the man "thinks a 'germ' is 'all bosh' and that what he doesn't know isn't worth a great deal." Others were grateful that someone finally acknowledged the problems of rural people. But J. V. Jacobs described farmers in Rensselaer County who "view[ed] the proposed acts of the commission as being something in line of settlement work in our large cities and rather object to their being investigated, as they feel amply able to take care of themselves." Systematic evidence is difficult to gather, but the enthusiasm of the Tompkins County man and the hostility of Rensselaer County farmers probably represented extremes. The attitude of local Granges tended to be one of polite but listless attention. Grangers who discussed the commission's questions on rural roads, social life, cooperative agriculture, and taxes did so in a perfunctory manner. They simply refined cherished themes: taxes were indeed too high, roads were poor, and help was hard to find. The rethinking of rural life that the commission hoped would come of their questions did not occur in New York, at least not in Grange halls.[25]

The agitation of rural reformers proved insufficient to alter the political and social habits of rural New Yorkers. For the reformers, mindful of recent urban advances, it was an exercise in frustration: the countryside seemed filled with stubbornly unproductive farmers, women whose strenuous work was wasted effort, and voluntary organizations that resolutely shunned activities that would benefit their communities. Changes in rural men's and women's political behavior and beliefs, however, were slowly developing. Advancing at an uneven pace, reconsiderations of nineteenth-century truths about politics and society occurred largely in the 1910s, when state policies and institutions directly tested earlier beliefs. In the end, state government brought Progressivism to rural New York.

While the reformers made their suggestions, changes in the dairy industry challenged rural men's political customs. In the late nineteenth century, dairy farming was the most important endeavor of New York farmers, as it would be in the twentieth century. But dairymen found few occasions for direct political action. Throughout most of the state, dairymen used local markets to dispose of their surplusses. They sold milk to village stores, nearby cheese factories, or their own cooperative plants. Farm wives churned butter. None of this called for mass political organization. Cheese factory owners tried to cultivate foreign markets, while the Grange inveighed against "filled" cheese and "counterfeit butter," or oleomargarine. Despite the size of the dairy industry in the state, neither politics nor a great push toward improving productivity seemed crucial in the late nineteenth century.[26]

The profitable sale of fluid milk to urban markets brought new regulations and pricing problems that changed farmers' work and politics. Men and women concerned about public health issues, along with dairy farmers, labored to rid New York City of impure and adulterated milk as early as the mid–nineteenth century. The problems were twofold: some dealers sold milk laced with dangerous colorings and flavorings, and others marketed skimmed or watered-down milk. The state and city responded with regulations and inspections that removed perhaps the worst offenders: "dairies" attached to breweries that milked diseased cows. But calls for stricter regulations mounted. In 1884, state lawmakers answered by creating the Dairy Commission, charged with inspecting dairies and milk dealers and formulating standards of "pure" milk. Complaining that a tiny staff precluded any attempt to monitor farm dairies, the commission's inspectors trained their attention on city dealers and milk depots. This focus on city merchants suited farmers: they believed the dealers tainted milk. When the inspectors hinted they would widen their work to farms, dairymen tried to rein in the commission by making its administrator subject to elections. Nineteenth-century ventures to regulate milk sales stayed in the cities.[27]

As these efforts to purify the city's milk supply continued, innovations occurred in the marketing of milk. Initially, only the farmers nearest to the cities were able to sell fluid milk to urban dealers. Orange County farmers, for example, began to ship milk to New York city when the market for their butter collapsed in the late nineteenth century. At first fluid milk was a profitable item. The increasing city population and tales about breweries' "swill" milk created demand for country milk. Limits on the distance over which milk could be safely shipped allowed Orange County farmers to set their own prices. Soon those farmers lost that luxury. In 1882, city dealers formed the New York Milk Exchange, frankly formed to fix prices dealers would pay. When Orange County farmers protested, dealers simply invited more-distant farmers to supply them. By 1890, refrigerated cars expanded the milk shed to encompass counties as far west as Broome and as far north as Cortland. Orange County farmers tried to organize as well, but with no success. Too many other farmers willingly supplied the New York market. The experience of Orange County dairymen would become familiar in other parts of the state. As farmers entered the city market, they lost control of prices. When they attempted to counter with their own organization, the dairymen failed.[28]

As city demand for milk gave dairymen new opportunities and problems, regulators began to take a closer look at the operation of dairy farms. In the 1900s, scientists determined that the strain of the tuberculosis bacillus found in contaminated cow's milk could transmit the disease to humans. Scientists commonly believed that the cows kept in dirty barns developed tuberculosis, so inspectors from New York City set out in 1907 to examine the conditions of dairies that shipped milk to the city. The city Health Department first sent instructions to dairymen that set out minimum levels of sanitation. "[M]ost fair minded dairymen," one newspaper guessed, "were inclined to admit these were reasonable demands providing a sufficient price was paid for their milk." But in addition, managers of village milk depots were to give the inspectors reports filed by farmers on the presence of infectious diseases in the area. Dairymen resented the trouble of filling out the necessary forms. "Some treat the instructions as a joke and after wading through the maze of printed matter . . . contemptuously threw the letter, blanks and all aside," a newspaper article asserted. Farmers claimed they did not have the time to deal with such paperwork. The complications of supplying New York City with milk began to mount.[29]

Dairymen soon learned that the city inspectors had more rules in mind. In 1907, the Health Department issued additional regulations, including one asking farmers to clip the tails of cows in order to retard the spread of disease. For Grangers in Madison County, the city regulators had gone too far. "There is plenty of brains and brawn among the hard working farmers, sufficient to find a way to earn their living without getting down as serfs for the city again," a speaker announced. The urban dealers should first clean their own houses: "what about the deadly microbes and disease germs sent back from New York to the country in the filthy milk cans for the farmers' wives to cleanse?" he asked. An Odd Fellows chapter planned a parade that featured a "nice clean cow [leading] the procession with a blanket labeled, 'What New York City Demands!' followed by a company of men carrying a large brush labeled 'Tooth Brush for Cows'; also a box marked 'Manicure Set for Cows.'" Faced with new regulations, dairymen directed their anger toward slovenly city dealers and chemists who knew much about germs but little about farming.[30]

Some dairymen did more than carp about urban arrogance. In 1907, some Orange County dairy farmers again attempted to organize. Both low prices paid to farmers and the increasingly intrusive regulations demanded collective action, these farmers believed. The Dairymen's League was to provide a means for farmers to communicate their concerns in Albany and allow them to determine their own prices. To accomplish their first goal, the Dairymen's League avoided partisanship and used pressure-group tactics targeting the legislature and state agricultural agencies. As for the latter, the Dairymen's League acted as the purchasing agent and sought to gain uniform contracts for dairymen. The local league's officers attempted to induce dealers to sign contracts with the league rather than with individual dairymen. The league was small in 1907—only 691 farmers joined—but gradually became a major force in agricultural policy.[31]

In the meantime, farmers were wary about the league's organization and its ability to deliver all it promised. Farmers had long been keen on the idea that they should be able to set their own prices the same way that manufacturers did. Still, some remained leery of collective bargaining and holding their milk off the market when prices were too low. That would be forming a trust, and farmers, as one logically consistent Granger explained, "condemn all other trusts." Others thought the whole idea hopeless—supply and demand determined prices, not organization. Additional critics of the Dairymen's League complained about the membership fees, which they thought too high, and suggested that farmers could cut better deals as individuals. Later, the high salaries of league officials would be added to the enumeration of problems. Principle and practical concerns made New York farmers suspicious of the league.[32]

Such considerations dampened the Dairymen's League's appeal for almost a decade. But what regulations and dealers' prices failed to do, changes in the dairy industry accomplished. Pasteurization became an increasingly important step in supplying milk to urban markets. The process demanded expensive machinery, which helped eliminate competition. Two major creameries supplied New York City by 1917—Borden and Sheffield Farms—and the companies determined the prices paid to farmers. In the summer of 1916, however, the league decided to take action against low prices through a milk strike: its members would refuse to sign contracts with dealers until the creameries agreed to recognize the Dairymen's League and pay a specified price. The league had the state on its side. The New York Senate had recently completed hearings that confirmed the dairymen's contention that the two large firms fixed prices and paid farmers less than their cost of production. The College of Agriculture assisted in determining what that cost was. The Department of Foods and Markets helped the most. John Dillon, head of that department, warned processors that beginning October 1, they would have to buy all milk through his office and the league—paying one cent more per quart. If they insisted on dealing only with individual farmers, Dillon threatened to devise his own distribution plan that would bypass uncooperative creameries.[33]

Plans for the strike moved forward in the fall. The large processors insisted they would not deal with the Dairymen's League and hinted that a strike might be a violation of existing antitrust laws. Farmers' complaints, moreover, were unwarranted. Most of them kept records too poorly to know whether or not they lost money, and they were better off selling to the large creameries, anyway. Meanwhile, the league held meetings in towns across the state and signed new members. If the dealers refused to cooperate, they would process and sell milk themselves. Thus on October 1, members of the league stopped shipping milk to dealers who rejected contracts with the organization. In addition, league members guarded roadways and stopped delivery trucks, effectively preventing nonmembers from supplying the offending creameries. League members also processed milk themselves. The strike lasted eleven days, until the processors settled on the league's terms. Making skillful use of state agencies, the College of Agriculture, and the Farm Bureau, the dairymen had managed to force the creameries to compromise.[34]

As a bonus, the Dairymen's League grew rapidly after the strike, going from roughly 15,000 members to more than 32,000 by 1917. With victory came a sense of power. The "big city dealers saw the folly of holding out any longer," a sympathetic newspaper claimed. Organized farmers now commanded politicians' attention and could dictate terms to processors and middlemen. Indeed, with the Dairymen's League, farmers could achieve the long-held dream of eliminating the middleman by processing their own milk. But New York dairymen would find such hopes dashed. The league began to suffer from both internal and external difficulties. It devised a system of pooling milk and determining the money paid to farmers on the basis of how milk was used (milk ultimately condensed or made into butter paid less than that sold as fluid milk). This plan drew criticism from some dairymen, as did the costs when the cooperative began to process milk products. The commercial creameries' grip was far from broken, and the league would be forced to strike again in future years. Nonmembers continued to believe that they received better prices by working out their own contracts.[35]

But the Dairymen's League was a new type of farmers' organization. It rejected the building of fraternity that was so important to the Grange, did not take the advancement of science as a goal, and pressed instead for better prices and favorable legislation for dairy farmers. There was a political lesson in all of this: legislatures could address farmers' economic needs. Regulation, monopoly, and price-fixing would help persuade rural men to see politics as a contest of material interests rather than a mechanism by which the morally worthy won rewards, and government as important ally instead of a barely restrained conspiracy of organized greed.

While the Dairymen's League worked to enhance farmers' incomes, the Farm Bureau aimed to both organize and educate rural men and women. The Binghamton Chamber of Commerce and the Delaware, Lackawanna, and Western Railroad formed the first Farm Bureau in Broome County in 1910. Its leaders argued that businessmen, railroads, and farmers shared similar interests, especially increasing farmers' production and profits. The farm bureaus received the help of the United States Department of Agriculture in their work, along with limited assistance from the New York College of Agriculture. The college's role in the Farm Bureau grew, however, after 1912 when counties began to support local bureaus. Fearing that the United States Department of Agriculture (USDA) would gain control, the college began to supply agents to counties that voted to support Farm Bureaus. The early farm bureaus thus tapped money from both public and private sources and expertise from the state and federal levels.[36]

Only a handful of counties saw fit to break new ground and spend money on farm bureaus during the first few years. The federal government, however, extended encouragement in 1914, when Woodrow Wilson signed the Smith–Lever Act. The measure provided money for agricultural extension, which was to be a cooperative venture of state agricultural schools and experiment stations and the USDA. In New York, the College of Agriculture appointed the county agents. These men, with the guidance of extension leaders and specialists in particular areas at Cornell, devised projects for their counties. Ideally, Granges and other agricultural organizations worked with county agents. Such cooperation—and divided authority—at times caused conflicts among the college's extension service, county agents, and federal authorities. Clashes erupted throughout the 1920s, but the Farm Bureau remained a fixture in rural counties.[37]

County agents in New York chiefly attended to educational projects: speaking to Granges, advising individual farmers, and performing experiments. Together with college administrators, agents first set out to interest farmers in Farm Bureau associations. The local groups were to support the work of the county agents and also spread news of advanced agricultural techniques to nonmembers. When a Farm Bureau had been established, the organizers ran drives modeled on political campaigns. A local "campaign manager" would divide the county into districts, persuade "committeemen" to contact farmers, and arrange for advertising. For the last, Farm Bureau leaders cultivated local newspaper editors, ran essay contests for children, and affixed posters to buildings and trees. The campaigns culminated in county meetings at which men joined Farm Bureau associations. With a Farm Bureau successfully organized (as they were in all farming counties by 1918), the search for new members resumed. Here the agents sought the help of the Grange and other agricultural groups. The Farm Bureau enjoyed a surge of interest during the war years, but membership slipped in the 1920s. Farmers objected to the fees—commonly five dollars. Since county agents were public employees, nonmembers who wanted their aid had it for the asking. By 1919, the Farm Bureau was a growing, albeit divided, organization. County agents, paid with public funds, engaged in projects designed to bring new agricultural methods to farmers. County Farm Bureau associations, with close but undefined connections to the county agents, sought to influence agricultural policies and helped form marketing and purchasing cooperatives. The dual roles of education and political and economic action did not sit well together, but by 1919, the Farm Bureau was an interest group and educational organization that drew together chiefly the already scientifically minded farmers.[38]

County agents were educators first, and they preached the gospel of scientific agriculture to all who would sit still to listen. A shortcut was to work through existing organizations; so agents often joined Granges, attended meetings, and turned the discussion to topics like fertilizers, proper accounting, silos, and the like. In addition to lecturing, county agents assigned projects to Grangers. The Cortland County agent set the members of the Marathon Grange to work on better recordkeeping. When the agent left them alone, Grangers debated the value of carefully recording expenses and the value of extension work itself. One man believed that the county agent "could help any of us if we would follow his advice." Another disagreed: he replied that he "never rec'd a cents worth of help from the Farm Bureau." While the men assigned to the task dutifully reported the cost of the milk their cows produced, others scoffed at the endeavor. One man explained that he "did not think much of keeping account of every little piece of work done on the farm." County agents helped bring the results of agricultural research to farmers, although with mixed success.[39]

While some farmers gingerly accepted new methods, others maintained that they already produced enough. They needed advice on how to market their produce, not on how to grow more. The Farm Bureau responded to these demands. County agents advised groups of farmers on operating purchasing and marketing cooperatives. Especially in the late 1910s, county agents played important roles in aiding cooperative producers' groups. Farm Bureau associations participated in cooperatives. Such work was controversial—businessmen cringed at the thought that government employees were helping create competitors for their trade. Fearing that the ventures of Farm Bureau associations would hurt extension efforts, the College of Agriculture distanced itself from such activities. State and national administrators of the extension program tried to clarify the relationship between the county agents and the farmers' organizations and specify the duties of the agents. While denounced by all of the partners in extension service, advice and direct assistance to producers' cooperatives in New York continued.[40]

By the 1920s, the American Farm Bureau Federation was an important force in national politics. The AFBF lobbied for price supports, tariff protection, and other laws it deemed essential to agriculture. In New York, the Farm Bureau had reservations about such actions. Its leaders were squeamish about mixing in politics, seeing their proper function as limited to education. Moreover, New Yorkers responded to the AFBF's proposals much as they did to the Populists': such measures might help Southern and Western farmers, but they were irrelevant or even harmful to Eastern agriculture. The New York Farm Bureau Federation (NYFBF) nonetheless took stands on state and national issues, as did a blanket organization of major state agricultural groups, the New York State Conference Board of Farm Organizations. This group evaluated federal policies, from tariff schedules to the Clayton Antitrust Act, in terms of what the legislation meant for New York agriculture and farm groups. The Conference Board, like its member organizations, concentrated on issues and ignored the parties.[41]

The Farm Bureau had transported some elements of Progressive thinking and behavior to rural residents by the 1920s: faith in the scientific method, nonpartisanship, and interest-group politics. County agents and the NYFBF made good use of larger groups already in place: the Grange, schools, and women's groups. But state and federal policies, not exhortation, prompted men to organize and conceive of politics in new ways. The NYFBF, in part a creation of the federal and state governments, engaged in single-issue politics. County agents helped organize other specialized agricultural groups that did the same. Much of this activity occurred in the 1910s, as state and federal interest in agriculture quickened.[42]

The expansion of state functions challenged rural men's earlier veneration of small and frugal government. What good was local government or individual effort against the large creameries that controlled the market? Why not take advantage of the help the state was willing to provide to modernize farming practices, if those new techniques meant greater profits? What sense did it make to promote local control when it meant that the cities would take advantage of the state's largesse? Rural men seemed uncertain how to respond. While the members of the Dairymen's League tried to get state agencies to work for them, others pondered the negative ramifications of governmental activism. For a *Morris Chronicle* writer in 1915, a large government meant an intrusive government that multiplied the existing problem of too many laws:

> To-day no man walks our streets who is not a lawbreaker, so interminable have become the laws. If he figures, if he hunts, if he traps, if he sells anything, if he buys anything, if he spits, ... if he runs a business, if he speaks emphatically, if he rides, if he goes cross-lots, if he is sick, if he dies and is buried—if he does any of these things he is certain along the line to violate the law. Is it any wonder that there is a growing disrespect for the law?[43]

Along with the complicated profusion of laws, men decried the increasing expense of government. At Grange meetings and in newspapers, men castigated costly new agencies. "To the harassments of over-government," an editor declared in 1916, "may be attributed in large measure the present high taxes and high cost of living." State and federal agencies shared the blame with partisan hacks for expensive and wasteful government. The *St. Lawrence Plaindealer,* like other Republican weeklies, blamed Tammany's various patronage schemes for high taxes. Rural editors still published partisan newspapers, but they subdued their praise of their favored candidates. Their parties' nominees deserved votes because they were the most efficient and qualified, not necessarily the most loyal. Cynical accounts of the nature of politicians remained numerous. Thus state agencies tended toward profligacy, and partisanship needed to be qualified. When rural men suspected that partisan politicians staffed agencies, their criticism grew all the more strident.[44]

Rural men complained, but they realized that some new governmental initiatives benefited them. Parcel post and rural free delivery, uniformly popular among farmers, were two such federal policies. Considered vicious threats by village merchants, these programs made it easier for country residents to make purchases through the mail; some even discussed the possibility of selling produce the same way. As dairymen relied more on the New York City market for their income, better roads—built at state expense—became vital. And New Yorkers took advantage of programs designed to bring science to the farms. Some attended farmers' institutes and demonstrations; some made use of the offerings of agricultural schools; a few found careers teaching agricultural science to others. With higher prices as an incentive, many New York farmers gave the scientists an extended hearing and implemented some of what they heard.

In the early twentieth century, it seemed that rural New Yorkers could both enjoy the assistance they wanted from government and, while fretting about the expense, watch their share of the tax burden decline. Through organization and concerted pressure on their representatives, rural men might get government to work in their favor. The victorious conclusion of the 1916 milk strike was one hint of the farmers' influence. Another was rural residents' successful effort in 1918 to repeal the township school bill of 1917. The state Grange, Farm Bureau, and educators promoted the school consolidation law, but the closing of small district schools still angered rural residents. The tiny schools provided a superior education; people took pride in the local schools; and transporting children to a central location would be a needless expense, they countered. Organized rural citizens seemed powerful enough to force positive political change, rather than merely, as in the nineteenth century, able to check county spending.[45]

Greatly expanded governmental activism during World War I brought further gains to farmers but also illustrated the limits of rural men's control over policies that affected them. Progressive-era policies had involved government in the regulation of the economy and social institutions. Yet the magnitude of the wartime undertakings and the new directions of public policy required far more central planning. Organizing industrial production and setting prices and wages, war-related agencies seemed to their staffers to open a new cooperative relationship between business, labor, and government. Changes were no less sweeping in agriculture. State and federal agencies controlled prices, found farm workers, and helped farmers increase their production. The planners balanced what they saw as the competing needs of all groups in American society—with results that rural men in New York found disappointing, if not totally unfair.[46]

The atmosphere of emergency and sacrifice of the war years pushed the Farm Bureau and other rural associations to higher levels of activity. County agents, anxious to address the food shortage, urged farmers to adopt new methods to raise productivity. They helped farmers upgrade their dairy herds and adopt new seeds and fertilizers. Their suggestions were printed in newspapers, recited at Grange meetings, and demonstrated at county gatherings. The war made help even scarcer on New York farms; the Farm Bureau and the state government assisted farmers in locating hands for harvests and using machines when that proved impossible. Agricultural organizations worked through government agencies to secure credit for farmers. Patriotism and economic necessity boosted farmers' acceptance of scientific agriculture during the war.[47]

Threads of cynicism ran through rural men's reactions to wartime propaganda and government efforts. In regard to the food shortage, one Granger believed that farmers should avoid "getting excited but go along in a good steady way." Another suggested that society ladies should be made to work in farm homes during harvests, freeing farm wives to work in the fields. But rural men mostly took the government's efforts and words seriously. "It's a big thing to be an American these days," began a newspaper article celebrating the departure of the first group of Yates County draftees. Patriotism swept up members of voluntary organizations. Many bought flags, sang patriotic songs, and scolded the "slackers" who damaged the war effort. For the first time, evidence that rural people thought of themselves as part of a nation appeared. In addition to symbolic gestures, men and women took part in more concrete activities. Voluntary societies bought war bonds; women worked for the Red Cross; the Grange raised money for an ambulance. Grangers read letters from members who went overseas, and newspapers printed such letters and followed the travels of local sons. Through those men and war work, rural people took part in a national effort. The war fostered a sense of identification with the nation.[48]

While New Yorkers got caught up in the wartime spirit, two issues remained so galling that no exhortation to sacrifice could quiet disaffection: milk prices and daylight saving time. Dairymen contended that milk prices remained too low, especially in light of the costs of feed and living expenses. The Dairymen's League failed to persuade state and federal office-holders to address their grievance, even as creameries raised the prices they charged consumers. George F. Warren, a College of Agriculture professor who sat on the Food Administration's Milk Committee, believed that the Food Administration purposely pegged food prices—milk in particular—below a reasonable level. The agency, he maintained, wanted to keep wages from soaring despite the wartime inflation: maintaining low food prices, whatever the drain on farmers, was one way of doing this. Dairymen, however, did not trouble themselves about why the Food Administration declined to help them. Rather, they worked for readjusted prices, and threatened to strike again in 1917. They gained little for their efforts, and the Dairymen's League finalized plans to market milk itself. With this rebuff, dairymen lost some of their earlier optimism about the benefits of government intervention in the market, and turned to dismantling the Food Administration as soon as the war was over. Government could be a problem for farmers as well as a solution.[49]

Rural opposition to daylight saving time had concrete as well as symbolic sources. On a practical level, farmers claimed that moving the clocks ahead one hour made them less productive. It disrupted their milking schedules, unsettled their cows, and took from them and their help an hour's work every day. More abstractly, disregarding "God's time" seemed to be one more example of urban contempt for rural people. It seemed incongruous that while the federal government endlessly reminded farmers of the importance of their work, the wishes of urbanites came first on this issue. During the war, Grangers debated whether to follow daylight saving time. When New York State held onto the system after the war, fighting the "noxious" daylight saving time law became the cause that most aroused Grangers' interest.[50]

Such wartime lessons contributed to dashing rural men's hopes for positive results from an activist government. With parties discredited and the agencies under suspicion, rural men again adopted weakening government as their favored political panacea. In time, additional developments confirmed men's querulous attitudes: the agricultural depression of the 1920s and the ascendancy of urban values during the same decade. But even then, government action and changed economic conditions encouraged rural men in the twentieth century, like nineteenth-century women, to either practice interest-group politics or dismiss the whole endeavor as hopeless. They expected an inexpensive government to deliver benefits to rural citizens and talked about politics in terms of interests, efficiency, and service. The events of the war and its aftermath soured men's political expectations, but the political habits developed during those years persisted.

Men's and women's politics drifted closer together in the early twentieth century. While men discovered their own reasons for echoing nineteenth-century women's fondness for government and contempt for partisan politics, women came to occupy a less anomalous place in rural political life. For New York women, the extension of the suffrage in 1917 transformed political participation and the ways in which they were viewed as political actors. At the same time, women's voluntary associations grew in number and membership. As was the case with men, the Farm Bureau played an important part in organizing rural women. Despite women's new public presence and organization, however, they wielded little new power in rural politics. Changes in the structure of government, popular ideas about women, and the concerns of women's groups blocked as well as opened public opportunities for rural women in the early twentieth century. But just as links between manhood and politics no longer gripped rural men, connections between domesticity and female public life gradually faded.

The eventual victory of woman suffrage helped further weaken traditional ties between gender and politics. That victory, however, seemed remote in the first decade of the twentieth century. Suffragists failed to induce the delegates of the New York State Constitutional Convention of 1894 to drop the word "male" from the state's voting requirements. Local and state suffrage organizations regarded school elections as too trivial for sustained effort. Rural and small-city women property-owners won the right to vote on bond issues in 1901, which ranked as the movement's weightiest achievement. Suffrage leaders debated new strategies in the 1900s, while rural Political Equality Club members studied civics books and the condition of women in various times and places, and read their favorite authors.[51]

In the 1910s, suffragists shook off this lethargy. The New York State Woman Suffrage Association (with the national movement) slowly united on a fresh set of tactics. Stepping out of parlors, the movement now courted publicity: suffragists marched in parades, spoke at large rallies, and sought newspaper coverage. NYSWSA also drew the local clubs into a tighter organization. Affiliates worked on state, not local, projects. To stimulate debate in rural places, the state organization produced articles for local use. Suffragists in small towns persuaded newspaper editors to print these items, invited state leaders to speak at public meetings, and raised money for NYSWSA, while continuing their traditional parlor meetings and work at county fairs. The arguments in favor of woman suffrage had changed only in the extent to which suffragists linked the vote to other issues. Women merited the vote because of their purer, nonpartisan political attitudes, because modern politics needed feminine virtues, because it was just, and because farm women worked as hard and unselfishly as their husbands. Rural women, like suffragists elsewhere, mixed arguments based on natural rights, with others resting on ideas about woman's special nature, with still others hinting at improvements women voters would bring. New tactics guaranteed that more men heard the suffragists' claims.[52]

In 1915, men had a chance to vote on the question as well as listen to debates. The legislature agreed to allow voters to decide whether women should have the ballot. In cities, suffragists worked hard to gain men's attention. They staged a large parade in New York City and kept squads of speakers busy on street corners and in halls. They followed the lead of the political parties by organizing down to the election district level. In small towns and villages, too, suffrage workers got out the word, although their campaigns followed traditional tactics more faithfully. Retaining the staple parlor meetings, rural women spoke and distributed pamphlets at county fairs. Innovation came from the outside: arriving on special trains, state speakers appeared in villages to debate anti-suffragists or simply to present pro-suffrage arguments. Members of local and state groups used automobiles (still a notable sight) to cover more territory. While suffrage supporters spent more time and effort in New York's cities, they also stumped the villages and hamlets.[53]

The question of women's right to vote received detailed coverage in rural newspapers. Editorials, however, treated the issue cautiously, if at all. A few editors declared outright opposition: the editor of the Cooperstown *Freeman's Journal,* for example, surmised that most women did not wish to be bothered with politics. But most withheld opinions. They published the prepared articles passed on by both suffrage and anti-suffrage organizations, sometimes tending to print more material from one of the sides. The issue was important enough to spend a great deal of ink on but many editors apparently saw taking a stand as unwise and divisive. The editor of the *Plattsburgh Press* thought it unnecessary for him to declare his position: woman suffrage was not a political issue. Not directly involving the parties or economic issues, "votes for women" fell outside of the usual run of political news.[54]

Rural editors who supported suffrage—mostly Republicans and independents—submitted the same wide range of arguments that suffragists did. It was a matter of justice and fairness; it was a gesture in keeping with modern life; it would purify politics by balancing partisan men with uncorrupted women; it would speed the progress of temperance. Poor roads would vanish if women voted. Changes in the functions of government, moreover, made woman suffrage necessary. The editor of the *Cortland Standard* noted that

> [n]early all of the home and social side of life is now involved in politics. A stream of politics pours into the kitchen sink every time the faucet is turned on to wash the dinner dishes for the water is "city water." Politics is left at the kitchen door every morning in small wide-mouthed bottles labelled "Milk–Grade A" . . . . There is no keeping politics out of the home and out of the children's stomachs in this day of communal living.[55]

With government entrenched in kitchens, electoral politics demanded women's special knowledge. Since government performed some of the tasks that formerly belonged to women's groups or homes, electoral politics was now safe and proper for women. Changes in some men's views of the purpose of politics, moreover, made the thought of women's casting ballots seem less absurd than it once did. For the Progressives, political participation no longer required the character traits thought to be exclusively held by men. Instead, voting required intelligence, attention to broader public needs, and a willingness to review the relevant facts before casting a ballot. Politics thus adhered more closely to nineteenth-century women's vision than to men's ideal of loyalty and friendship.[56]

Yet the Progressive view of politics had hardly erased earlier assumptions about the connection between politics and manhood. The 1915 referendum on woman suffrage lost: nearly 58% of the men who answered the question voted no. It carried in five upstate counties—Chautauqua, Schenectady, Chemung, Broome, and Tompkins. In four counties, Columbia, Lewis, Sullivan, and Ulster, fewer than one-third of

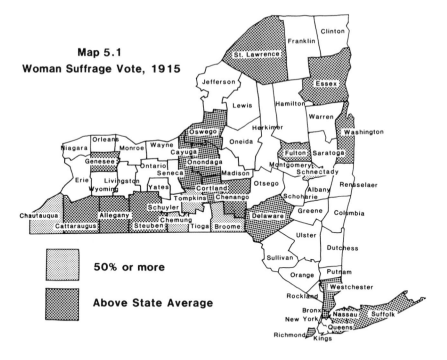

Map 5.1
Woman Suffrage Vote, 1915

50% or more

Above State Average

the men endorsed the change. In upstate New York, the pattern of support for woman suffrage resembled that for the Greenback Party: the southern tier produced victories and near victories. Cortland, Chenango, Allegany, Genesee, Cattaraugus counties tallied a higher percentage of suffrage votes than the state as a whole, and four of the five pro-suffrage counties were also located in that region. Otherwise, voters in the central and northern counties soundly rejected woman suffrage, as did those in New York City (5.1). Support for woman suffrage thus appeared most pronounced in places where men had shown a willingness to part with the Democrats and Republicans in the past: the southern tier, where Greenbackers had gained votes; and Bronx and Schenectady counties, where Socialists ran well. Many people linked woman suffrage and temperance as compatible causes, but areas of Prohibition Party strength were not necessarily bastions of suffrage support. On the whole, however, areas where men had broken with partisanship—and conceived of different purposes for government and politics—woman suffrage won votes.[57]

A closer examination of town-level returns for a number of counties can illustrate this point more clearly. Five counties in different parts of the state suggest some of the patterns in the vote on the referendum. Chautauqua, located in the far western end of the southern tier, was the banner suffrage county; Cortland, in the center of the state, split almost evenly; Montgomery, in central New York, closely matched the statewide vote; Clinton, in the northeasternmost corner, fell below the state average; and Lewis, on the eastern shore of Lake Ontario, produced one of the worst suffrage defeats in 1915. In each county, support for woman suffrage appeared to be linked to "modern" political patterns.

In all but four of Chautauqua's twenty-eight towns, a majority of men voted for woman suffrage. And even where the referendum lost—the city of Dunkirk and the towns of Clymer, Sherman, and Westfield—the percentage of votes in favor was higher than in the state as a whole (Table 5.1). In Chautauqua, a number of developments had early encouraged men in the rural towns to question nineteenth-century ideas about politics. Chautauqua County fruit-growers adopted producers' cooperatives, scientific agriculture, and interest-group activity far in advance of farmers in other parts of the state. In addition, Chautauqua men joined politically active Granges that consistently favored woman suffrage. With the aid of Buffalo organizers, suffragists also ran a visible campaign in the county's towns and cities. That contest was also not the county's introduction to woman suffrage: there, as in the rest of the southern tier, the movement had been prominent for decades. In the rural towns of Chautauqua County, a tradition of progressive politics (which included higher-than-average support for Greenback and Populist candidates), innovation in agricultural practices, and a spirited campaign helped make it the leading woman-suffrage county in both 1915 and 1917.

The referendum on woman suffrage fared far worse in rural town-

TABLE 5.1   Vote on 1915 Woman Suffrage Referendum in Five Counties

	Percent Yes	Number Yes	Number of Towns	Total Votes
Chautauqua County total	58.2	9,912	27	16,973
Small city/large village	58.1	3,373	4	9,247
Rural/small village	58.7	4,539	23	7,726
Clinton County total	39.2	2,657	15	6,783
Small city/large village	43.3	796	2	1,829
Rural/small village	37.5	1,861	13	4,754
Cortland County total	49.8	2,822	16	5,670
Small city/large village	54.5	1,943	3	3,578
Rural/small village	40.7	879	13	2,092
Lewis County total	29.9	1,604	18	5,372
Small city/large village	0	0	0	0
Rural/small village	29.9	1,604	18	5,372
Montgomery County total	44.1	3,588	11	8,300
Small city/large village	45.6	2,572	5	5,644
Rural/small village	38.2	1,016	6	2,656
State as whole	42.5	553,348		1,301,680

Sources: Official canvasses contained in county supervisor's reports.

*Large villages were those that exceeded 2,500 residents in the 1915 state census.

ships elsewhere. In two Cortland County agricultural townships—Scott and Solon—a majority of voters favored woman suffrage. In the rest of Cortland, most rural men rejected woman suffrage. Lewis County gave suffragists uniformly bad news—seventy percent of the men voted no and the referendum lost in every town. The small city of Plattsburgh contributed the only Clinton County suffrage victory; in Montgomery, the city of Amsterdam and St. Johnsville, a large town, alone produced suffrage majorities. In these counties, men in small cities, not in the countryside, were willing to see women vote.[58]

The agricultural townships in Clinton, Montgomery, and especially Lewis were not nearly so prosperous or organized as those in Chautauqua. Much of Lewis County proved barely suitable for pasture, let alone field crops; and a sizable number of its townships, like those in Clinton County, had poor access to transportation and markets. Farmers in Montgomery County generally worked better soil and enjoyed access to markets, but like farmers in many places where diversified farming was practiced, they avoided agricultural groups. The Farm Bureau found it difficult to organize Montgomery County, and had no easier time in Lewis and Clinton. Men in these declining townships, in short, had few good reasons to adopt modern agriculture and organization, or the ways of thinking they encouraged. In such townships, men were less than enthusiastic about most innovations in government. A change as drastic as woman suffrage, with unknown political consequences, was best resisted. In declining towns, nineteenth-century political attitudes held fast.[59]

In 1917, the woman suffrage referendum was back on the ballot. This time, the election approached with little fanfare. Rural newspapers again published suffrage and anti-suffrage items. But an anti-suffrage group in Cazenovia, which in 1915 had pressed its case at county fairs and mass meetings, in Grange halls and in print, decided in 1916 that "it was not wise to agitate the subject" further, since men had already spoken. Suffragists, however, still addressed meetings in villages and traveled through the countryside. Yet the war absorbed far more attention in 1917. Members of Political Equality Clubs sponsored state speakers and rallies, but they divided their time between campaigning and war work. As signs of their unselfish citizenship, they rolled bandages and knitted sweaters for the Red Cross. In so doing, they followed the lead of NYSWSA, which ran an organized but less attention-grabbing campaign. Suffragists hammered away at the same themes as the 1915 campaign, adding only that extending the vote to women would be a patriotic gesture, and inevitable in a modern society.[60]

Perhaps the most important difference between the 1915 and 1917 campaigns for woman suffrage was the position of the political parties. Both the Democratic and the Republican parties endorsed woman suffrage, and in New York City, Tammany leaders chose not to oppose the referendum. The 1917 campaign competed with news of the war in

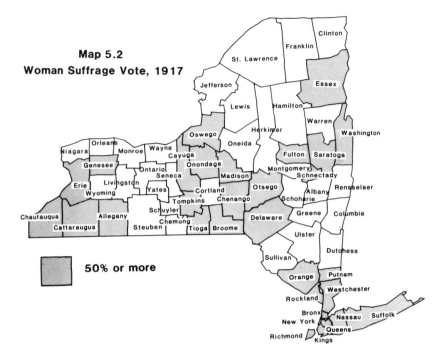

Map 5.2
Woman Suffrage Vote, 1917

50% or more

rural weeklies and hence received less space than in 1915. On the basis of party loyalty, some editors now gave a grudging blessing to woman suffrage. The editor of the *Freeman's Journal*, for example, still felt uneasy about the prospect of women voters—electoral politics was "a responsibility that the men should continue to assume, leaving the women the better performance of the higher and nobler responsibilities that are theirs by the laws of creation." But as a good Democrat, he would follow his party and vote for changing the state constitution. Women had proven their good citizenship through Red Cross work. Better still, women in Western states had shown themselves to be wise voters by preferring Woodrow Wilson to Charles Evans Hughes in the 1916 election. As distasteful as the sight of women voters might be, their votes could help the Democratic party.[61]

On the basis of victories in New York City and its environs, the woman suffrage amendment passed in 1917 with more than 53% of the vote. The greatest change occurred in the metropolitan counties—New York, Kings, Bronx, Westchester, Nassau, and Richmond. The gains made in these counties carried the referendum, although it also ran well again in the southern tier. Elsewhere in rural New York, the pro-suffrage vote was generally higher than that of 1915. Yet woman suffrage sentiment was not notably stronger in central and northern sections of the state: while party leaders modified their positions on woman suffrage, partisans in these rural towns had not. Despite these pockets of resistance, after decades of agitation, New York State women had finally won the vote.[62]

Victory posed a new set of questions that both suffrage and party leaders had to answer. What relationship would women have to the political parties? Would their votes make a difference in elections? For suffragists, the idea of forming a separate political party had only narrow appeal; NYSWSA, as its last major effort, held "suffrage schools" to provide training on the political system and voting. Otherwise, some suffragists formed the League of Women Voters, which rejected partisanship in favor of dispensing independent information about candidates and issues.[63]

Male partisans, meanwhile, tried to make sense of the new situation. A Penn Yan newspaper editor rightly noted that the "Socialistic vote" had much to do with the woman suffrage victory. He also had advice: he hoped that no "radical change will be brought about by the vote of the women. They have much to learn in politics, and they will do well to go slowly in forming any sort of radical opinion either of their authority or of their duty." Just after the election, the editor of the *Schoharie Republican* described the reaction in his anti-suffrage county. "If it is some good cuss words you want to learn," he wrote, one should speak with men who discovered that their votes were "but a drop in the bucket." Such men would "say lots of things about women that he wouldn't want his better half to hear and end up saying." While individual men lamented the passing of the older division of power between the sexes, politicians faced their own problems. "At one blow political organization went askew," the editor continued. " 'We used to be able to get along in the situation but now how are the women going to vote?' " he quoted a local politician as asking. Given this uncertainty, politicians, the editor believed, aimed to win the favor of women voters by allowing women to vote in the upcoming primaries which were to be held before the constitutional change took effect. And they stuffed candy along with cigars in their pockets to hand out to potential voters.[64]

Tokens of respect for women voters appeared in rural New York. Although women had been eligible for school positions for decades, school district meetings suddenly began to routinely elect women to office. This gesture had lasting effects in some districts, since women joined the groups that rotated the offices among themselves. More often, men soon regained the trusteeships, and women served, at most, as collectors and secretaries. No formal restriction ever barred women from holding nonceremonial offices in Granges, either. But few Granges ever elected women until after 1917. Small acts of recognition of women's new political standing, then, were the immediate consequences of their enfranchisement.[65]

The spring town meetings in 1918 provided a somewhat more serious test of women's political tendencies. If nothing else, partisans watched the elections closely to see whether women would turn out. Few men attended township and village elections in normal years, but the spectacle of women casting ballots drew both men and women to the polls. In

Otsego County, for example, a record number participated in most of the town meetings—a record that would have stood even without counting the women, who made up nearly half of the total. These men and women took the time to go to the polls, moreover, for an election in which there was only one nonpartisan ticket in the field. In Gouverneur, women ran for office as well as voted—indeed, a woman ran for each of the village offices. Special interest in the election developed around the position of village trustee, since the incumbent was challenged by his wife. As in school elections in the nineteenth century, women candidates sparked interest in the dullest of elections. At first, at least, women took the opportunity to exercise their franchise.[66]

It is difficult to determine what, if any, difference women's votes made. Minority parties in some places nominated female candidates with the hope that women voters would produce a rare victory. This strategy worked on occasion, just as it did in school elections. In Otsego County, for example, a woman running for a local office was the only Democrat elected in 1918. Elsewhere, the prohibition issue and the presence of the Catholic and "wet" Al Smith, Democrat, on the ballot for governor makes it difficult to determine whether shifts toward the Republicans had much to do with women's votes. In Schoharie County, for example, one of the last rural counties in which the Democratic Party remained dominant, voters deserted the Party in 1918. They supported Charles S. Whitman, the Republican incumbent for governor, over Al Smith, and chose Republicans for the state senate and assembly. In 1919, the Republican Party nominated a woman for county clerk. Her election would be due recognition for half of the electorate, according to a Republican newspaper. She understood the duties of the office; one which properly tapped feminine abilities: "Certainly a lady would make a far better clerk than sheriff," the editor argued. By 1920, the Republican Party was a force in Schoharie County politics. According to local newspapers, female voters deserved the credit—or blame—for this shift. Nonetheless, other issues probably brought about the shift toward the Republicans in this anomalous Democratic county.[67]

Interest in women candidates and voters soon faded. Few stories in rural weeklies during campaigns in 1925—or even 1921—reminded readers that women could vote, much less run for office. A flurry of activity ensued at the federal level when the national amendment passed, most notably in providing mother's pensions. In rural New York, some party leaders soon concluded that women voters did not divide between the parties differently than their husbands or fathers did. Without a bloc of women voters, the sense of crisis passed. Upon winning the vote, women produced no widely followed strategy for using it. They did not build a base in minority parties, turn to third parties in significant numbers, or change the direction of majority parties. The civics-book vision of politics that rural suffrage clubs promoted did not suggest a strategy for using the vote other than rational deliberation. Moreover, men's and women's ideas about the uses of politics and government had moved closer by 1917. Woman suffrage brought neither the disaster opponents imagined nor the era of Progressive policies suffragists hoped for.

While the enfranchisement of women did not bring lasting policy changes, it was far from unimportant. Woman suffrage severed some of the remaining connections between electoral politics and manhood. If some men had already rejected earlier ideals as ill-suited for modern life, the women's entry into the electorate forced the rest to rethink the male vision of politics. Definitions of manhood and womanhood would have to be found in places other than in one's ability to vote and hold office. Progressive ideals of efficiency, expertise, and public service—ideals long touted by women involved in the public sphere—now competed with the nineteenth-century values of friendship, loyalty, and partisanship for men's attention. These new political ideas would draw clear distinctions between public and private: rationality, service, and expertise on one side and personal feeling on the other. They would displace "proper manhood and womanhood" from their earlier positions of eminence in public life.

If the advent of woman suffrage was a watershed in men's understanding of politics, rural women seemed unimpressed. Female diarists did not insert the result of the 1917 election into accounts of visits, weather, and chores. They noted without elaboration the first time they went to the polls, usually accompanied by their husbands. Suffragists, some of whom devoted their lives to the cause, understandably saw their enfranchisement in a different light. For women distant from the campaign, having the right to vote did not represent a notable break with the past. The normal routines of their lives went on as always.[68]

Even while the campaign for woman suffrage went forward, other developments were changing rural women's understandings of domesticity, public life, and the relationship between the two. Beginning in the 1900s and increasing throughout the next two decades, both farm and village women joined single-sex organizations in greater numbers than they had in the nineteenth century. These groups, moreover, sought out local projects. Village improvement societies, chapters of the Daughters of the American Revolution, and other groups took on projects designed to make their villages and townships more modern and comfortable. The Home Bureau, the women's branch of the Farm Bureau, shared in this work, and undertook to introduce science into rural life. The Home Bureau formed women's clubs dedicated to bettering farm wives' performance as housekeepers and encouraging members to tackle community projects. Built on the ethic of cooperation rather than on the extension of feminine virtues to the wider world, these groups provided rural women with little new public influence. But they did signal a change in the nineteenth-century relation between gender and politics.

Women's organizations attacked shortcomings in their villages and townships in the early twentieth century. Village improvement societies formed by women in most of the larger villages attempted to enhance the physical appearance of houses, vacant lots, and streets and to raise community spirit in the process. The Civic Improvement Society of Morrisville, active in the first decade of the twentieth century, went about its work in typical fashion. Ella Harwood founded the group, which soon attracted "progressive men" as well as women. They planted trees, raised money for fountains, repaired hedges, and helped homeowners clean their yards. Such efforts were hardly controversial; indeed, they meshed nicely with the attempts of the Business Men's Association to boost the village. The way the Society executed its projects made criticism even less likely. It strained to engage everyone in its ventures, thereby enhancing community pride and preventing the society from being considered snobbish and exclusive, like typical women's clubs. Hence the society tried to "interest everybody down to the smallest children . . . and the most sluggish and heedless," and put all villagers on committees to accomplish specific tasks. Avoiding the slightest hint of disagreement with anyone either in the work they chose or how they accomplished it, the Morrisville group, like other village improvement societies, drew praise from their community. By the early twentieth century, village women's groups had the means, perhaps because of the support of village boosters, to take on local projects. Professing no larger political goals, such societies also escaped community criticism.[69]

Chapters of the Daughters of the American Revolution joined village improvement societies in community betterment plans. In addition to sponsoring essay contests in the schools, DARs built parks and playgrounds, raised money for local and distant charities, contributed to libraries, collected local historical documents, and furnished hospital rooms. They also pursued political issues, chiefly prohibition and immigration. During World War I, DAR members in rural New York quickly adopted Red Cross projects; those in Otsego determined they "were so interested in the work" that they formed a Red Cross chapter after the war. The community involvement of DAR chapters dropped off sharply in the 1920s, as the national organization discouraged local enterprises that might be duplicated by other groups. But for a time, they, too, contributed to civic improvement projects.[70]

External influences, whether communities or parent organizations, shaped the role the groups played in public life. A good illustration of the leverage of outside organizations—and changes in women's groups in the twentieth century—was the Twentieth Century Club of Cortland County. The members, mostly Cortland residents, divided the club into seven sections; all but the Domestic Science department stuck chiefly to literary pursuits. The members of the Domestic Science section worked to hone their own housekeeping skills and to improve the community as a whole. Thus they read papers like "Ptomaine and Ptomaine Poisoning" and "The Effects of Food Upon Character," while also running cooking classes and a sewing school for girls. They studied "Municipal Housekeeping," but also discussed "How to Put Your Home on a Business Basis." The women raised money for their favorite outside charity—a school in Appalachia—and sponsored projects for the Cortland poor. In 1919, one member argued that they had "outgrown the thought that we should live for ourselves alone. We should live to help others." Concentrating on housekeeping, personal and civic, the Domestic Science section proposed to do just that.[71]

In the process, the Domestic Science clubwomen redefined domesticity and the home for themselves and their community. Through their work as housekeepers, women could introduce modern values into the broader society. The first duty of housewives was not to work hard and see that duty was learned and bad habits squelched. Rather, modern homes required "efficiency and conservation of strength, for systematic but not arbitrary effort, and in home life for respecting individuality, encouraging rather than curbing." The clubwomen carried these ideals into the homes of Italian women, to whom they demonstrated labor-saving housekeeping techniques and introduced American food. They did the same with farm girls (who apparently also lacked an understanding of proper American housekeeping).[72]

In redesigning the good home, members of the Domestic Science section received the help of the Home Bureau and extension workers from the College of Agriculture. Home economists confirmed the clubwomen's view that running a proper home took a tremendous amount of effort, yet ultimately fixed the future of the nation. As Vera McCrea of the Home Bureau put it: "A Community is not stronger than its weakest home. . . . If homes are right the community will be right, if the communities are right then the town will be right, and so on up the scale until we have a nation that is right." By the 1920s, the Domestic Science section had all but dropped community work in favor of further study of homemaking. It was a rare meeting that did not include an outside speaker of some sort: a salesman from Wear-Ever cookware, a professor of home economics from Cornell, a banker, a doctor, or an expert on some aspect of the many complexities of running a house and raising a family. The members of the Domestic Science department did not seem unhappy with this dependence on outside speakers and the turn away from public action. Indeed, visitors structured their meetings and provided both entertainment and what the members saw as necessary education. With the help of outside leaders, the Cortland women returned domesticity to the home.[73]

Many of the small women's groups in the villages and townships stuck with the staples—socials and book reviews—and eschewed both community involvement and efforts to modernize the home. But the large number of clubs affiliated with the Home Bureau shared the Cortland club's aims. The Farm Bureau included home demonstrations in its work as early as 1914. The Home Bureau organized separately in 1918. By 1921 it claimed more than 17,000 women had joined Home Bureau clubs in New York State. Present in only a handful of counties before World War

I, Home Bureau agents found their services in demand during the war years. With the help of an additional emergency appropriation, home extension agents organized clubs throughout upstate New York and instructed women in the conservation of food, home production, and the construction of balanced menus despite shortages and restrictions. Present both in upstate cities and in the villages and towns, the Home Bureau organized on a permanent basis immediately after the war.[74]

Home Bureaus were organized in much the same fashion as farm bureaus. County "home agents" designed yearly programs and supervised extension teaching. They derived funding from federal, state, and county sources, although Home Bureau agents had to argue separately from the farm bureau for backing before county boards of supervisors. For a modest fee, women joined home bureaus and also participated by forming smaller community groups with the counsel of county bureaus. Thus the Gee Hill Friendship Club in Cortland County studied various aspects of homemaking with the help of the county home agent. Such clubs served hot lunches in district schools, studied civics as well as homemaking, and arranged socials and pageants.[75]

Like the Domestic Science Club, groups affiliated with the Home Bureau studied various aspects of homemaking and civic improvement. Extension service bulletins urged housewives to carry pedometers as they went about their daily tasks and to devise ways to save steps. In addition to learning about household Taylorism, rural women received instruction on nutrition and the proper preparation of food, home decoration, and novel devices like vacuum cleaners and "fireless cookers." Club members, in turn, conducted demonstrations for other neighborhood women, while Home Bureau agents visited Granges, gave talks, and hunted for recruits.[76]

The purpose of the Home Bureau, according to one extension leader in 1919, was both to improve rural women's household habits and to "awak[en] women to civic responsibility." Farm women needed such guidance. Commenting on a rural survey done in 1919, extension service leaders felt that "desolation, sickness, untidiness and discouragement . . . characterized altogether too many of the homes visited." In addition, according to the letters published as part of *Reading Course for Farmers' Wives*, rural women appreciated the chance to talk about their problems at home. Women discovered new arguments with which to coax their husbands to install running water. Some writers believed that the suggestions offered to farm wives were impractical and beyond the means of many farmers. But rural women joined Home Bureau–guided clubs just the same, finding in them a new reason to meet with neighbors and take part in a club that had practical and clear directions.[77]

Through these groups and their talks, the Home Bureau agents sought to show rural women that homemaking could be a high art. Once they learned the essentials, such as rudimentary tidiness, they could move on to the "spirtual side." The vision of proper womanhood and

domesticity touted by extension agents is neatly summed up in the praise
for an early home agent, Mrs. A. E. Nield, in the *Extension Service Newsletter.* "Aside from her public service, Mrs. Nield is a capable housekeeper
and a mother who is a real companion to the members of her family."
Homemakers did more than clean houses. Indeed, too much straightening up was the mark of a fussy woman who slighted the essential points
of homemaking: the play, companionship, and relaxation that made for
a home people wanted to be in. The description of Mrs. Nield closed:
"[H]er son Walter remarks, in a time of strikes for more pay for less
work, 'I think I'll strike for more mother.' "[78]

Properly understood, maintaining a home was a compelling occupation and allowed wives time to build better family relationships. Women
could also use their spare time to help others in the neighborhood:
joining Parent-Teacher Associations, organizing pageants and "community sings," and demonstrating to others what they learned about housekeeping. This was a vision in many ways narrower than the nineteenth-century understanding of domesticity, which stressed women's ability to
sacrifice and above all their moral superiority to men. Female public
action, as envisioned by the Home Bureau, demanded cooperation with
community leaders and other organizations. It avoided both twentieth-century feminism and nineteenth-century moralism: it did not entail
using moral force or legislation to limit the behavior of morally weak men.
Maurice C. Burritt, Director of Extension, summed up the twentieth-century approach to politics and gender roles. He cautioned Home Bureau leaders in 1919 to "shun politics and to maintain a non-partisan and
non-political basis, and above all do nothing that could be construed as
starting sex antagonisms." From available evidence, it seems that the
Home Bureau's clubs followed his directive.[79]

Thus by 1920, the Home Bureau clubs, along with groups like the
Domestic Science section in Cortland, helped make domesticity more
important to rural women. For those who could afford them, modern
labor-saving devices made it possible for women to complete household
chores without the help of men. In theory, they would devote their freed
energy to enriching family relationships and beautifying their communities. But while women focused more than ever on their homes—and
even organized on the basis of housework—domesticity lost its political
edge. A greater level of outside involvement masked an inward turn.
Emphasizing cooperation rather than moral righteousness, the more
numerous women's organizations of the twentieth century did not challenge or antagonize the male leadership of rural towns. Just as it was
falling out of fashion in urban centers, domesticity gained a new lease on
life in rural New York. While it had some applications to public life for
nineteenth-century women (and even those of the Progressive era), by
the twentieth century, domesticity was strictly confined to the home.
Neither the vote nor separate organizations enhanced activist rural
women's public influence.[80]

If the new restricted understanding of domesticity made women's community projects less controversial, so did changes in men's views of public life. Leaders of rural communities welcomed activities that made their towns seem up-to-date, whether instigated by men or by women. Such work became fodder for booster pamphlets, not evidence of local divisions. In this sense—in a desire to see local voluntary action—men's and women's public activities grew closer together by 1920. Distinctive conceptions of the purpose of government and politics faded as well. Both men and women used interest groups to effect changes in legislation. Their organizations were used by groups like the Anti-Saloon League when situations called for massive mail campaigns. Some men joined women in seeing politics as beyond redemption, and hence not worth the effort of participation. Both rural men and women spoke of politics using words like "efficiency," "expertise," and "public service," and expected their representatives to prove their fidelity to rural people's interests. Both shared hopes for new influence in the 1910s and saw those expectations disappointed.

The minimization of differences between men's and women's politics in rural New York brought another, equally significant, change: the redrawing of boundaries between public and private life. For women, the personal and moral convictions that once made women's public activity unwelcome were now safely trained on keeping better homes. Domesticity, stronger than ever in the twentieth century, applied to private behavior, not public questions. The values that once grounded men's political behavior—loyalty and friendship—were by the 1920s properly left out of public life. New rules governed what rightfully belonged in the public sphere. The relationship between gender roles and politics had changed. Gender roles had grown more specialized as the separate work of men and women required training and careful study. Faithful fulfillment of gender roles no longer deserved public reward. These new relationships between gender and politics, and the public and private spheres, became clearer in the 1920s, as the new political order in rural New York took hold.

CHAPTER 6

Progressivism and the Countryside in the 1920s

The effects of changes that reshaped rural New York by the 1920s were as stark as those in any industrializing city. New technologies transformed the landscape itself. Silos loomed over farmhouses, registered Holsteins grazed in properly seeded pastures, and tractors carved contours in well-drained fields. Telephone lines hung between poles lining roadsides. Paved roads connected farms to villages with moviehouses, gas stations, and chain stores. Rural poverty, meanwhile, was not far away from tidy, scientific farms. One could see it in dilapidated houses, some occupied, some not, nudged against steep hillsides; in fields overrun with weeds; in rusted machinery strewn in yards; and in boarded-up stores in once-handsome village blocks. The increasing amount of land that had reverted to forest told the future of many marginal farms. In smaller villages, failed businesses signaled long-term slides. Rural New York appeared much like it does today.

Shifts in mood less tangible than changes in the landscape had also taken hold by the 1920s. But just as the land offered contradictory testimony about the nature of those changes, these attitudes admitted of no single direction. Consider the content of rural weekly newspapers. With daily newspapers from cities telling farmers and villagers of the wider world, good weeklies concentrated on their towns. Local political and social events received far more coverage than they had in the nineteenth century, as did state and national developments that affected rural people. The minutiae of rural communities got its due: "Local Citizens Provide Awnings," one headline ran. Local suicides made the front page alongside inspirational stories about noble older residents. Boosterism vied with panic. Articles about how urban merchants and consumers threatened to impoverish farmers shared pages with accounts of Old Home Weeks. Poorer weeklies avoided coverage of both the anxiety and the serenity. If lazy editors in the nineteenth century had relied on partisan boilerplate, those of the 1920s used the copy of any contributor: recipes and beauty hints from the Home Bureau, farming advice from the USDA, and harangues from organizations seeking to crush the menace of Communism. Weeklies at once suggested smug confidence and nervous dread; renewed localism and loss of local identity; control and disarray.

The paradoxical messages of the landscape and the weeklies reflected economic and political developments that had reshaped rural public life. New York suffered in the agricultural depression of the 1920s. Productive farmers tried to market more milk than dealers claimed they could sell. As milk prices dropped after World War I, taxes rose abruptly, reflecting postwar inflation and the cost of newer services. On the modern farms, men and women increasingly grew irritated with government's role in their plight. The state provided little assistance, these farm families believed, yet demanded additional revenue. Farmers who ignored pleas to expand their acreage or adopt new techniques in the 1910s did not face the loan repayments that dogged scientific farmers, but they still felt the pinch of rising taxes. Despite the economic problems of the 1920s, new products found eager rural consumers. Radios, inexpensive automobiles, tractors, and home appliances altered men's and women's patterns of work and leisure. They also brought rural families firmly into the new mass-consumption economy and clouded the future of small villages.[1]

The same social and economic changes that reshaped both rural and urban America in the 1920s thus swept through rural New York. Stereotypes of rural people, by then a minority of America's population, present them as crusaders for lost values against the onslaught of a new morality: men who left revival meetings to discuss future actions with fellow Ku Klux Klansmen; women who gathered to plot ways to keep liquor from the thirsty, new immigrants from American shores, and the evils of makeup, short hemlines, and loose habits from their daughters. Some rural New Yorkers did attend fundamentalist revivals and join the Klan, assault government's intrusions into the economy, and combat immigrants, Catholics, and liquor—as did many urban Americans. Yet they also recognized the state government as crucial to the future of New York agriculture, and launched new cooperative ventures. Progressive ideas about work and religion won converts in rural townships. The technical modernization of rural life had helped secure an esteemed older belief: mechanization of farms and homes made the boundaries between men's and women's work firmer than ever. The changing economic and political context opened new possibilities but exposed formerly shrouded conflicts.

In all of this seesawing, one development stood firm: men's and women's fulfillment of their roles no longer grounded nineteenth-century gender-based political attitudes and behavior. Earlier connections between gender roles and politics, between personal attributes and public life, had broken. New Yorkers—like other Americans—failed to agree on any other single way to imagine links between the public and private spheres. The center had in a sense fallen through, leaving obvious and uncomfortable disputes about politics and values; conflicts earlier assumed to be the work of a handful of malcontents. All bonds between the public and private spheres had not been sundered, but different links took the place of gender.

Indications of rural disaffection with the course of government in the 1920s were plain and wide-ranging. Most immediately, people complained of the wasteful spending of government at all levels. Such extravagance needlessly made taxes high and the prospects of New York agriculture bleak. Some rural men worked vainly to transfer control over certain policies back to their villages and townships. Rural men and women sensed the decline of civilization in Socialism, the decrease in respect for the law after Prohibition, and the content of motion pictures. Rural New Yorkers had soured on the idea of a more powerful and generous state government. They returned to trimming it back and exercising greater control in their communities, even while angling to secure further state assistance.

That government agencies spent too much money and enriched only the powerful again became the conventional wisdom in rural New York. Reeling from the effects of the agricultural depression, embittered by what seemed the unkept promises of a stronger state government, and without the soothing balm of partisanship, rural people lashed out at commissions and agencies more virulently than in the nineteenth century. A "prairie schooner" carrying farmers' petitions and the message "Let's go back to the ways of our fathers—Simplicity, Honesty, and Economy in Government" toured New York agricultural meetings in 1924. The Farm Bureau of Otsego County passed a resolution in 1920 favoring economy and the "abolition of many of the existing boards, commissioners, and departments and the concentration of the state business within as few department heads as possible." Individual work and character were "of no value when every man works by governmental regulations," according to the state Grange. The war-related agencies were a special target at first, but it seemed that state government in general had gotten out of hand.[2]

Men took the time to speak their minds more frequently than women. Denunciations of government came from all quarters—from polished spokesmen of the Dairymen's League and ordinary rural men alike. A letter from a farmer in Afton to his assemblyman captures the spirit of revised rural attitudes toward government following World War I. H. S. Linger had heard that the assembly was considering creating a new commission to fix the price of milk in much the same way as utility prices. He was not pleased:

> [I]t appears to me that as a Representative of a Agricultural district you should do all that is in your power to defeat such legislation. Comisions are nothing more or less than establishing dictators over the people. if the State or rather the Citty of New York wishes to fix prices for the farmers labor or

his prudct which is his labor then the prices of all other labor would have to be included such as Lawyers fees and Doctors fees and all classes of labor. . . . Cammishions are always Corrupt in unwise ways While some one might think they would do a grate service to the people they are only making things worse.

Linger's distrust of the government's ability to serve citizens in a positive way sprang from his views on the work of the wartime commissions. Those that determined food policies, he believed, were staffed by "profiters or Crooks" who deliberately set out to hurt farmers. Leaving milk prices to the market had its own problems—the small creameries fell under the assault of the large ones. But that course, he believed, was infinitely more desirable than permitting distant, unelected officials to exercise power.[3]

New Yorkers' crusade against high taxes and costly commissions extended to contests over the control of schools. Regaining local authority over the schools promised to both reduce taxes and return decisions to those who knew the children's needs best. Although the New York State Grange stood ready as always to support agricultural education, local Granges still debated the wisdom of agricultural and vocational programs in the high schools. "[S]elf-determination by the community concerned was established as the only safe conclusion" at a meeting of the Cattaraugus Grange in 1921. The Committee of Twenty-One—a group consisting of delegates of agricultural and educational organizations—kept alive the hope of some for consolidated rural schools. Members of local Granges, with other rural New Yorkers, still largely opposed any consolidation plan or regulations that would snatch decisions away from the districts.[4]

New Yorkers raised a series of questions related to their schools: whether rural districts should pay the same wages to teachers as urban ones, and whether teachers trained in Normal Schools were better qualified than others. The thread that connected the various fears and hopes for rural schools was politics—the conviction that "politics" ought not be part of the operation of schools. Local control would best guard against unwelcome intrusions of politics. An editor explained his reason for rejecting the idea of federal aid to education in 1926:

> Local government of our schools will be surrendered, in small part at first but eventually in whole. It will be a bureau at the national capital which will tell what students are to be taught, how they are to be taught, and, perhaps, who is to do the teaching. And it probably wouldn't be long until it gets into politics, and appointing teachers will be pretty much the same as naming postmasters—and as crooked.

Predictably, H. S. Linger concurred with this fear of outside control. "[I]f the State would take all of the arbirytary power away from the commishinor of education and bring it back to the people where it belongs . . . then the public schools will come back to a better standard."[4]

As in the nineteenth-century, "politics" was a curse hurled at policies New Yorkers distrusted. As they assumed that all new policies would be costly, their invective grew more heated by the 1920s.[5]

Other state programs excited the economizing urge of rural New Yorkers. Some argued that primary elections were too expensive and should be abolished. The costly and "farcical" system inspired "disgust" that was "almost universal and deep-rooted, hatred for it having been deliberately nursed from the moment it was put upon the statute books" according to the *Delaware Republican*. Other rural men doubted the usefulness of the Extension Service's bulletins and suggested that the state no longer pick up the tab for distributing them to farmers. The bulletins were "[n]ot studied very carefully, and not at all by a large percentage of people that receive them and I think it is a waste of money to distribute them," wrote one man. Others felt that farmers, unable to find help, worked themselves "half to death" and could spare no time to read. In a series of letters on the question, most farmers claimed to read the bulletins sometimes, but guessed that almost no one else did. The vast majority believed that for the sake of economy the state should stop providing what farmers might have considered a benefit to them. Once again, rural men called for lower taxes and fewer laws; complaining that, as one editorial summarized, "Too Many People Live Off Government."[6]

The proclivity to spend had to be arrested at the local as well as the state level. County appropriations for the Farm Bureau aroused debate at meetings of boards of supervisors. Indeed, Niagara County actually discontinued its support for the bureau, while others targeted the Home Bureau and Junior Extension programs. For one man, the Farm Bureau existed only to "give jobs to people to conduct them" and to "swell the taxes and appropriations to sustain them." He was probably not far off the mark in asserting that "25 years ago more or less a supervisor would not vote for such appropriations[; he] would never be elected by the people again." Otsego County supervisors grudgingly voted to fund the Junior Extension program for another year in 1920 over the criticisms of those who felt that farmers cared more about "lesser taxes and something to eat" than wholesome activities for children. Retrenchment also struck other county institutions. In Cortland, a newspaper noted with some glee that "[t]he Prison Commission again condemns our jail," calling it "a disgrace to the State of New York." Surely the Cortland supervisors could not be accused of needless spending.[7]

Government spent too much and needlessly complicated everyday life: rural men's complaints in the 1920s had a familiar sound. After a brief flirtation with larger government, rural men—local party operatives and ordinary farmers and villagers alike—returned to nineteenth-century truths. If anything, their protests had a sharper edge, as they now attacked agencies and policies that clearly affected the conduct of their public and private lives. But differences other than the shrillness of words separated nineteenth- from twentieth-century attacks on the state.

Men tried to accomplish their goals in the context of a new political tradition—one in which issues, promises, and personality governed tactics and language. An imaginative politics had given way to a literal politics, which altered relationships between citizens and government.

Pruning the functions of government required the cooperation of politicians, and now rural voters could learn more about candidates' positions than the citizens in the nineteenth century could. Keeping local Granges up-to-date on current legislation were the state and national Granges, the Farm Bureau, and the Dairymen's League, as well as groups dedicated to ending daylight saving time, restricting immigration, raising teachers' salaries, revamping the state's tax code, and building more and better roads, among other goals. Rural New Yorkers appreciated the importance of state government, even if some hoped to shorten its reach. A Norwich man wrote to his assemblyman in 1920 to learn what sort of system legislators used to keep track of bills. As there would be measures of "vital interest" to him coming up, he wanted to buy an indexed binder to help him order his files.[8]

Rural weekly newspapers added to voters' knowledge of pending legislation. Weeklies that relied on canned columns from outside sources like the USDA reprinted items about the political economy of agriculture as well as farming hints. More substantial newspapers devoted their columns to township, county, and state political developments. One could now follow the lines of debate on local issues and read accounts of arguments at county supervisors' meetings. In contrast to nineteenth-century reticence on such matters, local newspapers in the 1920s explained where and why new roads would be built and the controversies surrounding tax assessment decisions. Actions of township and county politicians became mainstays of country newspaper columns.[9]

When elections neared, newspapers—even partisan ones—now stressed the qualifications and experience of nominees, rather than the candidates' long partisanship and manly qualities. In commending an incumbent, one editor declared that "Congressman Clarke's idea of public office is that it comes with it a delegation to those he represents." The *Hancock Herald* heaped additional praise on the central New York legislator before his bid for re-election in 1924. "Congressman Clarke's bill establishing a national reforestation policy is a constructive achievement ranking with the Homestead law," the editor claimed. Candidates without legislative credentials had other broad qualifications: "Mr. Currie is a careful student of the science of government and well grounded in the fundamentals of the organic law of our commonwealth," ran a recommendation for an assembly candidate. Candidates tried to impress upon voters their knowledge of the needs of agricultural areas and their fidelity to their constituents.[10]

Adding substance to these expressions of devotion, candidates made promises about specific pieces of legislation. One newspaper detailed

gubernatorial candidate Theodore Roosevelt, Jr.'s, plans for using the
state government to help farmers market their produce in 1924; Roosevelt himself described the programs he would advance to return law and
order to New York. The Anti-Saloon League, the WCTU, agricultural
associations, and other organizations strained to extract pledges from
candidates—the Anti-Saloon League was an especially refined model of
persistence. The Yates County WCTU reminded their representatives in
1925 that, to Union members, "principle means more than party and
that no man or woman should get our votes that does not stand decidedly for temperance purity and the uplift of the oppressed." One editor
called for an accounting of legislative performance: "It's beginning to
look as though Congressmen seeking election will have to stutter when
they start telling what they did for the farmer." he surmised. Pat phrases
still fattened political speeches, but voters and interest groups sought
significant proposals on issues that worried them. Voting for a candidate
had once been an implicit bargain between men; by the 1920s it was a
result of explicit promises made by candidates to constituents.[11]

Yet demands for specific assurances produced a curious backlash
among both candidates and voters. One candidate promised to make no
promises: "I have not made a single promise to any individual or organized minority, from the time I first became a candidate for public office,
nor will I," his advertisement avowed. The would-be congressman
claimed that promises led to bad legislation and maintained that he
would somehow both be faithful to his constituents and let his conscience
be his guide. Commitments made in the heat of campaigns also fostered
voter cynicism. "Every newspaper, every campaign speaker and radio
should be enlisted to pin candidates down and make them show the
practicability or possibility of carrying out political promises which they
make in appealing for votes," an editor pronounced. Bored with promises, he demanded further specifics. Office-seekers struggled to seem
independent and to please important groups. Voters distrusted promises
and sought concrete guarantees and the same sort of accountability they
once felt they had from township and county office-holders.[12]

While candidates promised and proposed, campaigns ceased to command popular enthusiasm. Sometimes with regret and sometimes with
satisfaction, editors noted the passing of nineteenth-century male political traditions, as some newspapermen had since the turn of the century.
"You can't make a man believe now that the country is going to the dogs
the day after election if his favorite candidate doesn't win," one noted
with approval. Voters had "lost interest in old-time political methods" by
the 1920s and were "more for business than politics." Another article
described the 1922 tour of Republican candidates as involving "an appeal to judgment and reason through the presentation of cold truths."
Yet rural and urban newspapermen, together with political scientists,
fretted about low voter turnout and the lack of interest in politics. As
government tangibly affected everyday life and campaigns more directly

addressed certain complicated policy questions, fewer people bothered to participate. Rural editors, like those in cities, felt it necessary to urge all voters, regardless of party, to get out and vote. Vote—"or shut up!"—one admonished.[13]

Despite the emphasis on performance and pledges, descriptions of nominees' personal characteristics had hardly disappeared. But these, too, had assumed new forms. Editors pointed to candidates' pleasing personalities rather than their manly (or womanly) traits and focused chiefly on the nominees for the major offices. Herbert B. Leary, an assembly candidate, was a "practical up-to-date farmer who has made a careful study of farm conditions." But he was also "a brilliant young man" and one of "fine appearance." While baldly put, this description paled in contrast to those of presidential aspirants. Writers pulled out the stops in depicting these men: the recommendations combined nineteenth-century ideas about character and personal example with twentieth-century attention to performance in office. One article related stories about the Coolidge family's penchant for hard work, unpretentiously accomplished. Such traits made Calvin Coolidge a superior president. He did not seek to "curry favor with the people and with Congress"; instead, he let his actions after Warren Harding's death illustrate that he was a man gifted with "a keen intelligence, a grasp of economic laws, an impressive sense of the right, and a calm courage that instantly created confidence in his ability, his wisdom and his integrity." He was, for another writer, "a safe, well-balanced official" who understood the responsibilities of the Presidency and met them "squarely and without excitement or prejudice." Editors continued to depict those who sought the highest offices as men who bore lightly their intelligence and sterling character. Sheriffs, assemblymen, supervisors, and congressmen, however, less frequently shared the traits formerly granted to all partisan public figures.[14]

Newspapermen (and the candidates themselves) claimed that nominees for high office embodied many fine traits, but they did not summarize these characteristics with the word "manhood." More men than women may have possessed the requisite character, but women were not by nature excluded, nor did politics provide a space to exhibit true manhood. Just as depictions of manly attributes no longer graced the pages of rural weeklies, the men and women who wrote to politicians had ceased making claims on the basis of their admirable representation of their gender roles. Few job letters made their way to one assemblyman, Bert Lord, who served in the 1910s and 1920s—civil service rules had taken care of that. Neither did requests for advice on knotty personal questions. Politicians at this level represented their constituents, no more or less; they were not necessarily wiser than voters or sources of general good judgment. Thus numerous letters on specific pieces of legislation arrived at Lord's office. These letters typically indicated the name and number of the bill in question and stated the authors' views. Writers knew these specifics and the exact content of bills because of newspaper coverage of legislation. Along with keeping rural residents posted on new bills, interest groups also provided forms for "personally" written letters.[15]

Given the ways politicians' roles, voters' expectations, and the transmission of political news had changed, it is not surprising that men's and women's letters had become indistinguishable. One woman's letter to Lord furnishes a good example of the waning of claims based on gender in political correspondence:

> I learned three things from talking to you yesterday afternoon. 1. You don't like long letters such as I have been writing to you. 2. You don't like women's welfare organizations. 3. You do like to have the opinions of responsible state officers about your bills.
>
> *On these points I have to say the following.*
>
> 1. I will try to make this short. 2. I enclose a list of organizations behind these bills and I don't know of any organization of men, women, or children opposed to them. 3. Fiscal Supervisor Utter and Secretary Johnson of the State Board of Charities have agreed to tell you what a good thing you have done introducing these bills, and how fine it would be if you would help to get them reported out and passed by the legislature at the earliest possible moment.

Feminine helplessness and self-sacrifice had no place in political requests made by women; neither men or women bothered to lard their letters with tributes to the politician's stature and sagacity. Friendship was the outcome of personal relationships, not of votes cast on election days.[16]

Politics mattered more to rural men and women in the 1920s, but it also mattered less. The actions of government directly touched most rural people's lives, but voters were less likely to participate in formal politics. If anything, expressions of cynicism mounted. Never trusting politicians, voters asked for more specifics now that government actually did things that directly affected their well-being. Yet specific promises seemed to only increase disillusionment with government and politicians. Discussions of precise issues and policies that reduced politics to a relatively narrow and technical matter diminished the capacity of formal politics to address broad questions that still greatly engaged voters: for example, the social and economic direction of the nation and the place of moral teachings in public life. Enthusiasm seemed out of place in a politics conducted without the orotund rhetoric of the nineteenth century. So did the notion that gender roles should be honored in public life. Ideas about gender no longer connected rural people's public and private lives; economic interests, and, sometimes, nominees' personalities, did. Rural people came to terms with modern politics, but also lost interest.

If gender roles no longer seemed relevant to the conduct of politics, it did not follow that women had a greater place in public life. To the extent that rural politics turned on matters of money, it remained the province of men who demanded frugality. Republican women at the state and national level mixed Progressive-era housekeeping rhetoric with party politics—"[W]omen want the government to be managed as simply and as inexpensively as they manage their own homes," an ad assured. But while the notion that women's knowledge of the home earned them a say in social policies, the idea did not effortlessly transfer to budgets, expenditures, and taxes. Winning the vote had hardly dispelled stereotypes: "Now that America has two women in the diplomatic service, we suppose there will be no danger of secret meetings." Moreover, while the literal politics of issues, pledges, and interest groups did not automatically exclude women, they were hard to find. A few rose in party politics after winning the vote: in state agencies where college-educated women used their expertise gained as reformers and social workers and as powers behind male politicians. Others appeared, as candidates of minority parties and county and township office-holders. In all, it seems the separation of gender from politics served to enhance men's grip on formal political power.[17]

But women, along with men, still participated in politics from outside of the parties. Women pursued social and economic goals through interest groups, joined by men who saw the advantages of working for their ends while bypassing the weakened parties. Many groups courted rural support on myriad issues: the agricultural economy, Communism, and the observance of moral customs, among others. On such issues, even more than with attitudes about politics, contradictions ruled the day. Despite the decided rural fondness for economy, individuals and organizations sought state aid. While decrying modernist tendencies, men and women used new technologies to reach their political goals. In the absence of the appearance of cultural agreement, some strained to create homogeneity. Modern life had its appeals, but it also inspired attempts to combat it.

As nineteenth-century male assumptions about public life had become debatable points by the 1920s, rural New Yorkers failed to discover substitutes for partisan politics and economical government that could attain substantial agreement. Differences of opinion cut across gender lines. Few men or women would have been willing to return to the small government of the nineteenth century, but devotion to economy remained a rural concern in the 1920s. In 1933, local Granges would again turn to cutting the salaries of public officials as the first step in combatting the Depression. "[E]xtravagances are practiced in the matter of the governmental administration of our county officers inordinately and unnecessarily augmenting the tax burdens of our County," one Grange claimed. For some, nineteenth-century wisdom held, even in the Great Depression.[18]

Like most people, then as now, rural New Yorkers were no slaves to consistency. When the time came, few counties spurned federal money for local projects, and New York farmers did not reject price supports for dairy products. In the 1920s, New Yorkers remained loyal to certain programs that had become fixtures of rural life: rural free delivery and parcel post, and state support for roads, education, and public health. The *Carthage Republican* writer who rejected federal aid to education impeccably expressed the tension between rural townships, need for fiscal support and their fear of outside control. An education agency in Washington would "mean more pork-barrel grabbing" and "cripple self-government by towns and counties." Yet rural New Yorkers should tell their representatives "they are willing to accept federal aid for their highways, but they prefer to have Uncle Sam let the present school system alone." Rural residents should be able to pick and choose.[19]

While seeking the state's assistance, rural organizations searched for ways to protect themselves from the market's vagaries. The Grange had implemented various marketing and purchasing cooperatives since its founding; none, however, had achieved much success. In 1917, the state Grange organized the Grange Exchange, a statewide group that purchased seed, animal feed matching Cornell-approved formulas, coal, and household goods. This arrangement, too, ran into difficulties—including the opposition of merchants and suppliers. To get around these problems, the Exchange's managers opted to produce their own feed. This step, however, required more money than the Grange had at its disposal. The Grange looked to other agricultural organizations for help; the Grange League Federation (G.L.F.), a purchasing cooperative, was the result. Taking its name from the cooperating organizations, the Grange, the Dairymen's League, and the New York State Farm Bureau Federation, the G.L.F. allowed any farmer to join by purchasing stock. The cooperative manufactured as well as sold farm products. Its organizers utilized available state assistance: the Extension Service offered advice and aid in raising subscriptions. In bringing together the state's largest agricultural and educational organizations and in having the cooperative run by professional managers, the G.L.F. was a model Progressive organization.[20]

Rural groups hoped that modern advertising, along with modern management and organization, would ease economic distress. Feeling that dairymen themselves deserved some of the blame, an officer of the Dairymen's League focused his attention on inconsistent farmers. "As a rule the farmer who delivers his milk at the station and comes back with five pounds of oleo, howls the loudest because milk is so low." The League also assessed its members a fee to pay for advertising campaigns to persuade consumers to drink more milk. Everyone needed to drink a pint a day, admen declared. Drinking milk promoted patriotism, in another ad: "More milk must be consumed if we are to have a healthier and a better citizenry." Drawing on the talents of Extension Service home economists, ads extolled milk's low cost and nutritional value.[21]

Village boards of trade and newspapermen advertised their towns in order to attract businesses and maintain local morale. One pamphlet touted the virtues of Mayville in Chautauqua County. "Do you throw away money in the city on high rents, high assessed valuations, high labor turnover?" it asked. From there it explained why "far-sighted industrial leaders" located their factories in villages. Along with pleasant scenery, good roads, and low wages, Mayville offered its people as an inducement, "native born whites or descendants of northern European countries." Newspapermen, meanwhile, whose trade had long included village boosting, stepped up their efforts. One assured his readers that businessmen never selected "a town that is dead" when looking for sites, and used market metaphors to spur villagers to pull together. "Many people are apt to overlook the fact that they are stockholders in their town and that their fortune is bound up with those of the community as a whole." "We Are For Edmeston and Otsego County—Are You?" ran a newspaper masthead, formerly the space for declarations of partisan faith. Using advertising, organization, and tried-and-true boosting, local elites labored to increase their villages' chances for survival.[22]

Yet such efforts—even boosting—pointed to tensions within rural communities. Newspaper editors told the inspiring stories of men who left small villages to find wealth and fame but remained true to their roots. " 'I think a man's boyhood town holds first place in his affections no matter where he may live later,' " a weekly quoted a former Carthage resident. The editor nonetheless cautioned villagers to stay put—and perhaps to forgo the success that he had earlier lauded. "[F]or your own piece of mind—be content with the opportunities Carthage is offering you." The successes of some village natives who left might bring indirect renown, but few villages could afford a further population drain. At once traitors and paragons of achievement, ex-residents were best quoted when fondly recalling their former homes.[23]

If boosterism and advertising purveyed mixed messages, they were also inadequate without additional assistance. Neither dairymen nor village boosters wanted to part with Progressive-era programs, either funding for good roads or regulations that removed competitors of dairy products from grocers' shelves. Rural representatives pointed to their efforts to secure legislation that helped farmers and rural communities, such as federal rules against the sale of adulterated milk. Rural New Yorkers called for economy and expanded programs, free markets and protection from their instabilities, and government aid and local control.[24]

Combining qualms about overweening state power and demands for political action, rural men and women found some new uses for government. Just as men had not discarded an interest in frugal government, women had not suddenly abandoned nineteenth-century concerns about community morals. Activist women took conspicuous part in campaigns to rid their towns of new and old specimens of vice. Granges, DAR and WCTU chapters, and other clubs encouraged strict enforcement of Prohibition and debated the necessity of censoring movies. A north-country WCTU held a "Victory Meeting" in 1926 and concluded that, "[P]oorly as the law had been enforced, great benefits have been realized. Homes, children, churches and banks all admit [Prohibition] being the direct cause." Clubwomen in Westfield urged their village trustees to "investigate the source of liquor traffic among young boys." Rural organizations responded to the prodding of various state groups and sent petitions urging their representatives to enforce and maintain Prohibition legislation. The state Grange compared the passage of Prohibition with the abolition of slavery, and the Wyoming County chapter hoped the Grange would now move against cigarettes, a remaining "menace to the physical and moral health of our young people." The Monday Club of Salem discussed the "motion picture problem" in 1923. Its members favored better selection without outright censorship and rented proper films for their local theater. Uncertain about the state of local morality, groups turned to legal action to accomplish what communities could no longer assume.[25]

Such actions were commonly infused with a sense of dread about the future of the nation. A WCTU chapter resolved in September of 1928 that the "coming presidential election is the most critical since the election of Abraham Lincoln and the overthrow of slavery, for the election of Alfred E. Smith to the presidency of the United States would jeopardize all that has been accomplished by the temperance people for the past nearly 100 yrs." In 1926, the members of the Cortland County DAR found inspiration in a "call to the need of unity and likemindedness in women for personal sincerity and purity against each & every menace of the present." Where agreement on values no longer seemed to exist, these women asked for its creation and enforcement. Just as boosters implored towns to hold together through another period of emigration, this DAR chapter hoped for unanimity while values seemed in doubt.[26]

Nowhere was this tendency to assert the existence of agreement plainer than in rural New Yorkers' embrace of anti-Communism. Rural people hardly held a monopoly on Red-baiting, but "Socialists," "Communists," and "Reds" represented all that rural men and women saw as dangerous and wrongheaded about the twentieth century. For people who saw the eight-hour day as a pernicious doctrine, Socialists could only be seen as men who discredited the very idea of work. "I.W.W." (International Workers of the World), according to one newspaper, stood for "I Won't Work." For men unhappy with the performance of government agencies, the notion that the government should run basic industries seemed ludicrous. For women seeking to "Americanize" the growing number of southern and eastern European immigrants in rural towns, "foreign doctrines" represented the chief evil to be fought. The pious sensed an attack on Christian faith. Only recently having embraced national patriotism in obvious ways, rural residents disapproved of intimations of anti-Americanism. As an apparent threat to work, religion, and rural values, Socialism barely deserved a hearing.[27]

Yet rural people's attitudes on this matter were as splintered as their thoughts on politics and government. Should Socialists elected by their districts be allowed to sit in the state legislature? Some cadidates vowed to keep Socialists out of the assembly if elected. Some editors held that the Socialists should be seated—the voters' decision was inviolable—but immigration to the United States ought to be curbed. The Allegany and Clinton County Granges called for the deportation—or even death—of people who supported "Socialism, Anarchism, Internationalism, [or] Bolshevism." The few letters that constituents wrote to Assemblyman Bert Lord on the subject ran against the Socialists: "I, myself, have no use for a traitor to the country," concluded one. But mild as well as inflammatory stories appeared in newspapers. One related the experiences of Socialist speakers in Cortland—"good talkers" who got "a respectful hearing." The speeches were an occasion for gentle partisan ribbing: "When they lambasted the [Wilson] administration, the Republicans and Socialists cheered. When they paid their respects to the Republican party, the Democrats and Socialists applauded." When a speaker turned to "scoring" Cortland's Republican assemblyman, "A chap in the crowd left, saying: 'Gosh, that fellow's a Democrat.' " While it is difficult to detect pro-Socialist sentiment in the 1920s, battling a "Red menace" seemed a less than pressing concern in rural New York.[28]

Without searching too long or too hard, one can find ample evidence that rural New Yorkers believed that their world had grown distressingly inexplicable and strange. In writing to representatives about "[g]etting rid of the five undesirable socialists," in clamoring for unity and "likemindedness," and in searching for ways to enforce the moral order, some rural residents appeared to be taking aim at changes in twentieth-century life that brought formerly concealed conflicts to the surface. A local correspondent for the *Cortland Democrat* simply threw up his hands: "This old world of ours seems upside down, everybody has a scheme for righting it. Some thought woman suffrage would solve all problems, others thought prohibition, while some think that militarism with big armies and navies, and yet we are no nearer the solution as how to right things." Others' failures did not leave him completely bereft of suggestions, however: "Let us down the profiteers first and then try religion." But for all the complaints and wringing of hands, indications that New Yorkers adjusted smoothly, even cheerfully, to modern developments were as numerous as the signs of pained disorientation. While singling out certain forms of modernism for attack, rural New Yorkers adopted new attitudes toward work and faith. In making these adjustments, they redefined the boundaries between their public and private lives.[29]

New Yorkers had not rejected the notion that hard work brought moral if not material rewards. But, slowly adopting the Progressives' arguments about the benefits of leisure, farm families packed their cars and drove off on summer vacations. Camping in state parks and staying with relatives, some rural New Yorkers had come to see vacations as pleasant relaxation, not as the morally questionable custom of lazy city people. What rural people considered entertainment had also changed. Grangers in the late nineteenth century, for example, regarded discussions of philosophical questions, agriculture, and religion—along with eating—as the entertainment portion of their meetings. By the 1920s, Grangers themselves composed few such talks; when they occured, they were given by representatives of the Farm or Home Bureau. The lure of a meal still enticed Patrons to meetings, but now they listened to radios and Victrolas, held contests (needle-threading, for example), played cards, and held dances. Salesmen stopped by to pitch house siding; power company representatives showed movies. The Granges survived the 1920s—some even prospered. But it was a different kind of organization. The Patrons' meetings testified to a new understanding of amusement, one at odds with that held by their fathers and mothers. For the earlier generation, even pleasure was work; a notion foreign to their children.[30]

Some forms of entertainment (commercial dance halls, for example) still raised eyebrows in rural communities. But perhaps because they combined work and leisure, other twentieth-century innovations, such as automobiles and radios, enjoyed wide acceptance. Cars soon became an essential part of rural life. While less useful than horses in mud and snow, cars helped in the conduct of farming and facilitated visits among scattered neighbors and relatives. An editor was heartened to see that rural people "welcom[ed], instead of discourag[ed]" radios, the "newest and greatest means of communication." The radio was useful as well as fun. It "not only brings pleasure, it brings all sections of the United States into closer touch with each other: It brings additional education to the young people of every home in which it is installed; it carries the gospel of good citizenship as well as the gospel of Christ to shut ins and those in far away places who cannot get to church."[31]

Signs that life seemed less severe cropped up in other contexts as well. Notices of members' deaths written up by voluntary organizations afford a case in point. Nineteenth-century memorials almost uniformly treated death as a release from life's problems. A poem written by a Granger in 1887 upon a member's death concluded that "The Reaper" had freed the woman "from the days of weary suffering, and nights of restlessness." Death also served a stern warning to the living: " 'Be ye also ready,' " ended another tribute. For the writers of these memorials in the 1920s, the deceased had not really died; rather, he or she had merely "gone away." "How comforting to know / We do not lose them / When our loved ones go," wrote a member of a DAR chapter in 1928. Assuming that no new interest in spiritualism had developed among the women of the DAR, changes in the memorials can be read as evidence of a more positive view of life's trials, as well as of a waning of the earlier strict and pervasive Christian heritage.[32]

Evidence of such moderation in Protestant teaching appeared in rural acceptance of another Progressive idea—the consolidated church. As the number of people living in rural townships continued to decline in the 1920s, additional congregations closed their churches. The members of the mainline Protestant congregations gradually turned their churches into community social centers. Ladies' Aid Societies raised money to expand kitchens and build meeting rooms. Youth groups made use of these facilities, as did other community organizations. Women's groups also sponsored movies (again of the "right kind") that were open to the public. While the average Protestant congregation did not fulfill the expansive objectives of community unification and moral regeneration reformers hoped for, these congregations demonstrated greater local involvement than they had in the nineteenth century. The social gospel had arrived.[33]

Two other developments in rural religion had greater long-term importance. The first—the growth and prosperity of Catholic churches—occurred as families of southern and eastern European backgrounds moved in greater numbers to occupy farms given up by the native-born. Their arrival introduced greater diversity to rural towns, but had little immediate political impact.[34] More relevant to rural politics was the appearance of the large and elaborate revival meeting. These were not the kind of community events that Progressives had in mind, but revivals brought Protestant believers together as nothing else did. Revivals replaced partisan campaigns as community rituals and provided sustenance for men and women set to do battle with those who would dismiss traditional values.

Protestant revivals had never really disappeared from rural religion. In addition to the great wave in the early nineteenth century, all the evangelically inclined congregations sponsored them on an almost regular basis through the end of that century. But the spectacular revivals waited until the twentieth century. Pioneering the use of radio and mass marketing techniques in forming public opinion—tactics later employed by politicians—individual evangelists gained national fame. A look at an early revival—a "tabernacle meeting" in Delhi in 1915—illustrates some of the ways religious enthusiasm reflected and replaced political campaigns.[35]

Weeks in advance, a local newspaper introduced Luther Peacock, the evangelist and assistant to the famous Billy Sunday. When the meetings commenced, Peacock spoke, not to all the village at once, but to groups of townspeople. He, like other evangelists, set special nights aside for women, men, fraternal organizations, young people, and old people. Suffragists had their own meeting, as did members of the Village Improvement Society. Peacock excelled at short, quotable statements that could be easily remembered and reprinted. "God has no place for loafers," he reminded his listeners. His sloganeering and addresses to specific groups with presumably separate needs—interest groups of a sort—paralleled trends in modern politics. By creating a sense of excitement and involving large numbers of citizens, he occupied the void left by the subsidence of partisan politics. Villagers encouraged neighbors to turn out, as they had for elections. Peacock enjoyed press coverage that politicians might have envied. Just as newspapers had reprinted the full speeches of nineteenth-century politicians, Peacock's sermons nearly filled entire pages. Townspeople turned out for the meetings and were not disappointed. As political rhetoric had once provided an imaginative vision of a well-ordered society, evangelical Protestantism now created a future in which justice was served, in heaven and on earth. Such a claim would have been too extravagant for an ordinary church service, but it fit the mood of a mass meeting.[36]

If politics no longer reminded men and women of their proper roles, evangelical religion filled the gap. True religion required the traits of manhood, in much the same way that partisanship had. Bible study, Peacock claimed, "produces a virility, a ruggedness of character, an altruistic spirit, a hopeful temper, a power of patience and endurance, a fearlessness, a stability of manhood that nothing else gives." Not forgetting the ladies, he commanded village women to teach the Bible to their children. He told them of the blessings of motherhood ("God wanted us to honor motherhood") and women's duty to sacrifice for their families. Fulfillment of gender roles might not constitute a claim for political favors, but it satisfied God's plan.[37]

It was fitting that religion—traditionally considered a "private" matter—would have reminded men and women about their proper roles and supplied some of the public ritual that partisan politics used to provide. It was emblematic of changes in how rural people drew distinctions between the public and private spheres. Some of the bitterest and most divisive disputes of the 1920s, such as those over gender roles and other elements of community morality, were conducted outside of partisan politics. If these debates touched on formal politics at all, it was through interest groups. In the nineteenth century, battles about woman's place were joined, in part, in politics—in disputes over woman suffrage and in the rhetoric of manhood in partisan politics. Such contests were now waged outside of politics—in homes, workplaces, and the mass media—not in the increasingly stiff and formal world of promises and legislation. Men's and women's roles became more sharply divided in the 1920s, yet more open to question. But the links that bound these debates to public life had broken.

Only the most isolated rural resident could have been oblivious to the furore over the "new woman" of the 1920s. Held up as a model, damned as a symptom of moral decay, or merely scrutinized as a curiousity, this departure from nineteenth-century womanhood was the subject of magazine articles, novels, movies, and sermons. Even if flappers or glamorous, independent women preferred cities to farms or sleepy villages, rural New Yorkers could hardly have missed the news about women who challenged traditional notions of woman's place and sexual morality. If rural women themselves did not blatantly challenge sexual and gender constraints, there are hints that they did so in smaller ways. Scraps of negative evidence suggest some dissension, such as a newspaper article warning of the dire consequences awaiting women who put work before children.[38]

On the more positive side, the conflicts in Jennette Howell Deal Prior's marriage hint at a stirring of dissatisfaction with some of the tenets of traditional womanhood. Jennette, a teacher, married Lewis Prior in the 1910s when she was in her early thirties and moved to her husband's farm. The life of a farm wife was isolating for a woman who had grown accustomed to the camaraderie of village female organizations and the satisfactions and frustrations of her work. But she abandoned teaching— and a whole range of voluntary activities—to take care of his two sons, their newborn daughter, and a staggering load of farm chores. As her daughter reached young womanhood and her troublesome stepsons gained independence, she again joined church and women's societies. Despite some signs of prosperity—they purchased a car in 1922 and took vacations—the Priors suffered financial setbacks, worsened by Lewis' frequent illnesses. Jennette resumed teaching in 1922 for reasons she did not reveal. She did complain, however, about problems in juggling home and job: "School went well," she reported, "but of course it is hard to do so much at home and teach, too." She resolved this tension in 1926 by boarding in a village near her school during the week and returning home on weekends. Was boarding a matter of adding to the family's finances as best she could? Or was it a way to regain some independence and to reduce strife at home? She did not explain her decision, but she did note that "Lewis and I have quarreled again. I wish there was some way to settle our troubles but I can't see any way out but death." That same day she renewed her teaching contract.[39]

Too much could be made of such evidence. But it does indicate some friction concerning women's roles. Discord ensued not only as the "new woman" achieved notoriety, but also as household and agricultural technologies allowed for greater separation of rural men's and women's work. Nineteenth-century farm wives made butter and sold eggs, as women had done for generations. These tasks took up a good deal of farm women's time, and the energy they invested provided regular income for their families. By the twentieth century, chicken farming had become a major industry and an attractive alternative to dairying. Large creameries manufactured butter. As these changes occurred, men, rather than women, ran the chicken farms and sold cream to, and worked in, the factories.

Women, however, did not gain new idle hours. Few women surveyed in 1929 by social scientists with the New York State College of Home Economics claimed to enjoy more than one hour of "free time" each day. Farm and home chores remained, while new tasks, such as the shopping formerly done by men on trips to town, became women's responsibility. Their husbands might join them on the year's major excursion to a large city, but otherwise farm women did the day-to-day purchasing for their families. Shopping became a larger chore, as women now purchased many of the items they once had produced themselves, such as bread and canned food. Women increasingly accomplished all of their chores alone—as they no longer had the household help that they once received from their husbands, and hired girls became harder to find. Machinery powered by electricity or gasoline engines allowed women to finish their work alone: washing machines, for example, removed some of the hard labor that made washdays dreaded events in the nineteenth century. Thus women still helped with farm chores, and some worked on a seasonal basis in nearby vegetable canneries. But keeping a home—a task that required study and dedication—was women's duty alone.[40]

Twentieth-century agriculture required the same careful attention from men. Agricultural reformers had claimed for decades that successful farming demanded that the farmer develop the skills of a businessman and scientist in addition to hard work. By the 1920s, their words seem to have reached an increasing number of rural men. New machinery both lightened and complicated the farmers' work; paying off equipment loans required closer attention to the question of what their profits really were. Because of the higher investments involved, errors in calculations about what crops or techniques would prove profitable were less easily forgiven. Like homemaking, farming demanded a high level of expertise if done well; farmers and their wives crossed each others' boundaries less frequently.[41]

However complex their work, twentieth-century culture glorified neither men's nor women's labors. Their duties required effort and study, not good character or the proper set of personal traits, to be performed well. Farming was a business; it did not presuppose a man's special relationship to the land or a particular devotion to independence and hard work. The demands of motherhood called for certain skills, but they, too, could be learned and were not a natural part of every woman's character. The nineteenth-century notions of women's moral superiority and farmers' special contributions to the nation had ceased to be persuasive in an urban society in which expertise and personality, not character, were the ruling fictions. Rural men and women did not attempt to block these changes in values; many cooperated in bringing them about.[42]

While the ideal and reality of domesticity remained every bit as pervasive throughout the 1920s, it had lost its place in public life. Technological changes had made the practice of domesticity open to more women who now even studied the proper techniques for running homes and raising children. But as politics became a matter of public service—a notion women had argued for—women's piety and moral stature had no more place in political life than male friendship and loyalty. Changes in the cultural standard of the ideal woman in the 1920s—the "new" woman who worked outside of the home and threw off the constraints of nineteenth-century propriety—helped attenuate a distinctive set of political expectations held by women. By the 1920s, domesticity was reduced to a private occupation, not a collection of admirable cultural attributes.

Understanding how domesticity came to be confined to the home helps account for why single-sex organizations brought so little new influence to rural women. If anything, rural women were organized more than ever before in the 1920s—a Home Bureau agent imagined that "rural women of the state, the first to federate, are already being considered as a powerful factor by legislative agencies and others." In villages and in the countryside, women's groups paid increasing attention to the needs of their communities. Their activities, however, had no broader purpose than serving hot lunches or planting trees. They were simply good deeds; not, as in the nineteenth century, expressions of a moral mission or intent to limit men's behavior. However confining, domesticity had provided wider reasons for even the smallest tasks women performed for their communities in the nineteenth century. Without this, men and women alike saw women's community projects as useful services, but services that lacked a larger agenda. In rural New York, separatism was a less useful strategy for gaining public influence than the vote.[43]

Even if domesticity had retained a moral edge, it was unlikely that its public authority could have endured in the political context of the 1920s. In the conventional wisdom of the time—recited to farmers and merchants, as well as to politically active women—lean and efficient organization held the key to political and financial success. Applied to politics, this dictum generated organizations with professional staffs to watch over everything from membership to legislative agendas. Concentrating resources at the state and national offices made sense in light of the growing importance of lawmakers and agencies at these levels. If one wanted Prohibition enforced, county sheriffs mattered, but state laws and federal agents mattered more. But this focus on state and national politics gave women's groups (like those of farmers and other men) a much more pronounced top-down flavor in the 1920s. Village female societies in the late nineteenth century mixed self-direction with action at the state level: even while bypassing their towns, they chose their own outside projects. By contrast, twentieth-century national or state organizations had a far greater hand in determining suitable projects and the public positions local affiliates should take. Some groups responded by refraining from political activities; others went on as always, dutifully raising money, holding socials, discussing problems, and sipping tea. However local groups reacted, the more hierarchical organizations of the 1920s produced a group of women of real stature in state and national politics. But the local groups appeared to become observers rather than participants, organized publics mobilized by larger associations. One cannot gauge the vitality of voluntary societies as easily as one can measure political interest by counting the number of voters who turned out for elections. Yet it seems that both voters and members of organizations had turned away from active participation in public affairs.[44]

Gender-based understandings of the purpose of government and politics had waned by the 1920s in rural New York. Successful politicians were people who represented accurately the wishes of their constituents, not men of exceptional wisdom and manly virtue. Neither men nor women made requests of public figures by pointing to their own admirable manhood or womanhood. Women gained the right to participate in what had been an exclusively male ritual, while men adopted the interest-group tactics that activist women had practiced. Village boosters now encouraged women's involvement in community projects. Both men and women repeated the notion that good citizens made choices in voting booths on the basis of reason and interests—with some adding Protestant convictions. Party loyalty retained a hereditary quality, but neither men nor women publicly proclaimed the desirability of party loyalty. Rural New Yorkers might have still admired personal virtue and given some men and women public acclaim. But no one assumed that there was a necessary connection between personal righteousness and reward with a political office or favor.

Manhood and womanhood became private matters defined and contested outside of politics, not traits represented in public life. In the nineteenth century, gender rules were clearly defined ideas—there was no shortage of tracts explaining what the proper traits of men and women were. But in rural New York, gender roles remained porous in practice. Especially on farms, there was simply too much work to be done to demand that men and women always stand at their proper stations. New Yorkers' public life paid tribute to popular ideas about the separate natures of men and women. Electoral politics, the sphere limited to men, supplied an imaginative world where all men were equal, where those with the greatest virtues received their just reward, and where the traits of manhood were defined and reinforced. Women's politics occupied a space apart from voting and office-holding. Through their groups and direct pressure on lawmakers, organized women sought to bring the female characteristics of piety and moral righteousness to public life.

The links between these personal traits and public life weakened in the twentieth century. Electoral politics, ideally, proceeded without reference to personal characteristics—intelligence and expertise, things that one learned, were said to matter more in public life. Discussions of material interests were allowable, even encouraged, in choosing office-holders; talk about friendship and loyalty were not. Strict separation of the sexes was an idea that had grown unfashionable. Women did not have to uphold a stricter standard of morality, according to the conventional wisdom of the 1920s; they were not in essence different from men. While women could participate in electoral politics on an equal footing with men, however, they apparently lacked the necessary expertise and proper public presence to hold office. Since women and men did not have separate natures, there were few reasons for women to support other women's efforts to gain office. The waning of the nineteenth-

century myth of womanhood united by domestic concerns meant that
women's organizations could no longer pretend that they commanded a
large, unified female constituency. In the end, men held public power
perhaps more firmly than before.

By the 1920s, rural men and women paid attention to state and national issues and expected political representation and benefits—or
tuned out formal politics completely. These were changes in political
ideas and behavior that the state government, along with minor local
politicians, had pushed forward. When they arrived in rural New York,
farmers, local partisan operatives, and organized women alike depended
increasingly on political direction from the state or from organizations
that were nationwide in scope. Each organization argued for a specific
political agenda, often directly contrary to that of another group, which
lent a chaotic quality to 1920s politics. Despite the clamor of rival voices,
rural politics had, in another sense, become more homogeneous. All
groups, male or female, farm or village, used (or were used by) hierarchical organizations to gain the attention of state or federal officials. Rural
groups now shared tactics, strategies, expectations, and a political language, even if their goals diverged.

Neither men nor women gained the ability to control the changes over-
taking their communities as a result of this new relationship between
citizens and government. Rural New Yorkers today remain as dependent
on—and sometimes as angry with—the state as they were in the 1920s.
Rivalries among declining townships for state prisons are an example of
continued dependency. The easy political demand for longer sentences
for criminals has put upstate towns into competition with each other to
become the next Attica. In Allegany County, for example, dead last in
per capita income among New York's fifty-two counties, local political
leaders have worked energetically to bring a prison to one of their towns.
The supervisor from Friendship has traveled to Albany to impress directly upon the authorities her town's suitability for a state prison. Despite the inconveniences that jails located in out-of-the-way places cause
for prisoners' families, leaders of rural townships see prisons as clean
industries that bring jobs. Winning state institutions remains a crucial
strategy for achieving economic stability, especially in poor rural areas.[45]

Other Allegany citizens have organized to prevent the construction of
a less welcome state institution—a low-level nuclear waste dump. Even
hard times have failed to make nuclear or toxic waste facilities attractive.
When the state government announced that three of the five finalists for
New York's dump were in Allegany, residents held mass meetings,
posted antinuclear signs on their houses, and tried to persuade Governor Mario Cuomo's administration to put the waste anywhere but
Allegany County. Arguments against an Allegany site combine older and
newer approaches to politics. They include traditional city-bashing (nuclear waste is produced in urban and suburban areas), appeals to gender

(the dump would pose a threat to mothers and babies), populism (Allegany has been picked on because it is sparsely populated and poor), history (an abolitionist past), and calls to serve the public good (the county supplies milk, which could be contaminated, to the entire state). Allegany residents also add newer appeals to expertise (a geologist has determined that a fault line runs through the county). The prospect of having a dump in their county has turned Allegany citizens into opponents of nuclear technologies in general. The cases of prisons and dumps point to how developments outside of rural communities—new technologies and punitive methods of dealing with crime—have changed even remote rural places. They also highlight continuities, especially the sad economic circumstances and ambivalence toward government in rural New York politics.

Elsewhere in New York, some townships almost prospered during the 1980s as economically comfortable urbanites opened inns and purchased and restored houses. Older village industries—cheese factories or mop wringer plants—struggled to hang on while others failed. Regional hospitals brought stability to other villages; nearby state parks benefited still others. Until the cutbacks of the Reagan Administration, support payments assisted owners of large farms. Other farmers stayed afloat by strictly following consumer fads—fresh herbs, goat cheese, and the like. But tottering silos, rusted vintage tractors littering yards, and kitchen appliances on porches of rundown houses suggest that neither science nor market savvy provided a universal solution in a depressed economy. Villagers mutter about the hill people who collect welfare but live in shacks wired to satellite dishes (the rural version of the welfare Cadillac). The new politics provided the means for some townships, villages, and groups to adapt to changes in the American economy. Neither the old politics nor the new saved the rest.

Appendix

TABLE 1   Vote for Governor, 1914, and Woman Suffrage, 1915

County	Rep%	Dem%	Soc%	Proh%	Prog%	Amer%	IndL%	Yes%
Chautauqua	60.6%	12.0%	**4.3%**	**11.8%**	4.0%	4.0%	3.4%	58.3%
Schenectady	38.4%	19.4%	**13.1%**	**19.1%**	3.3%	5.9%	0.9%	55.0%
Chemung	34.2%	27.0%	0.8%	**18.0%**	1.3%	13.5%	5.2%	51.9%
Broome	39.1%	18.3%	0.9%	**11.4%**	1.6%	17.4%	11.3%	51.3%
Tompkins	49.0%	19.3%	1.5%	**13.5%**	5.3%	7.7%	3.7%	50.8%
Cortland	60.3%	12.4%	0.5%	**4.3%**	2.4%	8.6%	11.4%	49.8%
Oswego	55.0%	21.0%	0.2%	**5.9%**	2.4%	6.7%	8.9%	48.2%
Chenango	43.5%	10.4%	0.4%	**10.0%**	3.9%	24.5%	7.3%	46.9%
Fulton	48.9%	19.1%	**8.6%**	**7.8%**	9.3%	3.8%	2.6%	46.9%
Allegany	54.6%	13.4%	1.3%	**10.9%**	6.9%	8.5%	4.4%	46.8%
Genesee	63.9%	16.7%	0.5%	**5.7%**	5.3%	3.5%	4.4%	46.7%
Onondaga	53.2%	29.3%	2.3%	**4.1%**	4.4%	2.3%	4.5%	46.7%
Nassau	52.0%	28.8%	0.5%	1.8%	4.6%	4.0%	8.3%	46.1%
Westchester	53.2%	29.9%	1.4%	1.2%	4.1%	2.0%	8.2%	45.7%
Cattaraugus	53.1%	18.5%	2.4%	**8.2%**	3.8%	8.0%	6.0%	45.6%
Bronx	38.9%	34.4%	6.4%	0.7%	2.5%	4.9%	12.2%	45.6%
Rockland	45.4%	22.1%	0.9%	**8.7%**	4.2%	10.6%	8.1%	45.5%
Essex	55.2%	17.9%	0.6%	3.1%	9.7%	4.5%	8.9%	45.4%
Richmond	39.1%	41.2%	1.2%	1.2%	1.8%	2.7%	12.8%	45.0%
Suffolk	54.3%	32.4%	0.7%	**10.0%**	2.6%	0.0%	0.0%	44.6%
Orange	53.2%	27.2%	0.8%	**11.6%**	7.1%	0.0%	0.0%	44.3%
Montgomery	52.6%	23.7%	1.9%	**6.9%**	3.5%	7.1%	5.0%	44.1%
St. Lawrence	62.7%	19.5%	0.5%	3.6%	4.8%	2.7%	6.2%	43.4%
Cayuga	57.4%	19.6%	1.4%	**5.4%**	2.9%	4.1%	9.2%	43.2%
Washington	61.6%	19.1%	0.5%	2.7%	2.8%	4.5%	8.9%	43.1%
Tioga	42.2%	16.0%	0.7%	**12.5%**	2.4%	19.3%	6.9%	43.1%
New York	37.3%	39.6%	3.8%	0.6%	2.4%	4.3%	11.8%	43.0%
Delaware	47.7%	11.6%	0.9%	**10.1%**	2.8%	20.7%	6.1%	42.7%
Steuben	34.3%	19.6%	1.9%	**23.8%**	4.0%	11.2%	5.1%	42.6%
Niagara	60.4%	18.5%	1.3%	3.0%	2.4%	4.6%	9.7%	42.6%
Putnam	45.3%	21.7%	0.3%	3.0%	2.5%	13.8%	13.4%	42.4%
Herkimer	47.7%	28.1%	1.8%	**7.2%**	7.9%	3.1%	4.2%	42.4%
Schuyler	41.9%	11.6%	0.2%	**19.7%**	1.3%	18.6%	6.7%	42.4%
Monroe	62.8%	18.3%	2.7%	2.8%	5.7%	1.9%	5.8%	42.4%
Madison	56.3%	18.9%	1.2%	**4.6%**	4.6%	5.9%	8.5%	42.1%
Orleans	63.0%	17.9%	0.3%	**4.6%**	2.4%	4.6%	7.3%	41.8%
Kings	43.5%	33.5%	3.8%	0.9%	2.2%	4.3%	11.9%	41.8%
Otsego	41.6%	15.0%	0.4%	**12.0%**	3.4%	22.4%	5.2%	41.5%
Erie	55.9%	26.3%	2.2%	2.6%	3.6%	1.0%	8.4%	41.3%
Hamilton	39.1%	41.2%	0.3%	**8.2%**	4.1%	0.2%	6.9%	41.2%
Saratoga	54.3%	25.0%	1.0%	3.2%	1.5%	6.4%	8.6%	40.6%
Franklin	59.5%	26.9%	0.2%	3.0%	3.1%	1.5%	5.7%	40.3%

Dutchess	57.4%	22.1%	0.8%	3.2%	2.0%	4.5%	10.1%	40.1%
Wyoming	62.5%	15.3%	0.3%	**6.8%**	4.1%	6.1%	4.7%	39.7%
Queens	40.0%	39.5%	**3.5%**	0.9%	1.8%	2.8%	11.5%	39.3%
Clinton	51.4%	31.3%	0.2%	**3.9%**	1.3%	2.6%	9.3%	39.2%
Seneca	51.6%	22.5%	0.4%	**10.2%**	1.7%	8.0%	5.6%	39.0%
Ontario	56.5%	19.3%	0.4%	3.6%	4.5%	7.4%	8.3%	37.9%
Jefferson	58.5%	17.9%	1.4%	**3.9%**	3.3%	6.3%	8.6%	37.3%
Rensselaer	49.2%	39.2%	1.0%	2.4%	4.8%	2.4%	1.1%	37.2%
Livingston	56.3%	21.1%	0.2%	**5.2%**	4.0%	5.7%	7.4%	37.1%
Schoharie	39.7%	15.7%	0.3%	**14.2%**	1.3%	23.5%	5.4%	36.8%
Oneida	49.3%	24.8%	1.3%	**5.6%**	6.8%	3.3%	9.0%	36.4%
Greene	51.0%	19.0%	0.9%	**6.0%**	1.3%	11.6%	10.2%	36.1%
Yates	59.9%	13.5%	0.5%	**7.5%**	3.9%	8.7%	6.0%	34.6%
Warren	58.8%	19.6%	1.1%	2.6%	2.4%	6.3%	9.3%	34.5%
Wayne	61.6%	16.2%	0.5%	**6.2%**	6.5%	5.1%	4.0%	34.4%
Albany	59.3%	26.6%	0.6%	2.7%	1.1%	4.6%	5.2%	34.2%
Ulster	55.6%	20.7%	0.3%	**4.2%**	1.5%	8.2%	9.5%	33.3%
Sullivan	44.1%	27.4%	1.1%	**6.4%**	1.8%	10.6%	8.5%	32.6%
Lewis	51.4%	25.2%	0.1%	3.6%	5.9%	4.6%	9.2%	29.9%
Columbia	51.6%	25.6%	0.2%	3.0%	2.2%	90.4%	8.1%	26.6%
State Total	47.9%	28.8%	2.6%	3.8%	3.2%	4.9%	8.7%	42.5%

Source: Manual for the Use of the Legislature of the State of New York, 1916 (Albany, 1916).

Boldface: Socialist and Prohibition vote above state average.

There were no statewide offices contested in 1915.

TABLE 2   Vote for Attorney General and Woman Suffrage, 1917

County	Rep%	Dem%	Soc%	Proh%	Yes%
Chautauqua	68.4%	17.1%	9.5%	**5.1%**	62.0%
Tompkins	59.6%	33.0%	2.2%	**5.1%**	60.8%
Richmond	31.3%	60.0%	7.2%	1.5%	60.1%
Westchester	59.4%	34.7%	5.1%	0.7%	59.5%
New York	32.8%	48.7%	**18.2%**	0.3%	59.2%
Bronx	27.6%	45.1%	**27.0%**	0.4%	59.2%
Cortland	67.4%	23.3%	2.9%	**6.5%**	58.7%
Kings	38.0%	43.9%	**17.6%**	0.5%	58.4%
Broome	64.1%	28.5%	2.4%	**5.0%**	57.9%
Nassau	63.5%	30.0%	5.4%	1.1%	57.8%
Cattaraugus	62.1%	28.1%	6.0%	**3.9%**	57.7%
Chenango	66.2%	26.6%	1.7%	**5.5%**	56.4%
Allegany	28.3%	49.5%	7.0%	**15.2%**	56.2%
Queens	28.6%	53.9%	**17.1%**	0.5%	56.0%
Oswego	64.0%	26.2%	1.3%	**8.5%**	55.6%
Suffolk	60.8%	30.3%	6.8%	**2.1%**	55.6%
Schenectady	50.8%	25.0%	**21.4%**	2.9%	55.3%
Putnam	63.1%	34.7%	1.0%	1.2%	55.1%
Saratoga	64.8%	30.6%	1.9%	**2.7%**	53.9%
Delaware	63.0%	31.0%	2.5%	**3.5%**	53.8%
Erie	49.1%	32.5%	**16.1%**	2.3%	53.6%
Rockland	54.9%	37.5%	5.7%	1.8%	53.2%
Onondaga	57.7%	28.0%	9.5%	**4.7%**	52.3%
Cayuga	65.4%	30.8%	1.7%	**2.1%**	52.0%
Tioga	64.5%	27.2%	2.5%	**5.8%**	51.5%
Orange	62.6%	31.4%	3.8%	**2.2%**	51.5%
Washington	71.2%	24.2%	2.0%	**2.5%**	51.3%
Madison	65.6%	27.8%	2.5%	**4.1%**	51.1%
Fulton	61.4%	24.2%	9.6%	**4.8%**	50.9%
Essex	74.6%	21.8%	1.4%	**2.2%**	50.2%
Otsego	58.3%	36.7%	1.2%	**3.7%**	50.1%
Genesee	72.3%	22.9%	2.0%	**2.7%**	50.1%
Warren	66.5%	28.2%	3.3%	**2.0%**	49.9%
Steuben	63.5%	29.7%	2.1%	**4.7%**	49.6%
Niagara	59.0%	30.7%	8.2%	**2.2%**	49.3%
Franklin	67.3%	28.5%	0.9%	**3.3%**	48.4%
Montgomery	57.9%	36.3%	4.4%	1.4%	48.2%
Schuyler	63.4%	31.3%	0.9%	**4.5%**	47.7%
Dutchess	57.0%	38.2%	3.2%	1.7%	47.7%
Herkimer	63.6%	31.2%	2.9%	**2.4%**	47.5%
Sullivan	53.5%	37.2%	7.3%	**1.9%**	47.0%
Wyoming	67.0%	27.0%	2.7%	**3.3%**	46.6%
Chemung	52.9%	38.0%	3.3%	**5.8%**	46.6%
Greene	56.2%	39.7%	2.2%	**2.0%**	46.2%
Hamilton	54.3%	42.6%	0.9%	**2.1%**	45.6%
Monroe	62.2%	19.9%	**14.7%**	3.2%	45.0%
Orleans	73.2%	21.9%	2.2%	**2.7%**	45.0%
Clinton	62.8%	34.2%	0.6%	**2.5%**	44.9%
Schoharie	46.5%	47.2%	1.0%	**5.2%**	44.9%
Seneca	58.7%	34.8%	0.8%	**5.6%**	44.1%
St. Lawrence	73.4%	22.1%	1.2%	**3.2%**	44.0%

Oneida	55.7%	38.3%	3.8%	**2.2%**	43.6%
Rensselaer	54.6%	42.0%	2.4%	0.9%	43.2%
Jefferson	64.3%	28.7%	3.0%	**4.0%**	42.2%
Ontario	65.9%	30.6%	1.2%	**2.4%**	41.8%
Albany	0.5%	87.8%	9.6%	**2.1%**	41.3%
Wayne	70.4%	24.8%	1.3%	**3.5%**	41.2%
Columbia	58.9%	38.4%	1.4%	1.3%	40.0%
Lewis	58.9%	37.7%	0.8%	**2.7%**	39.6%
Yates	71.2%	24.3%	1.2%	**3.3%**	39.1%
Ulster	60.7%	33.6%	2.4%	**3.3%**	37.9%
Livingston	68.9%	26.1%	2.2%	**2.9%**	35.8%
State Total	48.6%	37.8%	11.8%	1.8%	53.9%

Source: Manual for the Use of the Legislature of the State of New York, 1918 (Albany, 1918).

Boldface: third party vote above state average.

Abbreviations

AU	Alfred University
CCHS	Cortland County Historical Society
ChCHS	Chautauqua County Historical Society
CU	Cornell University, Olin Library, Collection of Regional History and the University Archives
CUAES	Cornell University Agricultural Experiment Station
DAR	Daughters of the American Revolution
DCHS	Delaware County Historical Society
JCHM	Jefferson County Historical Museum
MCHS	Madison County Historical Society
NYSG	New York State Grange
NYSHA	New York State Historical Association (Cooperstown)
NYSL	New York State Library (Albany)
NYSWSA	New York State Woman Suffrage Association
PFL	Patterson Free Library (Westfield)
SCHS	Schoharie County Historical Society
SUNYO	State University of New York at Oswego, Penfield Library
WCTU	Women's Christian Temperance Union

Notes

Introduction

1. Ben Marvin Post #209, Grand Army of the Republic, Minutes, January 30, 1893; William Ralston Balch, *Life of President Garfield* (Philadelphia, 1888), publisher's preface. Also see Henry Davenport Northrop, *Life and Public Service of James G. Blaine, "The Plumed Knight"* (Chicago, Philadelphia, and Stockton, Calif., 1893), whose "most marked characteristic was his manliness," p. 451 and Chaps. XX–XXIII generally; William Thayer, *From Log-Cabin to the White House: Life of James A. Garfield: Boyhood, Youth, Manhood, Assassination, Death, Funeral* (Boston, 1881).

2. See in addition to the works cited in note 1, Gen. Lew Wallace, *Life of Gen. Ben Harrison* (Hartford, Conn., 1888), 57; Northrop, *Life and Public Service of James G. Blaine*, 513; and for an extreme case, Murat Halstead, *The Illustrious Life of William McKinley, Our Martyred President* (n.p., 1901), Chap. XIV; and the portrait, "William McKinley, Wife and Mother," on p. 256.

3. See, for example, Lori Ginzberg, " 'Moral Suasion is Moral Balderdash': Women, Politics, and Social Activism in the 1850s," *Journal of American History* 73 (1986): 601–22; Nancy A. Hewitt, *Women's Activism and Social Change: Rochester, New York, 1822–1872* (Ithaca, N.Y., 1984); Suzanne Lebsock, *The Free Women of Petersburg: Status and Culture in a Southern Town, 1784–1860* (New York, 1984); Mary P. Ryan, *Cradle of the Middle Class: The Family in Oneida County, New York, 1790–1865* (Cambridge, England, 1981).

4. Like "urban," "rural" is as much a concept as a definition, and its meaning could easily be debated as heatedly as "urban" has been. But working out a universally valid definition would serve no useful purpose here. Indeed, the concept itself gained new meaning as the proportion of the population living in cities grew. This study relies on census definitions: "rural" designates places with fewer than 2,500 inhabitants, "small towns" and "large villages" are those with a population of 5,000 or less. I have omitted, however, places that were indisputably suburbs by the early twentieth century—towns in Nassau, Suffolk, Orange, Westchester, and Rockland counties. Villages that achieved the status of small city before 1900 were also not considered: Amsterdam, Batavia, Catskill, Corning, Dunkirk, Endicott, Fredonia, Geneva, Glens Falls, Herkimer, Hornell, Hudson Falls (Sandy Hill), Ithaca, Johnson City, Kingston, Little Falls, Mechanicville, Medina, Olean, Oneonta, Owego, Malone, North Tonowanda, Solvay, and Whitehall. The definition of "rural" used here is far from ideal, but it is perhaps the most inclusive one that still leaves out places that were clearly part of New York's large cities.

5. There were notable exceptions: Seventh-Day Adventists dominated some towns in western New York; Catholics became a substantial presence in some areas; Italian and eastern European immigrants made homes in rural communi-

ties. On ethnicity, see Wilbert A. Anderson, "Movement of Population to and from New York State," Cornell University Agricultural Experiment Station (CUAES) *Bulletin* 591 (Ithaca, N.Y., 1934); E. C. Young, "The Movement of Farm Population," CUAES, *Bulletin* 426 (Ithaca, N.Y., 1924); David M. Gold, "Jewish Agriculture in the Catskills, 1900–1920," *Agricultural History* 55 (1981): 31–49; Arthur J. Vidich and Joseph Bensman, *Small Town in Mass Society: Class, Power and Religion in a Rural Community*, rev. ed. (Princeton, N.J. 1958, 1968).

6. On patterns of male politics in the North, see Michael E. McGerr, *The Decline of Popular Politics: The American North, 1865–1928* (New York, 1986); John F. Reynolds, *Testing Democracy: Electoral Behavior and Progressive Reform in New Jersey, 1880–1920* (Chapel Hill, N.C., 1988).

7. Class differences certainly existed in New York towns, but they do not figure prominently in this study. Careful local research of mobility and village conflicts could illuminate class tensions and perceptions of social class. That research would have dictated a focus on a handful of towns, and, done with the attention the subject deserves, pushed this study too far away from gender, politics, and government.

8. *Westfield Republican*, March 19, 1884.

9. To avoid an intrusive and repetitious use of *sic*, I have left intact the spelling and grammar of the original documents.

10. For such lack of interest, if not cynicism, in the early nineteenth century, see Lewis O. Saum, *The Popular Mood of Pre–Civil War America* (Westport, Conn., 1980); and the better-known distrust of politics of Gilded Age mugwumps in John G. Sproat, *"The Best Men": Liberal Reformers in the Gilded Age* (New York, 1968); Geoffrey Blodgett, "Reform Thought and the Genteel Tradition," in H. Wayne Morgan, ed., *The Gilded Age*, rev. and enlarged ed. (Syracuse, N.Y., 1970), 55–76.

11. On urban women's activism, see Mary R. Beard, *Women's Work in Municipalities* (New York, 1915); Karen Blair, *The Clubwoman as Feminist: True Womanhood Redefined, 1868–1914* (New York, 1980); Mari Jo Buhle, *Women and American Socialism, 1870–1920* (Urbana, Ill., 1981); Nancy Shrom Dye, *As Equals and as Sisters: Feminism, Unionism, and the Women's Trade Union League of New York* (Columbia, Mo., 1980); Marlene Stein Wortman, "Domesticating the Nineteenth-Century American City," *Prospects* 3 (1977): 531–72.

12. Exceptions include Cindy Sondik Aron, *Ladies and Gentlemen of the Civil Service: Middle-Class Workers in Victorian America* (New York, 1987); Ellen DuBois, "Working Women, Class Relations, and Suffrage Militance: Harriot Stanton Blatch and the New York Woman Suffrage Movement, 1894–1909," *Journal of American History* 74 (1987): 34–58; Kathryn Kish Sklar, "Hull House in the 1890s: A Community of Women Reformers," *Signs* 10 (1985): 658–77.

13. On economic and demographic changes in New York, see Clarence Danhof, *Change in Agriculture: The Northern United States, 1820–1870* (Cambridge, Mass., 1969); Ulysses Prentice Hedrick, *A History of Agriculture in the State of New York* (Albany, N.Y., 1933); Elmer O. Fippin, *Rural New York* (New York, 1921); Eric Brunger, "Changes in the New York State Dairying Industry, 1850–1900," (Ph.D. diss., Syracuse University, 1954); Wilbert A. Anderson, "Population Trends in New York State, 1900–1930," CUAES, *Bulletin* 547 (Ithaca, N.Y., 1932); Bruce Melvin, "The Sociology of a Village and the Surrounding Territory," CUAES, *Bulletin* 523 (Ithaca, N.Y., 1931); and *idem*, "Rural Population of New York, 1885–1925," CUAES, *Memoir* 116 (Ithaca, N.Y., 1928); Dwight San-

derson, "Rural Social and Economic Areas in Central New York," CUAES, *Bulletin* 614 (Ithaca, N.Y., 1934); Lawrence M. Vaughan, "Abandoned Farm Areas in New York," CUAES, *Bulletin* 490 (Ithaca, N.Y., 1929).

Chapter 1: Limited Horizons of Rural Life

1. Discussions of rural decay include Amos N. Currier, "The Decline of Rural New England," *Popular Science Monthly* 38 (1891): 384–89; Henry U. Fletcher, "The Doom of the Small Town," *Forum* 19 (1895): 214–23; Josiah Strong, *The New Era; or, The Coming Kingdom* (New York, 1893), 164–202; Rodney Welsh, "The Farmer's Changed Condition," *Forum* 10 (1891): 689–700. On the literature of rural decline, see Hal S. Barron, *Those Who Stayed Behind: Rural Society in Nineteenth Century New England* (Cambridge and New York, 1984), 31–50.

2. See Fippin, *Rural New York*, 73, 76; Melvin, "Rural Population of New York, 1855–1925."

3. Richard A. Easterline, "Population Change and Farm Settlement in the Northeastern United States," *Journal of Economic History* 36 (1976): 45–83; Melvin, "Rural Population of New York, 1855–1925"; Anderson, "Population Trends in New York State, 1900–1930"; Young, "Movement of Farm Population."

4. General histories of Northeastern and New York agriculture are: Danhof, *Change in Agriculture;* Fippin, *Rural New York;* Hedrick, *History of Agriculture in New York.* On dairy farming, see Eric Brunger, "Changes in the New York State Dairying Industry"; Eric E. Lampard, *The Rise of the Dairy Industry in Wisconsin: A Study in Agricultural Change, 1820–1920* (Madison, Wisc., 1963).

5. For prices for New York State farm products, see George F. Warren, "Prices of Farm Products in New York," CUAES *Bulletin* 416 (Ithaca, N.Y., 1923); Samuel E. Ronk, "Prices Received by Producers in New York State, 1841–1933," (Ph.D. diss., Cornell University, 1935).

6. On social conditions in different kinds of rural towns in the late nineteenth and early twentieth centuries, see E. L. Kirkpatrick, "The Standard of Life in a Typical Section of Diversified Farming," CUAES *Bulletin* 423 (Ithaca, N.Y., 1923); Bruce L. Melvin, "Village Service Agencies, New York, 1925," CUAES *Bulletin* 493 (Ithaca, N.Y., 1929); Sanderson, "Rural Social and Economic Areas"; F. E. Shapleigh, "Community Survey in Cattaraugus County," Shapleigh Papers; Ray E. Wakeley, "The Communities of Schuyler County, New York, 1927," CUAES *Bulletin* 524 (Ithaca, N.Y., 1931).

7. *Cuba Patriot,* December 27, 1888. The editor scaled back expectations by 1893; then he saw "No Reason for Residents to Entertain Fits of Despondency," *Cuba Patriot,* March 16, 1893. On assessments, see, for example, New York State Assessors, *Annual Report for the Year 1881* (Albany, N.Y. 1882), 8–11; *idem, Annual Report for the Year 1889* (Albany, N.Y. 1890), 10–25. Discussions of boosterism in nineteenth-century towns and villages include Don Harrison Doyle, *The Social Order of a Frontier Community: Jacksonville, Illinois, 1825–1870* (Urbana, Ill., 1978), 62–91; Robert R. Dykstra, *The Cattle Towns* (New York, 1968); John C. Hudson, *Plains Country Towns,* (Minneapolis, Minn., 1985), Chap. VII; James Mickel Williams, *The Expansion of Rural Life: The Social Psychology of Rural Development* (New York, 1926), 23–26.

8. These points are discussed further in Chapter IV. Taken together, other studies suggest that growing communities experienced a good deal of conflict in

the late nineteenth century, while stable and declining places did not. Contrast Dykstra, *Cattle Towns;* with Barron, *Those Who Stayed Behind;* and Doyle, *Social Order of a Frontier Community.*

9. Social patterns in stable rural communities will receive further attention in later chapters, but also see Williams, *Expansion of Rural Life,* for a discussion of social institutions and attitudes in a prosperous farming area and nearby villages in Madison County.

10. Accounts of secularism, challenges to Christianity, and the weakening though still dominant place of belief in the late nineteenth century include Paul F. Boller, "The New Science and American Thought," in Morgan, *Gilded Age* 239–74; William R. Hutchison, *The Modernist Impulse in American Protestantism* (Cambridge, Mass., 1976); James Turner, *Without God, Without Creed: The Origins of Unbelief in America* (Baltimore, Md., 1985).

11. For example, in two villages in Schoharie County—Middleburgh and Cobleskill—81.2 percent of the village's residents could not be found in the membership lists of the four Protestant churches in the 1890s. The villages had a small Catholic population, but the great majority of villagers clearly did not take the step of joining a congregation. Nonetheless, if newspaper reports and diarists' accounts are any indication, churches in these villages and in others across the state drew attendance far beyond their membership. The records of the Lutheran, Methodist, Reformed, and Baptist churches are located at the churches in Cobleskill and Middleburgh, and I discuss membership further in my "Culture of Politics in the Late Nineteenth Century: Community and Political Behavior in Rural New York," *Journal of Social History* 18 (1984–85): 174, 187–88. Also see Barron, *Those Who Stayed Behind.* On published sermons, see S. W. Hobbes Diary, Hobbes Family Papers, 1880–1888; Emma L. Smith to Belleville Baptist Church, January 1895, Belleville Baptist Church File. Sermons—along with poems— clipped from newspapers could be found tucked in the back pocket of numerous diaries.

12. Henry Benton Diaries, 1872 and 1896; Lucius Bushnell Diaries, 1877, on conversion, Bushnell Family Diaries; Jennette Howell Deal Prior Diaries, January 13 (quote), August 7, and December 12, 1892; March 11 and September 13, 1896; October 11, 1898; and all of 1902; Mrs. M. D. Spaford Diaries, December 7 (quote) and May 10, 1904 (quote); her detection of Satan afoot when work went badly, March 18, 1905, and *passim;* Aldrich Swann Diaries, 1870–1890; Catherine Wood Diary, January 14, 1884; and July 6, 1887, Wood Family Diaries.

13. Central New York Farmers' Club Minutes, February 1, 1895. Also see *Freeman's Journal,* November 10, 1898; report on a Farmers' Institute held in Steuben County in 1890 in *Steuben Farmers' Advocate,* January 15, 1890; Williams, *Expansion of Rural Life,* 239.

14. See, for example, the Sunday entries in the Edward J. Filkins Diary, 1872; Stephen Hait Diaries, 1891–1893, Abram Karker Diaries, 1872–1888; Mrs. P. Palmer Diary, 1877; Prior Diaries, 1892–1900; Spaford Diaries, February 19 and April 2, 1905, for her bitterness about not being able to take part in her usual Sabbath activities.

15. For varied activities, see Prior Diaries, 1892–1912. On participation in church organizations by members and nonmembers of a particular congregation, see Sunday entries in Hait Diaries, 1891–1893; Swann Diaries, especially through the 1880s; Addison Winfield Diaries, 1888, 1893; Wood Diaries, 1884–1888. Every country weekly also featured news of the activities of church organizations.

16. Prior Diaries, March 9, 1892. Entries by numerous diarists who attended many churches are included in Hait Diaries, especially June 30, 1891; Karker Diaries; Palmer Diary; Swann Diaries; and Wood Diaries, especially August 7 and September 18, 1887. An exception was Edward J. Filkins, who disdained all but the Reformed church: Filkins Diary, August 25, 1872. An example of persisting internal disputes involving the use of language in a Welsh church is *Madison County Leader*, August 2 and 9, 1906. On the reduction of tensions between churches, see my "Culture of Politics"; Barron, *Those Who Stayed Behind;* Geoffrey Louis Rossano, "A Subtle Revolution: The Urban Transformation of Rural Life, New Gloucester, Maine, 1775–1930," (Ph.D. diss., University of North Carolina, Chapel Hill, 1980), 202–9; Williams, *Expansion of Rural Life*, 89–90. These accounts of relative placidity in Northeastern churches contrast with findings of fierce doctrinal disputes in the Midwest that spilled over into politics. See Richard J. Jensen, *The Winning of the Midwest: Social and Political Conflict, 1888–1896* (Chicago, 1971); and Paul Kleppner, *The Third Electoral System, 1853–1892: Parties, Voters, and Political Cultures* (Chapel Hill, N.C., 1979), for discussions of religious conflict and politics. While doctrinal conflict tore through the upper reaches of church organizations in the Northeast as well as in the Midwest, such acrimony did not filter down to the ordinary churchgoer.

17. *Record of Proceedings of the New York State Grange, Patrons of Husbandry, Albany, 1876* (Elmira, N.Y.), 63–64 (quote); Venelia R. Case, *Grange Poems* (Bloomfield, Conn., 1892). Also relevant is the mistrust of science some rural people expressed. In a letter to the editor, a reader of the *Cortland Democrat* dismissed recent findings of geologists on the age of the earth. "But whether this new philosophy was designed for only the learned or otherwise, the Bible is, we are sure, designed for all; and we choose to be wise above what is written." *Cortland Democrat*, August 1, 1879. Also see *Westfield Republican*, January 16, 1884; the discussion by a reader of the separate concerns of and necessary tensions between sociology and religion in *Madison County Leader*, December 20, 1894. Recorders of sermons included Prior Diaries, October 30, 1892, and *passim;* Swann Diaries; Wood Diaries, 1884–1888.

18. Virgil Grange #457, Patrons of Husbandry, Minutes, February 18, 1889, NYSG Records. Beginning in the 1890s—and becoming much more prominent by the 1910s—the number and size of organizations within Protestant churches expanded. This held true for both large and small villages. These groups, at least until the 1920s, hardly directed their attention to reform. Rather, they held prayer meetings, raised money, and held socials. The social gospel—at least as it concerned community involvement—had little impact in rural New York in the late nineteenth century. The work of church organizations is described in Chapter III.

19. On tolerance of spiritualism, see Mr. and Mrs. Bernard Burns to Nixon, March 8, 1901; Lilian McEwen to Nixon, March 19, 1901 (quote); R. Gage to Nixon, March 8, 1901; H. W. Richardson to S. Fred Nixon, February 28, 1901, all in Nixon Papers. Also see Williams, *Expansion of Rural Life*, 244. Freethinkers and agnostics were also dismissed. See *Westfield Republican*, February 20, 1884; *Cortland Democrat*, December 5, 1879, and July 9, 1880.

20. Catherine Wood explained the illness of a neighbor by noting that "[t]he lords wiaze are misterious for us to finding out." Wood Diaries, January 14, 1884. Also see Prior Diaries, especially March 3–27, 1907; Spaford Diaries, especially February 14, March 18, and October 13, 1905; the account of the Johnstown flood in *Cuba Patriot*, June 6, 1889.

21. *Freeman's Journal* January 10, 1917. In one case at least, in the village of Preble, Cortland County, a minister was apparently dismissed for pushing his political beliefs too hard. See the report in the *Cortland Democrat,* July 18, 1879.

22. *Ballston Journal,* March 5, 1870. Women's political attitudes are covered in Chapter III.

23. *Cuba Patriot,* May 10, 1888 (quote); Manchester Grange #501, Patrons of Husbandry, Minutes, November 24, 1900 (quote), NYSG Records; Prior Diaries, August 15, 1907. Also see the account of the Eleventh Annual Otsego County Farmer's and Dairyman's Association Meeting provided in *Freeman's Journal,* December 10, 1891. Christianity, of course, admitted of a wide variety of interpretations other than one of limited expectations. See Herbert G. Gutman, "Protestantism and the American Labor Movement: The Christian Spirit in the Gilded Age," *American Historical Review* 72 (1966); Nick Salvatore, *Eugene V. Debs: Citizen and Socialist* (Urbana, Ill. 1982); Donald E. Winters, Jr., *The Soul of the Wobblies: The I.W.W., Religion, and American Culture in the Progressive Era, 1905–1917* (Westport, Conn., 1985).

24. *Cortland Democrat,* August 15, 1879; Manchester Grange, Minutes, November 11, 1899, NYSG Records; *Cuba Patriot,* March 9, 1893.

25. *Yates County Chronicle,* April 24, 1895.

26. *Journal of Proceedings of the Thirteenth Annual Session of the New York State Grange of the Patrons of Husbandry, Cortland, 1886* (Elmira, N.Y. 1886), 44.

27. *Cuba Patriot,* May 10, 1888. Also see *Freeman's Journal,* December 31, 1891. On the morbid side of rural life, see Michael Lesy, *Wisconsin Death Trip* (New York, 1973).

28. Filkins Diary, January 1, 3, 4, 14, and 28 (first quote), August 25 (second quote), September 12, November 9, December 9, 1872; Charles H. Broughton Diaries, February 18, 1876 (quote); Edna M. Hoffnagle Diary, November 19, 1904; Catherine Wood Diary, October 8, 1884, when she noted that "[t]hey say that old Mrs. Thompson was to be married to Knight to Nelson Crandle but will not for he is dead."

29. Wellington Richards Diary, June 19 (quote) and 20, 1894; Charles Spencer Diaries, March 30, 1909. For an exceptionally full and emotional account of the death of a family member, see Prior Diaries, February 26, 1907. For the pious, it seemed that death brought the end of work, pain, and suffering; the joining with Jesus for the saved; and for one woman, rebirth in a place "where their is no winter": Spaford Diary, January 6, 1905.

30. All diaries enumerated chores. The discussions of Carlyle occurred in the *Westfield Republican,* November 21, 1884. A woman thought Carlyle's ideas were fine, but Carlyle himself failed to live up to them: his wife did all of the family's work.

31. *Freeman's Journal,* September 17, 1891. Other views of work and the work ethic are analyzed in Leon Fink, *Workingmen's Democracy: The Knights of Labor and American Politics* (Urbana, Ill., 1983); James B. Gilbert, *Work Without Salvation: America's Intellectuals and Industrial Alienation, 1880–1910* (Baltimore, Md., 1977); Daniel T. Rogers, *The Work Ethic in Industrial America, 1850–1920* (Chicago, 1974).

32. *Bolivar Breeze,* August 27, September 3 (quote), 1892; *Cuba Patriot,* February 23, 1893.

33. *Cortland Democrat,* September 5, 1879 (quote); *Steuben Farmers' Advocate,* January 3, 1879; *Yates County Chronicle,* April 24, 1895, which counseled its read-

ers to "decrease the outgo and not expect too much of the income." Also see *Journal of Proceedings of the Fifth Annual Session of the New York State Grange of the Patrons of Husbandry, Rochester, 1878* (Elmira, N.Y., 1878), 9; Little York Grange #441, Patrons of Husbandry, Minutes, September 18, 1888, NYSG Records. On child-rearing, see *Journal of Proceedings of the Ninth Annual Meeting of the New York State Grange of the Patrons of Husbandry, Lyons, 1882* (Elmira, N.Y. 1882), 78 (quote); *Cuba Patriot,* July 12, 1888; *Canastota Bee,* June 23, 1906, which assured its readers that all successful men, as boys, had been "thrashed"; Clymer Grange #169, Patrons of Husbandry, Minutes, March 26, 1887, NYSG Records; *Freeman's Journal,* March 10, 1892. On learning character, also see Williams, *Expansion of Rural Life,* 94.

34. *Cortland Democrat,* December 3, 1880. On the differing points of view of farmers and villagers on work, see Williams, *Expansion of Rural Life.*

35. *Freeman's Journal,* November 19, 1896; Cortland County Farmers' Club, Minutes, reprinted in *Cortland Democrat,* September 5, 1879. Also see "Character-Making," in *Freeman's Journal,* November 12, 1891.

36. Grangers, for example, spent a good deal of time discussing other factors that contributed to their economic hardships. Most prominent among their conclusions were unfair competition from the makers of oleomargarine and "filled cheese," high taxes, exorbitant salaries paid government officials, and the unfair advantages awarded Western and Midwestern farmers. See, for example, the discussion of why "[f]armers should exercise an economy bordering on squalor in order that other classes may live in luxurious ease," Clymer Grange, Minutes, January 24, 1880, NYSG Records.

37. S. W. Hobbes Diaries, December 9, 1885 (quote).

38. Manchester Grange, Minutes, February 24, 1893 (quote), NYSG Records; Jessie Burnell Diaries, January 28 (quote), August 23 and October 19, 1884, and *passim;* Palmer Diaries, 1877. In personal statements—those in diaries rather than those in public talks—women were far more likely than men to complain about work. Recognition of this odd silence and a suggestion that men were less than sincere in glorifying how hard they worked is in Domestic Grange #98, Patrons of Husbandry, Minutes, January 10, 1885, NYSG Records.

39. The petition originated with the Cherry Creek Grange, and it circulated through the other Granges in Chautauqua County. The text was copied in Clymer Grange, Minutes, December 16, 1889, NYSG Records. The state Grange often embellished its statements with similar rhetoric; see, for example, *Journal of Proceedings of the Second Annual Session of the New York State Grange, Patrons of Husbandry, Syracuse, 1875* (Elmira, N.Y., 1875), 9–10; *Journal of Proceedings of the Fifth Annual Session of the New York State Grange,* 16–17; *Journal of Proceedings of the Seventeenth Annual Session of the New York State Grange of the Patrons of Husbandry, Watertown, 1890* (Elmira, N.Y., 1890), 51–60.

40. In their rhetoric, at least, the New York State farmers shared a good deal with Southern Populists. Agrarian critiques of capitalism and the late nineteenth-century social order—critiques that drew on republicanism and traditional ideas about equality and justice—are discussed in most detail in Bruce Palmer, *"Man Over Money": The Southern Populist Critique of American Capitalism* (Chapel Hill, N.C., 1980). Also see Lawrence Goodwyn, *Democratic Promise: The Populist Moment in America* (New York, 1976); Stephen Hahn, *The Roots of Southern Populism: Yeoman Farmers and the Transformation of the Georgia Upcountry, 1850–1890* (New York, 1983), 1–11 and 232–89. Recent discussions of labor and agrarian radical-

ism are Fink, *Workingmen's Democracy;* James R. Green, *Grass-Roots Socialism: Radical Movements in the Southwest, 1895–1943* (Baton Rouge, La., 1978). The ways New Yorkers turned anti-monopoly, and sometimes anti-capitalist language, as well as republicanism, to generally conservative ends is described in Chapter II.

41. Speech reprinted in *Freeman's Journal,* August 27, 1891. Debates on progress are described in Manchester Grange, Minutes, March 10, 1900; but also see March 25, 1899.

42. Isaac P. Richards Diary, Helen Tooke Butler Family Papers, December 31, 1880 (quote); Burnell Diaries, January 1, 1884 (quote); Mary Moores Diary, Moores Family Papers, September 3, 1867 (quote); S. W. Hobbes Diaries, December 31, 1885; Prior Diaries, June 30, 1892; Unidentified Woman, Diary, January 1, 1877, and January 1, 1878.

43. On scientific agriculture and the persistent efforts to modernize farming in the late nineteenth and early twentieth centuries, see Wayne D. Rasmussen, "The Impact of Technological Change in American Agriculture, 1862–1962," *Journal of Economic History* 22 (1962): 578–91; Roy V. Scott, *The Reluctant Farmer: The Rise of Agricultural Extension to 1914* (Urbana, Ill., 1970); John L. Shover, *First Majority—Last Minority: The Transforming of Rural Life in America* (DeKalb, Ill., 1976), especially Chap. IV. On New York, see Gould P. Colman, *Education and Agriculture: A History of the New York State College of Agriculture at Cornell University* (Ithaca, N.Y., 1963); Ruby Green Smith, *The People's Colleges: A History of the New York State Extension Service in Cornell University and the State, 1876–1948* (Ithaca, N.Y., 1949).

44. *Westfield Republican,* January 9, 1884 (quote); Clymer Grange, Minutes, April 13, 1895 (quote); January 27, 1906, for a defense of farming guided by the phases of the moon; Mexico Grange #218, Patrons of Husbandry, Minutes, January 20, 1894, for a debate on the "general purpose vs. the special purpose Cow"; Domestic Grange, Minutes, February 5 and March 12, 1887. Most late nineteenth-century farmers failed to keep records in any systematic fashion, and as late as 1918, only six percent of their dairy cows were purebred and their overall productivity was 4,500 pounds—as opposed to 12,000 to 18,000 for a good commercial herd. Fippin, *Rural New York,* 75–78. On resistance to scientific agriculture elsewhere, see David B. Danbom, *The Resisted Revolution: Urban America and the Industrialization of Agriculture, 1900–1930* (Ames, Iowa, 1979); David Thelen, *Paths of Resistance: Tradition and Dignity in Industrializing Missouri* (New York, 1986), 14–17.

45. Debate continues on the character of agriculture and aspirations and motives of farmers in the nineteenth-century North. For arguments regarding market intrusion, the decline of self-sufficiency, and the adoption of market values in the early nineteenth century, see Michael Merrill, "Cash Is Good to Eat: Self-Sufficiency and Exchange in the Rural Economy of the United States," *Radical History Review* III (1977): 42–66; and Christopher Clark, "Household Economy, Market Exchange, and the Rise of Capitalism in the Connecticut Valley, 1800–1860," *Journal of Social History* VIII (1979): 169–89. In a similar way, Stephen Hahn describes how the intrusion of the market into the Georgia upcountry victimized formerly self-sufficient small landholders; see *Roots of Southern Populism.* James A. Henretta, "Families and Farms: Mentalite in Preindustrial America," *William and Mary Quarterly,* 3rd Ser., Vol. 35 (1978): 3–32, argues for a family-based system of agriculture—rather than one that rested on individual aspirations—in the eighteenth century; for the nineteenth century,

see Barron, *Those Who Stayed Behind.* The point to be stressed here is that while New York farmers followed conservative farming practices and often distrusted promises of economic (and political) change, they did so in the hope of both moral and material improvement. A general discussion of fads in farming is in Earl W. Hayter, *The Troubled Farmer, 1850–1900: Rural Adjustment to Industrialism* (DeKalb, Ill., 1973).

46. The vast majority of diaries that have survived in rural New York are of the chores–weather–visits variety; to this core, some added religious reflections. A handful reflected on the writers' feelings and reactions to public events or events in their own lives. In a number of cases, it seemed clear that diaries were family records—a number of family members provided entries on visits and chores or whatever—which doubtless further constrained psychological reflection.

47. George Pomeroy Keese, "Funeral Oration for Benjamin F. Murdock," ca. 1900, George Pomeroy Keese Collection. Village newspaper editors, however, generally carried on as the representatives and advocates of "progressive" ideas and "wide-awake" commercial and business actions. As such, they did constant battle with those they described as the local "kickers," or "moss backs," or "grumblers." For a discussion of editors' places in their communities, see Sally F. Griffith, *Home Town News: William Allen White and the Emporia Gazette* (New York, 1989).

48. For the history of the New York State Grange, see Leonard L. Allen, *History of the New York State Grange* (Watertown, N.Y., 1934); also contained in L. Ray Alexander, ed., *100-Year History of the New York State Grange* (n.p., n.d.). The classic history of the early years of the Grange is Solon Justus Buck, *The Granger Movement: A Study of Agricultural Organization and Its Political, Economic, and Social Manifestations, 1870–1880* (Cambridge, Mass., 1913); also see D. Sven Norden, *Rich Harvest* (Jackson, Miss., 1974). Like the organization across the nation, the New York State Grange grew rapidly in the early 1870s and reached its first peak in the number of locals and members in about 1875. In the 1870s, the New York Grange, like those in the Midwest, lobbied for railroad regulation and political reform. The Grangers were hardly alone in this effort: on this point and the early political activity of the New York State Grange, see Lee Benson, *Merchants, Farmers, & Railroads: Railroad Regulation and New York Politics, 1850–1887* (Cambridge, Mass., 1955). Through the later 1870s and 1880s, the New York State Grange drifted into decline, although local Granges did continue limited joint purchasing. Overall, however, the group stressed the educational and social functions of fellowship. The Grange recovered in the early twentieth century, and surpassed even the 1870s membership totals in the 1910s. Also see Robert L. Tontz, "Memberships of General Farmers' Organizations, United States, 1874–1960," *Agricultural History* 38 (1964): 143–56; Morton Rothstein, "Farmers' Movements and Organizations: Numbers, Gains, Losses," *Agricultural History* 62 (1988): 161–81.

49. Bowens Corners Grange, Minutes, through January 1892 and 1893; also see November 16, 1896, through 1904; Three Mile Bay Grange #126, Patrons of Husbandry, Minutes, October 12, 1878, and February 22, 1878, through 1900; Charlotte Center Grange #669, Minutes, October 13, 1892, and *passim,* all in NYSG Records.

50. Reports of both prosperous and failing Granges are found in the Proceedings of the New York State Grange. For example, see *Journal of Proceedings of the*

Second Annual Meeting of the New York State Grange of the Patrons of Husbandry, 1875 (Elmira, N.Y., 1875), 32–40; *Journal of Proceedings of the Sixth Annual Session of the New York State Grange of the Patrons of Husbandry, Ithaca, 1879* (Elmira, N.Y., 1879), 26–48; *Journal of Proceedings of the Twelfth Annual Session of the New York State Grange of the Patrons of Husbandry, Canadaigua, 1885* (Elmira, N.Y., 1885), 80–95. Each year's proceedings contained a list of active Granges and their locations. Examples of Granges the proceeded more quickly are Clymer Grange, Minutes, February 12, 1876; February 12, 1887; December 24, 1890; January 10, 1891; and April 14, 1900; Cherry Creek Grange, Minutes, especially January 17, 1891; Domestic Grange, Minutes, February 23, 1884, all in NYSG Records.

51. State Grange accounts of weak and folded Granges include *Journal of Proceedings of the Seventh Annual Session of the New York State Grange of the Patrons of Husbandry, Rochester, 1880* (Elmira, N.Y., 1880), 37–42; and *Journal of Proceedings of the Sixteenth Annual Session of the New York State Grange of the Patrons of Husbandry, Syracuse, 1889* (Elmira, N.Y., 1889), 87–88, 94–95, 98. Also see St. Lawrence Grange #396, Patrons of Husbandry, Minutes, February 24, 1883, NYSG Records, on personal quarrels and the closing of a Grange; "19th Anniversary, Sinclairville Grange No. 401, Sinclairville, New York," (n.p., 1895), 3–6, on disagreements about purchasing, leadership, and temperance.

52. Numerous Granges arrived at a "dormant" stage in the 1880s only to reorganize in the early twentieth century; their cases are described in the county reports cited in note 51. Also see Manchester Grange, Minutes, February 17, 1888, NYSG Records; *Official Directory and History of Oswego County Granges from Organization to Date* (n.p., 1936), 83–84, on the closing of the North Scriba Grange in 1878 after failures with cooperative purchasing, and its recovery in 1890.

Chapter 2: The Moral Vision of Men's Politics

1. Good discussions of late nineteenth-century political campaigns include Jensen, *Winning of the Midwest*, 1–33; *idem*, "Armies, Admen, and Crusaders: Types of Presidential Election Campaigns," *History Teacher* 2 (1969): 33–50; McGerr, *Decline of Popular Politics*. For reports on rural New York campaigns, see, for example, *Bolivar Breeze*, November 5, 1892; *Cuba Daily News*, October 29, 1880; *Freeman's Journal*, October 28, 1880.

2. Well-known works on the matter of partisan affiliation include Paul Kleppner, *The Third Electoral System, 1853–1892: Parties, Voters, and Political Cultures* (Chapel Hill, N.C., 1979), which posits that ethnic and religious influences shaped party identification; Samuel T. McSeveney, *The Politics of Depression: Political Behavior in the Northeast, 1893–1896* (New York, 1972); Melvyn Hammarberg, *The Indiana Voter: The Historical Dynamics of Partisan Allegiance in the 1870s* (Chicago, 1977), which examines voters' economic motivations. On turnout and Gilded Age politics, see Paul Kleppner, *Who Voted? The Dynamics of Electoral Turnout, 1870–1980* (New York, 1982), Chap. III; Walter Dean Burnham, *Critical Elections and the Mainsprings of American Politics* (New York, 1982); Robert D. Marcus, *Grand Old Party: Political Structure in the Gilded Age, 1880–1896* (New York, 1971); Walter T. K. Nugent, "Money, Politics, and Society: The Currency Question," in Morgan, *Gilded Age*, 109–28; R. Hal Williams, *Years of Decision: American Politics in the 1890s* (New York, 1978).

3. Virtually all of the records of local Granges contained discussions of public questions, and in a few cases, protests when the discussions turned partisan. See Cherry Creek Grange #527, Patrons of Husbandry, July 30, 1889; Virgil Grange #457, Patrons of Husbandry, May 8, 1888, both in NYSG Records. An injunction to avoid politics was part of the Grange's statement of principles. A discussion of the difference between politics and public issues in New York is in *Journal Proceedings of the Fifteenth Annual Session of the New York State Grange, Patrons of Husbandry, Jamestown, 1888* (Elmira, N.Y., 1888), 15–16. Also see Buck, *Granger Movement,* 82, 108–11.

4. A thoughtful analysis of the uses of political theory, which this discussion indirectly draws on, is Norman Jacobson, *Pride and Solace: The Functions and Limits of Political Theory* (Berkeley and Los Angeles, 1978).

5. *Freeman's Journal,* October 14, 1880, and November 3, 1883.

6. *Freeman's Journal,* October 13, 1883.

7. *Freeman's Journal,* November 10, 1883.

8. *Delaware Gazette,* October 28, 1891 (quote); *Cuba Patriot,* December 13, 1888 (quote), and August 29, 1889 (quote); *Cobleskill Index,* October 12, 1893 (quote). Similar descriptions were printed in all newspapers before elections; see, for example, *Ballston Journal,* October 8 and 29, 1870; *Cortland Democrat,* October 3, 1879; *Freeman's Journal,* September 24, 1891; *Middleburgh News,* September 8, 1892; *Schoharie Republican,* October 26, 1893; [Wellsville] *Daily Reporter,* November 3, 1893; *Western New Yorker,* October 9, 1893; *Yates County Chronicle,* September 4, 1895. Also see Young Men's Democratic Club of Volney, Records, December 5, 1891. Similar characterizations appeared in campaign biographies; see, for example, Halstead, *Illustrious Life of William McKinley,* which described his hard work, devotion to his wife and mother, and popularity among men; Thayer, *Life of James A. Garfield,* which the author hoped would inspire boys to achieve better character; Gen. Lew Wallace and George Alfred Townsend, *Life of Gen. Ben Harrison, Also Life of Hon. Levi P. Morton* (Cleveland, 1888), which provided accounts of Harrison's military career, both men's character, statements on public questions, and electoral statistics. On personal character and politics, also see Patrick F. Palmero, "The Rules of the Game: Local Republican Political Culture in the Gilded Age," *The Historian* LXVII (1985): 479–98.

9. Republican County Committee, "To Schoharie Party Republicans," October 1892, in my possession; *Cuba Patriot,* October 11, 1888.

10. Chautauqua County Republican Party Committee Book, August 11, 1896 (quote); June 27, 1900 (quote); August 5, 1884 (quote). Also see the entries for September 17, 1887; August 7, 1894. A similar newspaper account of a county convention is in *Westfield Republican,* October 10, 1883.

11. *Cortland Democrat,* May 30, 1879. Politicians could also set examples for children and thus lead them on the path to virtue. A public school in Albany had an S. Fred Nixon Club, named after the Speaker of the Assembly. In recognition of the photographs of himself Nixon had sent to the club, a teacher indicated her "hope that the boys of the club will be as valorous and successful in life as you, and the girls of the club are trying their best to amount to something." May VanDerbilt to Nixon, December 19, 1900, Nixon Papers.

12. On work and success, see John G. Cawelti, *Apostles of the Self-Made Man; Changing Concepts of Success in America* (Chicago, 1965); Daniel T. Rogers, *Work Ethic in Industrial America.* The ideals of domesticity and separate spheres are discussed in Nancy F. Cott, *The Bonds of Womanhood: 'Woman's Sphere' in New*

England, 1790–1835 (New Haven, Conn., 1975); Kathryn Kish Sklar, *Catherine Beecher: A Study in American Domesticity* (New Haven, Conn., 1973); Barbara Welter, "The Cult of True Womanhood, 1820–1860," *American Quarterly* 18 (1966): 151–74.

13. These connections between manhood and politics were not limited to rural men in the late nineteenth century. For an extended discussion of this point, see my "Domestication of Politics: Women and American Political Society, 1780–1920," *American Historical Review* 89 (1984): 620–47.

14. Chautauqua County Republican Party Committee Book, August 9, 1905, (quote); C. F. Peck to Hill, August 20, 1891, Box 1 (quote); F. D. Beagle to Hill, February 16, 1894, Box 3; John Kelly to Hill, November 10, 1893, Box 3, all in Hill Papers. Also see *Washington County* [Cambridge] *Post*, October 27, 1893. Descriptions of masculine images in campaign material (though not usually in those terms) are in Jensen, "Armies, Admen, and Crusaders"; *idem, Winning of the Midwest*, 1–33; McGerr, *Decline of Popular Politics*, Chap. II.

15. The song was reprinted in the campaign supplement in the *Cuba Patriot*, September 20, 1888. Also see *Headquarters Republican Handbook*, (n.p., 1892), copy in the Robinson Family Papers, Box 2. Edward Applegood to Nixon, January 31, 1901, Nixon Papers.

16. *Cortland Democrat*, February 20, 1880.

17. R. M. Smith to Hill, September 7, 1891, Box 1, Hill Papers. Jones' talks are reprinted in *Journal of Proceedings of the Sixteenth Annual Session of the New York State Grange, Patrons of Husbandry, Syracuse, 1889* (Elmira, N.Y., 1889), 54–60, 70–72; *Journal of Proceedings of the Seventeenth Annual Session of the New York State Grange, Patrons of Husbandry, Watertown, 1890* (Elmira, N.Y., 1890), 51–60.

18. C. F. Peck to Hill, August 23, 1891, Box 1, Hill Papers. On the unit rule, see *Cortland Democrat*, April 2, 1880, a reprinted story from the *Syracuse Courier*. On principle and partisanship, also see Irving H. Palmer to Hill, February 28, 1894, Box 3, Hill Papers.

19. John Macklin to Hill, April 22, 1891, Box 1, Hill Papers. On loyalty, see also Palmero, "Rules of the Game," 485.

20. *Freeman's Journal*, September 3, 1891. On the highly competitive elections in New York State in the 1880s, see Albert C. E. Parker, "Empire Stalemate: Voting Behavior in New York State, 1860–1892," (Ph.D. diss., Washington University, 1975); McSeveney, *Politics of Depression*, especially 8–20.

21. Willis H. Tennant to Nixon, December 30, 1898, Nixon Papers.

22. Chautauqua County Republican Party Committee Book, September 15, 1885 (quote); September 17, 1887; August 22, 1896.

23. One letter that nicely combined heroism, principle, and devotion to party was O. H. Perry to Hill, December 1, 1894, written after Hill had been defeated in his race for governor. "[Y]ou made a Noble Sacrifice and worked as no other Man ever did before to save our party. . . . I do hope you have not injured your health in what you have passed through and that when you go into the Senate Chamber the people of the United States will know that there is a *Democrat* at last who is not afraid to stand by his convictions." Box 3, Hill Papers.

24. F. R. Green to Nixon, March 10, 1898; Charles Ehlers and George G. Phillipbar to Nixon, June 22, 1903; William W. Phipps to Nixon, July 10, 1902; J. A. McGinnies to Nixon, February 8, 1901 (quote), S. S. Talyor to Nixon, December 3, 1898, Nixon Papers; T. Boardman to Thomas Collier Platt, March 25, 1881, Box 1, Platt Papers; Walter H. Bun to Hill, July 18, 1894, Box 3, Hill

Papers. Not all men who wrote to politicians for favors put entitlement in terms of character and manhood. See, for example, Gustaf Gustafson (to Nixon), December 30, 1899; John L. Rattenbar to Nixon, March 5, 1901; and Milton E. Vennan[?] to Nixon, January 9, 1899, who simply asked for jobs; H. B. Gibbs to Nixon, February 21, 1901, who wanted a state-published history of Gettysburg because he was a veteran: all in Nixon Papers. On the ritual language in letters between politicians, also see Palmero, "Rules of the Game."

25. Unsigned to William Morgan, September 28, 1898, Morgan Papers (quote). Contemporary accounts of friendship and politics, both focusing on urban machine politics, are Mary Kingsbury Simkhovitch, "Friendship and Politics," *Political Science Quarterly* 17 (1902): 189–205; Theodore Roosevelt, "Machine Politics in New York City," in Hermann Hagedorn, ed. *The Works of Theodore Roosevelt: Memorial Edition*, 24 vols. (New York, 1923–1926), XV:114–40. Also see Palmero, "Rules of the Game."

26. Lynn L. Kitland to Hill, March 5, 1895 (quote), Box 3, Hill Papers; William H. Niegel to Flower, December 30, 1889 (quote), Flower Papers, Edward Forester File, JCHM; A. Cheeseman to Flower, June 30, 1891, Box 1, Flower Papers, SUNYO; Frank Fielder to James A. Roberts, October 28, 1898; Albert D. Shaw to William Morgan, Oct. 2, 1898, Morgan Papers; William W. Phipps to Nixon, July 10, 1902, Nixon Papers. The supplicant's expecting too many favors was one reason to deny requests; see Charles W. Bemus to Nixon, January 3, 1901, Nixon Papers.

27. Charles W. Hurlburt to Nixon, August 3, 1900 (quote); M. C. Donovan to Nixon, January 7, 1903 (quote); B. W. Turner to Nixon, January 17, 1902; Charles Phillips to Nixon, January 19, 1902; H. S. Bennett to Nixon, January 8, 1902; C. B. Perrin to Nixon, January 7, 1902; W. A. Whitney to Nixon, January 13, 1902; A. H. Steffins to Nixon, April 7, 1899, all in Nixon Papers. H. D. Brewster to Flower, June 20, 1891, Box 1, Flower Papers, SUNYO. Thomas Greenwood to Hill, December 19, 1893; Edson Potter to Hill, December 3, 1893; Luin Babcock to Hill, January 22, 1893; M. B. Govern to Hill, December 17, 1894, Box 3, all in Hill Papers. Charles E. Parker to Benjamin Harrison, December 19, 1888; R. C. Thompson to Harrison, December 20, 1888; A. Roberts to Harrison, January 1, 1889, Box 1, all in Platt Papers. Reversing the process, a Prohibitionist promised to "further your interest in any way my little influence may do it" in return for a favor: W. J. Ball to Flower, July 17, 1891, Box 1, Flower Papers, SUNYO.

28. William Bastian to Flower, December 22, 1890; S. Lockett to Flower, January 22, 1890, Box 3, Flower Papers, JCHM; John Halward to Flower, July 8, 1891, Box 1, Flower Papers, SUNYO.

29. H. E. Everhart to Nixon, November 5, 1902, Nixon Papers. Other, somewhat threatening letters, written in regard to a battle over the postmastership in the small city of Jamestown, are E. H. Bemus to Nixon, February 1, 1902, and February 5, 1902; F. R. Sweet to Nixon, January 30, 1902, all in Nixon Papers.

30. H. W. Thompson to Nixon, March 10, 1902; John C. Davies to Nixon, December 28, 1900, both in Nixon Papers. Also see A. O. Bunnell to Chauncey M. Depew, November 21, 1904, Box 2, Depew Papers.

31. Ira C. Miles to Nixon, November 27, 1898, Nixon Papers.

32. James T. Rogers to Nixon, undated, Nixon Papers. The Nixon papers contained numerous other letters, concerning both rural and urban assemblymen on committee assignments that were similar in tone. See George S. Sands to

Nixon, November 23, 1898; William F. Sheehan to Nixon, December 21, 1898; and, on bad character, Fremont Cole to Nixon, December 3, 1898, all in Nixon Papers. Also see Nixon's tribute to the friendship of Chautauqua County Republicans in Chautauqua County Republican Committee Book, June 27, 1900.

33. Carroll Smith-Rosenberg, "The Female World of Love and Ritual: Relations Between Women in Nineteenth Century America," *Signs: A Journal of Women in Culture and Society* 1 (1975): 1–29, analyzes women's letters and the relationships they described. Women's letters to politicians are discussed in Chapter III.

34. H. D. Brewster to Flower, June 20, 1891, Flower Papers, Box 1, SUNYO; A. J. Markham to Flower, March 20, 1890, Box 3, JCHM.

35. Junius Carroll to Hill, December 16, 1891 (quote), Box 1; John Bacon to Hill, December 28, 1889, Box 1, both in Hill Papers. Other examples include A. Cheeseman to Flower, June 30, 1891, Box 1, Flower Papers, SUNYO; closing of Henry Tappen to Hill, May 2, 1888; Giles L. Marsh to Hill, December 29, 1891, Box 1, both in Hill Papers; W. W. Clark to Nixon, March 12, 1899; Cavos[?] A. Bergy[?] to Nixon, February 28, 1900, both in Nixon Papers.

36. J. Edward Young to Hill, April 23, 1894, Box 3, Hill Papers.

37. Maynard's speech was reprinted by the *Freeman's Journal,* October 13, 1883. The letter defending personal character is C. E. Remick to Hill, September 4, 1893, Box 3, Hill Papers. Examples of devotion to leaders are Oscar O. Olson to Nixon, August 19, 1902 (quote); A. H. Stellins to Nixon, August 29, 1902, all in Nixon Papers; William Bastian to Flower, December 22, 1890, Box 3, Flower Papers, JCHM; William M. Cameron to Hill, June 1, 1892 (quote), Box 2; Ira Brown to Hill, November 7, 1894, Box 3, Hill Papers.

38. On the functions and ritual of conventions, see *Cattaraugus Republican,* September 29, 1893; *Cuba Patriot,* August 29, 1889; Chautauqua County Republican Party Committee Book, October 2, 1871, and August 9, 1905. A general account is Harold Foote Gosnell, *Boss Platt and His New York Machine: A Study of the Political Leadership of Thomas C. Platt, Theodore Roosevelt, and Others* (Chicago, 1924), 89–109.

39. The work of local political clubs is described by the Jeffersonian Club of Cooperstown, Minutes, 1889–1895, Jeffersonian Club Papers; Young Men's Democratic Reform Club of Volney, Records. Diaries that describe rural men's participation in campaigns include Lucius Bushnell Diary, August 12, October 29, and November 2, 1880; S. W. Hobbes Diaries, Hobbes Family Papers, October 26, 1880; and October 25 and 28, 1884; F. W. Squires Diaries, October 25, 1892; Addison Winfield Diaries, October 25, 1888. Accounts of campaigns in the late nineteenth century are cited in footnote 1, this chapter.

40. The nuts and bolts of the work of the parties in preparing for an election are described in H. L. Chadeayne Diaries, Chadeayne Family of Cornwall Papers, especially September 4 through November 7, 1882; October 31 through November 6, 1883; and August 30 through November 8, 1884. Rural elections are reported in men's diaries; for examples, see Stephen Hait Diaries, November 3, 1891; Hobbes Diaries, November 4–8, 1882; November 3, 1885; and November 6–7 1888; Oscar Loveland Diary, October 18 and November 4, 1884; Winfield Diaries, November 6, 1888. On election bets, see *Cuba Patriot,* November 15, 1888; *Bolivar Breeze,* September 3, 1892. Women's participation in elections were mentioned in newspapers, sometimes sarcastically. "One of the most onerous duties that men are called upon to perform is attending to the affairs of

state. These things require a clear head, a strong moral courage, and unselfish desire for ultimate good not encountered in every day life. Town meetings furnish one of these times of fiery trial. . . . [T]he ladies of Ripley, famous for their culinary proficiency, kept a generous supply of good things to eat, within close proximity of the polls, to thus fortify the men to bear the burdens which the ladies would willingly share, were men not so magnanimous as to insist on bearing them alone." *The Grape Belt,* February 24, 1893. For women's participation in and observation of campaigns, see Anna Moores Diary, October 31, 1888, Moores Family Papers; Jennette Howell Deal Prior Diaries, October 21, 1892. Also see McGerr, *Decline of Popular Politics,* 28, 208.

41. On the social attractions of elections, see my "Culture of Politics in the Late Nineteenth Century," 167–95; McGerr, *Popular Politics,* Chap. II and *passim.*

42. An insightful discussion of the connections between partisanship and patriotism in an earlier period is Jean H. Baker, *Affairs of Party: The Political Culture of Northern Democrats in the Mid-Nineteenth Century* (Ithaca, N.Y., 1983), Chapters I and II. On the wonder of elections, see *Cuba Daily News,* November 2, 1880; C. W. Hazard to Virgil Kellogg, September 14, 1896, Kellogg Letters.

43. On the identification of male characteristics with the necessary public virtue in Revolutionary America, see Linda K. Kerber, *Women of the Republic: Intellect and Ideology in Revolutionary America* (Chapel Hill, N.C., 1980), Chap. II. Republicanism in all its variations, of course, involved much more than the idea that personal virtue made self-government possible. But New Yorkers' insistence on individual character as a crucial part of politics had a direct connection to nineteenth-century ideas about the importance of character in general, which in turn drew on a number of sources, including Christianity and ideas about respectability. On "character," see Warren I. Susman, " 'Personality' and the Making of Twentieth-Century Culture," in *idem, Culture as History: The Transformation of American Society in the Twentieth Century* (New York, 1985), 271–85.

44. Joseph W. Kay to Hill, January 6, 1895 (quote); F. D. Beagle to Hill, February 16, 1894 (quote), Box 3, Hill Papers; *Cuba Patriot,* February 23, 1893 (quote), and April 5, 1888; *Madison County Leader,* October 19 and 26, 1901. For charges of effeminacy in general see Blodgett, "Reform Thought and the Genteel Tradition," 56–57; Richard Hofstadter, *Anti-Intellectualism in American Life* (New York, 1963), 179–91; Alan Trachtenberg, *The Incorporation of America: Culture and Society in the Gilded Age* (New York, 1982), 163–65.

45. On the regularity of "bolting" one's party in the late nineteenth century, as shown through the propensity of voters to split their tickets, see John F. Reynolds and Richard L. McCormick, "Outlawing 'Treachery': Split Tickets and Ballot Laws in New York and New Jersey, 1880–1910," *Journal of American History,* 72 (1986), 838–48. Also see Herbert J. Bass, *"I Am a Democrat": The Political Career of David Bennett Hill* (Syracuse, N.Y.), 120–25.

46. *Cortland Democrat,* August 1 and 8, 1879 (quotes); *Freeman's Journal,* November 10, 1898; [Wellsville] *Daily Reporter,* November 1, 1880.

47. *Westfield Republican,* March 19, 1884. Similar comments on the character of office-seekers are in the Hobbes Diaries, February 11, 1884; *Cortland Democrat,* June 25, 1880. On the Grange and political meetings, see Domestic Grange #96, Patrons of Husbandry, Minutes, October 11, 1884, NYSG Records.

48. *Westfield Republican,* February 13, 1884 (quote), and January 9, 1884. Domestic Grange, Minutes, September 29, 1881, and August 8, 1885 (quote); Clymer Grange #169, Patrons of Husbandry, Minutes, November 27, 1897

(quote), NYSG Records. Also see Farmers' National Alliance, Castile Local 141 Records, November 22, 1893; debate on a new school law in *Cortland Standard,* May 16, 1880; and editorial in *Freeman's Journal,* December 23, 1880.

49. See Benson, *Merchants, Farmers, & Railroads,* Chap. IV; and Norden, *Rich Harvest.*

50. Cherry Creek Grange, Minutes, March 21, 1896 (quote), February 2 and December 7, 1889; Domestic Grange, Minutes, September 29, 1881 (quote), and February 1, 1896, all in NYSG Records. Also see Farmer's Club of Hanover to "The Farmers, Farmers Clubs & Grangers of Chautauqua Co.," January 11, 1890; Clymer Grange, Minutes, December 16, 1889, and April 12, 1890, NYSG Records; *Steuben Farmer's Advocate,* February 21, 1879, for a report on the Prattsburg Grange's resolutions.

51. On support for an income tax, see Little York Grange #441, Patrons of Husbandry, Minutes, October 5, 1886, NYSG Records; and Roger Earl Sipher, "Popular Voting Behavior in New York, 1890–1896: A Case Study of Two Counties" (Ph.D diss., Syracuse University, 1971), 73. Complaints about high and unequal taxes ran through state Grange meetings. See, for example, *Report of Proceedings of the New York State Grange, Patrons of Husbandry, Albany, 1874* (n.p., n.d.), 36; *Journal of Proceedings of the Second Annual Session of the New York State Grange, Patrons of Husbandry, Syracuse, 1875* (Elmira, N.Y., 1875), 51–52; *Journal of Proceedings of the Ninth Annual Session of the New York State Grange, Patrons of Husbandry, Lyons, 1882* (Elmira, N.Y., 1882), 67; *Journal of Proceedings of the Seventeenth Annual Session of the New York State Grange,* 7. In addition, a committee on taxation and assessments made annual reports, and it was a rare address by the Worthy Master that failed to mention taxes. Also see Benson, *Merchants, Farmers, & Railroads,* 95–96 and 99–100.

52. Three Mile Bay Grange, Patrons of Husbandry, #126, Minutes, February 6, 1897, NYSG Records. Arguments against "good roads" included references to higher taxes, fear of state control, anti-monopoly sentiment, and distrust of politicians. One Granger noted that "a vote for State roads would be playing into the hands of corporations": Manchester Grange, Patrons of Husbandry #501, Minutes, January 23, 1897. Also see Charlotte Center Grange, Patrons of Husbandry #669, Minutes, June 9, 1893; Bowens Corners Grange, Patrons of Husbandry #99, Minutes, January 28, 1893; Willett Grange, Patrons of Husbandry #591, Minutes, September 25, 1897, all in NYSG Records. On the refusal of further funding for the Erie Canal, see *Yates County Chronicle,* July 30, 1895; Cherry Creek Grange, Minutes, April 6, 1900; Mexico Grange, Patrons of Husbandry #218, Minutes, February 1, 1902; Three Mile Bay Grange, February 16, 1901, all in NYSG Records; Central New York Farmer's Club, Minutes, February 20, 1903, which also reported mass meetings sponsored by local Granges to protest further funding. The state Grange, however, supported additional funds for the Canal. See *Proceedings of the New York State Grange . . . 1874,* 35; *Journal of Proceedings of the Thirteenth Annual Session of the New York State Grange, Patrons of Husbandry, Cortland, 1886* (Elmira, N.Y., 1886), 106. Also see Benson, *Merchants, Farmers, & Railroads,* 171–72.

53. *Cuba Patriot,* January 10, 1889 (quote). Also on convict labor, see *Yates County Chronicle,* March 27, 1895; S. L. Mead to Nixon, April 17, 1901, Nixon Papers. Mead explained that "[i]dleness is a relic of Barbarism & a breeder of Criminals. . . . *Build roads* & make this country a palace, with these men, & not plan to take hard earned cash from the poor." On support of economy and

ability to question even local state-funded institutions, see M. O. Greenwald to Nixon, November 26, 1898, Nixon Papers.

54. These points will receive further attention in Chapter IV. Local Granges that attempted to persuade county or township governments to reduce their expenditures included Cherry Creek Grange, September 21 and October 7, 1896; Clymer Grange, January 23 and February 18, 1892; and Charlotte Center Grange, January 23, 1892. Also see Farmers' National Alliance, Castile Local 141 Records, undated resolution.

55. For background on the Greenback movement, see Irwin Unger, *The Greenback Era: A Social and Political History of American Finance, 1865–1879* (Princeton, N.J., 1964).

56. Benson, *Merchants, Farmers, & Railroads*, 102–4; and Charles Vincent Groat, "Political Greenbackism in New York State, 1876–1884," (Ph.D. diss., Syracuse University, 1963), 24–99, on the party's relative success in 1877 and 1878. While the Greenback candidate for Justice of the Court of Appeals (the highest state office contested) gained 9.1 percent of the state's total vote, he captured 32.8 percent in Chemung County and 29.8 percent in Chenango. Further north, the Greenback ticket also did well in Oswego County (24.3 percent) and to the east in Sullivan County (28.2 percent). Oswego, Auburn, and Elmira chose Greenback mayors in that election, and the party's assembly candidates won in Oswego, Chemung, Cortland, and New York counties. Greenback candidates also drew respectable returns in Chautauqua, Wayne, Warren, Tioga, Steuben, and Tompkins, as well as in Albany and Monroe counties, which contained the cities of Albany and Rochester. Of the largely rural counties, all but Oswego, Wayne, and Warren were located in the southern tier.

57. Local returns are from the official canvasses in the *Journal of Proceedings of the Chautauqua County Board of Supervisors; Proceedings of the Board of Supervisors of Cortland County* (various publishers, 1876–1879). On Greenback county supervisors, see Groat, "Political Greenbackism," 100–5.

58. Groat, "Political Greenbackism," 106–8.

59. [New York] *Tribune Almanac and Political Register* (New York, 1893–1895), 319–38; 357–60; and 339–52. Rural men in the western end of the southern tier were more likely to vote for a Populist candidate than those in the east or north. Allegany, Cattaraugus, Yates, Ontario, and to a lesser extent, Chautauqua, Livingston, and Orleans counties were the relative strongholds of the party.

60. The different needs of farmers in the various agricultural regions of the state also helped discourage united political action—and, even more, economic cooperation. See Lee Benson, "The New York Farmers' Rejection of Populism: The Background" (M.A. thesis, Columbia University, 1948); James Dale Yoder, "Rural Pennsylvania Politics in a Decade of Discontent, 1890–1900," (Ph.D. diss., Lehigh University, 1969).

61. Clymer Grange, Minutes, October 10, 1891. The alliance with the Jamestown Knights of Labor was discussed on February 8 and March 8, 1890; the debate on Western grain took place on January 14, 1888. Also see Laonia Lodge 488 of the Farmer's Alliance and Industrial Union of the State of New York, Minutes, which voted on August 14, 1894, that "mettall itself is what gives [money] value."

62. On the electoral successes of the Prohibition Party, see John Joseph Coffey, "A Political History of the Temperance Movement in New York State, 1808–1912," (Ph.D. diss., Pennsylvania State University, 1976); Richard L. McCormick,

From Realignment to Reform: Political Change in New York State, 1893–1910 (Ithaca, N.Y., 1981), 33–34, McSeveney, *Politics of Depression,* 20–25, 116–18; Sipher, "Popular Voting Behavior," 93–117.

63. Schoharie County Republican Party Canvass Books, 1894; Sipher, "Popular Voting Behavior," 100–105 and 109–13. The Raines law is discussed in Coffey, "Political History of the Temperance Movement"; Gosnell, *Boss Platt and His New York Machine,* 162–64; McCormick, *From Realignment to Reform,* 94–98.

64. *Steuben Farmer's Advocate,* January 15, 1890 (quote). Calls for nonpartisanship were routine features of the meetings of the state Grange, and speakers also made an effort to link nonpartisanship with manhood. "The time has come when this order may exert a powerful influence in shaping public affairs, if its members will abide by principle uninfluenced by leadership that seeks only partisan advantage. Such independence is an attribute of the highest manhood and its fruits contribute to the public weal." *Journal of Proceedings of the Ninth Annual Session of the New York State Grange of Patrons of Husbandry, Lyon, 1882* (Elmira, N.Y., 1882), 9. Also see *Journal of Proceedings of the Seventh Annual Session of the New York State Grange of Patrons of Husbandry, Rochester, 1880* (Elmira, N.Y., 1880), 10; *Proceedings of the Sixteenth Annual Session of the New York State Grange,* 18, in which the Worthy Master referred to selling one's vote as "barter[ing] manhood."

65. Central New York Farmer's Club, Minutes, December 18, 1896 (quote); Willett Grange, Minutes, September 25, 1897; Domestic Grange, Minutes, September 29 and December 10, 1881; February 25, 1882; Cherry Creek Grange, Minutes, September 21, 1896, all in NYSG Records.

66. Domestic Grange, Minutes, August 24, 1898 (quote). Late nineteenth-century split-ticket voting, which concentrated on local offices, is analyzed in Reynolds and McCormick, "Outlawing 'Treachery'." On partisan alignments in the 1880s and 1890s in rural New York, see McCormick, *From Realignment to Reform;* McSeveney, *Politics of Depression,* 40–68; Parker, "Empire Stalemate." On the Grange's alleged achievement of railroad regulation, see Benson, *Merchants, Farmers, & Railroads.* Boasts of legislative achievements can be found scattered throughout the state Grange's *Proceedings;* a compilation is in Allen, *History of the New York State Grange,* 55–56, 58–62, and 64.

67. For examples of local nonpartisanship, see *Steuben Farmer's Advocate,* February 14, 1879; *Delaware Gazette,* February 17, 1892; *Unadilla Times,* March 5, 1891; *Freeman's Journal,* November 12, 1891; *Watkins Express,* February 12, 1874. A description of how nonpartisan local elections worked in an affluent town is Carol A. O'Connor, *A Sort of Utopia: Scarsdale, 1891–1981* (Albany, N.Y., 1983), 8–12, and passim.

68. *Freeman's Journal,* November 17, 1898; Central New York Farmer's Club, Minutes, February 15, 1895; *Cortland Democrat,* August 8, 1879.

69. Willett Grange, Minutes, September 25, 1897 (quote); Virgil Grange, Minutes, June 18, 1898; Bowens Corners Grange, Minutes, January 28, 1893, all in NYSG Records; Central New York Farmer's Club, February 2, 1894 and December 18, 1896 (quote). For the example of the town of Lansing, Tompkins County, see Sipher, "Popular Voting Behavior," 85.

70. Clymer Grange, Minutes, April 27, 1889 (quote), NYSG Records; *Freeman's Journal,* February 4 (quote); February 11 and 18, 1892; and November 26, 1896 (quote).

71. Domestic Grange, Minutes, February 1, 1896 (quote); Central New York

Farmer's Club, Minutes, February 19, 1897 (quote); *Freeman's Journal,* December 2, 1880 (quote); *Yates County Chronicle,* March 27, 1895.

72. The work of various groups and individuals to make farming more scientific and village life more modern will receive attention in Chapter V. Farmers' institutes, sponsored by the state, were one way for advocates of scientific agriculture to bring their message to farmers. See *Steuben Farmers' Advocate,* January 15, 1890, for talks given at a local Farmers' Institute; and Central New York Farmer's Club, Minutes, January 23, 1894.

73. Clymer Grange, Minutes, December 16, 1889 (quote); Cherry Creek Grange, Minutes, October 7, 1896, NYSG Records.

74. On the nonpartisanship of male reformers, see Blodgett, "Reform Thought in the Gilded Age"; Richard L. McCormick, "Anti-Party Thought in the Gilded Age," in *idem, The Party Period and Public Policy: American Politics from the Age of Jackson to the Progressive Era* (New York, 1986), 228–59; Gerald W. McFarland, *Mugwumps, Morals, and Politics, 1884–1920* (Amherst, Mass., 1975); Sproat, *"The Best Men."*

75. Fink, *Workingmen's Democracy;* Hahn, *Roots of Southern Populism;* and Palmer, *"Man Over Money."* That republicanism could lend itself to various uses is a point made by Sean Wilentz, *Chants Democratic: New York City & the Rise of the American Working Class, 1788–1850* (New York, 1984).

Chapter 3: The Feminine Virtues and Public Life

1. *Watkins Express,* February 5, (quote) and Feb. 12, 1874. Temperance sentiment in Watkins is discussed in Shirley Rice, "The Political Culture of Watkins, New York, 1872–1877" (graduate seminar paper, SUNY, Albany, 1984).

2. *Watkins Express,* April 9 and 16, 1874.

3. *Watkins Express,* July 2, 1874. Also see Rice, "Political Culture of Watkins."

4. On the women's crusade, see Eliza Daniel ("Mother") Stewart, *Memories of the Crusade: A Thrilling Account of the Great Uprising of the Women of Ohio in 1873 Against the Liquor Crime* (Columbus, Ohio, 1888, reprint ed., 1972); Jed Dannenbaum, *Drink and Disorder: Temperance Reform in Cincinnati from the Washington Revival to the W.C.T.U.* (Urbana, Ill., 1984); *idem,* "The Origins of Temperance Activism and Militancy among American Women," *Journal of Social History* 15 (1981–82): 235–52; Barbara Leslie Epstein, *The Politics of Domesticity: Women, Evangelism, and Temperance in Nineteenth-Century America* (Middletown, Conn., 1981), 95–107.

5. On urban women, see, for example, Allen F. Davis, *Spearheads for Reform: The Social Settlement and the Progressive Movement, 1890–1914* (New York, 1967); David Pivar, *The Purity Crusade: Sexual Morality and Social Control, 1868–1900* (Westport, Conn., 1973); Margaret Gibbons Wilson, *The American Woman in Transition: The Urban Influence, 1870–1920* (Westport, Conn., 1979), as well as works cited in note 60.

6. For an analysis of club membership in Wellsville, see Naomi Rosenthal, Meryl Fingruntd, Michele Ethier, Roberta Karant, and David McDonald, "Social Movements and Network Analysis: A Case Study of Nineteenth-Century Women's Reform in New York State," *American Journal of Sociology* 90 (1985), 1,045–50. Also see membership lists in the Alfred Centre Women's Christian Temperance Union minutes. On difficulties in participating in voluntary organizations, see, for example, Nina Burton Diaries, 1908–1921; Mrs. P. Palmer

Diary, 1877. Such selective patterns in club membership had changed little from those in the earlier nineteenth century. See Hewitt, *Women's Activism and Social Change;* Ann M. Boylan, "Timid Girls, Venerable Widows and Dignified Matrons: Life Cycle Patterns among Organized Women in New York and Boston, 1797–1840," *American Quarterly* 38 (1986): 779–97.

7. Descriptions of women's work were provided in Jessie Burnell Diary, 1884; Frances Moores Diaries, 1880, Moores Diaries; Mrs. M. D. Spaford Diary, 1904–1905; Catherine Wood Diaries, 1884–1885; and Wood Family of Butternuts Diaries. Most men's diaries were silent about women's work. For discussions of women's work, see Bowens Corners Grange #99, Patrons of Husbandry, Minutes, December 10, 1904, (quote); Mexico Grange #218, Patrons of Husbandry, Minutes, January 27, 1894, both in NYSG Records.

8. Burnell Diary, January 19, 1884 (quote); Catherine Wood Diaries, January 16, 1884 (quote). Also see Palmer Diaries, especially January 1, March 15–30, and October 2, 1877. For a man who complained regularly, see Elbridge Hunter Diaries, especially August 6 and December 31, 1886.

9. Jennette Howell Deal Prior Diaries, 1892–1912, describe in numerous places her voluntary activities. See especially May 8, 1892; January 3, 1895; February 5, 1896; January 6 and February 18, 1905.

10. Prior Diaries, 1912–1925, especially October 8, 1912 (quote); July 22, 1912; February 19, 1913; March 2, 1914; December 4, 1919; February 18, 1921 (quote).

11. See *Journal of Proceedings of the Second Annual Session of the New York State Grange, Patrons of Husbandry, Syracuse, 1875* (Elmira, N.Y., 1875), 48–50; *Journal of Proceedings of the Third Annual Session of the New York State Grange, Patrons of Husbandry, Auburn, 1876* (Elmira, N.Y., 1876), 8–9. On the early election of a woman as Worthy Master of a local Grange—and the ensuing discussion—see Clymer Grange #169, Patrons of Husbandry, Minutes, January 24, 1880. For examples of talks about meeting times and topics for discussions, see Clymer Grange, Minutes, April 28, 1884; Domestic Grange #98, Patrons of Husbandry, Minutes, July 19, 1884; Little York Grange #441, Patrons of Husbandry, Minutes, November 30, 1886, all in NYSG Records.

12. On sources of female identity and their implications for public life, see Suzanne Lebsock, "Women and American Politics, 1880–1920," in Louise Tilly and Patricia Gurin, eds., *Women, Politics, and Change in Twentieth-Century America* (New York, forthcoming).

13. See, for example, Manchester Grange #501, Patrons of Husbandry, Minutes, January 27 and March 11, 1893, NYSG Records; Political Equality Club of Cattaraugus County, New York, Minutes, 1891–1895; DAR, Tioughnioga Chapter, Minutes; Anthony Club Records, January 22 and April 30, 1901.

14. On women's piety as a reason for public involvement throughout the nineteenth century, see (among the many works) Epstein, *Politics of Domesticity,* Chaps. IV and V; Ryan, *Cradle of the Middle Class,* Chap. III; *idem,* "The Power of Female Networks: A Case Study of Female Moral Reform in Antebellum America," *Feminist Studies* 5 (1979): 66–85.

15. Most references to the work of Ladies' Aid Societies are scattered through the local columns of newspapers; but see Ladies' Aid Society of the Methodist Episcopal Church, Cooperstown, New York, Minutes; Philathea Class, Minutes, Cornwallville Methodist-Episcopal Church, Minutes; and Ladies of the United Presbyterian Church, 1897–1914 (Salem), United Presbyterian Church Papers.

16. See, for example, Women's Foreign Missionary Society of the Methodist Episcopal Church, Minutes, November 4, 1902, and May 5, 1903, Cooperstown United Methodist Church Records; Ladies' Union of the First Baptist Church (Ithaca), Minutes, May 12, 1892. Also Cherry Creek Grange #527, Patrons of Husbandry, Minutes, January 17, 1891 and March 3, 1894; Domestic Grange, Minutes, October 28 and 29, 1892; all in NYSG Records; WCTU of Hartwick, Secretary's Book, November 22, 1907.

17. George A. Soule to "Dear Friends," November 12, 1894, Secretary's Report of the Torry Mission Band, Presbyterian Church of Cazenovia Records.

18. *Delaware Gazette,* February 17 and March 2, 1892; *Madison County Leader,* April 25, 1907; Cherry Creek Grange, Minutes, February 5, 1898.

19. Secretary's Report of the Torry Mission Band, October 21, 1881; January 7 (quote), February 4, March 18, 1882; and February 2, 1884 (quote).

20. Maggie Douds to Presbyterian Ladies' Missionary Society, June 29, 1889; Josie Lawrence to "Friends," October 20, 1893; James M. Bain to Mrs. L. H. Yates, November 24, 1894; Flossie Wingfield to "Friend," December 22, 1892 (quote), and June 29, 1889; all in Records of the Presbyterian Ladies' Missionary Soceity (Cooperstown).

21. Alfred Centre WCTU, Minutes, December 16, 1885; Palmero WCTU, Secretary's Book, April 16, 1898; WCTU of Hartwick, August 23, 1907; Secretary's Report of the Torry Mission Band, August 18, and November 17, 1887. Charlotte Center Grange #669, Patrons of Husbandry, Minutes, May 14 and July 9, 1892; Domestic Grange, Minutes, October 24, 1890; all in NYSG Records. On the request from a national organization for greater system in giving, see Linda B. Green to Mrs. Erastus F. Beadle, August 25, 1880, Records of the Presbyterian Ladies' Missionary Society (Cooperstown).

22. "To the Hon. Excise Board of Cortland Village," April 12, 1871 (quote), Cortland City Records; *Cortland Democrat,* July 18, 1879; *Every Week,* February 9, 1887; *Delaware Dairyman,* January 8, 1892; Alfred Centre WCTU, Minutes, October 10, 1882; Minutes of the Long Eddy WCTU, October 28, 1909, May Morgan McKoon Temperance Papers. County reports at the state WCTU convention also detailed local activities; see, for example, WCTU of the State of New York, *Report of the 11th Annual Meeting,* Hornellsville, 1884 (Oswego, N.Y., 1884), 21–28.

23. *Every Week,* March 15, 1887. In nearby Belmont, the editor claimed that forty men and boys formed the "Iron Clad Reserve" and marched as a unit to the polls to vote for pro-licence commissioners. Also see *Cuba Daily News,* March 1, 1880; and the lengthy account of a WCTU's effort to vote a village dry—one that went from prayer, to drawing up a dry ticket, to enlisting male allies to work the polls, in WCTU of Penn Yan, Minutes, March 3–April 14, 1874, and February 23, 1875.

24. August 23, 1889, May Morgan McKoon Scrapbook, McKoon Temperance Papers.

25. *Cortland Democrat,* June 13, July 18 (quote), and July 27, 1879.

26. Oaksville Reform Club, Minutes, 1878. The first page of the minutes book had a membership list; the secretary recorded the club's statement of purpose on September 14, 1878.

27. Oaksville Reform Club, Minutes, March 30, May 3, and May 17, 1879; September 11 and October 25, 1880.

28. See Commissioner of Excise of the State of New York, *Second Annual Report, January 1898* (Albany, 1898), 21–22; Coffey, "Temperance Movement in

New York State," 275–76; G[allus] T[homann], *The Local Option Movement in New York*, (New York, 1894), 6–9. On the subversion of local laws, see Chapter IV.

29. Analyses of the impact of the temperance issue on electoral politics include Bass, *"I Am a Democrat,"* 62–65, 112–17, 136–37; Coffey, "Political History of the Temperance Movement," Chaps. VI–VII; McCormick, *From Realignment to Reform*, 94–100; McSeveney, *Politics of Depression*, 20–22, 24–25, 115–17, 204.

30. "A Lady" to Hill, February 5, 1888; Thomas J. Clark to Hill, April 29, 1888; James J. Gill to Hill, May 10, 1888; "Citizen of Brownsville" to Hill, May 21, 1888, all in Hill Papers, Box 12. Members of WCTU chapters had canvassed their villages, and those petitions are also in the Hill Papers.

31. Clymer Grange, Minutes, June 8, 1889; Domestic Grange, March 9, 1894; Virgil Grange #457, Patrons of Husbandry, Minutes, February 28, 1888, all in NYSG Records. Alfred Centre WCTU, Minutes, October 10, 1882; February 18, 1885; June 16, 1886. Also see WCTU of the State of New York, *Report of the 11th Annual Meeting*, 56–58; WCTU of the State of New York, *Report of the 18th Annual Meeting, New York, 1891* (Oswego, N.Y., 1891), 76.

32. For one county leader's account of the importance of the WCTU in state politics, see May 31, 1889, McKoon Scrapbook, McKoon Temperance Papers. Also see Minutes of the Long Eddy WCTU, March 18 and September 8, 1910, McKoon Temperance Papers; WCTU of Hartwick, Secretary's Book, January 8–February 5, 1909; *Grape Belt*, February 24, 1893. Also see Coffey, "Political History of the Temperance Movement," 164–76; Frances W. Graham, *A History of Sixty Years' Work of the Women's Christian Temperance Union of the State of New York* (Lockport, N.Y., 1934).

33. *Cuba Patriot*, March 2, 1893 (quote); *Every Week*, January 4, 1887; Clymer Grange, Minutes, February 8, 1890, NYSG Records.

34. Julia P. Freer to W. Martin Jones, April 1, 1887 (quote); Emily Howland to Jones, February 18, 1888 (quote); Mrs. E. V. L. Hoxie to Jones, February 8, 1886; Lydia E. East to Jones, January 6, 1886, all in McKoon Temperance Papers. Also see *Delaware Gazette*, September 28, 1892; report on WCTU in Woodhull in *Every Week*, April 26, 1887; WCTU of Penn Yan, Minutes, March 17, April 4, April 7, 1875; Alfred Centre WCTU, Minutes, June 13, 1882.

35. *Every Week*, February 22, 1887; Minutes of the Long Eddy WCTU, October 28, 1909, McKoon Temperance Papers; Palmero WCTU, Secretary's Book, February 19, 1898; Alfred Centre WCTU, Minutes, February 13, 1883; May 21, 1884; February 18 and December 16, 1885 (quote).

36. Domestic Grange, Minutes, December 11, 1886 (quote); Clymer Grange, Minutes, January 27, 1894, all in NYSG Records; *Watkins Express*, February 12 (quote) and March 5, 1874 (quote).

37. On the WCTU, see Jack S. Blocker, "The Politics of Reform: Populists, Prohibitionists, and Woman Suffrage, 1891–1892," *Historian* 34 (1975): 614–32; Ruth Bordin, *Women and Temperance: The Quest for Power and Liberty, 1873–1900* (Philadelphia, Pa., 1981); *idem, Frances Willard: A Biography* (Chapel Hill, N.C., 1986); Buhle, *Women and American Socialism*, 60–69, 80–89; Epstein, *Politics of Domesticity*, 115–46.

38. On the veneration of Willard, see, for example, Palmero WCTU, Secretary's Book, March 5, 1898; WCTU of Hartwick, Secretary's Book, February 12, 1908. State WCTU leaders were initially hostile to woman suffrage: see WCTU of the State of New York, *Report of the Ninth Annual Meeting, 1882* (Brooklyn, N.Y., 1882), 11–13. For changing views, see the work of local unions in WCTU of

the State of New York, *Report of the Twelfth Annual Meeting, 1885* (Oswego, N.Y., 1885), 50, 61; WCTU of the State of New York, *Report of the Sixteenth Annual Meeting, 1889* (Oswego, N.Y., 1889), 132–33 (quote).

39. See, for example, Alfred Centre WCTU, Minutes, September 14, 1886, and May 18, 1887; McKoon Scrapbook, May 10, 1889, McKoon Temperance Papers; *Every Week,* January 16, 1887 (quote); and *Delaware Dairyman,* October 28, 1892. Also see talk given by Chautauqua County suffragist Martha Beaujeans to a local WCTU on June 8, 1909, Beaujeans Family Papers.

40. *Every Week,* August 9 (quote) and January 16, 1887. Also see Central New York Farmer's Club, Minutes, January 17, 1896, on women's political roles.

41. *Journal of Proceedings of the Second Annual Session of the New York State Grange, Patrons of Husbandry, Syracuse, 1875* (Elmira, N.Y., 1875), 48–50, for a women's committee that asked for "a more active part" in the Grange, so that they might "advance our common cause . . . like Ruth, to follow the reapers, and pick up what we may of the scatterings of the golden grain." Also see *Journal of Proceedings of the Third Annual Session of the New York State Grange, Patrons of Husbandry, Auburn, 1876* (Elmira, N.Y., 1876), 8–9, when Worthy Master Armstrong suggested that the Grange would "become a barren, dreary waste" if it lost women's "cheery influence." But also see *Journal of Proceedings of the Sixth Annual Session of the New York State Grange, Patrons of Husbandry, Ithaca, 1879* (Elmira, N.Y., 1879), 87.

42. *Journal of Proceedings of the Tenth Annual Session of the New York State Grange, Patrons of Husbandry, Rochester, 1883* (Elmira, N.Y., 1883), 15; *Journal of Proceedings of the Thirteenth Annual Session of the New York State Grange, Patrons of Husbandry, Cortland, 1886* (Elmira, N.Y., 1886), 39.

43. Domestic Grange, Minutes, February 19, 1881 (quote); February 11, 1882; January 27, 1894 (quote); Clymer Grange, Minutes, November 14, 1891 (quote). Granges that offered pro-suffrage resolutions included Cherry Creek Grange, Minutes, March 2, 1895; Charlotte Center Grange, Minutes, October 5, 1891. Resolutions on woman suffrage lost in the Little York Grange, Minutes, February 2, 1886.

44. See, for example, Political Equality Club of Bath, October 28, 1898; January 27, 1899; and January 1906, when, after eight years, they decided to replace Fiske with another text and had a roll call, "Items on the life of John Fiske"; Susan Look Avery Club, Minutes, April 15, 1901; Political Equality Club, Oneida, Minutes, April 30, May 7, and May 28, 1898; Political Equality Club of Cattaraugus County, Minutes, May 14, 1892; Robert A. Huff, "Anne Miller and the Geneva Political Equality Club, 1897–1912," *New York History* 65(1984):325–48.

45. See Susan B. Anthony and Ida Husted Harper, eds., *The History of Woman Suffrage* 4 (Rochester, 1902), 860–67.

46. The 1880 law was vague on the issue of qualifications of voters, and the legislature clarified it in 1881: taxpaying women and those who had charge of school-age children could vote. School commissioners were chosen from districts that corresponded with assembly districts. Counties held one to four assembly districts. For the final judgment on the 1892 law, see *Re* Gage (1894), 141 N.Y. 112.

47. Political Equality Club of Cattaraugus County, Minutes, May 25 (quote) and October 20, 1893; Political Equality Club of Oneida, March 12, 1898; Secretary's Books of the Warsaw Political Equality Club, May 27, 1892, and July 13, 1894; Al-

fred Centre WCTU, Minutes, July 5, 1887 (quote), and August 27, 1888. Also see WCTU of the State of New York, *Report of the 18th Annual Meeting, 1891,* 158–59; WCTU of the State of New York, *Report of the 12th Annual Meeting, 1885* (Oswego, N.Y., 1885), 50–61, for county reports of women's voting at district meetings.

48. On the elections in the early 1880s, see *Woman's Journal,* March 20, 1880, p. 96; Elizabeth Cady Stanton, Susan B. Anthony, and Matilda Joslyn Gage, eds., *History of Woman Suffrage* 3 (Rochester, N.Y., 1886), 427–30; Barbara S. Rivette, "Fayetteville's First Woman Voter—Matilda Joslyn Gage" (Fayetteville, N.Y., 1985), 4–5. Also see New York State Woman Suffrage Association (NYSWSA), *Report of the 28th Annual Convention, Rochester, 1896* (Auburn, N.Y., 1897), p. 36 on Chautauqua County; NYSWSA, *Report of the 30th Annual Convention, Hudson, 1898* (Auburn, N.Y., 1899), p. 59 on Steuben; WCTU of the State of New York, *Report of the 23rd Annual Meeting, 1896,* 240–48. For an account of women's votes as decisive in a school meeting, see Thomas Lee, "Political Decisions and Their Makers in Glens Falls, New York, 1876–1885" (graduate seminar paper, SUNY at Albany, 1984). For district school elections, see, for example, School District Records, School District #6, Town of Truxton Records; School District #5 and #22, Town of Virgil Records; School District Minutes, District #4, Town of Preble Records; Hartwick District #6, Minutes; and Minden-Danube School District, Minutes. For elections in which the normal routine shattered (usually because of divisive spending decisions) and where losers challenged election results on a variety of grounds, see Thomas E. Finegan, *Judicial Decisions of the State Superintendent of Common Schools, State Superintendent of Public Instruction, State Commissioner of Education from 1822 to 1913* (Albany, N.Y., 1914).

49. Warsaw Political Equality Club, Annual Report, 1892–93 (quote); Report of the Annual Banquet of the [Wyoming] County Club [1893]. Also see *Western New Yorker,* November 2 and 9, 1893; NYSWSA, *Report of the 25th Annual Convention, Brooklyn, 1893* (Syracuse, N.Y., n.d.), 25–31.

50. *Cattaraugus Republican,* September 22 (quote), September 29 (quote), October 6 (quote), November 3 (quote), and story on Van Rensselaer's opponent, November 10, 1893. Along with Van Rensselaer, Myra Ingalsbe of Washington County, Roxie Tuttle of Warren County, and Julia West of Richmond County won in 1893; they joined two women who gained seats in 1890. Another woman took a position in 1894 upon the death of her husband. For accounts of other winning campaigns, see [Glen Falls] *Morning Star,* October 11 and October 23, 1893; NYSWSA, *Report of the 25 Annual Convention,* 25–31.

51. *Middleburgh News,* October 5 (quote), and October 26, 1893. The largest Democratic papers in the county, perhaps not seeing a Republican candidate as a threat, barely mentioned Sias' candidacy and did not make sex an issue in the race. See the coverage of the election in the October issues of the *Schoharie Republican* and the *Cobleskill Index.* Also see comparisons of different female candidates' skill at electioneering in *Friendship Weekly Register,* November 16, 1893. On the women voters, candidates, and school officials generally, see my "Gender Differences and School Politics in Late Nineteenth Century New York State" (paper presented at the Eighty-first Annual Meeting of the Organization of American Historians, Reno, Nevada, 1988).

52. *Middleburgh News,* November 9, 1893 (quote), discussing item from *Gilboa Monitor;* Manchester Grange, Minutes, November 3, 1893, for Granges who determined that women could not vote for school commissioners until 1894; *Western New Yorker,* October 16, 1893 (quote); Warsaw Political Equality Club,

Minutes, Annual Report, 1892–93. On further debate about the meaning of the 1892 law, see Anthony and Harper, *History of Woman Suffrage*, 866–68, 1094–96; *Canisteo Times*, a Prohibition newspaper that termed rumors about an unfavorable court decision a "trick," November 2, 1893; and *Washington County Post* (Cambridge), which reprinted the Williams decision, November 3, 1893.

53. See *Re* Cancellaton of Names (1893), 5 Misc. 375. Other decisions and opinions provided support to woman suffragists. See *Re* Woods (1893), 5 Misc. 575; *Re* Inspectors of Election (1893), 25 N.Y. Supp. 1063; *New York Times*, October 21, 1893, 8:4, for Attorney General Rosendale's advice to treat the law as constitutional. On opposition to women voters under partial suffrage, see Eleanor Flexner, *Century of Struggle: The Woman's Rights Movement in the United States*, rev. ed. (Cambridge, Mass., 1975), 179–180; and NYSWSA, *Report of the 25th Annual Convention*, 26–30, for reports of harassment and legal barriers in many counties, especially Madison, p. 26; Niagara, p. 28; Otsego (quote), 29; and Washington, p. 30. For claims regarding registration of female voters, see *Woman's Journal*, November 28, 1893, p. 362.

54. Some inspectors of elections who believed that women's votes might be invalidated tallied their ballots separately. See *Cattaraugus Republican*, November 10, 1893; [Glens Falls] *Morning Star*, November 7, 1893, for returns in Cattaraugus and Washington counties.

55. *Cuba Patriot*, September 19, 1889; and on another successful race in a small city, Huff, "Anne Miller and the Geneva Political Equality Club," 335–39. For a discussion of these later office holders, see my "Gender Differences and School Politics."

56. *Delaware Republican*, May 6, 1915.

57. On the radicalism of woman suffrage, see Ellen Carol DuBois, *Feminism and Suffrage: The Emergence of an Independent Women's Movement in America, 1848–1869* (Ithaca, N.Y., 1978). On "manhood" and men's opposition to woman suffrage, see my "Domestication of Politics," 620–47.

58. For criticism of school suffrage outside of rural areas, see *Woman's Journal*, July 21, 1883, p. 22 (article written by Henry B. Blackwell); Albany Woman Suffrage Society, Minutes, February 27, 1883; although given the lack of larger victories, suffragists nonetheless supported school suffrage laws. On Granges and schools, see, for example, Manchester Grange, Minutes, February 1, 1895, NYSG Records.

59. Also see Central New York Farmer's Club, Minutes, January 17, 1896, for a woman's speech on women and politics that outlined how mothers needed to train sons for good citizenship, while also working for world peace through women's organizations.

60. *Every Week*, July 26, 1887. On women's efforts in cities, see for example, Mary R. Beard, *Women's Work in Municipalities* (New York, 1915); Blair, *Clubwoman as Feminist;* Patricia M. Melvin, "Milk to Motherhood: The New York Milk Committee and the Beginning of Well-Child Programs," *Mid-America* 65 (1983): 113–34; Wortman, "Domesticating the Nineteenth-Century American City," 531–72.

61. Also see criticisms of women's organizations in *Westfield Republican*, December 19, 1883.

62. On religion in rural communities, see Chapter I.

63. Address of May Morgan McKoon to Convention of the Sullivan County WCTU, October 17, 1889, McKoon Temperance Papers.

64. *Every Week*, February 15 (quote), August 9 (quote), July 19 (quote), August

16, October 11, 1887. The *Friendship Weekly Register* and *Wellsville Democrat* contained especially pointed criticisms of Mrs. Rumpff and her politics. See *Cuba Patriot*, October 10 and 31, 1889, for charges that her nonpartisanship was in fact corruption, and that her choosing candidates from different parties was a foolish kind of personalism applied to politics.

65. On women's study of politics, see citations in note 44, this chapter. On the study of office-holders' duties and the American political system, see, for example, Political Equality Club of Bath, Journal, January 27 and February 8, 1899; Secretary's Books of the Warsaw Political Equality Club, November 5, 1892 (quote); and clipping on 1892 county convention. On qualifications of candidates, see Report of the Annual Banquet of the [Wyoming] County Club, July 19, 1893, Secretary's Books of the Warsaw Political Equality Club (quote).

66. *Every Week*, October 25, 1887; Annual Report, 1894–95, Secretary's Books of the Warsaw Political Equality Club; Alfred Centre WCTU, Minutes, December 17, 1884.

67. Prior Diaries, October 21, 1892 (quote); Report of the Annual Banquet of the [Wyoming] County Club, July 19, 1893, Secretary's Books of the Warsaw Political Equality Club; *Cuba Patriot*, October 25, 1888; Women's Republican Association of Alfred Centre, Minutes. There is no evidence of comparable Democratic clubs, at least in the rural part of the state. For an analysis of women's groups in the Socialist Party, see Buhle, *Women and American Socialism*, 14–20, 31–40.

68. Speech reprinted in *Cuba Patriot*, October 11, 1888. Also see form letter by Foster sent to Republican women's clubs, September 1, 1893, Women's Republican Association of Alfred Centre.

69. Women's Republican Association of Alfred Centre, Minutes, October 16 and 22, 1892; February 25 and September 30 (quote), 1893; March 31, April 28, October 27, and November 26, 1894; *Cuba Patriot*, October 25, 1888 (quote).

70. Domestic Grange, Minutes, September 2, 1882, NYSG Records.

71. Mary A. Stowell to Nixon, October 16, 1904 (quote); Elizabeth Barry to Nixon, March 2, 1901; Mrs. W. F. Eldrige to Nixon, n.d.; Mrs. A. T. Robinson to Nixon, February 6, 1901, all in Nixon Papers; Mrs. M. J. Denas to Roswell P. Flower, July 27, 1891, Flower Papers, Box 1, SUNYO. Among the more politically sophisticated, see, for example, Eva Coffeen to Nixon, July 14, 1902; and the series of letters by and about Martha Almy, a Chautauqua County suffragist, concerning the attempt by the Commissioner of the Department of Labor to remove her from her position as factory inspector—especially Almy to Nixon, March 30, 1901, Nixon Papers.

72. Mrs. L. P. Austin to Nixon, January 2, 1902 (quote); Mrs. M. G. Baker to Nixon, July 28, 1902; Ellen Cheney to Nixon, July 7, 1902, Nixon Papers; Mrs. Delia M. Shurtiff to Flower, n.d., Flower Papers, JCHM, Box 3. On femininity and women's requests for political favors, also see Aron, *Ladies and Gentlemen of the Civil Service*. Chapter III.

73. Elizabeth Barry to Nixon, March 2 and February 16, 1901; Jennie M. Francis to Nixon, February 5, 1902 (quote); Mrs. Harper to Nixon, March 4, 1901 (quote); Mrs. A. T. Robinson to Nixon, March 9, 1901; (Miss) S. H. Rublee to Nixon, January 23, 1901; Annette (Mrs. Alfred) Rose to Nixon, April 2, 1903 (quote), all in Nixon Papers. Josephine A. Douglas to Hill, June 30, 1894 (quote), Box 3, Hill Papers; Miss Ruby Chaumont to Flower, July 13, 1891, Flower Papers, Box 1, SUNYO.

74. A. F. Dean to Flower, January 6, 1890 (quote); Welsey J. Bean to Flower,

January 8, 1890 (quote); both Flower Papers, Box 3, JCHM. Kate M. Ball to Flower, June 15, 1891 (quote), Flower Papers, Box 1, SUNYO; Mrs. Adda E. Boole to Flower, January 25 and February 6, 1890 (quote), Flower Papers, Box 3, JCHM. For further examples, see William Bastian to Flower, December 22, 1890; and for a man who persisted in his search for a loan, Sherman S. Cross to Flower, February 12 and April 11, 1890, Flower Papers, Box 3, JCHM. Men's letters that requested loans—not letters that asked for jobs—resembled the job letters described by Aron, *Ladies and Gentlemen of the Civil Service,* Chap. II.

75. Kate McGovern to Hill, April 5, 1893, Box 3, Hill Papers. A more assertive request was Florence M. Arnold to Flower, July 10, 1891, Flower Papers, Box 1, SUNYO. Examples of more straightforward letters are Eliza C. Gifford to Nixon, March 24, 1899; Mary Hillard Loines, Legislative Chair, NYSWSA, to Nixon, December 29, 1900; and Mrs. Carrie E. E. Twing, President of the New York State Association of Spiritualists, to Nixon, February 2, 1901, Nixon Papers.

Chapter 4: Economy and Harmony

1. I have examined closely county supervisors' reports from ten counties, representing different parts of the state and different economic conditions: Allegany, Cattaraugus, Chautauqua, Cortland, Lewis, Oswego, Otsego, St. Lawrence, Schoharie, and Washington.

2. Historians and sociologists who have examined local government have stressed power, leadership, and social structure. For the late nineteenth century, see Barron, *Those Who Stayed Behind;* Doyle, *Social Order of a Frontier Community;* Edward J. Davies II, *The Anthracite Aristocracy: Leadership and Social Change in the Hard Coal Regions of Northeastern Pennsylvania, 1800–1930* (DeKalb, Ill., 1985); Dykstra, *Cattle Towns* (New York, 1968); Estelle F. Feinstein, *Stamford in the Gilded Age: The Political Life of a Connecticut Town, 1868–1893* (Stamford, Conn, 1973); David C. Hammack, *Power and Society: Greater New York at the Turn of the Century* (New York, 1982); Carl V. Harris, *Political Power in Birmingham, 1871–1921* (Knoxville, 1977). David C. Hammack reviews the work of historians as well as the vast number of studies produced by social scientists on community power in "Problems in the Historical Study of Power in the Cities and Towns of the United States, 1800–1960," *American Historical Review* 83 (April, 1978): 323–49. Among the sociological and anthropological analyses, see, for example, Vidich and Bensman, *Small Town in Mass Society;* W. Lloyd Warner and Associates, *Democracy in Jonesville: A Study in Quality and Inequality* (New York, 1949); James West, *Plainville, U.S.A.* (New York, 1945).

3. From February 1888 through January 1889, the *Cuba Patriot* was a reliable source of stories and editorials stressing the connections between progress and the waterworks. A letter to the paper contained the criticism quoted; see *Cuba Patriot,* February 16, 1888.

4. *Cuba Patriot,* February 2 (1st quote), February 23 (2nd quote), March 15 (3rd quote), 1888.

5. *Cuba Patriot,* April 5, November 22, December 6, December 27 (quote), 1888.

6. *Ballston Journal,* March 5, 1870; *Westfield Republican,* March 5, 1884. Also see *Cuba Patriot,* 29, 1888.

7. An example of a letter to a newspaper that claimed to express the views of

the "laboring classes" in favor of spending on a Union Free School in Cortland is in *Cortland Democrat*, May 6, 1880. For an example of a town meeting attempting to determine what to do about railroad bonds, see Town Meeting Records, March 9, 1879, Town of Solon, Records. Also see St. Lawrence County Supervisors, *Proceedings . . . Annual Session, 1900* (Gouverneur, N.Y., 1900), 72–73.

8. As late as the 1930s, real property constituted 98 percent of all property tax. See Chester Baldwin Pond, *Full Value Real Estate Assessment as a Prerequisite to State Aid in New York* (Albany, 1931), 5; Don C. Sowers, *A Financial History of New York State from 1789 to 1912* (New York, 1914), 334–35.

9. *Cuba Patriot*, March 1 and 29, 1888 (quotes); *Delaware County Dairyman*, October 14, 1892; *Freeman's Journal*, January 13, 1881. Also see Cattaraugus County Board of Supervisors, *Journal of Proceedings, 1892* (Little Valley and Salamanca, N.Y.), 86–115; Chautauqua County Board of Supervisors, *Journal of Proceedings of the Annual Session of 1886* (Jamestown, N.Y., 1886), 38–45; Schoharie County Board of Supervisors, *Proceedings for the year 1880* (Gilboa, 1881), 46–49.

10. On petty local conflicts, see Milford E. Atherton *vs.* Marshall E. Walker, March 25, 1886; People *vs.* John Kuhlman, July 7, 1886; People *vs.* Frank Westbrook, November 8, 1895, Belfast Justice Court Records. For other discussions of the weeklies' avoidance of bad news, see Dykstra, *Cattle Towns*, especially 382–383; and Sally F. Griffith, *Home Town News*.

11. Discussions of New York State's tax laws include Irving J. Call, "Farm-Property Taxation in New York" (Ph.D. diss., Cornell University, 1927); Luigi Cossa, *Taxation, Its Principles and Methods* (London and New York, 1893); F. F. Hedlund, "The Development of Property and Collection of Taxes in Rural New York," CUAES *Bulletin* 681 (Ithaca, N.Y., 1937); John Archibald Fairlie, *The Centralization of Administration in New York State* (New York, 1898); Paul E. Malone, *The Fiscal Aspects of State and Local Relationship in New York* (Albany, 1937); John Christopher Schwab, *History of the New York State Property Tax: An Introduction to the History of State and Local Finance in New York* (Baltimore, 1890); Sowers, *Financial History of New York State*.

12. New York State Assessors, *Sixth Annual Report of the State Assessors* (Albany, 1879), 3 (quote), 4–28; New York State Assessors, *Report of the State Assessors for the Year 1880* (Albany, N.Y., 1881), 3–6. On the complaints of farmers, especially members of the Grange, see Chapter II. In addition to the works cited in note 11, which generally provide a progressive critique of New York's tax laws, see McCormick, *From Realignment to Reform*, 147–48, 169–76.

13. See Fairlie, *Centralization of Administration in New York;* Sowers, *Financial History of New York State.*

14. *Freeman's Journal*, November 18, November 25, December 16, 1880.

15. *Freeman's Journal*, December 2 and 16, 1880. This newspaper was unusual in publishing debates that took place at supervisors' meetings.

16. Board of Supervisors of St. Lawrence County, *Proceedings of the Annual Session of 1885* (Ogdensburg, N.Y., 1885), 54–55; also see Board of Supervisors of St. Lawrence County, *Proceedings of the Annual Session, 1895* (Gouverneur, N.Y., 1895), 75–78; *Freeman's Journal*, November 26, 1896 (quote); Lewis County Board of Supervisors, *Proceedings, Annual Session, 1885* (Lowville, N.Y., 1885), 31. Also see *Western New Yorker*, December 7, 1893; Board of Supervisors of Schoharie County, *Journal of Proceedings for the Year 1890* (Albany, N.Y., 1890), 14–16.

17. Other county boards of supervisors reprinted the Seneca petition in their minutes: see, for example, Board of Supervisors of St. Lawrence County, *Proceed-*

ings of the Annual Session of 1880 (Ogdensburg, N.Y., 1880), 41. On salaries for county officials (sheriffs and clerks), see Board of Supervisors of Washington County, *Proceedings for the Year 1896* (Fort Edward, N.Y., 1896), 14–21; Cherry Creek Grange #527, Patrons of Husbandry, Minutes, October 21, 1905; Clymer Grange #169, Minutes, April 12, 1890; and Three Mile Bay Grange #126, February 9, 1901 (for one group in favor of the fee system), all in NYSG Records. Also see *Yates County Chronicle,* March 27, 1895.

18. Lewis County Board of Supervisors, *Proceedings of 1885,* 24–45; *Freeman's Journal,* December 16, 1880; Board of Supervisors of Oswego County, *Journal of Proceedings . . . at the Annual Session . . . 1880* (Oswego, N.Y., 1881) 194–95, and 204–210; Board of Supervisors of Schoharie County, *Proceedings for the Year 1890,* 22–28; Board of Supervisors of Washington County, *Proceedings . . . November and December Sessions for the Year 1893* (Fort Edward, N.Y., 1893), 21–22; Board of Supervisors of Washington County, *Proceedings . . . of the Year 1896,* 6–8. Also see Clymer Grange, Minutes, February 18, 1892.

19. On the statewide pattern, see Sowers, *Financial History of New York State,* 334–35. On assessments, see Hudland, "Development of Assessments of Property"; New York State Assessors, *Annual Report of the State Assessors of New York for the Year 1889* (Albany, 1890), 10–23; Board of Supervisors of Washington County, *Proceedings . . . , November and December Sessions for the Year 1894* (Whitehall, N.Y., 1894), 57–58, for a threat to take town assessors to court for underestimating personal property.

20. Contemporary discussions of the tax burden in declining towns are Ralph Theodore Compton, *Fiscal Problems of Rural Decline, A Study of the Method of Financing the Costs of Government in the Economically Decadent Rural Areas of New York State* (Albany, N.Y., 1929); Call, "Farm Property Taxation in New York."

21. The relative absence of partisanship at the township level doubtless also sprang from one-party dominance in most townships. Even in banner Republican counties, one or two townships produced Democratic majorities (and county supervisors) throughout the late nineteenth century. In the same way, the few rural counties that produced Democratic majorities also contained "Republican towns"; few townships remained competitive. In the ten counties examined for this chapter, votes taken on printing contracts and the appointments of clerks were most often partisan; sectional disagreements arose over proposed changes in county seats and spending for special projects, such as roads and bridges; and township and village divisions appeared in discussions of taxes, with country representatives almost always rejecting new spending and working for lower assessments for their townships. Also see Peter A. Baynes, "An Analysis of the Political Culture of Albion, New York, 1872–1877," seminar paper, SUNY at Albany, 1984.

22. See Board of Supervisors of St. Lawrence County, *Proceedings of the Annual Session of 1890* (Gouverneur, N.Y., 1890), 24–27, for a long debate on the printing contract; *Proceedings of the Special Meeting of 1890* (Gouverneur, N.Y., 1890), 8–13, on the board's attempt to settle on a superintendent of the poor. Also see *Proceedings of the Annual Session of 1895* (Gouverneur, N.Y. 1895), 21–24; Board of Supervisors of Schoharie County, *Proceedings for the Year 1890,* 20–23.

23. An account of long-suffering village and town office-holders is in *Westfield Republican,* March 5, 1884; also see *Madison County Leader,* March 5, 1908. On irregular tickets, see Chapter II. Avoidance of conflict, partisanship, and decisions were stable features of village politics; for an account of township and

village governments in rural New York in the twentieth century, see Vidich and Bensman, *Small Town in Mass Society*, 109–223.

24. Edward J. Filkins, Diary, April 9 (first quote), April 12 (second quote), 1872. On contentious meetings, see, for example, Board of Supervisors of St. Lawrence County, *Proceedings . . . 1890, Special Meeting*, 53–55, during which the debate on assessments became so heated that the chairman offered his resignation.

25. An example of anger at a patronage slight is *Ballston Journal*, October 29 and December 3, 1870; for the resolution of a newspaper patronage dispute, see Schoharie County Board of Supervisors, *Proceedings for 1885* (Albany, 1885), 24–27. The Cattaraugus, Cortland, Chautauqua, and Oswego boards had especially large proportions of supervisors serving on the various committees that dealt with assessments. On informal agreements designed to lessen public conflict in the twentieth century, see Vidich and Bensman, *Small Town in Mass Society*, 124–40.

26. For contrast, see Schoharie County Board of Supervisors, *Proceedings for 1890;* where supervisors argued about heating the County Clerk's office; and Chautauqua County Board of Supervisors, *Proceedings . . . of the Annual Session, 1890* (Jamestown, N.Y., 1890).

27. See, for example, Truxton, N.Y., Board of Health Minutes, 1882–1890; Town of Solon Records, Town Meeting Records, Box 2, March 9, 1879; Town of Taylor Records, Town Minutes and Accounts, Box 2, February 19, 1879.

28. In addition to the collections cited in note 27, see Cortland Village Trustees, Minutes, May 24, 1870; and the long-lived debate on fishing rights in Otsego County in *Freeman's Journal*, December 2 and 16, 1880; and January 29, 1881.

29. A sense of how school districts conducted their meetings can be gained from Town of Truxton Records, School District Records, School District No. 6, 1882–1913; Town of Virgil Records, Box 1, School District No. 5, 1870–1900, and School District No. 22, 1880–1883; Cuyler Town Records, District No. 7 Minutes, 1897–1900; Town of Preble Records, School District Minutes, District No. 4, 1880–1900; Roxbury School Minutes of Meetings, 1883–1900; Hartwick School District No. 3, Minutes, 1870–1900 (quote); Minden-Danube School District Minutes, 1870–1900.

30. See Hartwick District No. 3, Minutes, March 25, 1902; Cuyler District No. 7, Minutes, June 4, 1918; Oxford and Greene School District No. 16 Records, August 30, 1887.

31. A selection of the many cases of irregular meetings, elections, and decisions by local school officials is Thomas E. Finegan, *Judicial Decisions of the State Superintendent of Common Schools, State Superintendent of Public Instruction, and State Commissioner of Education from 1822 to 1913* (Albany, 1914), *Re* Childs *v.* Residents of Scott, no. 3699, 328–29; *Re* Madigan, Ryan and Mahoney, no. 4504, 378–82 (quote, 380); also *Re* Penny *vs.* Board of Education of Union Free School District No. 6, Town of North Greenbush, no. 4445, 366–68; *Re* Middlemist, no. 4406, 350–56.

32. All diaries provide accounts of roads; especially the diarists' relief when enough snow had fallen to permit sleighing. See, for example, Elbridge Hunter Diaries, May 1, 1890, April 7, 1891; D. W. Oliver Diaries, January 13, 1880, and January 27, 1882; Addison Winfield Diaries, January 2, 1889.

33. See W. M. Curtiss, "Development of Highway Administration and Finance in New York," CUAES *Bulletin* 680 (Ithaca, 1937), 16–44; *Highway Manual of the State of New York* (Albany, 1893), 3–66.

34. In New York, Good Roads Associations located in various cities argued in

favor of expenditures for road improvements, which presumably would have increased traffic and business in the cities and larger towns. See the arguments in Central New York Farmers' Club, Minutes, February 2, 1894; January 23 and December 18, 1898. For general accounts, see Harold Parker, "Good Roads Movement," *Annals of the American Academy of Political and Social Science* 40 (1912): 51–57; Wayne E. Fuller, *RFD: The Changing Face of Rural America* (Bloomington, Ind., 1964), 177–98; Philip Parker Mason, "The League of American Wheelmen and the Good-Roads Movement, 1880–1905," Ph.D. diss., University of Michigan, 1957.

35. Charlotte Center Grange #669, Patrons of Husbandry, Minutes, June 9, 1893. On Grangers' dissatisfaction with state spending on roads, also see Chapter II; the discussions of the Central New York Farmers' Club cited in the previous note also included criticisms of reliance on state money and fear of increased local taxes. Also see Central New York Farmers' Club, Minutes, March 8, 1902, for one speaker's explanation of how state control of roads threatened the survival of the Republic. On the progress of road improvement, see Hal S. Barron, "And the Crooked Shall Be Made Straight: Public Road Administration and the Decline of Localism in the Rural North, 1870–1930," paper delivered at the Annual Meeting of the Organization of American Historians, April 1988.

36. Flower's address is included in *Highway Manual of the State of New York*, 268. For the complaints of a member of a Good Roads organization about the way that the Higbee–Armstrong legislation worked, see H. D. Ackerly to Nixon, January 23 and January 30, 1901, Nixon Papers. For one county government's indifference to "good roads," see Washington County Board of Supervisors, *Proceedings . . . November and December Sessions, 1895* (Whitehall, N.Y., 1895), 24–25.

37. *Laws of New York, 1898*, Chap. CXV, p. 607; Curtiss, "Development of Highway Administration," 23–24. The Fuller-Plank act provided direct aid to towns in 1898.

38. Barron, "And the Crooked Shall Be Made Straight"; Michael L. Berger, *The Devil Wagon in God's Country: The Automobile and Social Change in Rural America, 1893–1929* (Hamden, Conn., 1979), 88–94; Mason, "League of American Wheelmen."

39. Potter quoted in *Freeman's Journal*, November 5, 1891. On criticisms of state-built roads, see Chapter II, and note 36, this chapter. Also see *Freeman's Journal*, 27, 1898 (quote); *Friendship Weekly Register*, September 21, 1893.

40. See especially Manchester Grange #501, Patrons of Husbandry, Minutes, January 23, 1897; Virgil Grange, Minutes, June 18, 1898; the series of talks on road laws cited in note 35. At least one Grange decided in favor of "good roads," although they did not specify how they would be built. See Bowens Corners Grange #99, Patrons of Husbandry, Minutes, May 7, 1898, NYSG Records.

41. St. Lawrence County Supervisors, *Proceedings of the Board . . . Annual Session, 1900*, 55–57.

42. Cortland County Board of Supervisors, *Proceedings . . . 1900* (Cortland, N.Y., 1901), 91–92; also see St. Lawrence County Board of Supervisors, *Proceedings . . . 1895, Special Meeting*, (Gouverneur, N.Y., 1896), 53.

43. Cortland County Board of Supervisors, *Proceedings . . . 1900*, 127.

44. *Madison County Leader*, December 6, 1906 (quote), and on one town that retained the labor system even while requesting state aid, *ibid.*, January 10, 1907. Also see Malone, *Fiscal Aspects of State and Local Relationships*, 291–94.

45. An amendment to the state constitution passed in 1905 permitted New

York to issue a $50,000,000 bond for road construction; the Department of Highways established in 1908 oversaw a system of state, county, and town roads. An additional bond issue in 1912 provided money for rural roads on a more favorable basis to counties and towns. In 1916, the federal government also provided funds for highways. On the course of road funding, see Curtiss, "Development of Highway Administration."

46. See, for example, the large number of letters related to roads in the papers of an assemblyman from Chenango County, Bert Lord, from 1914 through 1916. Examples include James P. Hill to Lord, May 20, 1916; Lord to Homer Higley, May 25, 1916. Supervisors, however, spent a good deal of their time administering the state's programs. See Leslie Tse-Chiu Kuo, "An Analysis of Actions Taken by the Boards of Supervisors in Allegany and Saint Lawrence Counties, New York, 1937" (M.A. thesis, Cornell University, 1939).

47. Early temperance legislation is traced in Coffey, "Political History of the Temperance Movement," Chapters I–III.

48. Women's activities are discussed in Chapter III.

49. See Lee, "Political Decisions and Their Makers in Glens Falls;" *Cuba Patriot,* March 8, 1888; March 7 (quote) and March 14, 1889.

50. See *Cuba Patriot,* May 16, November 21 and 28, 1889; *Every Week,* February 9, 15, and 22, 1887.

51. *Westfield Republican,* February 13, 1884. Also see G[allus] T[homann], *Local Option Movement in New York,* 11–14.

52. *Westfield Republican,* February 20 and 27, 1884; *Cuba Patriot,* January 26, 1888.

53. Accounts of the Raines law include Coffey, "Political History of the Temperance Movement," 262–73; McCormick, *From Realignment to Reform,* 94–98. For indications of local confusion about how the Raines law worked, see R. H. Service to Virgil Kellogg, October 6, 1896; H. J. Hastings to Kellogg, March 27, 1897, Kellogg Letters.

54. In addition to the works cited in note 53, see, for example, Warsaw Political Equality Club, Minutes, January 31, 1896.

55. H. W. Thompson to Patrick W. Cullian, State Commissioner on Excise, June 28, 1902; A. O. Briggs, Second Deputy State Commissioner of Excise, to H. W. Thompson, June 23, 1902, Nixon Papers. Minutes of the Long Eddy Women's Christian Temperance Union, July 22 and September 8, 1910.

56. The classic work on the political tactics of the Anti-Saloon League is Peter H. Odegard, *Pressure Politics: The Story of the Anti-Saloon League* (New York, 1928). For the League's work in New York, also see Coffey, "Political History of the Temperance Movement," 281–302; Jennette Howell Deal Prior Diaries, January 19, 1919, and December 7, 1924; J. F. Burke, Attorney, Anti-Saloon League, to Bert Lord, September 12, 1914; Lord to Burke, September 16, 1914, Lord Papers; Ernest H. Cherrington, ed., *Anti-Saloon League Year Book, 1909* (Columbus and Chicago, 1909), 45–46.

57. On the expansion of government in the late nineteenth century, see William R. Brock, *Investigation and Responsibility: Public Responsibility in the United States, 1865–1900* (Cambridge and New York, 1984); Leonard D. White, *The Republican Era: A Study in Administrative History, 1869–1901* (New York, 1958).

58. Histories of Cortland Normal are Carey Wentworth Brush, "The Cortland Normal School Response to Changing Needs and Professional Standards, 1866–1942" (Ph.D diss., Columbia University Teachers College, 1961); and Bessie L.

Park, *Cortland—Our Alma Mater: A History of Cortland Normal School and State University of New York Teachers College at Cortland, 1869–1959* (Ithaca, N.Y. 1960).

59. Brush, "Cortland Normal School Response," 95–102.

60. *Cortland Democrat*, February 27, July 16 and 30, 1880; Brush, "Cortland Normal School Response," 104–6.

61. *Cortland Democrat*, July 23, 1880 (quote). A short discussion of Hoose's accomplishments and his differences with Gilmour is in Park, *Cortland*, 16–18, 54–59. Also see the more thorough treatment in Brush, "Cortland Normal School Response," 62–75. A pamphlet that covers that incident from Hoose's point of view is *The Cortland Normal School Controversy, Issued by the Local Board and Addressed to the Legislature of the State of New York*, (Syracuse, N.Y., 1880).

62. *Cortland Standard*, July 1, 1880; *Cortland Normal School Controversy*, 33–35; Brush, "Cortland Normal School Response," 106–10.

63. *Cortland Democrat*, August 13 and 27, 1880; *Cortland Normal School Controversy*, 43–59; and Brush, "Cortland Normal School Response," 111–16.

64. On earlier differences between the *Democrat* and the *Standard* on Gilmour, see *Cortland Democrat*, December 5, 1879; *Cortland Standard*, April 8, 1880. Also see *Cortland Standard*, August 19, 1880; *Cortland Democrat*, August 27, 1880 (quote); Brush, "Cortland Normal School Response," 111–14.

65. *Cortland Democrat*, September 24, 1880 (quotes).

66. *Cortland Democrat*, January 14, 1881; *Cortland Standard*, January 6, 1881; Brush, "Cortland Normal School Response," 117–23.

67. Brush, "Cortland Normal School Response," 123–29.

68. John Seiler Brubacker, *The Judicial Power of the New York State Commissioner of Education: Its Growth and Present Status with a Digest of Decisions* (New York, 1927); R. L. Finney and A. L. Schafer, *The Administration of Village and Consolidated Schools* (New York, 1920); A. G. Grace and G. A. Moe, *State Aid and School Costs* (New York, 1938); Harlan Updegraff, *Rural School Survey of New York State* (Ithaca, N.Y., 1922).

69. See letter to the editor, *Freeman's Journal*, November 17, 1898.

70. On the extent to which rural townships depended on money raised elsewhere, see Compton, *Fiscal Problems of Rural Decline*.

Chapter 5: Intelligent Farmer and His Intelligent Wife

1. Manchester Grange #501, Patrons of Husbandry, Minutes, May 4, 1910 (quote), and January 28, 1913 (quote); Bowens Corners Grange #99, Patrons of Husbandry, Minutes, June 20, 1900; Clymer Grange #169, Patrons of Husbandry, Minutes, March 14, 1896; Three Mile Bay Grange #126, Patrons of Husbandry, Minutes, February 16, 1901.

2. The "Progressive movement" had many faces—it appeared, historians have claimed, as a drive for social justice; for control over unruly or alien ideas and people; for political changes that would open formal politics to new groups, such as women; for changes that would close politics to blacks; for weakening the power of large corporations; for consolidating corporate power; and for systematizing governmental functions. As this list suggests, historians have conducted a lively debate over the character of the movement, its major actors, and its meaning and outcome, chiefly during the 1960s and 1970s. My research has not set about the futile task of solving the riddle of Progressivism. Rather, it draws upon

what passes for the conventional wisdom: Progressivism embodied contradictory tendencies and brought, among other things, larger, more active governments at all levels.

3. Cattaraugus Grange #865, Patrons of Husbandry, Minutes, May 3, 1905; Cherry Creek Grange #527, Patrons of Husbandry, Minutes, March 3, 1906; Manchester Grange, Minutes, November 24, 1900 (quote); Three Mile Bay Grange, Minutes, September 8, 1900 (quote). Also see Political Equality Club of Cattaraugus County, Minutes, September 26, 1894; Political Equality Club of Oneida, Minutes, March 5, 1898; Susan Look Avery Club, Minutes, September 21, 1903; Anthony Club, Records, October 4 and November 25, 1902.

4. On men's earlier cynicism about politics, see Chapter II. Nothing in the Granges' discussions of public questions in the early twentieth century suggested that men's views of politics had moved much beyond their earlier distrust. As was the case in the late nineteenth century, speakers urged that farmers vote for candidates who represented agricultural interests and argued that lawmakers in Albany and Washington failed to pay attention to farmers' needs and that middle-men robbed farmers of their just profits. No particular change in the tone of farmers' complaints marked the arrival of the Progressive period; no new inter-est in state or federal policies appeared in the Granges' records. If anything, fewer discussions of state and national issues occupied local Granges.

5. See, for example, the treatment of Progressive-era legislation and politi-cians in the Republican *Madison County Leader* and *Cuba Patriot* and the Demo-cratic *Freeman's Journal* and *Schoharie Republican;* also see *St. Lawrence Plaindealer,* September 22–October 27, 1908, on the Hughes campaign; *Dundee Observer,* November 16, 1905, on bosses.

6. See Wilbert A. Anderson, "Population Trends in New York State, 1900–1930"; Edward F. Keuchel, Jr., "The Development of the Canning Industry in New York State to 1960," (Ph.D diss., Cornell University, 1970); G. F. Warren, "Prices of Farm Products in New York," CUAES *Bulletin* 416 (Ithaca, N.Y., 1923).

7. J. F. Booth, "Farmers' Cooperative Business Organizations in New York," CUAES *Bulletin* 461 (Ithaca, N.Y., 1928), 26–31; *The Grape Belt,* January 6, 1893.

8. Jasper Cardot to Nixon, March 7 and February 25, 1902; J. G. Schurman to Nixon, June 10, 1902 (quote); Colman, *Education and Agriculture,* 122–28.

9. The question of how to rid western New York orchards of the San Jose Scale inspired a large number of letters to Nixon. On the nurseryman's side, see F. R. Green to Nixon, February 6, 1900, and February 8, 1901; Edward H. Pratt, Pres., T. H. Hubbard Nursery, to Nixon, February 16, 1900 (quote); William Pitkin to Nixon, March 10, 1901; Lewis Roesch to Nixon, February 16, 1900. For the point of view of the orchardists, see L. S. Allmott to Nixon, March 29, 1900; C. W. Jennings, State Reporter, Farmers' Institutes, March 28, 1900 (quote); J. M. Munger to Nixon, March 28, 1900. All in Nixon Papers.

10. *The Grape Belt,* January 6, 1893; W. J. Horton to Nixon, March 30, 1903, Nixon Papers. On the dramatic decline in turnout in Chautauqua County, see McCormick, *From Realignment to Reform,* 263.

11. *Madison County Leader,* October 21, 1901 (quote), April 18, 1907 (quote), and also on science, August 2, 1906, and March 4, 1907.

12. *Madison County Leader,* June 21 and 28 (quote), July 5 and 12, 1906. The issue obviously meant more to Broad than it did to a rival editor in Canastota. See *Canastota Bee,* January 13, 1906.

13. *Madison County Leader,* September 6, October 4, 11, 18, and 27 (quote); and

November 8, 1906. Also see pro-Gates ads in *Canastota Bee,* October 13, 20, and 27, 1906, which included instructions on how to vote a split ticket, and downplayed Gates's wealth.

14. *Madison County Leader,* November 15, 1906; January 24, March 7, June 27, July 4, September 19, October 3, 16, and 24, 1907.

15. *Madison County Leader,* November 7, 14, and 21, 1907.

16. *Madison County Leader,* January 23, February 20 and 27, March 26, April 2, 9, and 16, 1908. Also see Colman, *Education and Agriculture,* 181, 203.

17. *Madison County Leader,* April 23, 30 (quote), May 7 (quote), 21, and 28, 1908.

18. Few periods of American history are in greater need of fresh questions than the Progressive era. Debates about the movement's character and ultimate purpose appear to have ground to an inconclusive halt, and historians have yet to construct a compelling new agenda for research in the period. My work provides neither startling new twists on older questions nor a brash new approach. It does, however, indicate what the period's political ferment meant to a group of people not directly engaged in reform efforts. While the reform ethos had little impact upon them, the actions of government, which did, produced new ways of thinking about government and politics. That government—rather than reform agitation—had a similar impact on the political expectations of people in other rural places or cities seems plausible.

19. Histories of the country life movement include Barron, *Those Who Stayed Behind,* Chapter III; Bowers, *Country Life Movement in America;* Danbom, *Resisted Revolution.*

20. The history of the College of Agriculture is ably traced in Colman, *Education and Agriculture,* especially Chapters II–V. Also see Milton Conover, *The Office of Experiment Stations: Its History, Activities, and Organization* (Baltimore, 1924). On the problems faced by the agricultural scientists in general, see Charles E. Rosenberg, "Science, Technology, and Economic Growth: The Case of the Agricultural Experiment Station Scientist, 1875–1914," *Agricultural History* 45 (1971): 1–20. Also see Palmer C. Ricketts, President, Rensselaer Polytechnic Institute, to Nixon, February 2, 1903, Nixon Papers.

21. Educational programs connected with Cornell are described in Colman, *Education and Agriculture.* Also see Maurice C. Burritt, "The Rise and the Significance of Agricultural Extension," typescript, Burritt Papers; on extension programs across the United States, Roy V. Scott, *The Reluctant Farmer: The Rise of Agricultural Extension to 1914* (Urbana, Ill., 1970).

22. In addition to the works cited in note 19, see U.S. Congress, Senate, *Report of the Country Life Commission,* Sen. Doc. 705, 68th Congress, 2nd Session, 1909; Clayton S. Ellsworth, "Theodore Roosevelt's Country Life Commission," *Agricultural History* 34 (1960): 155–72.

23. On New York, see, for example, Liberty Hyde Bailey, *York State Rural Problems* 1 (Albany, 1913), especially Chapters VIII and XII; and *ibid.* 2 (Albany, 1915), Chapter VI; Amelia Shaw MacDonald, "Social Conditions Among the Country Folk of New York State," manuscript, ca. 1908, Liberty Hyde Bailey Papers; Frederick E. Shapleigh, "Community Surveys in Cattaraugus County," manuscript, ca. 1913, Shapleigh Papers; and Williams, *Expansion of Rural Life.* On the country lifers' problems with schools and churches, see David B. Tyack, *The One Best System: A History of American Urban Education* (Cambridge, Mass., 1974), Chapter II; James H. Madison, "Reformers and the Rural Church, 1900–

1950," *Journal of American History* 73 (1986): 645–68; Kenyon Butterfield, *The Country Church and the Rural Problem* (Chicago, 1911); Charles Otis Gill and Gifford Pinchot, *The Country Church: The Decline of Its Influence and the Remedy* (New York, 1913); Richard Morse, *Fear God in Your Own Village* (New York, 1918); Mabel Carney, *Country Life and the Country School: A Study of the Agencies of Rural Progress and of the Social Relationship of the School to the Country Community* (Chicago, 1912); Ellwood P. Cubberley, *Rural Life and Education: A Study of the Rural School Problem as a Phase of the Rural Life Problem* (Boston, 1914).

24. *Proceedings of the Fourth Annual Session of the New York State Grange of the Patrons of Husbandry, Rochester, 1877* (Elmira, N.Y. 1877), 52–54; S. W. Fletcher to R. A. Lawrence, December 15, 1904, Fletcher Agricultural Extension Letterbooks. The minutes of almost all Granges I examined suggested some interest in country-life questions, but that interest quickly disappeared. See, for example, the minutes of the Manchester Grange for the early twentieth century, Stone Ridge Grange #932, Patrons of Husbandry; and for the same period, Mexico Grange #218, Patrons of Husbandry, which also decided against subscribing to the Cornell Reading Course through 1902 and 1903. NYSG Records.

25. Jay F. Hammond to Bailey, November 11, 1908 (quote); J. V. Jacobs to Bailey, November 30, 1908 (quote). Letters from New Yorkers in support of the Commission's aims include F. A. Seeley to Commission on Country Life, December 3, 1908, who hoped that the Commission would highlight farmers' economic problems; and Harry B. Warner to the Commission on Country Life, November 5, 1908, who stressed teaching farmers the principle of cooperation. But see also G. Wendell Bush to Bailey, December 17, 1908, Bailey Papers. For an example of local Granges' reactions (few noted participation), see Bowens Corners Grange, Minutes, October 31 and November 7, 1908. On the Country Life Commission surveys, see Olaf F. Larson and Thomas B. Jones, "The Unpublished Data from Roosevelt's Commission on Country Life," *Agricultural History* 50 (1976): 583–99.

26. See Brunger, "Changes in the New York State Dairying Industry"; for an example of the New York State Grange's ongoing battle against oleomargarine, see, *Journal of Proceedings of the Fourteenth Annual Session of the New York State Grange of the Patrons of Husbandry, Canadaigua, 1887* (Elmira, N.Y., 1887), 17.

27. Brunger, "Changes in the New York State Dairying Industry," Chapter IV; Melvin, "Milk to Motherhood," 113–34. For similar campaigns elsewhere, see Judith Walzer Leavitt, *The Healthiest City: Milwaukee and the Politics of Health Reform* (Princeton, N.J. 1982).

28. J. F. Booth, "Farmers' Cooperative Business Organizations in New York," 19–25; Brunger, "Changes in the New York State Dairying Industry," Chapter V; Thomas E. Milliman, *What Went Before* (Ithaca, N.Y., 1962), 15–23; *The Dairymen's League News*, February and June 1917.

29. See New York Milk Committee, *Proceedings of the Conference on Milk Problems at New York City, 1910* (New York, n.d.); State of New York, Department of Agriculture, *Report of the Director of Farmers' Institutes and Normal Institutes for the Year 1903* (Albany, 1904), 349–59; State of New York, Department of Agriculture, *Report of the Director of Farmers' Institutes and Normal Institutes for the Year 1905* (Albany, 1906), 17–22; *Madison County Leader*, August 15 (quote), November 14, 1907; February 6 and 20, 1908.

30. *Madison County Leader*, August 22 (quote), and August 29 (quote), 1907.

31. On the history and policies of the Dairymen's League, see John J. Dillon, *Seven Decades of Milk: A History of New York's Dairy Industry* (New York, 1941);

Milliman, *What Went Before*, 15–23; *The Dairymen's League News*, February, 1917. Also see *Delaware Republican*, May 6, 1915.

32. Manchester Grange, Minutes, October 24, 1908 (quote); Marathon Grange #455, Patrons of Husbandry, Minutes, June 27, 1914; all in NYSG Records. The Dairymen's League was organized by the Orange County Pomona Grange, and by 1916 and 1917, most subordinate Granges lent their halls to the League free of charge. The method of pooling milk adopted by the League in the 1920s inspired criticism and the formation of the Non-Pooling Dairymen's League Association, which acted as a bargaining agent for farmers. By that time, too, the Dairymen's League dealt almost solely with Borden's, while farmers who supplied other creameries belonged to separate organizations. On some of the problems faced by the Dairymen's League in the 1920s and 1930s, see Lowell K. Dyson, "The Milk Strike of 1939 and the Destruction of the Dairy Farmers' Union," *New York History* 51 (1970): 523–44.

33. State of New York, *Preliminary Report of the Joint Legislative Committee on Dairy Products, Live Stock and Poultry, February, 1917* (Albany, 1917), 55–570, especially 301–36; Dillon, *Seven Decades of Milk*, 84–102; *Rural New Yorker*, August 19 and 26, October 7, 1916.

34. State of New York, *Preliminary Report*, 329–36; *Dairymen's League News*, February 1917; *Delaware County Dairyman*, October 13, 1916; *Freeman's Journal*, October 4, 1916.

35. *Delaware County Dairyman*, October 20, 1916 (quote); *Rural New Yorker*, October 14, 1916; *Dairymen's League News*, February 1917. Also see Colman, *Education and Agriculture*, 275–77. For urban consumers' discontent about rising milk prices, see City of New York, *Report of the Mayor's Committee on Milk* (New York, 1917). Also see *Dairymen's League News*, December 1918, and February 10, 1919; Dyson, "Milk Strike of 1939."

36. For background on the Farm Bureau, see Gladys Baker, *The County Agent* (Chicago, 1939); Burritt, "Rise and Significance of Agricultural Extension"; *idem*, *The County Agent and the Farm Bureau* (New York, 1922); Orville Merton Kile, *The Farm Bureau Movement* (New York, 1921); Grant McConnell, *The Decline of Agrarian Democracy* (Berkeley, Calif., 1953); Milliman, *What Went Before*, 24–32; Scott, *Reluctant Farmer*.

37. Burritt, "Rise and Significance of Agricultural Extension"; *idem*, *County Agent and the Farm Bureau;* Colman, *Education and Agriculture*, 261–64.

38. Burritt, *County Agent and the Farm Bureau; Extension Service Newsletter* (November, 1919); Organization Committee, NYSFBF, "Organization Suggestions by the New York State Farm Bureau Federation, August, 1921," Farm Bureau Records; Colman, *Education and Agriculture*, 265–71. The Farm Bureau remained relatively small in New York (it claimed 10,143 members in 1920, compared with 48,008 Grangers) until the 1940s and 1950s. See Robert L. Tontz, "Membership of General Farmers' Organizations," 154, 156.

39. Marathon Grange, Minutes, June 12 (quote), August 7, October 16 (quote), October 30, 1915; also see *Rural New Yorker*, July 29, 1916; and M. C. Howard to E. V. Underwood, September 1, 1923, Box 4, Farm Bureau Records. All Granges whose records I examined cooperated in some fashion with the county agents; the extension workers often joined Granges and also led discussions on agricultural topics. See, for example, Transit Grange #1092, Patrons of Husbandry, Minutes, October 18, 1917, NYSG Records.

40. See H. C. McKenzie to M. C. Burritt, October 28, 1919, Box 3, Farm

Bureau Records; Colman, *Education and Agriculture,* 274–80, 355–60. County agents in the Midwest did far more to promote cooperatives than those in New York. See Baker, *County Agent,* 46–56; Burritt, *County Agent and the Farm Bureau,* 93–110.

41. See New York State Conference Board of Farm Organizations, Minutes, 1922–1929. Also see James L. Guth, "The National Board of Farm Organizations: Experiment in Political Cooperation," *Agricultural History* 48 (1974): 418–40. On the political activity of the American Farm Bureau Federation, see McConnell, *Decline of Agrarian Democracy.*

42. On the AFBF as an interest group, see Kile, *Farm Bureau Movement;* and McConnell, *Decline of Agrarian Democracy.*

43. *Morris Chronicle,* quoted in *Worchester Times,* March 24, 1915.

44. See, for example, *Freeman's Journal,* December 6, 1916 (quote); *St. Lawrence Plaindealer,* September 26, 1911, and September 29, 1914; *Steuben Farmers' Advocate,* February 12, 1913; *Worchester Times,* October 20, 1915; *Canastota Bee,* January 13, 1906.

45. For examples of the local Granges' opposition to the township school law, see Marathon Grange, Minutes, January 19, 1918; Stone Ridge Grange, Minutes, April 8, 1918; Transit Grange, Minutes, January 17, 1918, NYSG Records. For a compilation of editorials and letters on the township law, see Thomas E. Finegan [The University of the State of New York, The State Department of Education], *The Township System: A Documentary History of the Endeavor to Establish a Township School System in the State of New York from the Early Periods through the Repeal of the Township Law in 1918* (Albany, 1921), 155–520.

46. On the work of wartime agencies, see Robert D. Cuff, *The War Industries Board: Business–Government Relations During World War I* (Baltimore, 1973); Danbom, *Resisted Revolution,* Chapter V.

47. See Colman, *Education and Agriculture,* 281–82; L. R. Simons, "Wartime and Other Emergency Activities of the New York State Extension Service," *Cornell Extension Bulletin,* 1015; for local examples, *Oswego County Farm Bureau News,* November 1917–June 1918.

48. Marathon Grange, Minutes, May 26, 1917 (quote); *Yates County Chronicle,* October 3, 1917 (quote). On patriotic activities, see, for example, Bowens Corners Grange, Minutes, July 3, 1917, and September 17, 1918; Domestic Grange #96, Patrons of Husbandry, Minutes, April 21, 1917; Findley Lake Grange #1129, Patrons of Husbandry, Minutes, April 23, 1918; Hermitage Grange #1086, Patrons of Husbandry, Minutes, July 6, 1917; Transit Grange, Minutes, October 18, 1917, all in NYSG Records.

49. George F. Warren, Diaries, October 13, 14, and 15, 1917; Warren to Clyde L. King, October 10, 1918, Warren Papers. Also see *Rural New Yorker,* July 14, 1917; *Dairymen's League News,* May, June, and December, 1918; *Delaware County Dairyman,* January 26, 1917.

50. For examples of rural opposition to daylight saving time, see Bowens Corners Grange, Minutes, June 17, 1919; Domestic Grange, Minutes, May 1, 1920; Virgil Grange #457, Patrons of Husbandry, Minutes, December 5, 1923, all NYSG Records; and the numerous petitions printed in *Journal of Proceedings of the Forty-seventh Annual Session of the New York State Grange of the Patrons of Husbandry, Rochester, 1920* (Syracuse, N.Y., 1920), 124; *Journal of Proceedings of the Forty-Eighth Annual Session of the New York State Grange of the Patrons of Husbandry Utica, 1921* (Syracuse, N.Y., 1921), 120–25.

51. Accounts of the New York suffrage campaign include Anthony and Harper, *History of Woman Suffrage* 4: 839–73; Ida Husted Harper, ed., *The History of Woman Suffrage* 5 (New York, 1922), 440–89; Carrie Chapman Catt, *Woman Suffrage and Politics: The Inner Story of the Suffrage Movement*, 2nd ed. (New York, 1926); and Flexner, *Century of Struggle*, 258–70, 279–83, and 300–301.

52. On the revitalization of the suffrage movement in New York and elsewhere, see Ellen DuBois, "Working Women, Class Relations, and Suffrage Militance"; Flexner, *Century of Struggle*, 222–31, 256–85. Aileen S. Kraditor, *The Ideas of the Woman Suffrage Movement, 1890–1920* (New York, 1965), argued that arguments based on expediency, rather than natural rights, dominated woman suffrage rhetoric by the early twentieth century, although no absolute shift took place. Suffragists in rural New York offered all varieties of arguments in the second phase of the suffrage campaign. On the effort in rural New York, see, for example, Susan Look Avery Club, Minutes, October 30, 1915; Warsaw Political Equality Club, Minutes; Political Equality Club of Bath, Journal, October 27, 1899, 1900–1907; Anthony Club, Minutes, November 25, 1902.

53. See Delhi Equal Suffrage Club, Minutes, August 5 and September 23, 1915; Woman Suffrage Party of the First Assembly District of Chautauqua County, Minutes, 1915; Warsaw Political Equality Club, Minutes, "Annual Report, 1915–1916"; *Delaware Republican*, July 3 and 10, 1915; *Baldwinsville Gazette and Farmers' Journal*, June 17, 1915. Carrie Chapman Catt to Campaign District Chairmen, March 18, 1915; Catt to All Up-State Leaders, April 19, 1915; "The Plan of the Campaign of 1915," manuscript, 1915[?], all in Box 2, Catt Papers. An excellent analysis of suffragists' tactics is David Kevin McDonald, "Organizing Womanhood: Women's Culture and the Politics of Woman Suffrage in New York State, 1865–1917" (Ph.D. diss., State University of New York at Stony Brook, 1987).

54. *Plattsburgh Press*, October 11, 1915 (quote). Also see, for the weeks of September and October, *Cortland Standard*, especially October 6, October 11, and October 25, 1915, for a range of pro-suffrage arguments; *St. Lawrence Plaindealer* (especially September 21 and October 5) a neutral newspaper that printed items from both sides; *Cobleskill Index*, an anti-suffrage newspaper that, inspite of its leanings, printed accounts of the local campaign, such as on September 30, 1915, but editorialized on women's lack of interest in politics on October 28, 1915.

55. *Cortland Standard*, October 7, 1915.

56. Among works that trace the transformation in the meaning of the vote from a partisan expression to an exercise in judgment, see McGerr, *Decline of Popular Politics;* Reynolds, *Testing Democracy.* For an extended discussion of this change to women's politics, see my "Domestication of Politics," 639–47.

57. See Appendix for county returns. Prohibition Party support—such as it was—appeared in rural counties, while suffrage support cut across the urban–rural divisions. On socialist voters in New York City, see Doris Daniels, "Building a Winning Coalition: The Suffrage Fight in New York State," *New York History* 60 (1979): 59–80; Elinor Lerner, "Immigrant and Working-Class Involvement in the New York City Suffrage Movement, 1905–1917," (Ph.D diss., University of California, Berkeley, 1981). Also see Eileen L. McDonagh and H. Douglas Price, "Woman Suffrage in the Progressive Era: Patterns of Opposition and Support in Referenda Voting, 1910–1918," *American Political Science Review* 79 (1985): 415–35.

58. The referendum carried Cortland and the townships of Cortlandville and

Homer, both of which contained relatively large villages. In Montgomery County, the total vote was 44.1 percent in favor of woman suffrage and 55.9 percent against. In Amsterdam, however, 49.9 percent of the voters voted yes.

59. On the Farm Bureau, see county reports for February 17, 1921, Box 1, Farm Bureau Records.

60. Organization of Women of Cazenovia Opposed to the Extension of Woman Suffrage, Minutes, January 19, 1916 (quote). For descriptions of campaigns in rural townships, see W. R. Ellis to Glendolen Bens, August 12, 1917; Adelaide S. Foote to Bens, August 15, 1917; and Mrs. Raymond Brown to Bens, September 5, 1917, all in Glendolen Bens Papers. Also see Warsaw Political Equality Club, Minutes, March 10, and November, 1917, and "Annual Report, 1917–1918"; Woman Suffrage Party of the First Assembly District of Chautauqua County, Minutes, December 9, 1916–December 9, 1917; *Freeman's Journal,* October 24, 1917. On the state campaign, see Daniels, "Building a Winning Coalition"; Harper, *History of Woman Suffrage,* 475–89; Flexner, *Century of Struggle,* 299–301, and Chapter XXI.

61. *Freeman's Journal,* October 31, 1917 (quote).

62. For an analysis of the victory, see Daniels, "Building a Winning Coalition."

63. See Frances E. Rhodes to Bens, January 7, 1918, Bens Papers; Woman Suffrage Party of the First Assembly District of Chautauqua County, Minutes, December 24, 1917, February 27, March 27, and August 28, 1918; Warsaw Political Equality Club, Minutes, December 18, 1917, and October 1, 1920, when the club was disbanded; and Susan Look Avery Club, Minutes, October 8, 1921, and January 27, 1923, after it had become a women's club without political goals. Also see S. E. Forman and Marjorie Shuler, *The Woman Voter's Manual* (New York, 1918).

64. *Yates County Chronicle,* November 14, 1917 (quote); *Schoharie Republican,* November 15, 1917 (quote).

65. See, for example, Virgil School District #12, 1923, Town of Virgil Records; District #7 Records, May 6, 1924, Cuyler Town Records; Hartwick #6 School Meeting Records, May 3, 1921. Some Granges resembled women's clubs by the 1920s. See, for example, Findley Lake Grange minutes after 1916; Willett Grange #1381, Patrons of Husbandry, minutes after 1920, both in NYSG Records.

66. *Freeman's Journal,* March 13, 1918; *Schoharie Republican,* March 21, 1918.

67. *Freeman's Journal* March 13, 1918; *Schoharie Republican* October 16, 1919; *Cobleskill Times,* October 9, 1919, quoted in Daniel Larkin, "A Political Analysis of Schoharie County, 1916–1920" (senior thesis, Hartwick College, Oneonte, New York, 1965), 27.

68. Compare, for example, Jennette Howell Deal Prior, Diaries, September 13 and November 8, 1921; Lizzie Thayer Webb, Diaries, November 5, 1918; and Edna M. Hoffnagle, Diaries, 1915, 1917; with Warsaw Political Equality Club, Minutes, November 1917.

69. See *Madison County Leader,* December 27, 1906 (quote). Also see *Delaware Republican,* October 24, December 5, 1914; January 16, 1915.

70. See Daughters of the American Revolution, Tioughnioga Chapter, Minutes, January 11 and September 11, 1904; November 15, 1905; March 9 and September 18, 1908; October 10, 1910; March 9, 1912; June 9, 1916; November 4, 1918; and December 1, 1920; DAR, Patterson Chapter, Minutes, May 15, 1917; February 1918; and September 1919; Cora E. Fowler, "History of the Otsego Chapter, Daughters of the American Revolution, Read at the Celebration

of the Fiftieth Anniversary of the Chapter" (1944); Catherine Schuyler Chapter of the National Society of the DAR, Records, May 17, 1902, and June 17, 1914.

71. Twentieth Century Club, Domestic Science Section, Minutes, April 4, 1907; January 2, 1908; October 21, December 2, 1909; November 4, 1915; September 20, 1917; October 2, November 6, 1919 (quote), Twentieth Century Club Records.

72. Twentieth Century Club, Domestic Science Section, Minutes, November 4, 1915 (quote); December 5, 1915; October 16, 1919; January 20, September 15, 1921, Twentieth Century Club Records.

73. Twentieth Century Club, Domestic Science Section, Minutes, December 18, 1919 (quote); April 21, September 21, 1921; February 19, 1925; and *passim* through 1928. For an earlier period, Mary P. Ryan has discussed women's voluntary organizations as preparation for domesticity: see Ryan, *Cradle of the Middle Class.*

74. For an example of a social club, see Country Community Club, Minutes, 1917–1922. On home extension at Cornell, see Martha Van Rensselaer, "Home Economics at the New York State College of Agriculture," *Cornell Countryman* 11 (1914): 260–63, 12; Colman, *Education and Agriculture,* 188–89, 283–85, 319–20; Ruby Green Smith, *The People's Colleges: A History of the New York State Extension Service in Cornell University and the State, 1876–1948* (Ithaca, 1949), 75–89, 136–74.

75. Smith, *People's Colleges,* 136–57; Ruth C. Jones, "History of the Cortland County Farm Bureau," undated manuscript, Jones Family Papers; "Otsego County: An Account of its Agriculture and its Farm Bureau," *Farm Bureau Circular* 11 (Ithaca, 1920), 14–15; accounts of the Gee Hill Friendship Club and other local home economics clubs, *Cortland Democrat,* February 27, March 12, April 9, and May 7, 1920. For an indication of some hostility toward home extension, see Adams Center Study Club, Minutes, December 2, 1918.

76. Jones, "History of the Cortland County Farm Bureau"; "Saving Strength," *Cornell Reading-Course for Farmers' Wives,* Series III, no. 15 (1905); "Suggestions on Home Sanitation," *Farmers' Wives' Reading-Course* Series III, no. 11 (1904). On work with Granges, see for example Cattaraugus Grange, Minutes, May 19, 1920; Marathon Grange, Minutes, March 15, 1919; Stone Ridge Grange, Minutes, November 7, 1921, May 15, 1922; Transit Grange, Minutes, May 18, 1922, December 19, 1924, all in NYSG Records.

77. *Extension Service Newsletter* (Nov., 1919) quote; (June, 1919) quote; *Cornell Reading-Course for Farmers' Wives,* Series I, no. 3 (1903).

78. *Extension Service Newsletter* (May, 1920); also see Jones, "History of the Cortland Country Farm Bureau," Jones Family Papers.

79. *Extension Service Newsletter* Series II (Nov. 1919).

80. On changes in homemaking in general, see Ruth Schwartz Cowan, *More Work for Mother: The Ironies of Household Technology from the Open Hearth to the Microwave* (New York, 1983); Glenna Matthews, *"Just a Housewife": The Rise and Fall of Domesticity in America* (New York, 1987).

Chapter 6: Progressivism and the Countryside in the 1920s

1. On the increasing proportion of farm income that taxes took in the early 1920s, see Call, "Farm Property Taxation in New York"; Compton, *Fiscal Problems*

of Rural Decline; M. Slade Kendrick, "An Index Number of Farm Taxes in New York, and Its Relation to Various Other Economic Factors," CUAES *Bulletin* 457, (Ithaca, 1926); and Pond, *Full Value Real Estate Assessment,* 82–85. On prices and consumption patterns, see George F. Warren, "Prices of Farm Products in New York," CUAES *Bulletin* 416 (Ithaca, 1923); Helen Canon, "Size of Purchasing Centers of New York Farm Families," CUAES *Bulletin* 472 (Ithaca, 1928); *idem* "The Family Finances of 195 Farm Families in Tompkins County, New York, 1927–1928," CUAES *Bulletin* 522 (Ithaca, 1931); New York State College of Home Economics, *Household Buying by Farm Families, 1929,* 14 vols. (Ithaca, 1929); Marion Fish, "Buying For the Household as Practiced by 368 Farm Families in New York, 1928–29," CUAES *Bulletin* 561 (Ithaca, N.Y., 1933); and Harold C. Hoffsomer, "Relation of Cities and Large Villages to Changes in Rural Trade and Social Areas in Wayne County, New York," CUAES *Bulletin* 582 (Ithaca, 1934).

2. *Delaware Republican,* March 1, 1924; *Freeman's Journal,* February 2, 1921; *Journal of Proceedings of the Forty-seventh Annual Session of the New York State Grange of the Patrons of Husbandry, Rochester, 1920* (Syracuse, N.Y. 1920), 7. Also see the report on a speech by Fred Rasmussen, former Secretary of Agriculture, in Ithaca, in *Cortland Democrat,* February 13, 1920; and the account of the Cortland Pomona Grange, *Cortland Democrat,* March 5, 1920.

3. H. S. Linger to Bert Lord, February 8, 1920, Lord Papers. On the same subject, see *Dairymen's League News,* December 25, 1919, and January 25, 1920; *Journal of Proceedings of the Forty-Seventh Annual Session of the New York State Grange,* 14–17.

4. Smith, *People's Colleges,* 312–19, is a sympathetic account of the Home Bureau's role in increasing the state's control over rural schools. Also see Colman, *Education and Agriculture,* 365; George A. Works, "The Committee on Rural Schools," *Cornell Countryman,* April, 1921; and *idem,* "New York Can Have Better Rural Schools," *Extension Service News,* July 1922; Updegraff, *Rural School Survey of New York State; Rural New Yorker,* September 8, 1923, December 6, 1924; New York State Conference Board of Farm Organizations, Minutes, February 2, 1922; and *Delaware Republican,* March 22, 1924, on Farm Bureau support for a rural school bill. For local reactions, see Cattaraugus Grange #865, Minutes, November 26, 1921 (quote); Marathon Grange #455, Minutes, May 7, 1921; Charlotte Center Grange #669, Patrons of Husbandry, Minutes, March 25, 1921; all in NYSG Records.

5. *Carthage Republican-Tribune,* March 4, 1926; and H. S. Linger to Bert Lord, February 8, 1920, Lord Papers.

6. *Delaware Republican,* April 5, 1924; Waldron Harrington to Lord, February 20, 1920 (quote); W. S. Peck, March 20, 1920 (quote); see also J. B. Amsden to Lord, February 23, 1920; Otto L. Ives to Lord, February 24, 1920; Edson Pearsall to Lord, February 23, 1920; all in Lord Papers; and *Carthage Republican-Tribune,* June 19, 1926 (quote). Also see complaint about licensing in *Edmeston Local,* March 6, 1920.

7. See reports from Farm Bureau leaders on membership drives, such as E. V. Underwood to Enos Lee, September 25, 1923, Box 3; and membership blanks in Box 1, December 15, 1920, NYSFB Records. S. K. Wilcox to Lord, February 24, 1920 (quote), Lord Papers; Colman, *Education and Agriculture,* 356–62; *Freeman's Journal,* December 8 and 15 (quote), 1920; *Cortland Democrat,* August 27, 1920.

8. R. C. Stofer to Lord, February 2, 1920 (quote); and among the numerous letters on specific legislation, see, for example, W. H. Dun to Lord, April 20, 1920; Carrie Lathrop to Lord, February 12, 1920; Lord to E. B. Clark, February 17, 1920, asking for a list of the positions of the Sherburne Grange; V. A. Mead to Lord, March 3, 1920, all in Lord Papers. All records of local Granges contained discussions of letters received; see, for example, Marathon Grange, Minutes; Hermitage Grange #1086, Patrons of Husbandry, Minutes; Transit Grange #1092, Minutes, all through the 1920s, NYSG Records.

9. The Cooperstown *Freeman's Journal*, for example, won a series of awards at the College of Agriculture's Farmer's Week in 1921 for its local coverage.

10. *Otsego Farmer*, November 3, 1922 (quote); *Hancock Herald*, quoted in *Delaware Republican*, August 16, 1924 (quote); *Cortland Democrat*, October 22, 1920 (quote); *Sidney Record*, November 4, 1922; and *Freeman's Journal*, October 27, 1920.

11. On Roosevelt, see *Carthage Republican-Tribune*, October 16 and 31, 1924. The Bert Lord papers contained numerous letters on specific pieces of legislation. In addition to the letters cited in note 8, see Thomas Colbus to Lord, February 28, 1920, Lord Papers; and the letters and petitions of numerous Granges, Farm Bureaus, chapters of the Dairymen's League, the Law and Order League, and WCTU chapters, among others, claiming the support of their members for certain pieces of legislation. One Oxford newspaper provided a petition against daylight saving time that readers could cut out and send to Lord. On holding candidates to account, see *Carthage Republican-Tribune*, June 17, 1926 (quote); Yates County Convention of the WCTU, September 16, 1925 (quote), and September 14, 1928, WCTU of Penn Yan, Minutes.

12. Ad for John D. Clarke, *Delaware Republican*, July 26, 1924 (quote); *Carthage Republican-Tribune*, October 23, 1924 (quote).

13. *Carthage Republican-Tribune*, October 9, 1924 (quote); and *Oneonta Star*, October 20, 1922, Clarke Papers (quote). On getting out the vote, see *Delaware Republican*, July 19, 1924; *Carthage Republican-Tribune*, October 31, 1924 (quote); Yates County WCTU Convention, September 24, 1926, WCTU of Penn Yan, Minutes; and, generally, on voter apathy and get-out-the-vote campaigns, McGerr, *Decline of Popular Politics*, Chapter VII.

14. *Freeman's Journal*, September 22, 1920 (quote); *Delaware Republican*, June 14, 1924 (quote), and August 2, 1924 (quote); and *Cortland Democrat*, October 15, 1920, on "Smith, Governor and Man."

15. See, for example, M. L. Simpson of the Chenango County Sheep Breeders' Association, to Lord, March 25, 1920; H. J. Kershaw of the Dairymen's League, to Lord, March 19, 1920; Mary E. Sachett of Afton to Lord, March 13, 1920; petition from the Oxford Grange to Lord, April 1, 1920, on Prohibition enforcement (along with numerous letters); and Mrs. F. E. Holmes of the Twentieth Century Club of New Berlin to Lord, March 20, 1920, on an education bill.

16. Mary Vida Clark to Lord, April 1, 1920 (quote); Sarah E. Dunne to Lord, March 26, 1920; and Mrs F. E. Holmes to Lord, March 20, 1920. Letters dating from Lord's earlier stint in the assembly and on the board of supervisors echo the nineteenth-century language of friendship, but these were written by friends. See, for example, James P. Hill to Lord, January 14, 1914; and later, Jesse Jacobs to Lord, February 1, 1920. For contrast, see one of the extremely

impersonal cover letters attached to nominating petitions: Charles L. Carrier to Lord, August 25, 1914.

17. *Delaware Republican*, August 16, 1924 (quote); *Carthage Republican-Tribune* January 28, 1926 (quote), and February 4, 1926, on the "considerable comment" that arose as the first woman elected to the county board of supervisors took her place at the year's meetings. On "female networks" in the upper echelons, see Susan Ware, *Beyond Suffrage: Women in the New Deal* (Cambridge, Mass., 1981); and *idem, Partner and I: Molly Dewson, Feminism, and New Deal Politics* (New Haven, Conn., 1987). See Elisabeth Israels Perry, *Belle Moskowitz: Feminine Politics and the Exercise of Power in the Age of Alfred E. Smith* (New York, 1987); Nancy F. Cott, *The Grounding of Modern Feminism* (New Haven, 1987), on the transformation of the nineteenth-century women's movement to feminism in general; on partisan politics in particular, see 108–14. On the fate of women in politics elsewhere, see Carole Nichols, "Votes and More for Women: Suffrage and After in Connecticut," *Women and History* 5 (Spring 1983); Felice Gordon, *After Winning: The Legacy of the New Jersey Suffragists* (New Brunswick, N.J., 1986).

18. Marathon Grange, Minutes, January 21, 1933 (quote); Stone Ridge Grange #932, Minutes, April 20, 1932, both in NYSG Records.

19. *Carthage Republican-Tribune*, March 4, 1926. On negative reactions to New Deal farm programs in western New York, see Peter B. Bulkley, "Agrarian Crisis in Western New York: New Deal Reinforcement of the Farm Depression," *New York History* 59 (1978): 381–407.

20. A sympathetic account of the Grange League Federation by one of its founders is Milliman, *What Went Before*. Also see Colman, *Education and Agriculture*, 277–80; and Joseph Knapp, *Seeds That Grew: A History of the Cooperative Grange League Federation Exchange* (Hinsdale, N.Y., 1960).

21. H. J. Kershaw of the Dairymen's League, quoted in *Edmeston Local*, March 13, 1920. A few ads from the *Cortland Democrat* provide good examples of the milk campaign: February 6, 1920, and February 27, 1920 (quote). Also see *Dairymen's League News*, December 25, 1919. Rural weeklies dependent on outside copy could be counted on for USDA columns; including women's sections that detailed, for example, how to use more milk and cheese. See, among many, *Edmeston Local*, April 10, 1920.

22. "Mayville, New York, The Gateway to Chautauqua Lake, An Ideal Industrial Location" (np: ca. 1927) (quote). The examples of boosterism—which could be found in any weekly—are taken from *Carthage Republican-Tribune*, June 5, 1924, as the newspaper joined a campaign to bring a hospital to Carthage; and *Edmeston Local*, January 24, 1920, which managed to turn the fact that Edmeston shopkeepers decided to keep shorter hours into an indication that village merchants were up-to-date in recognizing that "greater efficiency can be obtained by concentrated efforts for a shorter period of time."

23. *Carthage Republican-Tribune*, January 14, 1926 (quote), and March 11, 1926 (quote).

24. *Delaware Express*, August 20, 1924; and *Delaware Republican* September 6, 1924. Letters to Bert Lord, such as those cited in notes 8, 11, and 15, indicate some rural devotion to state agricultural programs. Also see the defense of the state agricultural school in Delhi when rumors flew that Governor Al Smith was threatening to eliminate state funding, in the *Delaware Republican*, February 23 and March 15, 1924.

25. *Carthage Republican-Tribune,* January 14, 1926 (quote); DAR, Patterson Chapter, Minutes, November 15, 1921 (quote); The Monday Club (Salem), Minutes, December 3, 1923, December 17, 1924, and February 18, 1924; *Journal of Proceedings of the Forty-Seventh Annual Session of the New York State Grange,* 7; *Journal of Proceedings of the Forty-Eighth Annual Session of the New York State Grange of the Patrons of Husbandry, Utica, 1921* (Syracuse, N.Y., 1921), 113. Also see Twentieth Century Club (Cortland), Domestic Science Section, Minutes, September 16, 1920; January 20, 1921.

26. Yates County Convention of the WCTU, September 14, 1928 (quote); DAR, Tioughnioga Chapter, Minutes, September 14, 1926 (quote); Catherine Schuyler Chapter of the National Society of the DAR Records, September 21, 1921; and *Journal of Proceedings of the Forty-Seventh Annual Session of the New York State Grange,* 128–29.

27. For one reaction to the socialist "threat" and the I.W.W., see *Cortland Democrat,* April 23, 1920 (quote). On the eight-hour day, see, for example, the transcripts of hearings held by the Farm Bureau throughout rural New York in 1921, especially those in Herkimer, Thompkins, and Lewis counties; Farm Bureau Records, Box 1. The DAR chapters took a special interest in Americanization: see DAR, Patterson Chapter, Minutes, January 17, 1922; DAR, Tioughnioga Chapter, Minutes, December 12, 1921; and Twentieth Century Club, Domestic Science Section, Records, January 20, 1921.

28. On the case of the expulsion of the five Socialists in general, see Robert K. Murray, *The Red Scare: A Study in National Hysteria, 1919–1920* (Minneapolis, 1955), 235–38; Thomas E. Vadney, "The Politics of Repression: A Case Study of the Red Scare in New York," *New York History* 49 (January 1968): 56–75. For a campaign promise to boot out Socialists, see *Edmeston Local,* February 14, 1920. A more moderate statement including immigration restrictions is in *Freeman's Journal,* September 29, 1920. For Grange petitions, see *Journal of Proceedings of the Forty-Seventh Annual Session of the New York State Grange,* 125–26. Negative letters to Lord were Charles G. Brooks to Lord, January 16, 1920; O. L. Richmond to Lord, March 25, 1920; Leland Landers to Lord, January 8, 1919. See also Lord to Leland Landers, January 28, 1920. All in Lord Papers. Also see Monday Night Club (Delhi), Minutes, November 10, 1919. The account of Socialist speakers is from *Cortland Democrat,* October 15, 1920. On the whole, the case of the Socialist assemblymen did not receive extraordinary attention in the weeklies, and letters about highways and the like far outweighed the ones about the Socialists in Lord's papers.

29. Richmond to Lord, March 25, 1920, Lord Papers; and *Cortland Democrat,* May 21, 1920.

30. On vacations, for example, see the Jeanette Howell Deal Prior Diaries. After buying an automobile in 1923, she and her husband began to visit friends and relatives far more frequently than in the past; and beginning in July of 1925, they took yearly vacations. Good examples of changes in the meetings of local Granges include Transit Grange, Minutes, 1920–1925; Stone Ridge Grange, Minutes, 1922–1930; South Kortright Grange #1363, Patrons of Husbandry, 1918–1930; Franklinville Grange #1478, Patrons of Husbandry, especially February 5, 1929; Cattaraugus Grange, especially February 1, 1922, all in NYSG Records. On changing patterns of leisure in general, see, for example, John F. Kasson, *Amusing the Million: Coney Island at the Turn of the Century* (New York, 1978); and Roy Rosenzweig, *Eight Hours for What We Will: Workers and Leisure in an Industrial City, 1870–1920* (Cambridge and New York, 1983).

31. On cars in rural places, see Michael L. Berger, *The Devil Wagon in God's Country: The Automobile and Social Change in Rural America, 1893–1929* (Hamden, Conn., 1979); and Joseph Interrante, "You Can't Go to Town in a Bathtub: Automobile Movement and the Reorganization of Rural American Space," *Radical History Review* 21 (Fall 1979): 151–68. On radio, see *Carthage Republican-Tribune*, February 28, 1926 (quote); and Reynold M. Wik, "The Radio in Rural America During the 1920s," *Agricultural History* 55 (1981): 339–50.

32. Little York Grange #441, Patrons of Husbandry, Minutes, March 1 (quote), and August 16, 1887 (quote), NYSG Records; DAR, Tioughnioga Chapter, Minutes, April 11, 1927 (quote); and October 8, 1928 (quote). On changes in ideas about death in the twentieth century, see James J. Farrell, *Inventing the American Way of Death, 1830–1920* (Philadelphia, 1980).

33. See, for example, through the 1920s, the Ladies' Union of the First Baptist Church (Ithaca), Records; Minutes of the Meetings of the Philathea Class, Cornwallville Methodist-Episcopal Church, Records, 1920–1923; and Women's Home Missionary Society, Subdistrict Meeting (Otsego County), Minutes, 1926–1933. Also see William G. Mather, Jr., "The Rural Churches of Allegany County," CUAES *Bulletin* 587 (Ithaca, 1934); and *Edmeston Local*, March 20, 1920.

34. See Young, "Movement of Farm Population"; and Dwight Sanderson, "A Population Study of Three Townships in Cortland County, New York," CUAES *Bulletin* (Ithaca, N.Y., 1928).

35. Less extravagant accounts of revival meetings are found in *Edmeston Local* April 10, 1920; and *Carthage Republican-Tribune*, January 14 and February 4, 1926.

36. On preparation for the meetings, see *Delaware Republican*, December 26, 1914, January 30 and February 6, 1915. Examples of Peacock's sermons were reprinted on February 20, February 27 (quote), March 6, and March 13, 1915. One woman reported a Klan night at one revival meeting: see Prior Diaries, November 19, 1924.

37. His talks on the roles of men and women were reprinted in *Delaware Republican*, February 27 and March 13, 1915.

38. The best account of debates about feminism and women's roles that incorporates current scholarship on the 1920s is Cott, *Grounding of Modern Feminism*. For grumbling about women and work, see *Carthage Republican-Tribune*, July 31, 1924.

39. Prior Diaries, September 26 and November 19 and 21, 1923 (quote); April 29, 1926 (quote).

40. For a survey detailing the work of farm women, see New York State College of Home Economics, *Household Buying by Farm Families;* Fish, "Buying for Households." On housewives' work, see Cowan, *More Work for Mother;* and Glenna Matthews, *"Just a Housewife."*

41. See C. W. Gilbert, "An Economic Study of Tractors on New York Farms," CUAES *Bulletin* 506 (Ithaca, N.Y., 1930).

42. On changing standards of womanhood in the 1920s, see Elaine Tyler May, *Great Expectations: Marriage and Divorce in Post-Victorian America* (Chicago, 1980); and Mary P. Ryan, "The Projection of a New Womanhood: The Movie Moderns in the 1920s," in Lois Scharf and Joan M. Jensen, *Decades of Discontent: The Women's Movement, 1920–1940* (Westport, Conn., 1983).

43. *Cortland Democrat*, June 25, 1920. On women's networks as a source of influence, see Estelle B. Freeman, "Separatism as Strategy: Female Institution-

Building and American Feminism, 1870–1930," *Feminist Studies* 5 (1979): 512–529; and Ware, *Beyond Suffrage.*

44. On the increasing tendency for women's organizations to follow national or state directives, see also Chapter V. One of the clearest examples is the WCTU of Penn Yan, which moved from uncommon militance in the 1870s, to less-confrontational political activity at the turn of the century, to being an organization that raised money and listened to speakers in the 1920s. See the excellent run of records for the WCTU (Penn Yan and Yates County). A classic account of "intensified social stratification" in agricultural organizations is Grant Mc-Connell, *The Decline of Agrarian Democracy* (Berkeley, 1953). While Nancy Cott rightly notes that women's organizations grew in number and membership in the 1920s, one wonders about the activities of club members. Her analysis shows a wide variety of causes espoused by national leaders; those leaders' success in mobilizing members and engaging their interest remains uncertain.

45. On prisons and dumps, see *Cuba Patriot,* August 9, 1989; *New York Times,* September 10 and 19, 1989.

Bibliography

Secondary sources relevant to this study are cited in the notes. Rather than provide an inventory of those books and articles, it seemed more useful to describe the primary documents that form the basis of this book. I began my research by following the *Guides to Historical Resources* produced by the New York Historical Resources Center, Cornell University, Olin Library. Each *Guide* lists the documents available in all of the museums and libraries for a given county. As of 1987, surveyors had examined the holdings of forty-eight counties. Given the massive scale of the task, there are inevitable discrepancies between what the *Guides* list and what archives actually hold or what an archivist can find in a collection. The problem should grow more severe over time: those who had charge of collections when the surveyors arrived will leave their work to others who might not recall where documents had been stored. Even now, some who oversee museums or libraries have never heard of the *Guides;* some simply chuckled when I asked about items listed in one; and items have disappeared from collections. Nonetheless, the *Guides* are the best place to begin to find the rich variety of sources available for the study of New York's history.

Newspapers (not listed in the Resource Center *Guides*) provided the most direct point of entry into New Yorkers' political ideas. Rural weeklies demanded care in their use: nineteenth-century newspapers were highly partisan and trumpeted the causes of local businessmen. Yet, within bounds, newspapers can be read as one source for New Yorkers' political and social convictions. Editors printed stories they believed would interest their readers and would correspond with their audiences' attitudes: it was fairly clear when editors strained to persuade readers to change their minds. Editorial biases also suggested additional insights. The ways editors framed arguments, the language they used, and the near-absence of discussions of local controversies were all important in trying to piece together local political life. Paying attention both to what editors omitted and included as well as to how they expressed their ideas required slow and careful reading. It also meant that I took embarrassingly extensive notes, since the significance of certain statements became clear only much later. And because discussions of political and social attitudes could appear anywhere—in columns devoted to the events in hamlets, to short stories, or to reports of events from nearby counties, as well as in editorials—I needed to give entire newspapers a close reading. Useful material was buried in columns that seemed to have little relation to politics. Because their editors wrote much of their own copy, the following newspapers proved especially useful: the *Angelica Every Week*, the *Cuba Patriot*, the Cooperstown *Freeman's Journal*, the *Westfield Republican*, and the Warsaw *Western New Yorker*.

Diaries often confirmed or corrected the views expressed by the rural editors and suggested some of the day-to-day concerns of men and women. Because their authors needed both time and literacy, diaries are biased sources for discovering the ideas of uncelebrated people. Yet for the late nineteenth century, at least, it was clear that a wide variety of individuals kept diaries: children, the barely literate, small farmers, and women who made a living doing housework, as well as teachers, lawyers, and shopkeepers. Scores of rural people's diaries have been preserved, especially by local historical societies, although the vast majority of these are of the chores–weather–visits variety. Even these diaries, however, helped me see patterns of work and leisure and gain an understanding of rural politics and religion. Diaries covering the twentieth century were less numerous, either because fewer people kept them or because they have yet to make their way into historical societies. A few diaries were especially helpful. Those kept by Jennette Howell Deal Prior, covering the years from 1892 to 1941, provided a wealth of information on one woman's activities in voluntary organizations and her views on marriage, work, and child-rearing. The diary of the chronically depressed Jessie Burnell only covers one year (1884) but dispels romantic notions about rural communities. The Addison Winfield diaries (1888–1893) provide a good account of his political participation as well as of courtship and marriage. The journals of S. W. Hobbes (1880–1895), a usually out-of-work lawyer, also contain useful material on politics in addition to indications of the ways one village family parceled out housework.

The papers of politicians were helpful in gauging rural political concerns. I paid closest attention to letters often passed over by political historians: the innumerable requests for jobs and favors and missives about particular pieces of legislation. The structure and form of these letters and the ways writers made their claims were the most revealing aspects of this correspondence. The collections of prominent Republican assemblyman S. Fred Nixon, Democratic governor Roswell P. Flower, and Democratic governor and senator David Bennett Hill included a great number of constituents' letters, many of them from rural residents. Useful for a contrast to the nineteenth-century correspondence were constituents' letters in the papers of Bert Lord, an assemblyman from Chenango County in the 1910s and 1920s. Most local politicians (and for that matter, assemblymen) did not see fit to save their papers. One exception is H. L. Chadeayne, whose diaries (1876–1884), part of the Chadeayne Family Papers, provide a detailed picture of the work of a local party leader.

Records of rural voluntary organizations were crucial in enabling me to describe men's—and especially women's—political ideas and behavior. These documents pose special problems: the reader is at the mercy of the secretary of an organization. What appeared in the record to be inactivity might have been the sign of a particularly terse secretary. Often one reads "Discussed the woman suffrage question," without further remarks. Nonetheless, organization records contained information present in no other sources. Of singular value were the records of the defunct Granges of New York State—scores of minute books, membership lists, and treasurer's reports—at the Collection of Regional History at the Cornell University Archives. My analysis hardly begins to exploit these important sources for rural social organization and attitudes and politics. The records of women's groups are not so conveniently gathered together. The minutes of WCTUs, suffrage clubs, and other women's organizations are scattered in township and county historical societies throughout the state. The minutes of the Warsaw Political Equality Club, the Alfred Centre WCTU, and the WCTU of Penn Yan were especially detailed.

Government records were the final major set of primary sources important to this study. The proceedings of county boards of supervisors, which often contained township-level electoral statistics in addition to tax equalization reports, are readily available at county libraries, the New York State Library, and Olin Library at Cornell, among other places. No county supervisors' reports recorded the debates that took place—only motions and votes and the reports of various committees. Until the twentieth century, few newspapers did much more than simply reprint the proceedings of sessions (which would eventually be pulled together in a bound volume). The records of township officers, town meetings, and school districts, which are usually not very detailed, are most often found in township and county libraries.

The surveys and reports published by the Cornell University Agricultural Experiment Station (often dissertations done in the departments of Agricultural Economics, Farm Management, and Rural Sociology) were indispensable sources for tracing changes in rural communities and the farm economy. The personal papers of faculty—especially Liberty Hyde Bailey and George Warren—provided insights into rural reform and the work of the College of Agriculture. The published work of these men and other rural reformers also detail the Progressives' vision of the countryside. Most of these works (cited in the notes) tended to express disappointment in rural people's rejection of modernity and are of interest chiefly for that reason. One exceptionally useful book, however, was James Mickel Williams' *The Expansion of Rural Life: The Social Psychology of Rural Development* (New York, 1926), which discussed different types of rural places and offered a theory linking economic change and adaptations in individuals' personalities.

Primary Sources

Newspapers and Newsletters

Allegany County Republican (Angelica), 1880–1893.
Baldwinsville Gazette and Farmers' Journal, 1914–1917.
Ballston Journal, 1870–1875.
Bolivar Breeze, 1892–1894.
Canastota Bee, 1906–1908.
Canisteo Times, 1892–1894.
Carthage Republican-Tribune, 1920–1928.
The Castilian, 1880, 1884.
Cattaraugus Republican, 1888–1893.
Chautauquan Daily, 1911, 1913.
Cobleskill Index, 1880–1920.
Cornell Countryman, 1910–1920.
Cortland Democrat, 1876–1922.
Cortland Standard, 1880–1886, 1910–1920.
Cuba Daily News, 1880.
Cuba Patriot, 1880–1896.
Dairymen's League News, 1917–1925.
Delaware County Dairyman (Franklin), 1892–1918.
Delaware Gazette (Delhi), 1890–1895.
Delaware Republican, 1914–1924.
Dundee Observer, 1904–1908.
Edmeston Local, 1920–1925.

Every Week (Angelica), 1886–1887.
Extension Service News, 1919–1925.
Freeman's Journal (Cooperstown), 1880–1925.
Friendship Weekly Register, 1880–1895.
The Grape Belt (Brocton), 1893–1900.
Jefferson Courier, 1892–1896.
Madison County Leader (Morrisville), 1892–1910.
Middleburgh Gazette, 1892–1896.
Middleburgh News, 1892–1896.
Morning Star [Glens Falls], 1880, 1893–1896.
Oswego County Farm Bureau News, 1916–1920.
Otsego County Farm Bureau News, 1917–1920.
Otsego News, 1925–1928.
Plattsburgh Press, 1915–1918.
Richmond Springs Mercury and Daily, 1913–1915.
Rural New Yorker, 1915–1925.
St. Lawrence Plaindealer, 1914–1918.
Schoharie Republican, 1892–1920.
Sidney Record, 1915–1925.
Steuben Farmers' Advocate, 1879–1917.
Unadilla Times, 1891–1895.
Washington County Post (Cambridge), 1892–1897.
Watkins Express, 1873–1880.
[Wellsville] *Daily Reporter*, 1880–1896.
Westfield Republican, 1883–1890.
Western New Yorker (Warsaw), 1893–1896.
Woman's Journal, 1880–1893.
Worchester Times, 1914–1918.
Yates County Chronicle (Penn Yan), 1895–1900, 1917–1919.

Diaries

Bean Family Papers, Frank A. Bean Diaries, 1904–1910. CCHS.
Henry F. Benton Diaries, 1872, 1896, 1908. CCHS.
Sara Blackman Diaries, 1889–1918. Thelma Rogers Historical and Genealogical Society, Wellsville.
Charles H. Broughton Diaries, 1876–1901. NYSHA.
Jessie Burnell Diary, 1884. NYSHA.
Nina Burton Diaries, 1908–1921. MCHS.
Bushnell Diaries, 1857–1893. NYSHA.
Helen Tooke Butler, Collector. Family Papers. CU (including Isaac P. Richards Diary).
Chadeayne Family of Cornwall Diaries, 1876–1884. NYSHA.
Alexander H. Coffin Diary, 1878–1888. NYSHA.
Delphine Coney Diaries. CU.
Thomas Matthew Costello Diaries, 1870–1884. NYSL.
Truman Crumb Diaries, 1888–1912. MCHS.
Edward J. Filkins Diary, 1872. SCHS.

M. W. Frisbee Diary, 1870, 1882. NYSHA.
Stephen Hait Diaries, 1891–1893. NYSHA.
Connie K. Hinkley Diaries. ChCHS.
Hobbes Family Papers. CU (including S. W. Hobbes Diaries).
Edna M. Hoffnagle Diary, 1902–1918. NYSL.
Elbridge Hunter Diaries, 1875–1891. DCHS.
Abram B. Karker Diaries, 1852–1904. SCHS.
Celia Keynon, Diary 1899. Historical Society of South Jefferson.
Oscar Loveland Diary, 1884, in possession of Miss Ilene Smith, Adams Center.
Mary Mackin Diaries, 1913–1939. Thelma Rogers Historical and Genealogical
  Society, Wellsville.
Moores Diaries, 1863–1882. NYSHA.
D. W. Oliver Diaries, 1880–1882, copy in possession of author.
Mrs. P. Palmer Diary, 1877. NYSHA.
A. Parsons Diaries, 1858–1872. MCHS.
Jennette Howell Deal Prior Diaries. CU.
Wellington Richards Diaries, 1888–1924. NYSHA.
Edward Rutherford Diary, 1906. Belfast Town Hall.
F. W. Squires Diaries, 1840–1897. CU.
Mrs. M. D. Spaford Diary, 1904–1905. NYSHA.
Charles Spencer Diaries, 1902–1932. ChCHS.
Aldrich Swann Diaries, 1876–1920. Esperance Historical Museum.
Tenny Family Diaries, 1880–1885. NYSHA.
Lizzie Thayer Webb Diaries, 1896–1929. NYSHA.
Addison Winfield Diaries, 1888–1893. NYSHA.
Wood Family of Butternuts Diaries, 1884–1886. NYSHA.
Unidentified woman, Diary. 1877, Thelma Rogers Historical and Genealogical
  Society, Wellsville.

Personal Papers

Ackerly Papers. CU.
Liberty Hyde Bailey Papers. CU.
[Martha] Beaujeans Family Papers. ChCHS.
Lester Pratt Bennett Papers. CCHS.
Glendolen Bens Papers. Manuscripts and Archives Division, New York Public
  Library.
Alonzo D. Blodgett Family Papers. CCHS.
Maurice C. Burritt Papers. CU.
Carrie Chapman Catt Papers. Manuscript and Archives Division, New York Pub-
  lic Library.
[Mrs. Henry White] Cannon Collection. DCHS.
John and Marion Clark Papers. NYSHA.
Frank Norton Decker Papers. CU.
Chauncey M. Depew Papers. Sterling Memorial Library, Yale.
S. W. Fletcher Letterbooks. CU.
Roswell P. Flower Papers. SUNYO.
Roswell P. Flower Papers JCHM.
David Bennett Hill Papers. NYSL.

Raymond Clark Hitchings Papers. CU.
Jones Family Papers. CCHS.
George Pomeroy Keese Collection. NYSHA.
Virgil Kellogg Letters, 1896–98. Historical Society of South Jefferson.
Bert Lord Papers. CU.
William Morgan Papers. NYSL
S. Fred Nixon Papers (microfilm). CU. Originals at ChCHS.
Joseph McGinnies Papers (microfilm). CU. Originals at ChCHS.
May Morgan McKoon Temperance Papers. NYSL.
Thomas Collier Platt Papers. Sterling Memorial Library, Yale.
Henry S. Randall Correspondence. CCHS.
Frederick Elisha Shapleigh Papers. CU.
Charles Rufus Skinner Copy Book, 1881. NYSL.
Charles Rufus Skinner Papers. JCHM.
George Beal Sloan, Jr. Letters. SUNYO.
Temperance Correspondence. NYSL.
Horace Tennant Scrapbooks. SCHS.
George F. Warren Papers. CU.
Robinson Family Papers. CU.
Speeches Collection. JCHS.

Organizations

AGRICULTURAL

Central New York Farmers' Club Records. CU.
Cortland County Agricultural Society Records. CCHS.
Cortland County Farmers' Club Records. CCHS.
Department of Household Economics and Management Records. CU.
Dryden Mutual Protection Society Records. CU.
Farm Bureau Records. CU.
Farm Management Scrapbooks. CU.
Farmers' National Alliance, Castile Local 141, Records. CU.
Laonia Lodge 488 of Farmers' Alliance and Industrial Union of the State of New
     York, Minutes. Darwin K. Barker Library Historical Museum (Fredonia).
New York State College of Home Economics Extension Records. CU.
New York State Conference Board of Farm Organizations Records. CU.
New York State Grange Records. CU.
New York State Grange Readings Course. CU.
Rural Leadership Correspondence School Records. CU.
Volney Grange #165, Patrons of Husbandry, Records. Volney Town Hall (Volney
     Town Historian).

CHURCHES

Belleville Baptist Church File. Historical Society of South Jefferson.
Cooperstown United Methodist Church Records. NYSHA.
Cornwallville Methodist-Episcopal Church Minutes. NYSHA.
Cortland County Ministerial Association Minutes. CCHS.

Cortlandville Union Church Society Records. CCHS.
First Baptist Church of Ithaca Records. CU.
First Methodist Church of Cortland Records. CCHS.
Gilbertsville Baptist Church Society Minutes. NYSHA.
Presbyterian Church of Cazenovia Records. CU.
Presbyterian Ladies' Missionary Society Records. NYSHA.
Union Church Society of South Cortland Records. CCHS.
United Presbyterian Church, Salem, New York Papers. CU.

PARTISAN AND MISCELLANEOUS

Adams Center Study Club, Secretary and Treasurer's Records. Adams Center
    Free Library.
Belfast Board of Trade Minutes. Belfast Town Hall.
Ben Marvin Post #209, Grand Army of the Republic, Minutes. DCHS.
Chautauqua County Republican Party Committee Papers (microfilm). CU. Origi-
    nals at ChCS.
Chautauqua County Veterans' Union Records. ChCHS.
Cooperstown Literary Society Minutes. NYSHA.
Elections Collection. JCHM.
Grand Army of the Republic, Alfred Chapter, Minutes. AU.
Grand Army of the Republic, Knowlton Post, Minutes. Cazenovia Public Library.
Grand Army of the Republic, Department of New York, John A. Logan Post 477,
    Minutes. NYSL.
Jeffersonian Club of Cooperstown Minutes. NYSHA.
Kiatone Lodge #312, Independent Order of Good Templars, Minutes. ChCHS.
Oaksville Reform Club Records. NYSHA.
Oneida Republican Battery Records. MCHS.
Orophilian Lyceum Recordbook. AU.
Schoharie County Republican Party Committee Poll Books, 1894. SCHS.
Truxton Literary Club Minutes. CCHS.
Young Men's Democratic Reform Club of Volney, Records. Volney Town Hall
    (Volney Town Historian).

WOMEN'S CLUBS

Albany Woman Suffrage Society Records. NYSL.
Alfred Centre Women's Christian Temperance Union Records. AU.
Anthony Club Records. David A. Howe Public Library, Wellsville.
Susan Look Avery Club Records. Wyoming County Historical Center.
Cooperstown Y.M.C.A. Women's Auxiliary Minutes. NYSHA.
Cortland County Federation of Women's Clubs Records. CCHS.
Country Community Club Minutes. Darwin K. Barker Library Historical Mu-
    seum (Fredonia).
Daughters of the American Revolution, Patterson Chapter, Records. PFL.
Daughters of the American Revolution, Catherine Schuyler Chapter, Records.
    David A. Howe Public Library, Wellsville.
Daughters of the American Revolution, Tioughnioga Chapter, Records. CCHS.
Delhi Equal Suffrage Club Minutes. DCHS.
Hobart Women's Civic Club Minutes. DCHS.

Ladies' Literary Club Records. CCHS.

The Monday Club, Salem, New York, Records. CU.

Monday Club (Warsaw) Minutes. Warsaw Public Library.

Monday Club (Westfield) Minutes. PFL.

Monday Night Club (Delhi) Minutes. DCHS.

New York State Association Opposed to Woman Suffrage, Records. NYSL.

Oneida Women's Christian Temperance Union Minutes. MCHS.

Organization of Women of Cazenovia Against Woman Suffrage, Records. Cazenovia Public Library.

Palermo Woman's Christian Temperance Union Secretary's Book. SUNYO.

Political Equality Club of Cattaraugus County, New York, Records. NYSL.

Political Equality Society of Bath Journal. CU.

Political Equality Club of Oneida Records. MCHS.

Anna Shaw Club Minutes. Friendship Free Library.

Travellers' Club Minutes. PFL.

Twentieth Century Club Records. CCHS.

Warsaw Political Equality Club Minutes. Warsaw Public Library.

Westfield Book Club Minutes. PFL.

Woman's Christian Temperance Union (Penn Yan) Records. Yates County Genealogical and Historical Society.

Women's Republican Association of Alfred Centre Records. AU.

Woman Suffrage Party of the First Assembly District of Chautauqua County, Minutes. ChCHS.

Wyoming County Political Equality Club Minutes. Wyoming County Historical Center.

Government

Allegany County School Commissioner, District 1, Records. Belfast Town Hall.

[Belfast] Justice Court Records. Belfast Town Hall.

Belfast School District #11 Minutes. Belfast Town Hall.

Cortland City Records. Cortland County Court House.

Cortland County Public Health Association Records. CCHS.

Cortland Village Trustees Minutes. Cortland County Court House.

Gorham School District #9 Minutes. NYSHA.

Hartwick School District #3 Minutes. NYSHA.

Hartwick School District #6 Minutes. NYSHA.

Minden-Danube School District Minutes. NYSHA.

New York State Legislative Committee on Taxation, Book of Records of the Tax Commission, 1881. NYSL.

Oxford and Green School District #16 Minutes. NYSHA.

Roxbury School Minutes of Meetings. NYSHA.

Town of Belfast Records. Belfast Town Hall.

Town of Cuyler Collection. CCHS.

Town of Hartford Records. CCHS.

Town of Lapeer Records. CCHS.

Town of Marathon Records. CCHS.

Town of McGraw Records. CCHS.

Town of Preble Collection. CCHS.

Town of Preston Records. CCHS.
Town of Scott Records. CCHS.
Town of Solon Records. CCHS.
Town of Taylor Records. CCHS.
Town of Truxton Records. CCHS.
Town of Virgil Records. CCHS.
Village of Belfast Records. Belfast Town Hall.
Volney Town Clerk's Records. Volney Town Hall (Volney Town Historian).

Miscellaneous

Eleanor H. Blodgett. "Cortland Branch: American Red Cross, 1916–1925."
    Manuscript, 1966. CCHS.
Dewitt Carpenter. *Facts for Farmers: To the Farmers by a Farmer for the Farmer.* Pub.
    and distributed by Delaware, Lackawanna, and Western Railroad, 1910.
    CCHS.
Farmers' Club of Hanover. "To the Farmers, Farmers Clubs and Grangers of
    Chautauqua County." 1890. NYSHA.
"History of the Otsego Chapter, Daughters of the American Revolution, written
    by Miss Cora E. Fowler, Read at the Celebration of the Fiftieth Anniversary
    of the Chapter 1944." NYSHA.
"Mayville, New York, The Gateway to Chautauqua Lake, An Ideal Industrial
    Location." N.p., ca. 1927. ChCHS.

Published Reports and Speeches

Anti-Saloon League Yearbook. Chicago, 1906–1920.
William C. Bagley, Orville G. Brim, and Mabel Carney. *Rural School Survey of New
    York State: The Teaching Personnel, The Elementary Curriculum, Community Rela-
    tions.* Ithaca, 1923.
City of New York. *Report of the Mayor's Committee on Milk.* New York, 1917.
*The Cortland Normal School Controversy, Issued by the Local Board and Addressed to the
    Legislature of the State of New York.* Syracuse, 1880.
Department of Commerce, Bureau of the Census. *United States Census of Agricul-
    ture, 1925.* Part I, Northern States. Washington, D.C., 1926.
Frances W. Graham and Georgeanna M. Gardener. *Two Decades: A History of the
    First Twenty Years' Work of the Woman's Christian Temperance Union of the State of
    New York.* Oswego, N.Y., 1894.
J. A. McGinnies, compiler. *Laws and Resolutions of the Board of Supervisors of Chau-
    tauqua County.* Jamestown, 1924.
New York State Diary Commission. *First Annual Report, with Accompanying Docu-
    ments.* Albany, 1885.
New York State Food Supply Commission. *Census of the Agricultural Resources of
    New York, Census of 1917.* Albany, 1917.
———. *Census of the Agricultural Resources of New York State, Census of 1918.* Albany,
    1918.
New York Milk Committee. *Proceedings, Conference on Milk Problems.* New York,
    1910[?].

The New York Red Book, An Illustrated Legislative Manual. Albany, 1890–1930.

New York State. *Preliminary Report of the Joint Legislative Committee on Dairy Products, Live Stock and Poultry.* Albany, 1917.

————. *Report of the Director of Farmers' Institutes and Normal Institutes, 1900–1910.* Albany, 1900–1910.

New York State Assessors. *Annual Report.* Albany, 1875–1900.

New York State Education Department. *Annual Report* Albany, 1905–1930.

New York State Grange. *Record of Proceedings of the New York State Grange, Patrons of Husbandry.* 1874–1924.

New York State Improvement of Highways Committee. *Report, March 6, 1905.* Albany, 1906.

New York State Superintendent of Public Instruction. *Annual Report.* Albany, 1870–1904.

New York State Woman Suffrage Association. *Report of the New York State Woman Suffrage Association.* 1893–1900.

"Oration of Hon. Stephen L. Mayham, at Schoharie, N.Y., July 4, 1872, on the Centennial Anniversary of the Old Stone Fort, at Schoharie." Schoharie, 1872.

Proceedings of the Board of Supervisors of Cattaragus County, 1870–1930.

Proceedings of the Board of Supervisors of Cortland County, 1870–1930.

Proceedings of the Board of Supervisors of Chautauqua County, 1870–1930.

Proceedings of the Board of Supervisors of Lewis County, 1870–1930.

Proceedings of the Board of Supervisors of Oswego County, 1870–1930.

Proceedings of the Board of Supervisors of St. Lawrence County, 1870–1930.

Proceedings of the Board of Supervisors of Schoharie County, 1870–1930.

Proceedings of the Board of Supervisors of Washington County, 1870–1930.

Public Papers of Roswell P. Flower, Governor, 3 vols. Albany, 1893–1895.

United States Department of Agriculture. *Yearbook of the Department of Agriculture.* 1900–1940.

Woman's Christian Temperance Union of the State of New York. *Report of the Annual Meeting of the Woman's Christian Temperance Union of the State of New York.* 1885–1908.

Harlan Updegraff. *Rural School Survey of New York State: Financial Support.* Ithaca, 1922.

Unpublished Papers

Hal S. Barron, "And the Crooked Shall Be Made Straight: Public Road Administration and the Decline of Localism in the Rural North, 1870–1930." Paper delivered at the 1988 Annual Meeting of the Organization of American Historians, April 1988.

Peter Baynes, "An Analysis of the Political Culture of Albion, New York, 1872–1877." Graduate seminar paper, SUNV at Albany, 1984. Copies in possession of author and Robert Dykstra.

Thomas Lee. "Political Decisions and Their Makers in Glens Falls, New York, 1876–1885." Graduate seminar paper, SUNY at Albany, 1984. Copies in possession of author and Robert Dykstra.

Shirley Rice. "The Political Culture of Watkins, New York, 1872–1877." Graduate seminar paper, SUNY at Albany, 1984. Copies in possession of author and Robert Dykstra.

David Rockwell. "Adams: A Five-Year Study, 1880–1884." Graduate seminar paper, SUNY at Albany, 1984. Copies in possession of author and Robert Dykstra.

Index